Asian/Oceanian Historical Dictionaries
Edited by Jon Woronoff

Asia

1. *Vietnam*, by William J. Duiker. 1989
2. *Bangladesh*, 2nd ed., by Craig Baxter and Syedur Rahman. 1996
3. *Pakistan*, by Shahid Javed Burki. 1991
4. *Jordan*, by Peter Gubser. 1991
5. *Afghanistan*, by Ludwig W. Adamec. 1991
6. *Laos*, by Martin Stuart-Fox and Mary Kooyman. 1992
7. *Singapore*, by K. Mulliner and Lian The-Mulliner. 1991
8. *Israel*, by Bernard Reich. 1992
9. *Indonesia*, by Robert Cribb. 1992
10. *Hong Kong and Macau*, by Elfed Vaughan Roberts, Sum Ngai Ling, and Peter Bradshaw. 1992
11. *Korea*, by Andrew C. Nahm. 1993
12. *Taiwan*, by John F. Copper. 1993
13. *Malaysia*, by Amarjit Kaur. 1993
14. *Saudi Arabia*, by J. E. Peterson. 1993
15. *Myanmar*, by Jan Bečka. 1995
16. *Iran*, by John H. Lorentz. 1995
17. *Yemen*, by Robert D. Burrowes. 1995
18. *Thailand*, by May Kyi Win and Harold Smith. 1995
19. *Mongolia*, by Alan J. K. Sanders. 1996
20. *India*, by Surjit Mansingh. 1996
21. *Gulf Arab States*, by Malcolm C. Peck. 1996
22. *Syria*, by David Commins. 1996
23. *Palestine*, by Nafez Y. Nazzal and Laila A. Nazzal. 1997
24. *Philippines,* by Artemio R. Guillermo and May Kyi Win. 1997

Oceania

1. *Australia*, by James C. Docherty. 1992
2. *Polynesia*, by Robert D. Craig. 1993
3. *Guam and Micronesia*, by William Wuerch and Dirk Ballendorf. 1994
4. *Papua New Guinea*, by Ann Turner. 1994
5. *New Zealand*, by Keith Jackson and Alan McRobie. 1996

Historical Dictionary of Australia

Second Edition

James C. Docherty

Asian/Oceanian Dictionaries, No. 32

The Scarecrow Press, Inc.
Lanham, Maryland, and London
1999

SCARECROW PRESS, INC.

Published in the United States of America
by Scarecrow Press, Inc.
4720 Boston Way
Lanham, Maryland 20706

4 Pleydell Gardens, Folkestone
Kent CT20 2DN, England

British Library Cataloguing in Publication Information Available

Library of Congress Cataloging-in-Publication Data

Docherty, J. C.
    Historical dictionary of Australia / James C. Docherty. — 2nd ed.
      p.   cm. — (Asian/Oceanian historical dictionaries ; no. 32)
    Includes bibliographical references.
    ISBN 0-8108-3592-4 (cloth : alk. paper)
    1. Australia—History—Dictionaries. I. Title. II. Series.
DU90.D63   1999
994'.003—dc21   98-41796

For our daughter
Jessica Claire Docherty
born April 27, 1992
To her bright and shining future

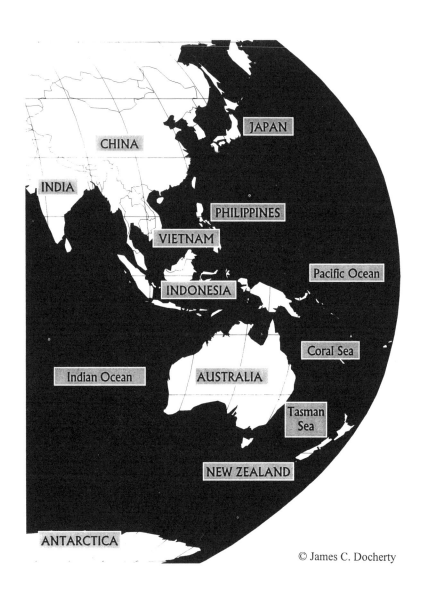

© James C. Docherty

CONTENTS

EDITOR'S FOREWORD

Although it was largely settled by Europeans and still has many links with Europe, Australia is becoming more linked to Asia with each passing year. This is shown by its foreign policy, economic and trade relations, increasingly the population, and a sea change in ways of thinking. Nonetheless, it remains a very special part of Asia, quite different from the rest, but with an important role to play. It is also a country with extraordinary potential, potential that frequently remains out of reach, but may one day be fulfilled.

Despite all this, it could hardly be claimed that Australia is well known abroad. It remains peripheral for most Europeans, Americans, and Asians. Yet it is a place that deserves to be much better understood, not only for what distinguishes it—from Aborigines to kangaroos—but for what it shares with other countries in the region and the world. That is the purpose of this book, a source of information and instruction, but one that is also surprisingly human in its treatment of Australia's many facets. This is done through a handy chronology, broad introduction, numerous dictionary entries, useful appendices, and an excellent, selective bibliography.

This volume was written by Dr. James Docherty, who works in the Department of Immigration and Multicultural Affairs in Canberra. He has also worked for the Department of Industrial Relations, the Department of Employment and Youth Affairs, and the Australian Bureau of Statistics. This means he is not an academic, like most other authors in this series. But it is his combination of an academic training with 20 years of varied work in Australia's national bureaucracy that gives him a unique perspective for writing this new edition of the *Historical Dictionary of Australia*.

Jon Woronoff
Series Editor

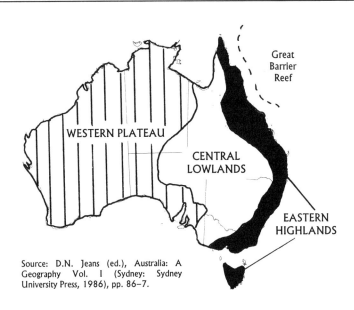

Source: D.N. Jeans (ed.), Australia: A Geography Vol. I (Sydney: Sydney University Press, 1986), pp. 86–7.

Source: D.N. Jeans (ed.), Australia: A Geography Vol. I (Sydney: Sydney University Press, 1986), p. 55.

III AUSTRALIA: EVOLUTION OF STATES, 1494-1863

AUSTRALIA: DIVISION BY
TREATY OF TORDESILAS, 1494

AUSTRALIA: DIVISION BY TREATY
OF SARAGOSSA, 1529

AUSTRALIA: BRITISH CLAIM, 1786   AUSTRALIA: BRITISH COLONIES, 1836

AUSTRALIA: COLONIES, 1859   AUSTRALIA: COLONIES, 1863

The Northern Territory was part
of South Australia until 1863

xi

Scale: 1 cm = 375 kilometers

© James C. Docherty

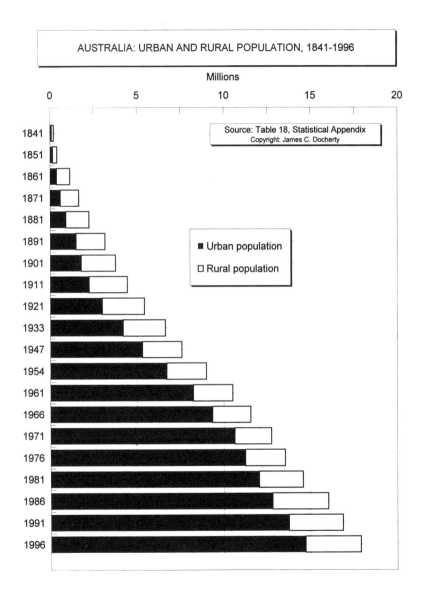

AUSTRALIA: URBAN AND RURAL POPULATION, 1841-1996

Millions

Source: Table 18, Statistical Appendix
Copyright: James C. Docherty

■ Urban population
□ Rural population

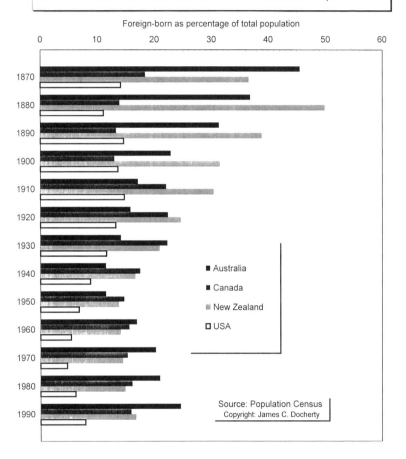

FOREIGN-BORN: AUSTRALIA AND SELECTED COUNTRIES, 1870-1990

Foreign-born as percentage of total population

- Australia
- Canada
- New Zealand
- USA

Source: Population Census
Copyright: James C. Docherty

PREFACE

This dictionary provides a guide to modern Australia and its past. When the first edition was published in late 1992, it was generally favorably received, but a number of reviewers complained that the body of the dictionary was too short. As I had given the former management of Scarecrow Press a work that was rather *longer* than originally asked for, it is satisfying to make good this deficiency now by means of a revised, much enlarged, and updated second edition.

The dictionary has a number of goals. First, in keeping with this series, it is an introduction to Australia and its history, and a reference work of first resort. It traces the history of Australia from the first human settlement about 80,000 years ago to the late 1990s through its 376 entries. There are other one-volume reference works about Australia, but these typically provide little assistance to readers about where to seek further information. Therefore, the second goal of this work is to enable readers to pursue areas of interest in greater depth through its extensive, analytical, and up-to-date bibliography which contains 1,167 items. An added feature of this work—also generally absent from other single-volume works on Australia—is its large, detailed, and easy to follow statistical appendix. As with other works in this series, the dictionary contains a chronology along with appendices listing governor-generals and prime ministers. Because finding out about Australia outside Australia can be difficult and even discouraging, the overriding aim of this work is to make that task as simple and as interesting as possible.

I have also taken the opportunity in preparing this second edition not just of incorporating a lot of additional material, but also to reconsider the perspective I used on the topic in the first edition. In the introduction to the bibliography of that work I complained about the narrow, nationalist approach of much of Australian historical writing. Although I still hold this view, my own work did precious little to remedy this defect. Accordingly, within the confines of this second edition, I have tried to make a greater effort to place Australia in an international context. For example, I have included an entry on emigration—a conspicuously neglected theme in Australian history and a useful one for my purposes in showing how Australians have made (and are making) an impact on other countries—in contrast to the usual domestic preoccupation only with immigration. Like other recent works in this series, cross references to other entries are in **bold**.

Even in its enlarged form, the dictionary remains a short work about a large topic and it makes no pretense to cover everything of importance. This is the only dictionary in this series that deals with a nation that spans a whole continent. Australia's European past is thoroughly documented. Its official statistics are among the best in the world and, although the body of research into Australian history has continued to grow, much remains to be done. The antiquity and complexity of its Aboriginal past is still being revealed.

The choice of what material to include always presents a special challenge in a work of this kind. The dictionary includes entries on all states and territories, urban centers with more than 100,000 people, leading exports, events, notable individuals, and other things that make Australia distinctive. As with the other volumes in this series, I have stressed relatively recent events and topics. Contemporary topics present special difficulties of their own. A topic that might seem important now might be forgotten after a few years. Similarly, a topic that might seem unimportant now may loom large later on. So in making their work up-to-date, the authors of historical dictionaries take their chances on the capricious passing of time.

Australian spelling normally follows British usage, but otherwise I have followed American usage. This second edition, like the first, was prepared in my spare time without sponsorship of any kind, and although I have used the information of others, the words, maps, and tables are my own. It would be expecting too much for the work to be free of errors. Some mistakes are bound to have escaped me; for these I apologize now. Finally, I have written this work with the conviction that Australian history really does have something useful to say to the world at large.

ABBREVIATIONS

AAW   *Australian Women's Weekly*

ABC   Australian Broadcasting Commission [renamed the
         Australian Broadcasting Corporation on July 1,1983]

ACM   Australian Chamber of Manufactures

ACT   Australian Capital Territory

ACTU   Australian Council of Trade Unions

AIF   Australian Imperial Force

ALP   Australian Labor Party [The official title since 1917; the
         use of different titles before that time has been ignored.]

AMA   Amalgamated Miners' Association

AMP   Australian Mutual Provident Society

AMWU   Amalgamated Metal Workers' Union

ANZAC   Australian and New Zealand Army Corps

AP   Australia Party

APA   Australian Patriotic Association

APEC   Asia Pacific Economic Cooperation

ASIO   Australian Security Intelligence Organisation

AWU   Australian Workers' Union

BCA   Business Council of Australia

BHP	Broken Hill Proprietary Company Limited
CAI	Confederation of Australian Industry
CPA	Communist Party of Australia
CSIRO	Commonwealth Scientific and Industrial Research Organisation
CWA	Country Women's Association
FMWU	Federated Miscellaneous Workers' Union
MTIA	Metal Trades Industry Association
NFF	National Farmers' Federation
NSW	New South Wales
NT	Northern Territory
Qld	Queensland
RAAF	Royal Australian Air Force
RAN	Royal Australian Navy
RSL	Returned Services League
SA	South Australia
Tas	Tasmania
UAP	United Australia Party
Vic	Victoria
WA	Western Australia

CURRENCY AND MEASUREMENT UNITS

Currency

Australia converted from the British pounds, shillings, and pence system to a decimal currency based on dollars and cents in February 1966. As a result of this conversion the main unit of currency, the pound, became $2, 10 shillings became $1, and 10 pence became 10¢. Unless otherwise stated, all the dollar amounts given in this dictionary refer to Australian dollars in current prices, that is they refer to the price at the date stated and have not been adjusted for inflation. A guide to changes in inflation and exchange rates is given in Tables 27 and 28 in Appendix 3 (Historical Statistics).

Measurement Units

Australia officially converted to the metric system between 1976 and 1981 and this system is used throughout the dictionary. Readers in countries with the Imperial or U.S. systems may find the following conversion factors useful:

1 hectare = 2.47 acres
1 kilometer = 0.62 miles
1 liter = 1.76 pints
1 tonne = 0.907 short ton (U.S.) or 0.984 long ton (British)

CHRONOLOGY

B.C.

c. 120,000-80,000
Migration of Aborigines into northern Australia from south-east Asia.

c. 22,000
Fall in the sea level during the Ice Age created a land link between the Australian mainland and Tasmania, enabling Tasmania to be settled by the Aborigines.

c. 10,000
Tasmania separated from the Australian mainland by a rise in the sea level

c. 6,000
Australia separated from New Guinea by a rise in the sea level.

A.D.

1494   Treaty of Tordesillas set the boundaries between Portuguese and Spanish lands in the western Atlantic and western Pacific oceans. The undiscovered Australian continent was divided so as to give the modern state of Western Australia to Portugal and the rest to Spain.

1516   Portuguese settlement on Timor, an island 460 kilometers from north-eastern Australia.

1529   Treaty of Saragossa between Portugal and Spain revised the boundary set by the Treaty of Tordesillas (1494). The line dividing Australia was moved eastward to place Cape York Peninsula and Torres Strait under Portuguese control.

1536   First appearance of Dieppe maps, which showed Portuguese knowledge of the coasts of north and north-west Australia and suggested that Portuguese navigators had knowledge of the eastern coast of Australia, then part of Spain's empire.

1606   First Dutch sighting of Australia by Willem Janszoon, who explored the western coast of Cape York Peninsula. In the same expedition, de Torres passed between Australia and New Guinea through the strait now named after him.

1616   Dutch captain, Dirck Hartog, landed on an island off the coast of western Australia, which is now named after him.

1642   Abel Tasman, a Dutch captain, discovered and claimed the modern island of Tasmania and named it Van Diemen's Land.

1688   William Dampier, an English explorer, spent three months in King Sound in Western Australia.

1699   Dampier explored the north-west coast of Australia.

1767   De Bougainville, a French navigator, sighted the Great Barrier Reef on the east coast of Australia.

1770   Captain James Cook explored the east coast of Australia from south to north. On April 29, he landed at Botany Bay; on August 22, he took possession of the eastern coast of Australia, that is, the part that had been given to Spain under the Treaty of Saragossa in 1529.

1779   Sir Joseph Banks recommended to a British parliamentary committee that the government set up a settlement at Botany Bay in eastern Australia using convicts.

1788   Arrival of the First Fleet with convicts at Botany Bay (January 18). Governor Phillip moved the fleet north to Port Jackson to found the settlement of Sydney (January 21). Phillip took possession of eastern Australia for Great Britain (January 26). Arrival of French explorer, La Perouse, at Botany Bay on the same day.

1789   Outbreak of smallpox among the Aborigines.

1790   Sydney affected by food shortages, which continued until 1794.

1791   First land grant of 30 acres made to ex-convict James Ruse. Arrival of the first convicts from Ireland.

1792   Antoine D'Entrecasteaux, a French navigator, explored the southern coast of Australia and Tasmania. First American trading ships reach Sydney.

1793   Arrival of the first free settlers from Britain. First sheep arrived in Australia.

1797   Discovery of coal at the mouth of the Hunter River north of Sydney.

1798   Bass and Flinders sailed around Van Diemen's Land (Tasmania) and proved it was an island.

1795   First printing press established in Australia.

1800   First issue of government copper coins in New South Wales.

1801   Nicholas Baudin, a French navigator, explored parts of the southern and northern Australian coasts until 1803.

1803   Matthew Flinders completed sailing around the Australian mainland (June 9). First newspaper published. First authorized Catholic Mass celebrated (May 15).

1804   Foundation of Hobart. Uprising by 200 Irish convicts in Sydney; nine were hanged. A program to vaccinate European children against smallpox was begun.

1807   First wool exports to Britain by James Macarthur.

1808   "Rum Rebellion" resulted in Governor William Bligh being deposed in a coup led by military officers of the New South Wales Corps.

1810   Recall of the New South Wales Corps to England. Lieutenant-Colonel Lachlan Macquarie became governor.

1813   Gregory Blaxland, William Wentworth, and Lieutenant William Lawson discovered a passage over the Blue Mountains, thereby opening up the interior for agriculture and sheep and cattle raising.

1814   Publication of Matthew Flinders's book, *A Voyage to Terra Australis*, which popularized the use of "Australia" for the whole continent.

1815   Road over the Blue Mountains from Sydney to Bathurst opened. First use of a steam engine.

1817   Foundation of the Bank of New South Wales (the ancestor of the modern Westpac Bank).

1819   Investigation of New South Wales administration by Commissioner John Thomas Bigge, which lasted until 1821; his reports criticized Governor Macquarie's administration and recommended spending less money on public works and greater use of convicts to assist private enterprise.

1824   Formation of Australian Agricultural Company in London. The Company was granted one million acres of land in northern New South Wales. Outpost settlements established on Melville Island (off the coast of the Northern Territory) and at Moreton Bay, Brisbane.

1826   Fear of possible French claims to Australian territory led to military settlements at Western Port Bay, Victoria, and King George Sound (modern Albany), Western Australia.

1827   First subscription library opened in Sydney.

1828   *Australian Courts Act* passed by British parliament. The *Act* was the basis for the appointment of legislative councils in Van Diemen's Land and New South Wales in 1829. First full-scale census of the European population. Total: 36,598 persons, of whom 15,728 were convicts.

1829   British government took possession of the western third of the Australian continent (May 2). Foundation of Perth, Western Australia.

1830   Charles Sturt followed the Murray River to the sea and proved it did not flow into an inland sea (February 9). First novel printed in Australia. First recorded labor union formed in Sydney.

1831   First issue of the *Sydney Herald* newspaper. It was renamed the *Sydney Morning Herald* in 1842. Ripon land regulations decreed that no more Crown lands were to be granted or leased without purchase. The money raised from land sales was to assist immigration.

1832   First Australian temperance society formed. First quarantine laws passed by New South Wales Legislative Council. First government-assisted immigrants bound for Australia left England.

1834   South Australia set up as a non-convict colony by the British South Australian Colonization Act.

1836   Formation of the Australian Patriotic Association to press for an elected legislature. John Batman arrived at Port Phillip and bought the land for the future city of Melbourne from the local Aborigines. Exploration by Thomas Mitchell of interior river systems and western Victoria. First settlers arrived in South Australia. Foundation of Adelaide, the new colony's capital.

1838   Massacre of 28 Aborigines at Myall Creek; seven Europeans were later hanged.

1840   Ending of the transportation of convicts to New South Wales.

1841   Explorer Edward John Eyre crossed the desert Nullarbor Plain from east to west.

1844   Journey of the German-born explorer Ludwig Leichhardt from Sydney to Port Essington in the Northern Territory. He completed it in 1845.

1848   First iron foundry began operations at Mittagong in southern New South Wales. Arrival of first Chinese laborers.

1849   Widespread protests in New South Wales against the renewal of transportation of convicts from Britain. Caroline Chisholm formed the Family Colonization Loan Society.

1850   *Australian Colonies Government Act.*

1851   Major bushfires in Victoria resulted in February 6 being called "Black Thursday." Discovery of payable gold (April 7) near Bathurst, New South Wales, began the gold rushes. Victoria became a separate colony from New South Wales.

1852   Arrival of last convicts in eastern Australia and Van Diemen's Land (1853). Melbourne *Age* founded. Foundation of the University of Sydney.

1853   Foundation of the University of Melbourne.

1854   Opening of first electric telegraph line between Melbourne and Williamstown in Victoria. Eureka Stockade incident at Ballarat, Victoria (December 3), between gold miners and government forces; 30 miners and five soldiers were killed.

1855   Opening of first public railway line in New South Wales.

1856   *Victorian Electoral Act* introduced the world's first secret ballot into elections.

1858   The European population of Australia reached one million.

1859   Importation and release of wild-bred rabbits introduced the rabbit pest into Australia.

1860   John McDouall Stuart reached the geographical center of Australia (April 22). Formation of a labor union by coal miners at Newcastle, New South Wales.

1861   Anti-Chinese riots at Lambing Flat goldfield. Death of explorers Burke and Wills in central Australia.

1862   John McDouall Stuart completed the first land crossing of Australia from south to north (July 24).

1863   First intercolonial conference in Melbourne (March). First Pacific Islanders (Kanakas) imported to work on Queensland sugar-cane plantations.

1865   First shale oil produced. William Arnott began Arnott's, the company, which by the 1980s produced 70 percent of Australia's cookies. Victoria introduced a protective tariff on imports.

1868   Arrival of last convicts in Australia, at Fremantle, Western Australia.

1870   Withdrawal of last British troops from Australia.

1872   Completion of overland telegraph line from Adelaide to Darwin.

1879   First intercolonial congress of labor unions.

1880   First issue of the nationalist weekly, the *Bulletin*. First export of frozen meat to Britain. First telephone exchange opened in Melbourne. Hanging of bushranger Ned Kelly.

1881   Most colonies passed laws to restrict the entry of Chinese.

1883   Discovery of huge deposits of silver and lead at Broken Hill, New South Wales, which became the basis of the Broken Hill Proprietary Company, Australia's largest company (formed 1885).

1885   Foundation of Victorian Employers' Union.

1886   Foundation of a wool shearers' union, which was the ancestor of the Australian Workers' Union.

1888   First general meeting of the Australasian Association for the Advancement of Science held in Sydney.

1889 First public exhibition of Australian "plein air" art; their work was attacked by the critics.

1890 General strike in eastern Australia based on maritime and pastoral employees. About 50,000 struck work (August to October).

1891 Major wool shearers' strike in Queensland resulted in defeat of the strikers (January). First attempts to federate the Australian colonies at the National Australasian Convention (March to April). Entry of organized labor into politics. First Labor candidates were elected to parliament in South Australia (May 9) and New South Wales (June 17).

1892 Queensland introduced preferential voting into Australian politics.

1893 Severe financial crisis in Victoria aggravated the economic depression that had begun in 1890. Discovery of gold in Kalgoorlie, Western Australia, produced the second great gold rush in Australian history.

1894 Women gained the right to vote in elections in South Australia (December 21).

1895 Beginning of a severe drought that lasted until 1903.

1898 A draft Federal constitution was passed by voters in Victoria, South Australia and Tasmania, but rejected in New South Wales.

1899 A second round of voting on the federation of the colonies produced majority votes in favor of a revised Constitution. Western Australia also voted reluctantly in favor of the draft constitution in July 1900. Labor formed the first Labor government in the world for one week in Queensland (December).

1900 The British parliament passed the *Act to Constitute the Commonwealth of Australia* (July 9). The *Act* set out the Australian Constitution.

1901 The Commonwealth of Australia came into being (January 1).

1902 William Farrer developed a new variety of wheat that was resistant to the disease rust.

1903 Establishment of High Court of Australia. End of the worst recorded drought in Australian history, which had begun in 1895.

1906 Commonwealth parliament passed laws to protect Australian industries from imported competition. Australia and South Africa signed a trade agreement, the first time Australia signed such an agreement with another country.

1908 Visit of the "Great White Fleet" from the United States.

1909 Commonwealth parliament passed laws to introduce national old age and invalid pensions. Major labor disputes in silver and lead mining at Broken Hill and coal mining at Newcastle, which lasted into 1910.

1910 Labor party elected to govern in the Commonwealth (April 13) and New South Wales parliaments (October 21). First national coinage issued.

1912 Walter Burley Griffin, an American architect, won an international competition for the design of the new federal capital, Canberra (May 14). Foundation of the Commonwealth Bank.

1913 First national paper currency and postage stamps issued by the Commonwealth. Formation of the first Country Party in Australia in Western Australia.

1914 Australia, following Britain, declared war on Germany (August 4). Australian forces captured German New Guinea (August 18). The Australian cruiser *Sydney* destroyed the German raider *Emden* off Cocos Island (November 9). Foundation of Coles, now one of Australia's largest retailers.

1915   First steel ingots produced at the new steelworks at Newcastle, New South Wales. Australian forces played a notable role in the massive Allied amphibious assault on the Gallipoli peninsula in north-western Turkey (April 25 to December 20). Total casualties: 27,859.

1916   Fifth Australian Division assaulted Fromelles on the Western Front in France (July 19): 22,826 were killed or wounded in the following seven weeks. Referendum on conscription for overseas military service narrowly defeated (October 28).

1917   Rising living costs heightened social divisions and helped prolong massive strikes in New South Wales and Victoria. Defeat of second referendum on conscription (November 29).

1918   Australian forces helped to defeat the last German offensive on the Western Front (March 21 to May 7) at a cost of 15,000 killed and wounded. First direct radio message from Britain to Australia (September 22). End of World War I (November 11). World War I cost Australia 59,342 men killed and 166,819 wounded. The first Australian permanent trade commissioner was appointed to the United States, the first Australian appointment for any country.

1919   Influenza epidemic killed over 11,500 by February 1920. By the Treaty of Versailles, Australia gained an official mandate over German New Guinea. First direct flight from Britain to Australia by Ross and Keith Smith (November 12 to December 10).

1920   Formation of the Australian Country Party (January 22-23). Formation of the Communist Party of Australia (October 30). Consumer price index reached double what it had been in 1911. Generally depressed economic conditions during 1920 and 1921.

1922   Abolition of the Queensland legislative council (March 22). Queensland remains the only Australian state without a legislative council to review laws proposed by the lower house. First reciprocal trade agreement signed between Australia and New Zealand. In Sydney a group of businessmen formed the Smith Family, now a major Australian charity.

1923   Formation of the Loan Council to coordinate Commonwealth and state government borrowings from overseas. First "Vegemite," a food product made from yeast, was produced.

1924   The retailer, Woolworths, began operations. Compulsory voting introduced for Federal elections.

1925   Federation of Business and Professional Women formed in Melbourne.

1927   Opening of Parliament House in Canberra (May 9). Up to this time, the Commonwealth parliament had convened in Melbourne. An Australian delegation representing employers, labor unions, and government visited the United States to investigate industrial conditions (February 10-August 7).

1928   A Commonwealth royal commission into the Australian film industry reported that Australian films were being squeezed out of the market by imported films, mainly from the United States. A British Economic Mission visited Australia to promote trade relations. First flight from California to Australia (May 31-June 9). The aviators were Charles Kingsford Smith and Charles P. Ulm. Massacre of 31 Aborigines in the Northern Territory in reprisal for the murder of a European.

1929   Major strikes among timber workers and coal miners (February-June 1930). Election of first Commonwealth Labor government since 1917 under James Scullin (November 21).

1930   Australia linked to Britain by telephone (April 30). Don Bradman broke the world record for an individual first-class cricket score. Sir Otto Niemeyer, of the Bank of England, visited Australia and advised balancing the budget to reduce debts owing to Britain.

1931   Reduction of 10 percent in the basic wage (January 22). The Depression was at its worst in Australia during 1931 and 1932. Sir Isaac Isaacs became the first Australian-born governor-general (January 22). A new conservative political party, the United Australia Party, was formed (April 19). Australian currency devalued 25 percent against Britain's pound sterling. The ratio between the two currencies remained fixed until 1967.

1932   Opening of the Sydney Harbour Bridge (March 19). Dismissal of New South Wales premier Jack Lang by the State governor for breaches of Commonwealth law (May 14). Unemployment among trade union members reached 28.1 percent (June), its highest point during the Depression.

1933   Controversial "bodyline" cricket tour by England caused much popular ill-feeling. In a protest vote, Western Australia voted in a referendum by two to one to secede from the Commonwealth but the move failed. Australia signed a trade agreement with Belgium, the first with a country outside the British Empire.

1934   Australian Eastern Mission to south-eastern Asia and Japan. First airmail service began between Australia and Britain (December).

1936   Commonwealth government agreed to allow entry of Jewish refugees from Germany, provided they were guaranteed by friends or relatives not to become a burden on the state.

1938   At Wollongong, New South Wales, waterfront workers refused to load pig iron bound for Japan in protest against Japanese aggression in China (November 15). First passenger and mail flying boat service between Britain and Australia began (August).

1939   Major bushfires in Victoria (January 13). Australia declared war on Germany after its invasion of Poland (September 3).

1940   Australian military forces sent to Middle East. Australia declared war on Italy (June 11).

1941   Australian forces defeat Italians at Bardia, Libya (January 2-3), and went on to capture Tobruk (January 22). Introduction of national child endowment scheme (January 16). German Afrika Korps recapture most of the territory lost by the Italians. Tobruk held but was under siege until December 7. Australian forces sent to fight in Greece (March 7). Forced back by the invading

German army, most were evacuated to Crete (April 24-25). Crete was captured by the Germans between May 20 and June 1. Total Australian losses in Greece and Crete were 1,595 killed or wounded and 5,174 captured. Fall of United Australia Party and Country Party coalition government in the national parliament. It was replaced by a Labor Party government under John Curtin (October 3). Australia declared war on Japan (December 9). First public opinion poll published using the Gallup method.

1942   Japanese forces landed on New Britain and Bougainville, islands off the New Guinea coast, then part of Australian territory (January 23). Fall of Singapore to the Japanese (February 15); 15,384 Australians were among the 133,814 Allied troops captured. Massive Japanese air raid on Darwin, Northern Territory, killed 243 (February 19). During the war, other air raids were made on Townsville, Queensland, and Broome and Wydham in Western Australia. Australian government agreed to the appointment of General Douglas MacArthur as supreme commander of all Allied forces in the south-west Pacific (March 17). First American forces reached Australia (April 6). Commonwealth government took over taxation powers from the states (June 4). Japanese submarines attacked Sydney and Newcastle (June 8). Australian forces inflicted first land defeat of Japanese forces at Milne Bay, New Guinea (August 25 to September 6). Riot between American and Australian troops in Brisbane, Queensland (November 26). Brutal treatment of Australians along with thousands of other prisoners of war and conscripted Asian laborers in building the Burma-Thailand railway (November 1942 to November 1943).

1943   End of Japanese resistance in Papua. The fighting cost 2,165 Australian lives. Introduction of conscription for the war in the south-west Pacific (February 19). Japanese sank the *Centaur*, a hospital ship, off the coast of Queensland: 268 died. Introduction of pay-as-you-earn income tax.

1944   Continuation of battles with Japanese in New Guinea and islands in the south-west Pacific. Introduction of unemployment and sickness benefits by the Commonwealth government (March). Formation of Liberal Party by R. G. Menzies (December 14-16).

1945 Death march of remaining Australian prisoners of war by the Japanese army in Borneo; only six survive out of 2,000 (January). Australian troops land in Borneo (May 1). Howard Florey awarded the Nobel prize for the joint discovery and development of penicillin. End of the Second World War in the Pacific (August 15).

1946 First national celebration of January 26 as Australia Day. Renewal of assisted passage for British immigrants. Creation of the Australian National University (although the first permanent building was not opened until 1952).

1947 Australia's population: 7.6 million. Introduction of a large immigration program for European refugees (July 21), which had been foreshadowed in 1944. Beginning of Australian Broadcasting Corporation's independent news service (July 1).

1948 Herbert Vere Evatt, Australian minister for External Affairs, elected president of the United Nations General Assembly (September 21). First mass-produced car, the Holden, entered the Australian market. It was produced by General Motors-Holden. The *Nationality Citizenship Act* created the status of "Australian citizen" for the first time from January 26, 1949.

1949 Coal strike in New South Wales (June 26 to August 15). The strike was broken by the use of troops, and the economic dislocation helped to defeat the Federal Labor government at the election on December 10. At the election, the coalition Liberal-Country parties gained power and held it until 1972. Beginning of the Snowy Mountains Hydro-Electric scheme (July).

1950 Successful release of the myxomatosis virus helped to reduce the plague of millions of rabbits that threatened agriculture and the environment. Australian forces committed to the Korean war (July 26).

1951 Australia, New Zealand, and the United States signed the ANZUS Treaty for mutual defense in the Pacific region (September 1). Narrow defeat of a referendum to outlaw the Communist Party (September 22).

1952 First atomic test by Britain off the north-west coast of Western Australia (October 3).

1953 First discovery of oil in commercial quantities in Western Australia.

1954 Visit of Queen Elizabeth II and Prince Philip to Australia, the first by a reigning British monarch. Defection of Soviet diplomat Vladimir Petrov (April 13). The defection set off a chain of events that helped split the Labor Party.

1955 Split in the Australian Labor Party and creation of the Australian Labor Party (Anti-Communist), later called the Democratic Labor Party (1956); first performance of Ray Lawler's play, *Summer of the Seventeenth Doll*.

1956 First television broadcast in Australia (September 16). Olympic Games held in Melbourne (November to December).

1957 Australia and Japan signed a trade agreement to give "most favored nation" treatment of each other's goods (July 6).

1958 Harold Macmillan visited Australia, the first visit by a British prime minister.

1959 Formation of Reserve Bank of Australia to replace the central banking functions of the Commonwealth Bank.

1960 Macfarlane Burnet shared the Nobel prize for Medicine.

1961 Introduction of oral contraceptives for women. First investigative current affairs program on television, *Four Corners*, began broadcasting. Australia's population reached 10.5 million (June 30).

1962 The University of Sydney established the first chair of Australian Literature. The first Australian troops sent to Vietnam as advisers.

1963 Sir John Eccles shared the Nobel prize for Medicine. Commonwealth government gave approval to the United States to establish and run a naval communications base at North West Cape, Western Australia.

1964   First national newspaper, the *Australian*, began publication. Reintroduction of conscription based on a ballot of birthdays (November 10).

1965   Australian troops committed to Vietnam war (May). Vernon Committee of Economic Inquiry released its report (May 6). The report reviewed Australia's post-war economy, drew attention to weaknesses and suggested the introduction of a uniform tariff of about 30 percent.

1966   Retirement of Robert Gordon Menzies as prime minister (January 20). He had been in power since 1949. Visit of Lyndon B. Johnson to Australia (October), the first United States president to visit Australia. Japan replaced Britain as Australia's largest trading partner.

1967   A referendum passed by a 90.8 percent majority gave the Commonwealth government the power to make special laws for Aborigines (May 27). Establishment of joint Australian-United States space station at Pine Gap in central Australia to monitor Soviet missiles and intercept communications.

1968   Gough Whitlam became leader of the Australian Labor Party and took steps to revitalize the party. Woodchip industry began in south-eastern New South Wales.

1969   Commonwealth Arbitration Court introduced the principle of equal pay for equal work for women. Full pay for women was to be made by 1972.

1970   Pope Paul VI became the first pope to visit Australia (November).

1971   Neville Bonner became the first Aborigine to enter federal parliament when he was selected by the Queensland Liberal Party to fill a casual vacancy in the Senate (May). The leader of the federal opposition, Gough Whitlam, led a delegation to the

People's Republic of China (June), a month before the announced visit of President Nixon.

1972 Formation of the United Tasmania Group (March), the first "green" political party in the world. Labor Party under Gough Whitlam won power at the federal election of December 2 and began a program of widespread reforms.

1973 Opening of the Sydney Opera House (October 20). Federal government reduced tariffs on imports by 25 percent (July 18). Patrick White won the Nobel prize for Literature, the first Australian writer to do so.

1974 Devastation of Darwin, Northern Territory, by cyclone *Tracy* resulted in 50 deaths and the evacuation of 26,000 residents (December 24-25).

1975 Report of the National Population Inquiry (February 25). Color television began in Australia (March 1). The federal government introduced Medibank, a national hospital and medical benefit scheme (July 1). Sharp rise in unemployment to 5.2 percent of the workforce. Whitlam government dismissed by the governor-general, Sir John Kerr (November 11). The Liberal-National Country Party coalition, led by Malcolm Fraser, won the federal elections on December 13.

1976 The Labor Party won government in New South Wales under Neville Wran (May 1). Divorce procedures reformed by the Family Law Act. Treaty of friendship signed between Australia and Japan (June 16).

1977 Formation of a new moderate political party, the Australian Democrats (May 9).

1978 Northern Territory gained self-government (July 1). Australia declared a 200-mile economic zone around its coastline. First Gay-Lesbian Mardi Gras in Sydney (March); by the mid-1990s it had become a major tourist event.

1979   Conciliation and Arbitration Commission granted 12 months'
        unpaid maternity leave to women who had worked for one year
        (March 9). National Farmers' Federation formed.

1980   Elimination of tariff preference for British goods, which had
        begun in the 1930s. Multicultural television began broadcasting
        in Sydney and Melbourne. Beginning of a severe drought in
        eastern Australia, which did not break until 1983. State of Origin
        Rugby League matches begin.

1981   Campbell Committee of Inquiry into the Australian financial
        system recommended reducing the regulation of the industry.

1982   Environmental dispute between Commonwealth and Tasmanian
        governments over damming the Franklin river. The area
        proposed for the dam was successfully entered on the World
        Heritage List and the proposed dam was not built. In Victoria,
        the Labor Party under John Cain (1931-) won government after
        27 years in opposition (April 3). In Tasmania, the Labor Party
        lost government after having ruled the state for 45 of the
        previous 48 years (May 15). Opening of the Australian National
        Art Gallery in Canberra. *Freedom of Information Act* came into
        operation covering Commonwealth documents (December 1).

1983   Labor Party won government in Western Australia (February 19)
        under Brian Burke and in the Commonwealth (March 5) under
        Bob Hawke. *Sex Discrimination Act* passed by the national
        parliament (December 16).

1984   National Population Council established (June).

1985   Significant reduction of government regulation of the banking
        system. Substantial fall in the value of the Australian dollar.

1986   Last constitutional links with Britain broken. Australia's
        population reached 15.6 million (June 30) or double what it had
        been in 1947. Formation by Australia of the Cairns Group of
        Fair Traders in Agriculture (August 25-27). National Parliament
        passed the *Affirmative Action (Equal Opportunity for Women)
        Act.*

1987 Publication of 10-volume history, *Australians: An Historical Library.*

1988 Celebration of the Bicentenary of the European settlement of Australia (January 26): two million people watched the celebrations. In New South Wales, the Labor Party lost government to the coalition Liberal-National parties led by Nick Greiner (1947-) (March 19).

1989 Tasmanian elections (May 13) resulted in the Greens gaining 18 percent of the vote. The Liberal Party, which had held power since 1982 under Robin Gray (1940-), was defeated. Labor, under Michael Field (1948-), formed a government with the support of the Greens. In the Queensland elections (December 2), the Labor Party under Wayne Goss (1951-) won government for the first time since 1957. Newcastle, New South Wales, became the first Australian city to be damaged by an earthquake (December 28). The earthquake killed 12 people, injured 100 more and caused $1.1 billion worth of damage.

1990 Carmen Lawrence (1948-) became the first woman premier of an Australian State, Western Australia (February 12). Labor Party under Bob Hawke re-elected to the federal government for a fourth term (March 24). Amid financial crisis, Joan Kirner (1938-) replaced John Cain as premier of Victoria (August 9). Sale of State Bank of Victoria (established 1842) to the Commonwealth Bank (August 26). The economy officially entered a recession in September.

1991 The Australian economy remained in recession during 1991. In New South Wales, the Liberal-National parties were re-elected but were forced to depend upon the support of independents (May 25). National population census held (August 6). In federal politics, Paul Keating replaced Bob Hawke as prime minister (December 20). President George Bush made a goodwill visit to Australia (December 31, 1991–January 3, 1992) as part of a trip to Singapore, South Korea, and Japan.

1992 In Tasmania, the Labor Party was defeated by the Liberal Party (February 1). The Labor Party vote (29 percent) was the lowest it had received in 80 years. Formation of the Australian

Chamber of Commerce and Industry from the amalgamation of the Confederation of Australian Industry and the Australian Chamber of Commerce (September 1). In Victoria, the Labor Party was defeated by the Liberal and National Parties (October 3). The Mabo Decision of the High Court was delivered.

1993 Labor government in Western Australia defeated by the Liberal-National parties (February 6). Sydney was announced as the venue for summer Olympic Games in 2000 (September 24). The Labor government in South Australia was defeated by the Liberal-National Parties (December 11).

1994 Widespread destructive bush fires around Sydney (January). An Australian relay team won a bronze medal at the Winter Olympics in Norway, the first time Australia won a medal since the Games began in 1926.

1995 Mother Mary MacKillop (1842-1907) was made Australia's first saint by Pope John Paul during a visit to Australia (January). The Labor Party was narrowly returned to power in the elections in New South Wales (March 25) having been in opposition since 1988. Mutual defense treaty signed between the Australian and Indonesian governments (December).

1996 The Labor Party government in Queensland lost office after being defeated in a by-election and was a replaced by a National-Liberal coalition government (February). Australia's first voluntary euthanasia legislation introduced into the Northern Territory (February); the law became effective in July but was subject to legal challenges. Landslide victory of Liberal-National coalition over the Labor Party in the federal election (March 2); John Howard (1939-) became the first coalition prime minister since March 1983. A deranged gunman in Tasmania killed 35 people (April); this mass murder led to coordinated legislation by the states and territories to ban semi-automatic and automatic firearms. The national census showed that Australia's population had reached 17.9 million (August 6). Peter Doherty shared the Nobel prize for Medicine (October 7). Visit of U.S. President Bill Clinton (November 19-23). The High Court delivered the Wik Decision (23 December).

Aborigines near Kempsey, New South Wales, won the first land claim on mainland Australia under the *Native Title Act*.

1997 Geoffrey Rush won an Oscar for his role as the Australian pianist David Helfgott in *Shine* (March). Pauline Hanson, an independent member of the federal parliament, formed the One Nation Party (April 11). The Liberal Party was returned to government following the elections in South Australia, but with a substantially reduced majority (October 11). The federal government privatized one-third of Telstra, the government telecommunications instrumentality (October). The Australian Mutual Provident Society stockholders voted for demutualization and the listing of the Society on the stock exchange (November). Voluntary elections for the Constitutional Convention attracted a voter turnout of only 47 percent and voting favored supporters of a republic (November-December). End of a multi-million dollar contest between Rupert Murdoch's Super League and the Australian Rugby League (December).

1998 Australia pledged financial assistance to Indonesia because of the Asian currency crisis (January). Constitutional Convention on whether Australia should become a republic (February 2-13); the government agreed to hold a referendum. Australia sent 190 troops to the Persian Gulf in support of an appeal by the United States over the stockpiling of chemical weapons by the leader of Iraq, Saddam Hussein (February 17). Labor dispute between the federal government and the Maritime Union of Australia over work practices (February-June). The right-wing populist One Nation Party gained 22.6 percent of the vote in the Queensland state elections (June 13) and resulted in the defeat of the National party government and the installation of a minority Labor government. The senate passed amendments to the *Native Title Act 1996* to accommodate the Wik Case (2 July). The federal government announced its support for a referendum to give statehood to the Northern Territory (August 11) by 2001. In the state elections in Tasmania, the Liberal government was defeated by the Labor Party (August 29). Pat Rafter wins the U.S. Tennis Open for the second year in succession (September). The Liberal-National party coalition was returned for a second term following national elections but with a much reduced majority (October 3).

1999   Referendum scheduled on whether Australia should become a republic. Re-election of the Labor Party in New South Wales with an increased majority (March 27).

2000   Australia hosts the Olympic Games in Sydney (September-October).

INTRODUCTION

Australians are usually dismayed at how little is known of their country beyond its shores, and, if known, how little is understood. The stock images of tourist promotions—the vast, brown landscape, kangaroos, beaches, and Sydney harbor—are valid, but misleading and although books about Australia abound within Australia, only a few foreign libraries can boast extensive Australian collections. The foreign media pay little attention to Australia and, if they do, generally present a highly selective and often biased impression. This dictionary attempts to redress this imbalance within the limits of a single volume. It offers a reliable factual basis for the serious study of Australia, its past, its people, and its place in the modern world. Australia is a new nation in many ways and still in the process of defining its identity. This makes its presentation to an international audience daunting and exciting.

Australia has loomed small for most of recorded history. It belongs to the last part of that sweep of history from the late fifteenth to the late nineteenth centuries when Europeans carved out empires throughout the world. From that perspective, it has a history shared with the Americas, South Africa, and parts of the periphery of Eurasia.

Australia was the last continent to be claimed by Europeans and, from its earliest years, its history has always been distinctive while being like other Western societies. It is a paradoxical country. As a European society, its history is relatively recent—only beginning in 1788—but as a center of human habitation, it is an ancient land with the first inhabitants, the **Aborigines**, now believed to have arrived possibly as early as 120,000 years ago. Long largely oriented towards **Britain**, Australia has tried to come to terms with its physical closeness to south-east Asia in recent years.

It has a well-documented history, nearly all of it in English, which lends itself well to the testing of theories about general historical developments and offers an important case study of these developments in their own right. These include the treatment of indigenous peoples, the European colonization of a continent, the growth of cities and towns, as well as the challenge of conquering large distances, the growth of a home-owning, liberal democracy, the process of nation-building, and tackling racial divisions.

The remainder of this introduction is divided into four parts. The first two parts examine the setting of Australia, its physical and climatic features, and how these have influenced its history. The third

1

part reviews the historical framework of Australia from its origins as a British jail to the remarkable emergence of a liberal democracy. The fourth part presents a profile of the main features of Australian society at the start and at the end of the twentieth century.

THE PHYSICAL ENVIRONMENT

The setting of Australia

Two hundred and fifty million years ago, Australia, **Antarctica**, and southern Africa were joined together close to the South Pole. About 60 million years ago, this land mass began to break up. Australia, which then had a warm, wet climate, gradually drifted north and started to dry out. It reached its present position between the Indian and Pacific Oceans about 10 million years ago. The isolation of Australia over millions of years allowed the evolution of remarkable flora and fauna. Australia now accounts for half of the world's species of marsupials of which the best known is the **kangaroo**.

Australia divides the South Pacific and Indian Oceans. It is easily the largest land mass in the southwest Pacific region, but also the smallest of the world's continents. The island of New Guinea is the only land mass close to Australia but it is only one-tenth of the area of Australia. To the immediate north-west of Australia are the 13,667 islands that make up **Indonesia** (see Map 1). New Guinea and Indonesia are comparatively close to Australia. New Guinea is only 150 kilometers from Cape York, the northern tip of eastern Australia, and a number of Indonesia's largest southern islands, notably Timor, are within 500 kilometers of the northern Australian mainland.

In contrast to the nearness of south-east Asia and the Pacific, Britain, the country of greatest political, economic, and cultural importance to Australia for most of its history, is literally on the other side of the world, 17,000 kilometers away. The distance of Australia from Britain has been one of the most important influences on Australia's history and attitudes. The Asian north was seen as alien, its millions of inhabitants a threat to an isolated, empty land, a perception that gave rise to the **White Australia Policy**. The peoples of the Pacific were seen as primitive and harmless.

The land: dimensions and parts

Australia has an area of 7,682,300 square kilometers or 5.7 percent of the world's land surface without Antarctica. Its coastline is 36,700 kilometers long. At its greatest extent it stretches nearly 4,000 kilometers from west to east and nearly 3,200 kilometers from north to south. It is a low, flat continent. Almost 90 percent of its area is less than 500 meters above sea level. The lowest point is the normally dry Lake Eyre, which is 15 meters below sea level. The highest point is Mount Kosciusko (2,228 meters). Australia has a mean altitude of only 330 meters compared to 780 meters for North America; only 2 percent of its areas is over 1,000 meters compared to 27 percent for North America. Australia can be divided into three major physiographic regions (see Map 2):

1. The Western Plateau

The Western Plateau covers about half of Australia and includes the states of **Western Australia**, nearly all of the **Northern Territory**, and about half of **South Australia**. It is the oldest part of Australia with some of its rocks dating back 3,000 million years. It is generally arid and sparsely populated apart from the state capital cities of **Perth** and **Adelaide** in the south and the town of **Darwin** in the north. Mining, cattle raising, and tourism are important economic activities of the region.

2. The Central Lowlands

The Central Lowlands is made up of the interior flood plains from the Gulf of Carpentaria in the north to the plains of the Darling and Murray Rivers in the south, that is, about 35 percent of Australia. The region is the heart of Australia's wool and wheat industry. Other than country towns, the main centers of population are the mining centers of Mount Isa and Broken Hill.

3. The Eastern Highlands

The Eastern Highlands include the Great Dividing Range, the eastern coastal strip, and Tasmania. These Highlands cover about 15 percent of Australia. Better watered than the rest of the continent, this region is the home of most of Australia's 18 million people. It contains the three largest capital cities—**Sydney**, **Melbourne**, and **Brisbane**—as well as **Canberra,** the national capital—and the heavy industry cities of **Newcastle** and **Wollongong**.

The dry continent: climate

Australia's climates range from tropical in the north to desert in the interior to varieties of temperate climates in the south-east. Most of Australia is arid and the rainfall away from the coastal fringes is highly variable. Floods may make for dramatic news coverage on television, but the main threat of the climate is **drought**.

Australia is the world's hottest and driest inhabited continent. It has been estimated that 71 percent of its area receives less than 500mm of rain a year making those parts arid or semi-arid. Deserts dominate the interior landscape. Australia's average annual rainfall is only 425mm compared to 1,740mm for the United States. In other words, Australia receives only a quarter of the rainfall of the United States. Not only that, but the rainfall in Australia is highly variable across much of the continent and a high deviation from the "average" is usual. **Bush-fires** are a recurrent feature of Australia in summer.

Only 12 percent of the rain Australia receives becomes runoff in the form of streams and rivers compared to 52 percent in North America. There are no major rivers outside the eastern third of the continent. Most of the interior lakes and rivers shown on maps exist only after rain; otherwise they can be dry for years at a time. Only 11 percent of Australia has an average annual rainfall of 800mm or more and 68 percent receives less than 410mm a year.

THE CHALLENGE OF THE ENVIRONMENT

The lonely continent: distance and communications

Great distances, both outside and within Australia, are inescapable facts of Australian history. Before 1850, sea transport to Australia was slow and uncertain. In 1788 the **First Fleet** took eight months to reach Australia from England, but by 1849 the average voyage took only four. By comparison, the typical voyage from Western Europe to north America by sailing ship took between five and six weeks. Steam replaced sailing ships in the 1880s and reduced the time and increased the safety of the journey as did the opening of the Suez Canal in 1869. By 1914 steamers had cut the journey from Britain to Australia to just over five weeks.

Aircraft held the promise of faster individual travel and communications. The first direct flight from Britain to Australia was made in 1919 (four weeks); the first from the United States in 1928 (10 days). An air mail service between Britain and Australia was begun in 1934, as was a combined passenger and mail flying-boat service in 1938. It took about two weeks for mail from Australia to reach Britain. But ships were the main movers of people to and from Australia until the 1960s.

As a result of distance, the number of Australians who traveled overseas was very small. Between 1925 and 1949 the annual average number of Australians who traveled overseas was only about 20,000 or the equivalent to five adults in every thousand. Isolation, aggravated by strict **censorship**, encouraged an inward-looking society and a general lack of interest in, and knowledge of, the outside world. Until 1942 Australians' experience of wars had been confined to the troops it dispatched to distant battlefields. The war with **Japan** and its attacks on the Australian mainland forced governments to take a more active interest in world affairs. But for the great mass of Australians it was not until the early 1970s that it became possible through greater affluence, jumbo jets and mass **tourism** to experience European—and more recently, Asian—culture and way of life firsthand.

Communications, like transport, made slow progress. In 1872 the completion of the **Overland Telegraph** through the center of Australia and its linking to the international cable made it possible for Australia to receive news quickly. The first direct radio message from Britain to Australia was made in September 1918. The first telephone link between Britain and Australia was not made until 1930, but like other new technology, it was too expensive for mass usage for many years. It took 20 years for the number of connected telephones in Australia to double from half a million in 1930 to 1.1 million in 1950; by 1980 there were 7 million. In 1994, 96.6 percent of Australian households were connected to the telephone system and 7.4 percent had a modem connection (*see* Telecommunications).

Not only was Australia a long way from Western Europe, but distances within Australia were large too. The total area of Australia is greater than all of Western Europe. Further, unlike Western Europe and the United States, Australia does not have a network of permanent navigable inland rivers that could have provided cheap transport for people and goods. Until the 1870s, most land transport was horse-drawn. Rail was the main form of land transport from the 1880s to the 1960s, but progress was slow because of the cost of covering great distances and the small population. There was no east-west rail link until 1917 and the north-south rail link from **Darwin** to **Adelaide** was never completed, although Adelaide was connected to Alice Springs in the center of Australia in 1929.

Until World War II road building was carried out mainly in well-populated areas and it was only with the strategic implications of the war that a system of inter-state road links was begun or planned. An east-west road link was made between Adelaide and Perth during World War II, but the whole road was not bitumen sealed until 1976.

Similarly, there was no fully sealed north-south road link between Darwin and Adelaide until 1979 (*see* Roads).

Distance, and attempts to defeat it by better communications, pervade Australian history. It is no accident that the most honored personalities and institutions in Australian history were often connected with trying to improve communications (*see* Cobb and Co; Kingsford Smith; Royal Flying Doctor Service; School of the Air).

Environment and history

The physical facts of Australia have shaped its history in many ways. For the **Aborigines**, the harsh, dry land limited their mode of life to one of subsistence based on hunting and gathering wild crops. Isolated from the stimulus of contact with other cultures, their material culture remained primitive with the result that they were unable to offer effective resistance to the European occupation of their lands. Despite this, the harshness of the land encouraged the Aborigines to develop a rich spiritual culture.

For the Europeans, the dryness of much of Australia and its generally poor soils limited the nature and scale of settlement and agricultural development. Unlike the United States, Australia does not have wide belts of highly productive soils. In fact, it has been estimated that Australia has only about as much arable land as Illinois and Iowa combined. With low yields for most forms of agriculture, well-managed sheep, cattle, and wheat production made economic sense. Where agriculture could be practiced, it generally favored large landholders, not small ones.

Until recent times, Australians resisted the peculiarities of their large, hot, dry land. The first generations of European settlers tried to make their parts of the country like Britain. They imported plants and animals from Britain. Some of these animals, particularly rabbits and foxes, have done great damage to the native fauna and to the environment in general. European agricultural techniques and widespread deforestation also harmed the environment through soil erosion and dust storms. It took a century of European occupation for Australian artists fully to come to terms with, appreciate, and, finally, celebrate the unique Australian environment (*see* May Gibbs; *Jindyworobaks*; Tom Roberts). Governments were far slower to come to terms with the realities of the environment. Not until the 1930s did soil erosion become a topic of official concern, and critics of the official view that Australia had unlimited potential for economic growth because of its dry climate were scorned (*see* Thomas Griffith

Taylor).

Governments were not alone in refusing to accept the limitations imposed by Australia's dryness. Land was a goal of many nineteenth-century immigrants to Australia and North America. Possession of land and the agricultural life were seen as the bases for independence as opposed to the dependent life of the urban wage earner. Through the new colonial democracies set up in the 1850s, the immigrants were able to exert pressure for closer settlement of the land (*see* Free Selection). Unfortunately only about a tenth of the land was suitable for the kind of intensive agriculture they wanted.

In the 1820s and 1830s, large tracts of land claimed by the British crown were illegally occupied by ranchers for raising sheep and cattle by a process known as **squatting**. Although various laws eventually brought their activities under control, the dryness of the land worked in their favor. However unacceptable the squatters were to governments and the bulk of the urban-based and largely immigrant population, well-managed sheep and/or cattle-raising suited much of the environment.

By 1880, pastoral settlement included most of the land that could support it. Extension of this frontier in the 1880s into semi-arid and arid lands proved disastrous in the great drought of 1895 to 1903 when the number of sheep fell from 100 to 54 million. In the twentieth century, federal and state governments continued to sponsor closer land settlement schemes and projects designed to bring water to the interior. It assisted ex-soldiers after both world wars to settle on the land as farmers. In 1949 the federal government began building the massive Snowy Mountains hydro-electric scheme, whose purpose was to turn the waters of the Snowy River in south-eastern Australia inland to generate electricity and provide water for irrigation farming in southern central New South Wales (*see* Snowy Mountains Scheme). In the 1960s, governments supported the Ord River Irrigation Project (completed in 1972) in northern Western Australia, a project that has yielded few benefits for its cost.

The price of these policies has been a high degree of environmental destruction. A national study in 1975-78 of Australia's non-arid land (that is, only 30 percent of its total area), found that two-thirds had been degraded by either soil erosion or salinity. Further, 2,000 species of plants (a tenth of the total) are at risk of becoming extinct. Nineteen vertebrate animals are believed to have died out with a further 74 animals at risk. Since this survey, there has been greater official recognition of environmental problems and resolve to address them by measures such a massive tree-planting program.

Farm and mine: the economy and history

In spite of its environmental limitations, Australia has managed to be an important producer of minerals and agricultural products, particularly **sheep and wool** and **wheat**. It is richly endowed with an abundance of minerals, particularly bauxite, **aluminum**, copper, **gold**, **iron ore**, silver, lead, zinc, **coal**, **petroleum**, natural gas, **nickel**, **mineral sands**, **diamonds**, and uranium. Australia is a major supplier of the world's minerals, particularly bauxite and aluminum, mineral sands, coal (for export), diamonds, nickel, gold, and iron ore for much of its history. From the gold rushes of the 1850s, the mining of these minerals has been an important feature of the economy and the landscape. Mining was the economic base of many of the largest towns outside the capital cities. Coal mining was the basis for the pre-1900 settlements at **Newcastle** and **Wollongong** in New South Wales; gold was the basis for Ballarat and Bendigo in Victoria; and silver and lead was the basis for the inland mining towns of Broken Hill in New South Wales and Mount Isa in Queensland.

Agriculture, sheep and/or cattle raising, and mining have been vital to the Australian **economy** since the 1850s (*see* Appendix 3). Growth was generally rapid from 1860 to 1890, but thereafter Australia's economic record has been mixed. Severe depressions hit the economy very hard in the early 1890s and 1930s. As well as fluctuations in the world economy, Australia is susceptible to droughts, which retarded economic growth from 1895 to 1903, 1911 to 1916, and, most recently, from 1982 to 1983. The Australian economy has also suffered from its colonial origins. From the 1840s to the 1960s the main function of the Australian economy was to provide primary products for Britain in return for being a largely captive market for British manufactured goods. As a result, local **manufacturing** developed fairly slowly until the 1880s. In 1891 it accounted for only about 12 percent of gross domestic product or less than half that of the rural sector. An **iron and steel** industry developed after 1915 and there was some growth in the 1920s but the main growth period for manufacturing was from the late 1930s to the early 1970s.

Australia's economic performance has been the cause of widespread concern in recent years. Since the mid-1970s, manufacturing has failed to contribute adequately to economic growth. Built up behind walls of protection from overseas competition in the post-1945 years, much of Australian manufacturing developed to meet only the demands of a small domestic market rather than to compete on a world scale (*see* Protection). Also it was often foreign owned and dependent upon foreign technology. Between 1960-61 and 1997-98 the contribution made by manufacturing to gross domestic product fell from 30 to 13 percent.

In addition, the high subsidies to inefficient agricultural producers under the Common Agricultural Policy of the European Economic Community and the determination of the United States to fight this policy by subsidizing its own producers have harmed efficient agricultural producers and exporters like Australia.

Australia's economy has proven itself to be an efficient producer of raw commodities like minerals and agricultural products but a poor producer of high valued-added goods, a reflection of its colonial origins. At the same time, it is important to recognize that the dryness of Australia has ultimately prevented it from supporting a population and huge internal market on the scale of the United States and to be relatively more reliant on exports to maintain living standards.

THE HISTORICAL SETTING

The European colonization

Europeans carved up Australia before they had discovered it. Under the Treaty of Tordesillas (1494), the lands in the Atlantic and Pacific oceans were divided between Spain and Portugal (see Map 3). The western third of Australia (the present state of Western Australia) was given to Portugal and the remainder to Spain. The Portuguese were the first on the scene. In 1514 they reached Timor, an island in modern southern Indonesia. Thereafter they made a number of voyages to Australia. How much the Portuguese knew of Australia before 1570 is disputed, but their maps indicate they were familiar with much of the northern and western Australian coast. In addition, they may also have explored the eastern coast at least 250 years before the famous voyage of Captain James Cook in 1770, which resulted in British annexation and settlement in 1788. The French also began to take an interest in the south-west Pacific after 1766, but the turmoil of the French Revolution of 1789 and the European pre-occupations of Napoleon allowed the British a free hand to incorporate all of Australia into their empire by 1829, a year after their imperial neighbor, the Dutch, annexed the western half of the island of New Guinea.

Australia was founded not as the land of the free, but as the land of the controlled. British settlement in Australia began in 1788 in the form of a jail for British convicts. Previously such convicts had been sent to North America. First introduced into English law in 1597, the "transportation" or banishment of convicts became an instrument of imperial policy. Between 1655 and 1775 a total of about 55,000 convicts were "transported" to North America or the Caribbean as the range of crimes incurring transportation was broadened to include relatively minor offenses. During the eighteenth century the British government began to use convicts as a convenient means of populating strategic outposts in its empire. From the 1720s opposition to British convicts in North American colonies grew, although their labor was welcomed by plantation owners. The sending of British convicts and indentured servants to North America gave rise to the idea in Britain by the 1760s—and later applied to Australia—that its population was socially inferior to the mother country, being descended from convicts. In 1788 the American Congress resolved not to accept any more British convicts. Neither were British convicts wanted in Canada.

In North America, British convicts were so easily absorbed into the labor-hungry society of colonial America that they became untraceable, but they were a distinct class in early Australia. Often transported for minor offenses, they were the bulk of the colony's workers until the 1820s and even when they had completed their sentence or were pardoned, few were able to return to Britain. Convicts were the raw human material for a series of settlements along the coast of Australia, first at Port Jackson (Sydney) in 1788, and then at Hobart (1803), Newcastle (1804), Launceston (1806), Brisbane (1824), Melville Island, (1824), near modern Darwin, and Albany (1827). The purpose of these settlements was strategic: they were intended to strengthen the British naval presence in the Pacific, to keep competitors away from Australia, and to protect trade routes to China.

The British domination of Australia was based on sea power. All the colonies of Australia began as ports—Sydney (1788), Hobart (1804), Melbourne (1835), Brisbane (1824), Adelaide (1836), Darwin (1869), Perth (1829)—and settlement gradually moved inland. Up to the 1820s, the two earliest colonies of **New South Wales** and Van Diemen's Land (**Tasmania** after 1856) were primarily jails, but thereafter free immigration was encouraged to develop the economy.

The British Empire and Australia

The British Empire was the single most important influence on Australia's history from 1788 to the 1950s (*see* Britain). At every level—political, economic, and social—Australia operated as a loyal part of the British Empire. The constitutions of the original Australian colonies were granted to them as Acts of the British parliament as was the national Constitution in 1901. In that year, Australia made up one-quarter of the land area of the British Empire, but only 1 percent of its population.

Unlike the United States, there was never any suggestion of revolution or breaking with Britain. Most Australians, with the notable exception of the Catholic **Irish**, took great pride in being part of the British Empire. Indeed independence over matters of foreign policy was not formally granted to Australia until the Statute of Westminster in 1931 and not exercised until 1942.

Britain dominated the cultural life of Australia. One way of demonstrating this dominance is to consider the sources of imported printed materials, that is books, newspapers, periodicals, sheet music and atlases, by value. In 1900 no less than 93 percent of Australia's imports of printed materials came from Britain compared to only 4 percent from the United States; even by 1971 the British share of these imports had only fallen to 48 percent and the American share had risen to 30 percent. Britain set the standard for Australia's ideas and imagery.

The Australian economy was an important part of the British Empire. Up until about 1950, the dominant pattern of trade was for Australia to supply raw materials (wool, meat, and wheat) to Britain and for Britain to supply manufactured goods. Australia also attracted a significant share of overseas British investment. In 1938 Australia accounted for nearly 12 percent of British investment overseas. Economic ties were underlaid by agreements on preferential trading between the two countries.

British influence on Australian society was continually fed by immigration. Even in 1996 the British-born were the largest group among the foreign-born. British influence was felt in everything from customs and clothing, to technology and ideas. Australians took pride in being part of the British Empire, and visits by British royalty were greeted with great enthusiasm from all ranks of society. During the triumphant tour by Queen Elizabeth II in 1954, the first by a reigning English monarch, an estimated 70 percent of Australians saw the queen in person.

For Australia, being part of the British Empire had two advantages. First, it guaranteed a market for Australia's primary products. Second, Australia gained the protection of British armed forces for defense against Asia. Since the influx of **Chinese** into the gold fields in the 1850s, Australians saw Asia as a threat to their national interests. They saw their land as under-populated and empty, a tempting target for Asia's crowded millions.

After 1940, the closeness of Australia's relationship with Britain weakened. The capture of British Malaya and Singapore by the Japanese in February 1942 and their swift conquest of the Dutch East Indies (Indonesia) made Australia's worst nightmare come true: the Asian invader was at the door and the British Empire was beaten. From this time onward, Australia slowly began to build a closer relationship with the United States as a replacement for Britain as its protector. At the same time, the pace of this transition must not be exaggerated. Defense links with Britain remained very strong until the 1970s. In the 1950s and 1960s Australia provided the space for British nuclear weapons blasts and the testing of its guided missiles. Australia's economic links with Britain remained close until 1973 when Britain joined the European Economic Community. The last constitutional links between Australia and Britain were broken in 1986 when appeals to the Privy Council were stopped.

The emergence of a liberal democracy

As the economy developed from the 1830s, so did Australian colonial society and its political institutions. The previous form of government of an autocratic governor with a small nominated council became increasingly out of step with the economic and social progress of the colonies. Local groups, often led by **Emancipists**, began to press for political reforms. They wanted an end to the sending of British convicts to Australia. This was done in New South Wales in 1840 and an attempt to revive the convict system in 1852 met with mass protests. They also wanted "responsible" government, that is, for the British government to grant the colonies their own parliaments. Up to 1851, the development of Australia had been steady, not spectacular. The total European population was only about 400,000. All this changed with the discovery of gold in various parts of eastern Australia not long after the start of the Californian gold rushes. Gold transformed Australia. It attracted thousands of immigrants and speeded up the granting by Britain of self-government. New South Wales and Victoria were granted self-government in 1855, Tasmania and South Australia in 1856, and Queensland in 1859, by which time the population had reached one million. The late economic development of Western Australia delayed its granting of self-government until 1890.

Self-government was granted by legislation passed by the British parliament that contained written constitutions, itself a departure from the unwritten constitution of Britain. The new colonial parliaments were made up of a lower house (legislative assembly) and an upper house (legislative council). How the membership of these bodies was selected varied between the colonies, but most men aged 21 or over could vote in elections. In the absence of a House of Lords based on a hereditary aristocracy, the purpose of the upper house was to review laws proposed by the lower house and generally to guard the interests of those with property (*see* "Bunyip Aristocracy"). The colonies became states after 1901, but all except Queensland (which abolished its upper house in 1922) retained their upper houses.

At the same time, all the colonies retained governors as the representatives of the British crown. A bill passed by the colonial parliament did not become law until it was signed by the governor. When the colonies federated in 1901, the new Constitution established the office of governor-general to exercise the power of the British crown. The former colonies, now states, retained their governors too.

Although generally considered to be figureheads, **colonial/state governors** and **governor-generals** have exercised real political power in exceptional circumstances. On two occasions they have sacked elected governments. The first occasion was in 1932 when the governor of New South Wales, Sir Philip Game, sacked the government of **Jack Lang**. The second occasion was in 1975 when the Governor-General John Kerr sacked the government of **Gough Whitlam** and installed the opposition as the caretaker government until a new election could be called.

Nevertheless, in all other respects the progress of democracy was swifter in Australia than in Britain. Australia became a proving ground for a number of advanced reforms such as the vote to men aged 21 and over; the **secret ballot**, which was at first known as the "Australian ballot"; votes for **women**; payment of members of parliament; and the formation of a major new political party based on **labor unions**. Australian men over 21 gained the right to vote in Australia in the 1850s, 30 years before it was granted to British men. Australian women were first given the vote in South Australia in 1894 and in federal and New South Wales elections in 1902. Women over 21 did not get the right to vote in Britain until 1928. Payment of members of parliament—a reform that made it possible, at least in theory, for an elected representative to come from the less well-off—had been advocated in Australia since 1854. It was introduced into Victoria in 1880, Queensland in 1886, South Australia in 1887, New South Wales in 1889, Tasmania in 1890, and Western Australia in 1900. In contrast, payment of members of the British House of Commons was not introduced until 1911.

Up to the 1890s **political parties** in the modern sense did not exist. Government majorities were based on **factions** which were often based on prominent individuals. Apart from differing views over **Free Trade** and **Protection**, ideology was not a part of the political scene.

In the late 1880s the political landscape began to change. The formation of the **Australian Labor Party** (ALP), based on labor unions in 1891 and originally called the Political Labor League until 1917 marked the birth of modern social democratic party politics in Australia. The ALP required that its elected members support a specific program of reforms when in office. The first "labor" politicians were elected in South Australia and New South Wales in 1891; there was no comparable political party in Britain until 1900 when the British Labour Party was established.

With the **federation** of the Australian colonies on January 1, 1901, Australian government and politics assumed its present distinctive structure, which was quite unlike its British beginnings. There were three levels of government: federal, state, and local. There was the new federal government. The new states were the original Australian colonies of New South Wales, Victoria, Queensland, South Australia, Western Australia, and Tasmania (see Map 4). Local government was created by the various colonial governments after 1840 but, unlike Britain, has traditionally been the weakest of the three levels of Australian government.

The powers of the new federal government were set down in detail in section 51 of the **Australian Constitution**. Any powers that were not mentioned remained with the state governments, which retained their own written constitutions. Like the states, the new federal constitution was a law of the British parliament.

The federal parliament consists of two chambers: the **house of representatives** representing electorates in the states and **territories** based on population size and a **senate**, which is elected on the basis of states and territories. As their names indicate, the Constitution of the United States strongly influenced the drawing up of the Australian constitution.

Until federation, the colonial governments were the center of political power, particularly their capitals, which were also the largest cities in each colony. After federation, the new federal or Commonwealth government gradually acquired increasing power with the need for national leadership in two world wars and in economic management (for example, during the Depression). Ever since 1942 when the Commonwealth gained control of income tax, the power of the states has been declining (*see* Commonwealth-State Relations). The federal system has also provided the framework for much of Australia's political and institutional history. One other feature of Australian democracy needs to be mentioned: **compulsory voting**. Australia is unique among English-speaking democracies in legally requiring its citizens to vote in federal and state elections. Since the early 1990s there has been debate about whether or not Australia should become a republic, but the idea has yet to win mass interest and support (*see* Republicanism).

All in all, Australia provides a remarkable example of a country that has achieved a liberal democracy without the struggles which marked the histories of the United States or continental Europe. It owed this to a benign British imperial policy in the nineteenth century that was determined to avoid the mistakes that had been made with the American colonies in the eighteenth century and to some extent also to test political reforms that Britain might itself consider. The legacy of these policies was the creation of an enduring liberal democracy.

AUSTRALIAN SOCIETY

The new nation in 1901

Australia as federal nation was born with the twentieth century in 1901. It was a bad beginning. The economic boom the country had enjoyed from the 1860s to the late 1880s ended in depression in 1893. The depression was followed by the worst drought in Australian history from 1895 to 1903. Between 1891 and 1901 gross domestic product per head fell from $115 to $111 million. Instead of coming to Australia, people began to leave. With the exception of 1901, more people left Australia than arrived between 1898 and 1906. In 1901 there were at least 66,493 Australian-born living outside Australia, of whom 39 percent lived in New Zealand, 37 percent in the United Kingdom, 11 percent in the United States, and 10 percent in South Africa. Of the 7,041 Australian-born living in the United States, 32 percent lived in California, 10 percent in New York State, and 7 percent in Pennsylvania. Australia's expatriate population in 1901 was equivalent to 2.3 percent of the country's native-born population.

In 1901 there were 3.8 million people living in Australia of whom 23 percent were foreign-born. This high level of foreign-born was a reflection of sustained immigration from Britain and Europe throughout the nineteenth century. The level of foreign-born in 1901 Australia was comparable for the other similar nations at the time, namely, Argentina (25 percent), New Zealand (31 percent), and the European population of South Africa (26 percent). But it was significantly higher than the percentage of foreign-born in the United States (14 percent) and Canada (13 percent).

Although 77 percent of the population were Australian-born, the age structures of the two groups were markedly different. Half the Australian-born were less than 17 years old whereas half the foreign-born were less than 44 years old. In other words, the Australian-born were disproportionately more likely to be children and teenagers than the foreign-born. Seventy-nine percent of the foreign-born were either English, Welsh, Scottish, or Irish. Only 27 per cent of the British-born were Irish compared to 58 percent in the United States and 21 percent in New Zealand.

Although a newcomer as a nation in 1901, Australia was remarkable for its high degree of **urbanization**—48 percent of Australians were urban dwellers in 1901. This was a higher level of urbanization than France (41 percent) and the United States (40 percent), but less than England and Wales (78 percent) and Germany (56 percent).

Australia's urban population was also remarkable for the dominance of its large cities: 62 percent lived in cities with over 100,000 people. Although Melbourne remained the center of the federal government before its move to Canberra in 1927, Sydney had now caught up with Melbourne in population size—for the first time since the 1860s—and thereafter overtook it to become Australia's largest city, a place it has maintained to the present. **Home ownership** was also a significant feature of Australian society by 1901. The precise figure is not known in 1901, but by 1911, 49 percent of Australian homes were either owned or being bought by their occupiers, a level not attained in Britain until 1971. The main features of modern Australian society—an immigrant, highly urbanized, British-oriented, home-owning democracy—were already well established by 1901.

Current social profile

The 1996 census revealed that Australia's 17.9 million people were mainly Anglo-Celtic immigrants or their descendants. Aborigines and **Torres Strait Islanders**—the original peoples—together number only 353,000 or only 2 percent of the total population. Just over a quarter of Australians—26.1 percent or 3.9 million—were foreign-born with the largest groups from:

- the British Isles (28.8 percent);
- Southern Europe (16.5 percent);
- other Europe and the former Soviet Union (11.5 percent);
- South and South-East Asia (21.9 percent);
- New Zealand and the Pacific Islands (9.7 percent);
- the Middle East (4.9 percent);
- the Americas (3.9 percent); and
- Africa (2.8 percent).

Although Australia's population grew from 3.8 to 17.9 million between 1901 and 1996, its distribution among its states has changed relatively little in that time. As in 1901 New South Wales was the largest state with 34 percent of the population. Victoria was still the second largest state with 24 percent of the population. Queensland remained the third largest state with 19 percent of Australians. South Australia was the fourth largest state in 1901, but had been overtaken by Western Australia by 1986. Together, the three eastern mainland states of New South Wales, Victoria, and Queensland were home to 77 percent of Australians in 1996 compared to 81 percent in 1901.

Again, as in 1901, Australians continued to be predominantly urban dwellers as they have been for most of the country's history. Between 1901 and 1996 the proportion of urban dwellers in Australia has risen remorselessly from 47.7 to 82.3 percent. Since 1966 the level of urbanization has been at least 80 percent or higher. In 1996, 62 percent of Australians lived in the capital cities compared to 35 percent in 1901. Between them, Sydney and Melbourne were home to 38 percent of all Australians in 1996 compared to 26 percent in 1901. Rural or frontier stereotypes of Australia have persisted as popular images, such as the Australian setting in Australia's top international earning film, *Crocodile Dundee* (1985), but the urban reality—or more precisely suburban reality—of life for most Australians, both now and in the past, is undeniable (*see Ginger Meggs*).

Australians also continue to prefer to live near their coastline if possible. In 1996, 83 percent of the population lived within 50 kilometers of the coastline compared to about 41 percent in 1901. Better communications and suburban development, as well as declining prospects in agriculture and mining, have drained population away from the interior.

A successful immigrant nation

Australia is not just an immigrant nation—as often proclaimed within the country—it has been a highly successful one and a major player in global migration. Between 1846 and 1932, Australia absorbed 5.6 percent of total European emigration, and between 1946 and 1963, it absorbed no less than 21 percent.

Unlike most other English-speaking immigrant countries, **immigration** has continued to play a central part in the forming of Australian society since 1920. In that year 15.8 percent of the Australian population was foreign-born compared to 25 percent in New Zealand, 22 percent in Canada, and 13.2 percent in the United States. By 1990 the foreign-born made up 24.5 percent of Australia's population compared to 17 percent in New Zealand, 16 percent in Canada, and 8 percent in the United States.

Between 1800 and 1997 the European population of Australia grew from 5,200 to 18.5 million. Over a third of this increase—35.2 percent—came from immigration: 6.3 million people. Of these, 3.3 million have been assisted by governments under various schemes. It was not until 1871 that a majority of Australians (54 percent) were Australian-born, but most of these were children with the British-born dominating the older age groups until the 1900s.

Australia was an immigrant society cut off from its parent society by a long journey. The decision to come to Australia was not one to be taken lightly as there was little opportunity—unlike going to North America—for most to change their minds and return. Because land sales were used to subsidize immigration, land was expensive to buy, far more so than in North America. Distance from Britain fostered popular nostalgia for Britain among most immigrants with the exception of the Irish. Continued immigration from Britain reinforced these sentiments. Until the 1960s it was common in Australia for Britain to be referred to as "home."

Immigration is one of the central themes in Australian history, although its contribution to population growth has been variable. It has been particularly prominent in certain periods, namely 1852-60, 1876-90, 1909-13, 1919-29, and 1948-74, periods of comparative prosperity. At the first sign of a downturn in the economy, government assistance for immigration stopped. Because of the distance and cost of emigrating from Western Europe, entry to the Australian **labor force** could be far more easily restricted than into North America. As a result, labor unions were able to become important social and economic institutions. They also benefited from being part of, what was until the late nineteenth century, a transplanted British society.

These demographic facts color much of Australia's subsequent history. Although the proportion of foreign-born within the population fell, immigration from Britain continued to be important, particularly with assisted immigration schemes and the imposition of the White Australia Policy by the new federal government. In other respects Australia's progression to nationhood was slow and cautious.

Although Australia failed to realize the dreams of those in the 1920s that it might one day have the population and power of the United States, it was able to provide generally higher living standards for most of its British immigrants than if they had remained in Britain. Since 1945 it has also absorbed large numbers of immigrants from non-English speaking countries with a minimum of social tension. From being an insular, British-oriented society Australia has become one of the world's most successful immigrant nations. Since 1978 federal government policy has supported "multiculturalism" (that is, acceptance of immigrants' cultural diversity), whereas the previous policy was one of assimilation to an Australian way of life derived from Britain.

In recent years the difficulties and disappointments of the Australian economy have led to a questioning of immigration as a national policy, which assumed racist anti-Asian colors among a small minority of Australians. Immigration has been reduced—as it has on many previous occasions in the past—in response to the domestic demand for labor. In May 1997 the federal government reduced the intake level for non-humanitarian migration to 68,000 in 1997-98 compared to 82,560 in 1995-96. Nevertheless, Australia remains an outstanding example of a genuinely successful multicultural society. A poll taken in May 1997 found that although 64 percent of Australians thought that immigration was too high, 78 percent considered that multiculturalism was good for Australia.

Australia's development, from the most unpromising of beginnings as a British jail in 1788 to the liberal, tolerant, democracy of the present is as remarkable as is its success as a country of large-scale immigration. The challenge of the future will be to maintain these achievements and its free market economic policies in the face of the economic and political difficulties facing its Asian neighbors.

THE DICTIONARY

A

ABORIGINES   Aborigines were the first inhabitants of Australia and by far the largest group among its indigenous peoples, the other group being **Torres Strait Islanders**. The Aborigines are believed to have migrated from South-East Asia into northern Australia between 120,000 and 80,000 years ago. By about 38,000 years ago they had reached the south-eastern and south-western parts of the Australian mainland and around 21,000 years ago they had crossed into **Tasmania** using a land bridge caused by a fall in the sea level. When the sea level rose again about 10,000 years ago, these Aborigines were cut off in Tasmania.

It is not known for certain how many Aborigines there were by 1788 when the first permanent European settlement was made. It used to be thought that there were only about 300,000, but the distinguished economic historian **Noel Butlin** cast doubt on this figure in 1983 and it is now thought that there may have been between 500,00 and 750,000. As in the Americas, the arrival of the Europeans and their diseases, especially smallpox, had a devastating impact on the native population of Australia. One of the strongest arguments for a larger rather than smaller number of Aborigines before 1788 was a second outbreak of smallpox among the Aborigines of south-eastern Australia in the 1830s. Smallpox requires a minimum population of 250,000 to remain active.

By 1788 there were 600 distinct Aboriginal groups. They were most numerous in the areas of permanent water supply on the northern and eastern coasts. As the land was often dry and rainfall unpredictable, and the Aborigines were cut off from the challenges of other cultures, their material culture remained primitive although the **boomerang** (a curved wooden throwing tool) showed evidence of technological sophistication. Aborigines lived lives based on hunting and gathering. At the same time, they developed a rich spiritual culture with a high degree of complexity.

The first British governors in eastern Australia, following the eighteenth-century French philosopher Jean-Jacques Rousseau, saw the Aborigines as "noble savages," that is, unspoiled by civilization. In 1792 the Aborigine Bennelong (c.1764-1813) was taken to

England and met King George III. European attitudes towards the Aborigines soon changed. Governments and missionaries regarded them in paternal terms as a people who should be made Christian and encouraged to live like Europeans. For the settlers who came in increasing numbers after 1820, the Aborigines were competitors for the land. Fighting between settlers and Aborigines is estimated to have cost the lives of 20,000 Aborigines and 2,500 Europeans by 1900. Some Aborigines were the victims of massacre such as at **Myall Creek**. However, it was European diseases such as smallpox that killed most Aborigines.

By 1861 the number of Aborigines had fallen to about 180,000 and continued to fall thereafter, reaching its lowest point in 1933 when there were only 73,800. Although European diseases accounted for most of the deaths in the early years of contact, violence by settlers and the general destruction of the original environment by the process of settlement took away the Aborigines' traditional way of life in the best lands and forced a drastic decline in their numbers. Government policies did not support the violence done to the Aborigines but proved unable to stop it either. Since the 1930s, the number of Aborigines has recovered and grown steadily

With their primitive material culture, it was easy for the materially superior Europeans to see them as an inferior race unable to manage their own affairs and destined to die out. Governments tried to protect the Aborigines but their efforts were often disastrously misguided. For example, in Van Diemen's Land (Tasmania after 1856), the government removed the remaining Aborigines to Flinders Island where they eventually all died out (the last, Truganini, in 1876). The last full-blooded Tasmanian Aborigine died on another island in 1888.

In other parts of Australia, many Aborigines were confined to Christian missions or put on government reserves. During **World War II**, only one Aborigine became an officer in the Australian Army, Reginald Walter Saunders (1920-90) in 1944. Up to the 1960s the goal of the official policy was the "assimilation" of Aborigines into the values and lifestyles of Australian society.

Since the 1930s Aborigines began the slow business of establishing for themselves a better place in Australian society. In 1938 some protested about the 150th anniversary celebrations of European settlement. In the 1950s many Aborigines began moving into the cities in New South Wales and Victoria where they formed advancement groups. Inspired by the example of American black activists, Aboriginal activism became more strident. Charles Perkins (1936-), the first Aborigine to graduate from a university, helped organize "freedom rides" in rural New South Wales to draw attention to discrimination against Aborigines.

In 1967, 91 percent of voters in a national referendum approved a change to the **Australian Constitution** to grant the federal government the power to count Aborigines in the census and to make laws on their behalf.

Despite these advances, Aborigines remained (and remain) the most disadvantaged group in Australian society. Their health is poorer than Europeans, and they have far higher death, arrest, imprisonment, and unemployment rates, characteristics documented from the 1960s and confirmed by an official survey of 15,700 indigenous Australians in 1994.

In 1972 Aboriginal groups began a campaign for "land rights," that is, legal title to certain lands. When Australia was taken over by the British, the land was appropriated by the Crown on the grounds that no one "owned" it. There was no national treaty between Aborigines and Europeans. Since 1972 Aborigines have been granted freehold title to large tracts of land, mainly in the center of Australia. By 1984 about a tenth of Australia's land had been returned to the Aborigines, usually in the form of reserves or as freehold land. Two judgments by the **High Court of Australia**— the **Mabo Judgment** (1992) and the **Wik Case** (1996)—have brought the issue of Aboriginal land claims into the forefront of political debates in federal politics during 1997.

There have also been two important recent official inquiries into the conditions and treatment of Aborigines. The first was the royal commission into Aboriginal deaths in custody, which was established in 1987 and produced recommendations to prevent suicide by Aboriginal prisoners. The second inquiry was appointed in 1995 into the past policies of separating very young Aborigines from their families and having them brought up in European households.

An official survey of Aborigines and Torres Strait Islanders in 1994 found that of those aged 13 and over, nearly 60 percent identified with a clan, tribal, or language group, 84 percent saw elders as important, and 72 percent had attended an indigenous cultural activity in the previous 12 months. The survey also found that 75 percent of Aborigines and Torres Strait Islanders aged over 13 recognized an area as their homeland.

At the 1996 census there were 314,120 Aborigines (compared to 238,575 in 1991), that is, 1.8 percent of all Australians. A far higher proportion of Aborigines are rural dwellers, which contributes to their lower standard of living. In 1996 only a quarter of Aborigines lived in the capital cites and the administrative center of **Darwin** compared to 63 percent of all Australians. (*See also* Alfred Reginald Radcliffe- Brown)

ABORIGINAL AND TORRES STRAIT ISLANDER COMMISSION (ATSIC) ATSIC was formed by the *Aboriginal and Torres Strait Islander Act* in 1989 and began to function in March 1990, although its origins were in the federal department of Aboriginal Affairs (formed in 1972) and the Aboriginal Development Commission, which had been formed in 1980. ATSIC is made up of 35 regional councils elected by **Aborigines** and **Torres Strait Islanders**. The purpose of ATSIC is to put into effect the principle of self-determination for indigenous Australians, which has been a policy of federal governments since 1972, and to deliver federal government programs of assistance. In July 1994 the Torres Strait Regional Authority was set up to focus on the needs of Torres Strait Islanders. In July 1997 the **Howard** government announced that ATSIC would probably be divided into two organizations by 2000 with the intention of giving Torres Strait Islanders more autonomy.

ACCORD The name of a formal agreement between the **Australian Labor Party** (ALP) and the **Australian Council of Trade Unions** (ACTU) regarding economic and social policy released on February 22, 1983. The Accord set out details of policies to be implemented when the ALP was elected to the federal government. It covered prices, wages and working conditions, non-wage incomes (for example, earnings from dividends and interest), taxation, government expenditure, social security, and health. The Accord grew out of conferences between the ALP and the ACTU in 1979 over new approaches to economic management. The Accord was renegotiated seven times while the ALP was the federal government between 1983 and March 1996 under the **Hawke** and **Keating** administrations. The Accord has been credited with modest general increases in wages since 1983 in return for lower levels of **labor disputes** by **labor unions**. In this sense it was a continuation of the "Wages Pause" of the previous government of **Malcolm Fraser**, which was introduced in December 1982 to freeze wage increases and was supported by the **industrial tribunals** for six months.

ADELAIDE   Adelaide is the capital city of the state of **South Australia**. Its site was selected and planned by Colonel William Light (1786-1839) in 1837-38. A municipal corporation was up in 1840, the first local government authority in Australia. The city owed its early growth to British immigration and served as port for the **wheat** industry. By 1851 the population had reached 18,000; it doubled by 1861 and by 1901 had reached 141,400. In the 1870s much growth took place in the southern and northern suburbs when the total population increased from 51,100 to 91,800. Unlike other major Australian cities, Adelaide's growth rate in the 1880s was modest. It did, however, share in the general suburban growth from 1910 to 1914 and from 1921 to 1929. In 1954 the satellite town of Elizabeth (named after Queen Elizabeth II) was established north of Adelaide as a home for workers in the motor vehicle industry. Elizabeth became a city in 1964.

Between 1947 and 1971 the population rose from 382,500 to 842,700 in response to official encouragement of new industries in South Australia and consequent immigration. The downturn in manufacturing employment has hurt the economy since the mid-1970s and slowed population growth. In 1996 Adelaide had a total population of 1,045,900 compared to 1,003,800 in 1986 when it first reached the one million mark.

Famous for its churches and grid city plan, Adelaide's reputation as a cultural center was boosted by the beginning of the bi-annual Adelaide Festival of Arts in 1960. Adelaide was unusual for an Australian city in being systematically planned from its foundation—**Canberra** is the only other Australian capital city that has also been planned—and interest in planning continued. A town planning department was established in the state government in 1920 and government interest in planning the city continued after 1945. Dubbed the "Athens of the South" by the late 1920s, largely for its fine layout, the term is now meant more as a compliment for its cultural achievements. A large drama complex was opened in the inner city in 1974. The Adelaide Festival of Arts, which began in 1960, is held every two years and attracts international attention and performers.

AGE   One of Australia's most respected newspapers, the *Age* was first issued in **Melbourne**, **Victoria**, on October 17, 1852. In 1856 it was bought by two Scottish immigrants, David and Ebenezer Syme (1826-1860). David Syme (1827-1908), editor from 1860, was a major political figure in Victorian politics. Under him, the daily sales of the *Age* grew from 38,000 in 1880 to 120,000 by 1900. Syme denounced **squatting** and supported free compulsory and secular **education**. However, he was best known nationally as a supporter of **protection**. In 1996 the *Age* had daily sales between Monday and Friday of 206,500. (*See also* Press)

AGRICULTURE   Until the 1930s agriculture contributed more to Australia's gross domestic product and employment than **manufacturing**. This was despite the arid character of much of Australia which limited the kinds of agriculture that could be practiced as well as its scale. The unusual circumstances of European settlement also influenced the development of agriculture. In the older European societies, agriculture arose first and provided the foundation for towns and cities, but in Australia the urban centers came first and the rural areas followed.

Farming begun soon after the arrival of the **First Fleet** with the object of providing food. Even so, there were food shortages in **Sydney** between 1790 and 1794 and the early settlement was reliant on imported food. Neither was much of the land around Sydney particularly suitable for agriculture, despite the efforts of James Ruse (1760-1837), an ex-convict, who was granted land for a farm in 1791. Early agriculture had more success in **Tasmania** because of the better soils near the early centers of settlement. The statistics on agricultural production for this period are regarded as only approximate, but they indicate that by 1800 there had been sufficient production to remove the threat of starvation. For example, the number of cattle on private farms increased from 18 in 1795 to 227 by 1799, and the number of sheep from 688 to 4,588. Food and seeds also arrived by ship from **Britain**, but the same ships also brought **convicts** who had to be fed.

The other great breakthrough in the early history of Australian agriculture came in 1813 when a route was finally found over the rugged Blue Mountains. This discovery opened up the plains of south-eastern Australia to large-scale agriculture and **sheep and wool** production. There was rapid settlement of these plains between 1820 and 1850, usually by **squatting**. Between 1841 and 1861 the occupation of this area was largely responsible for raising the proportion of Australians living in rural areas from 61.4 to 66.8— its highest level—a growth which represented a rise in the rural population from 126,900 to 769,900. The last half of the nineteenth century saw a sharp increase in agricultural land use. Between 1850 and 1900, the total amount of land cultivated for crops rose from 400 to 8,670 hectares. The bulk of this land was sown for grain crops such as **wheat**. Over the same period, wool production rose from 19 to 201,960 million kilograms. Although the first Australian wool exports to Britain were made in 1807, it was this success that enabled large-scale production. Between 1815 and 1821 wool shipments from **New South Wales** to Britain increased from 15,000 to 79,600 kilograms, and by the 1840s Australia had become one of the largest suppliers of wool to the British market. Wool accounted for about 40 percent of Australia's entire export earnings between 1841 and 1911.

The proneness of Australia to **drought** severely limited the expansion of agriculture. This was especially notable during the great drought between 1895 and 1903, which had a spectacular effect on agricultural output. In 1894 wheat production reached 37.1 million bushels, but only 12.4 million were produced in 1903. In the same period, the number of beef and dairy cattle fell from 11.8 to 7.1 million, and the number of sheep fell from 99.5 to 53.7 million. Subsequent droughts have also depressed agricultural output, but none so much as in this period.

The potential of agriculture was also limited by the release of rabbits in 1859. Originally intended as game, they adapted quickly and lacking native predators had assumed plague proportions by 1900. Until the introduction of the disease myxomatosis in the 1950s, there was no other way to control their numbers except by shooting and trapping. Over time, the rabbits developed immunity to myxomatosis and biological controls in recent years have concentrated on the caleci virus.

Agriculture has been one of the most innovative sectors of Australian industry and many of the patents taken out in Australia before 1920 were intended for use in agriculture. In 1843 John Ridley (1806-1887) successfully tested a mechanical wheat harvester. The first mechanical sheep shearing machine was patented in 1868. One of the main technological breakthroughs of the period came in February 1880 when the first consignment of frozen Australian meat arrived in Britain, the culmination of efforts made since 1873. Refrigeration opened up export possibilities for other agricultural exports such as butter. The example of California provided the model for irrigation schemes using the Murray River. Technological innovation enabled the emergence of the dairy industry to service the urban population from the 1890s.

Increased use of mechanization from 1914 onwards reduced the demand for rural labor, but at the price of a higher loss of population to the larger towns and cities to the detriment of most country towns. Better communications—**roads** as well as **railroads**—also encouraged the centralization of Australia's population. Since 1911 the proportion of Australians living in rural areas has continued to fall steadily from nearly half to only one in five by the 1990s. Similarly, the proportion of Australians living in towns with between 2,500 and 10,000 people (mainly country towns) has also fallen. A widespread feeling of neglect from the 1900s led to the formation of the **Country Party** in 1920 and its rise as the third party of Australian politics. Despite the decline in the economic and social importance of agriculture in Australian society, rural politics remains a potent force and an important part of political policy making regardless of whether the **Liberal Party** or the **Australian Labor Party** are in government.

The general efficiency of Australian agriculture meant that it has continued to contribute strongly to the **economy** until the 1960s. It was particularly hard hit by the decision of Britain to join the European Economic Community in 1973 and by the massive subsidies made to agriculture by the Community, hence the formation of the **Cairns Group of Fair Traders in Agriculture** in 1986. Between 1921 and 1961 the contribution made by agriculture to gross domestic product fell from 30 to 13.8 percent. Since that time this contribution has declined until it reached only 3.7 percent in 1995-96. As an employer, agriculture employed 24.3 percent of the labor force in 1921, but only 11.3 percent by 1961 and 5 percent by 1995-96. Many of these changes in agriculture have been inevitable as a consequence of the maturing of Western economies and consequent changes in patterns of consumption and demand. This can be illustrated by the sharp fall in the demand for coarse wool over the past decade; in contrast, fine wool commands a high premium. Other success stories concerning agricultural products include rising exports for Australian **beer** and **wine**. Since 1979 the national voice of Australian agriculture has been the **National Farmers' Federation**.

ALL FOR AUSTRALIA LEAGUE A conservative political body, the League was set up originally in **Sydney** in early 1931 to oppose the **Australian Labor Party** federal and **New South Wales** governments and their policies dealing with the Depression. Branches of the League were later formed in other **states**. The League stood for "responsible" government, the repayment of overseas debts, and loyalty to the British Empire. The League was the main extra-parliamentary body behind the formation of the **United Australia Party**.

ALUMINUM The aluminum industry began in Australia in 1955 when a joint federal and state government enterprise began production of aluminum metal at Bell Bay in northern **Tasmania**. In the same year, a major deposit of bauxite was found at Weipa in northern **Queensland**. These, and other bauxite deposits in **Western Australia** and the **Northern Territory**, enabled the industry to become internationally significant. By 1980 Australia had become the largest producer of bauxite (30 percent of world production) and the largest exporter of alumina (about 20 percent of world output). In 1995 Australia was still the world's largest producer of bauxite and the fourth largest producer of aluminum. In 1997-98 Australia produced 44.9 million tonnes of bauxite and alumina accounted for 6.9 percent of Australia's merchandise exports in 1997-98. (*See also* Mining)

AMALGAMATED METAL WORKERS' UNION (AMWU) The AMWU is one of the largest and most influential **labor unions** in Australia. It began as the **New South Wales** branch of the English-based union the Amalgamated Society of Engineers in 1852 with 27 members. From 1920 to 1973 it was called the Amalgamated Engineering Union (AEU) and the AMWU from 1973 to 1990. Its members were skilled metal workers, and it was one of the few unions to offer members sickness, accident, unemployment, and strike payments. From 1915 it slowly began to admit lesser-skilled metal workers into its ranks. Between 1920 and 1968 its share of metal industry union members rose from 18 to 84 percent. In 1968 it formally severed its links with its British parent union.

Long a militant union, the AMWU was one of the leading unions in gaining higher pay and better conditions for its members since the 1940s. From 1972, it gained members by amalgamating with other unions in the metal industry. Reflecting fluctuations in manufacturing employment, the membership of the AMWU fell from 171,200 in 1973 to 163,400 in 1987. In 1990 the AMWU and the Association of Drafting, Supervisory and Technical Employees (20,000 members) amalgamated. In April 1991 the AMWU became the Metals and Engineering Workers' Union, which was later renamed the Australian Manufacturing Workers' Union. In 1997 this union had 191,800 members compared to 200,000 in 1995. (*See also* Metal Trades Industry Association)

ANGLICANISM (*See* Church of England)

ANGRY PENGUINS The Angry Penguins was a literary and artistic movement begun in Adelaide University in 1940, mainly by Max Harris (1921-1995). Unlike its contemporary, the **Jindyworobaks**, the Angry Penguins promoted internationalism and modernism; they saw the Jindyworobaks as narrow and provincial. In 1944 the Angry Penguins were the target of a successful literary hoax. Two Sydney poets, James McAuley and Harold Stewart, produced a series of poems drawn at random from a miscellany of unlikely sources and passed it off as the work of one "Ern Malley" whom they said had recently died. The purpose of the hoax was to test whether the Angry Penguins could in fact distinguish good modern poetry from bad. After they declared it to be of significance, the hoax was revealed. Later in 1944 Harris, as editor of *Angry Penguins*, was successfully, but unfairly, prosecuted for publishing indecent material; thereafter the Angry Penguins became a part of the broader literary and artistic Australian landscape.

ANTARCTICA Australians have been prominent land explorers of Antarctica since 1907-9 when Sir Douglas Mawson (1882-1958) and the geologist Professor Edgeworth David (1858-1934) went with Sir Ernest Shackleton's expedition. Mawson led a separate expedition in 1911-12. The British expedition to the South Pole of Robert Scott in 1910-12 included the Australian geographer and meteorologist **Thomas Griffith Taylor**. On the basis of Mawson's discoveries of 1929-31, **Britain** granted Australia control over about 40 percent of Antarctica (from 160 to 45 degrees east excluding a sector claimed by France) in 1933. Australia's territorial claims to Antarctica, like those of other nations, are not recognized by the **United States**. In 1989 the Australian government announced its opposition to proposals to conduct mining in Antarctica and in December 1992 became the first party to the Antarctic Treaty (1959) to ratify a protocol designed to protect the environment of Antarctica which came into force in April 1994. Australia maintains three permanent bases in Antarctica: Casey, Davis, and Mawson.

ANZAC   Anzac stands for Australian and New Zealand Army Corps. The word was first coined early in 1915. During the Allied landing at **Gallipoli**, Turkey, on April 25, 1915, Australian and **New Zealand** soldiers went into battle for the first time in **World War I**. The efforts of the Australian and New Zealand soldiers were much praised by the British, and Anzac became a general term for all Australian (or New Zealand) soldiers. In the fighting, which lasted until January 8, 1916, 8,418 Australians were killed and 19,441 were wounded. The Gallipoli campaign was quickly portrayed as much more than a military operation; it was held to have proved that Australia had now become a nation and no longer just a collection of colonies. The word "Anzac" was prohibited from commercial use under British (1916) and Australian law (1918, 1921), although "Anzac" cookies, a particular type of cookie, have been available in supermarkets since 1994.

Anzac Day—April 25—was observed as a public holiday by the early 1920s and a legal holiday in all **states** by 1927. It became Australia's true national day—in contrast to **Australia Day**— marked by marches of war veterans in all cities and towns. Attitudes to Anzac Day were the subject of a controversial play, *The One Day of the Year* by Alan Seymour (1927-) first produced in 1960. Since **World War II** Anzac Day has gradually evolved into a day of remembrance for those killed in war. Marches of veterans in the cities and towns draw huge crowds.

ANZAC PACT The Anzac Pact (also known as the Australia-New Zealand Agreement and the Canberra Pact) was a wartime security agreement signed in 1944 and a reaction to the exclusion of Australia and New Zealand from the Cairo Conference in November 1943. It was an initiative of **Herbert Vere Evatt**, then the Australian minister for external affairs, in an effort to promote regional defense and security. It was replaced by the **Anzus Treaty** in 1951. The most lasting effect of the Anzac Pact was the creation of the **South Pacific Forum** in 1947 which was designed to coordinate various kinds of assistance programs to the region.

ANZUS TREATY   The Anzus Treaty (or Anzus for short) was signed by Australia, **New Zealand**, and the **United States** in September 1951. Under it, the signatories bound themselves to "act to meet common danger" in the Pacific, that is, against the threat of communism. In effect the Treaty made Australia part of the American defense sphere. In 1985 New Zealand withdrew from Anzus over visits by American ships carrying nuclear weapons, but Australia and the United States remain signatories and the Anzus Treaty remains fundamental to the defense links between Australia and the United States. The sending of Australian troops to the Persian Gulf in response to a U.S. request in February 1998 can be seen in the context of Australia's commitment to Anzus.

ARCHIBALD, JULES FRANÇOIS (1856-1919)   Journalist and editor, Archibald was born John Feltham Archibald in Kildare, **Victoria**. He worked on provincial newspapers before moving to **Melbourne** in 1874, then **Queensland** and **Sydney** when he was one of the cofounders of the *Bulletin* in 1880. In 1883 he visited Britain, France, and the United States. He was editor of the *Bulletin* from 1886 to 1902; he sold his share in the *Bulletin* in 1914. Archibald was a great admirer of France and her culture as well as being a strong Australian nationalist. In his will, he left a bequest to be used as an annual prize for portrait painting, which continues to this day.

ARCHITECTURE   Because the **First Fleet** carried no builders or building materials, the first buildings erected at **Sydney** in the 1790s were crude huts, often little better than the shelters made by the **Aborigines** for thousands of years. Neither was the landscape bounteous with softwood timber; most of Australia's trees are species of gum tree, which is a hardwood. As the population grew and became better-off, the quality and scale of housing grew too. Apart from extensive terrace housing in the inner suburbs of the large cities, detached houses were the preferred form of housing and have remained so to the present. The architectural style before 1900 was transplanted directly from **Britain** with no allowance made for the great difference in climate or the different position of the sun. The importance of what is known as "northeast aspect" or siting the main part of a house to face the northeast so it would avoid the summer sun but catch the winter sun, was only advocated in 1902 even though it was a fundamental feature of solar planning for Australian buildings.

The dominance of the English example was inescapable in the urban landscape of what are now the inner areas of many Australian cities and towns and which look thoroughly English. Victorian architecture was particularly important in **Melbourne**, which boasts many magnificent examples of this kind of architecture. Similarly, Launceston, the second largest town in **Tasmania**, has fine examples of Edwardian architecture.

Since 1900 there was a greater willingness to experiment with other architectural forms. For example, in **Queensland** with its hot and humid climate, building houses on wooden stilts became common. More generally, there was a new form that was named "Federation" style after the **federation** of the Australian colonies in 1901. Although rooted in the Art Nouveau movement, this style incorporated motifs from Australian flora and fauna. Architecture itself gained a new status in 1918 when Leslie Wilkinson (1882-1973) was recruited from Britain by the University of Sydney to become Australia's first professor of architecture. Wilkinson was associated with the "Spanish Mission" style; with its emphasis on courtyards and verandahs, it was particularly suited to Australia's sunny climate. American influence on Australian architecture came from the Californian bungalow, which was first built in Australia using those built in Pasadena in 1911 as a model. It became a popular form of building in the 1920s. From the late 1930s the ideas of Frank Lloyd Wright also began to be applied to some of the more experimental homes of wealthy owners.

Relatively few Australian buildings were high-rise before 1920. Although the skyscrapers were begun in Melbourne in the late 1880s, credit for the first skyscraper actually completed has been claimed by Culwalla Chambers in Sydney, which was opened in 1913. But the detached house was the dominant type of Australian building despite the growth of flats in the larger cities since 1920.

In 1952 the noted Australian architect Robin Boyd (1919-1971) published *Australia's Home: Its Origins, Builders, and Occupiers*, a general history in which he summed it up as "a material triumph and an aesthetic calamity." He expanded on this theme in *The Australian Ugliness* (1960). What Boyd described was perhaps an unavoidable consequence of a democracy dominated by **home**

ownership and the need to make up for about a decade and a half of virtually suspended new building caused by the Depression and **World War II**. Since 1950 there has been a greater fusion between domestic and international architectural styles and their application to the realities of the Australian landscape and the needs of its people. Australia's best-known building remains the **Sydney Opera House**, which was begun in 1957 and finished in 1973.

ARNOTT'S Arnott's has dominated the Australian cookie market for over a century. The company was founded by William Arnott (1827-1901), a Scottish immigrant and unsuccessful gold miner. He opened a bakery in West Maitland, **New South Wales**, but was forced to relocate it to **Newcastle** because of repeated flooding. The business thrived through serving the growing market of **Sydney**. The modern well-known brands of "Ginger Nuts" and "Milk Arrowroot" were being produced by 1882. Other traditional Australian cookies such as "Iced Vovos," "Saos," "Jatz," "Salada," "Scotch Finger," and "Wheatmeal" were launched in 1906. In the same year, the bulk of the factory was relocated to Homebush, **Sydney**.

By 1991 Arnott's accounted for 65 percent of all Australian cookie sales, but inept management led to the demise of Arnott's as an Australian-owned company. An attempt to distribute its cookies in the **United States** was an expensive failure, and concerns over a hostile takeover by the Bond Corporation led to an agreement with the U.S. giant Campbell's Soup Company, which was officially allowed to acquire 40 percent of Arnott's in 1985. By 1992 Campbell's had acquired a controlling interest in Arnott's. In November 1997 the remaining 30 percent of Arnott's shareholders—mainly family members—sold their shares to Campbell's Soup Company.

ARTISTS (*See* Sidney Nolan, Tom Roberts)

ASIA PACIFIC ECONOMIC COOPERATION (APEC) APEC is a regional inter-governmental forum launched by the **Hawke** government. Its purpose is to maintain economic growth and development in the Asia-Pacific and North American region and to reduce regional trade barriers. The first meeting of APEC was held in **Canberra** in November 1989. APEC provides a framework for regular inter-governmental cooperation on a wide range of economic issues such as trade and investment data, investment and technology transfer, training, energy, and trade promotion. By 1990 APEC included Australia, **New Zealand**, **Japan**, the members of the Association of South-East Asian Nations (Brunei Darussalam, Indonesia, Malaysia, Philippines, Singapore, Thailand), the Republic of **Korea**, **United States**, and Canada; China, Taiwan, and Hong Kong were admitted to APEC at the Seoul meeting in November 1991. In 1993 a permanent secretariat was set up in Singapore. In May 1997 the trade ministers of APEC met in Montreal to work toward greater liberalization of trade. (*See also* Protection)

ASSIGNMENT SYSTEM The assignment system was a way of "assigning" or allocating **convicts** to work for free settlers in return for food, clothing, and accommodation. The purpose of the system was to reduce the burden of the convicts on the government and build up a more diversified economy. Convicts were not able to change the settler they were assigned to, and settlers were not allowed to punish convicts. By the 1830s most convicts were assigned in this way; in 1835 about 70 percent of the 20,000 convicts in **New South Wales** were assigned. The assignment system came under increased criticism, largely because it was considered too lenient and, in an **economy** short of labor, provided too many opportunities for convicts to advance themselves. The system was abandoned in 1840 in New South Wales.

AUSTRALIA The idea that there had to be a *terra australis*—a "south land"—in the southern hemisphere to counterbalance the continents of the northern hemisphere was an ancient one in European geographical thought, but finding the continent proved elusive, hence its other name of *terra australis incognita*, "the unknown south land." The term "Australia" came into use on European maps during the seventeenth century and was the general term by the late eighteenth century. Its status was boosted by its use in *Voyage of Terra Australia* by **Matthew Flinders** in 1814. The governor of **New South Wales**, **Lachlan Macquarie** officially approved the term in 1817.

AUSTRALIA DAY Australia Day is Australia's national day and is celebrated on January 26, the day when the **First Fleet** arrived in Sydney Cove, **New South Wales**, in 1788. Fifty years later, in

1838, it was proclaimed as Anniversary Day and made a public holiday in New South Wales, which then included the present **states** of **Victoria** and **Queensland**. In 1930 the **Australian Natives' Association** started a national campaign to have January 26 declared Australia Day. In 1932 the **premier** of New South Wales, **Jack Lang** adopted the idea, but after his dismissal, the day reverted to its former title of Anniversary Day. Australia Day has only been celebrated nationally since 1946 following agreement between the federal and state governments. The next Monday after January 26 is a public holiday. Australia Day is the most popular day for the holding of ceremonies to confer Australian **citizenship**. (*See also* Australian Flag)

AUSTRALIA FIRST MOVEMENT   The Australia First Movement was an extreme nationalist Australian group that was pro-fascist and anti-Semitic. It was formed in 1941 by W. J. Miles, the editor of a minor monthly publication called the *Publicist*. Although only numbering about 20, the movement's access to publicity as well as its extremism resulted in the **internment** of its members in 1942. Most were released after a few weeks, but P. R. Stephensen (1901-1965), considered its leader, was held until 1945.

AUSTRALIA PARTY (AP)   The AP was a progressive, moderate reformist political party, which was formed in July 1969 by a **New South Wales** businessman, Gordon Page Barton (1929-). The AP grew out of the Liberal Reform Group, which was formed in November 1966 following an open letter Barton had written to visiting U.S. President Lyndon B. Johnson protesting Australia being drawn into the **Vietnam** war. Many among the Liberal Reform Group were dissident members of the **Liberal Party**. By 1971, the AP had 1,700 members, 900 of them in New South Wales. In the December 1972 federal election for the **house of representatives**, the AP gained 159,916 votes or 2.4 percent of the formal primary vote and was able to direct enough of its preferences to the **Australian Labor Party** to assist it to win government. The AP suffered from a high turnover of membership and contested its last election in 1975 when it only gained 33,630 votes. Some of its members joined the **Australian Democrats**.

AUSTRALIAN   There have been two noteworthy newspapers in Australian history called the *Australian*. The first was established by William Charles Wentworth (c.1792-1872) and Robert Wardell (1794-1834) to champion the cause of **Emancipists**, **franchise** reform, and trial by jury. The paper closed in 1848. The second newspaper to be called the *Australian* was established by **Rupert Murdoch** in 1964 as Australia's first national daily newspaper; in 1996 it had daily sales of 122,500 from Monday to Friday and 311,000 on Saturdays. (*See also* Press)

AUSTRALIAN BALLOT   (*See* Secret Ballot)

AUSTRALIAN BROADCASTING COMMISSION (ABC)   The ABC is the government-owned broadcasting service of Australia. Modeled on the British Broadcasting Company, the ABC was formed in 1921. It began broadcasting by radio in 1932 and by television in 1956. Although the programs of the ABC cover a wide range of interests, they emphasize areas neglected by commercial broadcasters, such as the arts and documentaries. Investigative current affairs television was begun in Australia by the ABC in 1963 with its *Four Corners* program. On July 1, 1983, the ABC was renamed the Australian Broadcasting Corporation. In 1996 there was a federal government inquiry into the role of the ABC as Australia's national broadcaster. The result of this inquiry was that the budget of the ABC was substantially reduced.

AUSTRALIAN   BROADCASTING   CORPORATION   (*See* Australian Broadcasting Commission)

AUSTRALIAN CAPITAL TERRITORY (ACT)   The ACT is the territory that was proclaimed on January 1, 1911, as the site for Australia's federal or national government. It covers 2,538 square kilometers in inland south-eastern **New South Wales** and some land on the southern coast of New South Wales at Jervis Bay. Provision for the Territory was made in section 125 of the **Australian Constitution**. The present title dates from 1938. The main function of the ACT as an administrative unit is to accommodate the city of **Canberra**. Despite a referendum to the contrary supported by 63 percent of the residents in 1978, the federal government enacted legislation to give the ACT self-government in 1989. Since May 1995, Kate Carnell (1955-), the **chief minister**, has led a minority Liberal government in the ACT. At the 1996 census the ACT had a resident population of 299,200.

AUSTRALIAN CHAMBER OF MANUFACTURES (ACM)   The ACM is Australia's oldest continuous **employers' association**. It was formed in 1985 when the Victorian Chamber of Manufactures (6,000 members and founded in 1877) changed its name to the ACM and briefly merged with the **New South Wales** Chamber of Commerce (2,300 members and founded in 1885). Separate Chambers of Manufactures also exist in **South Australia** (founded 1869), **Tasmania** (founded 1899), **Western Australia** (founded 1900), and **Queensland** (founded 1911). In May 1998 the 3,200 members of the ACM agreed to merge with the its rival, the **Metal Trades Industry Association**, to form the Australian Industry Group.

AUSTRALIAN COLONIES GOVERNMENT ACT   This British law was drafted by the colonial secretary, Henry George Grey (1802-1894), and come into force in 1850. The law extended the **franchise**, created the modern state of **Victoria**, and invited the colonies to submit proposals for representative government.

AUSTRALIAN CONSTITUTION   Australia's constitutional history has evolved completely within the framework of British law. The *Commonwealth of Australia Constitution Act*, a piece of British law that received royal assent on July 9, 1900, set out the Australian Constitution, that is the constitution for the new **federation** of the Australian colonies.   The federal constitution was proclaimed in **Sydney** on January 1, 1901. By this time, written constitutions were a long-established part of Australian political life. The *Australian Colonies Government Act* of 1850 set up the framework for the granting by **Britain** of written constitutions for **New South Wales** and **Victoria** in 1855, **Tasmania** and **South Australia** in 1856, **Queensland** in 1859, and **Western Australia** in 1890.

   The product of three conferences between the colonies in 1891, 1895, and 1896-97, the Australian Constitution reflected various compromises and influences from the Constitution of the **United States**, most notably in its establishment of a two-chamber parliament: a **house of representatives** and a **senate**. It established an office of **governor-general**, which was to exercise the executive powers of the British monarch, but these powers were not precisely codified. It also established the **High Court of Australia** as Australia's supreme court in federal affairs.

Section 51 carefully enumerated the powers of the federal government. Briefly, these powers included: trade, taxation, defense, the postal service, telecommunications, the regulation of interaction with other countries (**immigration**, **emigration** and external affairs), the **census** and statistics, weights and measures, and, marriage and **divorce**. Not all powers were the exclusive preserve of the federal government, because much of the intent of the Constitution was to protect the interests of the **states** (the former **colonies**). Banking was envisaged as a shared function; there was no question of the federal government interfering with the states' banks in the eyes of the founders of the Constitution. **Labor disputes** were also envisaged as a shared function with the federal government only having the power to make laws with respect to disputes that extended beyond a single state.

Other matters dealt with in the Australian Constitution included the provision to admit new states and to provide that the Constitution could only be altered by a referendum that was passed by not only a majority of voters, but also by a majority of states. The founding fathers of the Australian Constitution clearly had in mind a very limited form of federal government as indicated by **Braddon's Blot**, for example, but because of different interpretations of the extent of federal powers by the High Court of Australia, and the development of Australia as a nation, the reach of the Constitution has extended far beyond their expectations. (*See also* Commonwealth-State Relations; Franchise)

AUSTRALIAN COUNCIL OF TRADE UNIONS (ACTU) The ACTU is the national body representing Australian **labor unions** and the Australian counterpart of organizations such as the American Federation of Labor-Congress of Industrial Organizations and the British Trades Union Congress. Founded in **Melbourne** in 1927, it grew steadily in influence under its first full-time president Albert E. Monk (who presided over it from 1949 to 1969) and his successor **Bob Hawke** who was its president from 1970 to 1980. The ACTU has been a member of the International Confederation of Free Trade Unions since 1953.

The success of the ACTU in representing unions in major wage cases before the federal **industrial tribunal** encouraged higher levels of affiliation by Australian unions. By 1981 all significant unions and union councils had become affiliated with the ACTU, that is, it represented about 2.5 million employees. The ACTU has been at its greatest influence since February 1983 when it negotiated the **Accord** with the Australian Labor Party (ALP). At the March 1983 federal election, the ALP won office and the former ACTU president, Bob Hawke became **prime minister**. A former ACTU advocate, Ralph Willis (1938-), became minister for industrial relations. At the federal elections on March 24, 1990, another ACTU president, Simon Crean (1949-), was elected to parliament and was made a junior minister.

Although the ACTU remains based in **Melbourne**, most large labor unions have their headquarters in **Sydney**. Between 1986 and 1991 the number of unions affiliated with the ACTU fell from 162 to 119. With the election of the Liberal-National Party government in March 1996, the political influence of the ACTU collapsed. (*See also* Confederation of Australian Industry)

AUSTRALIAN DEMOCRATS   The Australian Democrats are a moderate political party that has often held the balance of power in the **senate** since the March 1983 elections. The Democrats were formed by a former **Liberal Party** minister, Don Chipp (1925-), in 1977. The Democrats have always been opposed to nuclear weapons and the uranium industry. In recent years they have become the main "green" political party by their strong support of environmental issues. At their formation, the Democrats claimed 8,000 members. However, they have not been able to win any seats in the **house of representatives** from either the Liberal-National coalition or the **Australian Labor Party**. In October 1997, Cheryl Kernot, a senator, and the party's high-profile leader for the previous four years, defected to the Australian Labor Party. She was replaced by Meg Lees (1948-) who had been deputy leader since 1991. At the national elections on October 3, 1998, the Australian Democrats attracted only 5.1 percent of the votes for the house of representatives (compared to 6.8 percent in 1996) and 8.5 percent of the votes for the senate (compared to 10.8 percent in 1996). (*See also* Australia Party, Environment)

AUSTRALIAN EASTERN MISSION   The Australian Eastern Mission was an official goodwill mission led by the attorney-general and minister for external affairs and industry, John G. Latham (1877-1964) in 1934 to Singapore, Hong Kong, French Indo-China (modern **Vietnam**), China, and **Japan**. The Mission was unusual for the time in not being conducted through British representatives, although it had prior clearance from the British foreign office. Japanese-Australian trade was the main focus of the Mission, and it resulted in the appointment of an Australian trade commissioner to Tokyo in 1935.

AUSTRALIAN ENGLISH Australian English began to be recognized as a distinct variant of English from the 1890s. During his visit to Australia in 1897 Mark Twain observed a tendency to flatten certain vowels in Australian speech, but rejected this as an indigenous development and attributed it to the transplanting of London working-class speech. In contrast, other writers began to note an emerging pattern of Australian English. This was shown by the publication of *The Australian Slang Dictionary* by Cornelius Crowe in 1895 and *Austral English*, the first attempt to record Australian English on an historical basis, by Edward E. Morris in 1898.

The timing and scale of Australian historical development shaped the development of Australian English. Most of the immigration to Australia came after 1850, and most immigrants were working class. Social class, not region, defined Australian English. Unlike the **United States**, regional variations in English were few, and Australian English was always remarkable for its relative uniformity across the country. The **Aborigines** also made an important contribution to the vocabulary of Australian English, supplying words like **kangaroo**, koala, and many place names. From 1900 three forms of spoken English could be discerned in Australia: "educated" Australian (an imitation of received English pronunciation), "general" Australian (the speech of the majority) and "broad" Australian, a form of speech associated with the less educated working class.

Since the 1960s Australian sensitivity about the quality of Australian English has been replaced by a confidence in its value, a reflection of growing **nationalism** and the waning of British influence and prestige. The *Macquarie Dictionary*, the first general Australian dictionary, was published in 1981 and *The Australian National Dictionary*, a comprehensive historical record of the development of Australian English, was published in 1988. Over this same period, much of the former distinctiveness of Australian English has lessened through **urbanization**, **television**, and the ubiquitous penetration of American English, particularly American usage.

AUSTRALIAN FLAG Until the **federation** of the Australian colonies in 1901 there was no Australian flag. The British flag was used for all official occasions. At various times unofficial flags were used to promote political causes. The most enduring of these was the blue flag of the 1854 **Eureka Stockade**, which used the constellation of the Southern Cross as its motif, a flag still used today as a symbol of left-wing protest.

A competition for a new national flag was held in 1900 and attracted 32,823 entries. Because five of the winning designs were similar, their creators shared the prize money of 200 pounds. The flag, based on the British Blue Ensign, featured the British Union Jack in the top left quarter with the rest occupied by a design symbolizing the constellation of the Southern Cross. In 1953 the federal parliament passed the *Flags Act*, which officially established the Australian National Flag. The **governor-general** has a personal flag that was created in 1936.

In the armed forces, the army has always used the national flag, but the navy used the White Ensign of the British navy from 1910 to 1967 until given its own ensign, and the Air Force was granted royal approval for an ensign based on the British air force in 1949, and a red kangaroo was added to this ensign in 1981.

The proportion of Australians favoring the retention of the Union Jack in the flag has fallen from 72 percent in 1967 to 57 percent in 1992.

AUSTRALIAN HONORS SYSTEM Until 1975 Australian governments honored their citizens through the British system of knighthoods or by military decorations. Individuals could be nominated for honors by state governments as well as by federal governments. The **Whitlam** government abandoned this system because of the traditional opposition of the **Australian Labor Party** to the British honors system based on knighthoods and because of its preference for **republicanism**. It began a new honors system made up of the Order of Australia, the Australian Bravery Awards, and the National Medal. Although the succeeding **Fraser** government restored the British honors system, and some conservative state governments continued the practice, it was finally terminated by the **Hawke** government in 1986 and was never restored. Recipients of honors are announced by the **governor-general** on **Australia Day**.

AUSTRALIAN IMPERIAL FORCE (AIF) The AIF was the official title of the military forces raised in Australia during both world wars. Some 330,700 men served overseas in **World War I** of whom 54,000 were killed and 155,000 were wounded. During **World War II** a total of 690,000 men and women served in the Second AIF of whom 17,501 were killed and 13,997 were wounded. A total of 28,756 were captured of whom 8,031 died, mostly in Japanese hands. (*See also* ANZAC; Returned Services League)

AUSTRALIAN LABOR PARTY (ALP) The ALP is Australia's oldest continuous political party. It was founded in 1891 in **New South Wales** after the defeat of the **labor unions** in the **Maritime Strike** of 1890. Labor unions have continued to provide the basis of the ALP ever since. It represented the culmination of efforts to elect working class representatives to parliament, which began in the late 1870s. It drew part of its inspiration from the British Liberal Party, the main political outlet for the organized English working class in the nineteenth century. By the mid-1900s the ALP had been set up in all the **states**. Its features of a platform of policies and disciplined voting by its elected members began a new era among Australian **political parties**. In time the non-Labor parties also adopted platforms of policies and more disciplined voting by their elected members.

Though usually represented by its opponents as a "left wing" party, the ALP was from its beginnings a moderate social democratic party though it did contain some radical groups. There have been two major splits in the ALP. The first was in 1916 over **conscription** and the second occurred in 1955 over attitudes toward communism and led to the creation of the **Democratic Labor Party**. The split of 1955 was worst in **Victoria** and **Queensland** and was largely responsible for keeping the ALP out of power at the national level until 1972. The ALP has been a member of the Socialist International since 1966.

The ALP held federal government in 1904, 1908-9, 1910-13, 1914-15, 1929-32, 1941-49, 1972-74, and 1983-96. The ALP governed New South Wales in 1910-16, 1920-22, 1925-27, 1930-32, 1941-65, 1976-88, and 1995 to date; in Victoria in 1913, 1924, 1927-28, 1929-32, 1943, 1945-47, 1952-55, and 1982-92; in Queensland in 1915-29, 1932-57, 1989-96, and 1998 to date; in **South Australia** in 1905-9 (with the Liberal Party); 1910-12, 1915-

17, 1924-27, 1930-33, 1967-68, 1970-79, and 1982-93; in **Western Australia** in 1904-5, 1911-16, 1921-30, 1933-47, 1953-59, and 1983-93; in **Tasmania** in 1909, 1914-16, 1923-28, 1934-69, 1972-82, 1989-92 (with the support of the Greens), and 1998 to date.

Notable ALP prime ministers have been **William Morris Hughes** (1915-16), **James H. Scullin** (1929-32), **John Curtin** (1941-45), **Ben Chifley** (1945-49), **Gough Whitlam** (1972-74), and **Bob Hawke** (1983-91). At the national elections on March 2, 1996, the ALP was heavily defeated; it only attracted 38.8 percent of the vote for the **house of representatives** (compared to 44.9 percent in 1993) and 36.2 percent for the **senate** (compared to 43.5 percent in 1993). At the next national elections on October 3, 1998, the ALP vote recovered to 40.1 percent for the house of representatives and 37.3 percent for the senate, but this was insufficient for it to form government. Since March 12, 1996 Kim Beazley (1948-) has been leader of the federal parliamentary ALP.

Despite commanding the most votes of any single Australian political party, the ALP in the postwar period had the smallest membership of any of the three major parties, preferring to rely on labor unions, its traditional power base, rather than individual members. In 1954 the ALP had about 75,000 members but after the 1955 split, this fell to about 45,000; between 1982 and 1995 ALP membership fell from 55,000 to 35,000. (*See also* Accord, Australian Council of Trade Unions)

AUSTRALIAN MUTUAL PROVIDENT SOCIETY (AMP) The AMP is Australia's largest insurance company and, until 1998, was one of the largest mutual life insurance companies in the world. Founded in 1849 to help the less well-off to save for their old age on retirement and their dependents, the AMP was wholly devoted to life insurance until 1950. Since that time, it has diversified into other businesses. It is a major property owner and shareholder. In 1989 it acquired the British insurer the Pearl Group for 1.2 billion pounds. By 1996 42 percent of its business was conducted in the United Kingdom. The AMP is Australia's largest investment manager with $94.5 billion in assets. In November 1997 the policy holders of the AMP voted in favor of its de-mutualization and on January 1, 1998, the AMP became a share-owned company and issued one billion shares to 1.8 million members after making a profit of $1.8 billion. It was listed on the stock market on June 15, 1998.

AUSTRALIAN NATIVES' ASSOCIATION (ANA) The ANA is a friendly or mutual benefits society largely based in **Victoria** to provide medical insurance. Formed in **Melbourne** in 1871, it was of greatest importance between 1890 and 1914 when it actively campaigned for **federation**. It included **Alfred Deakin** among its members. In the 1930s it lobbied governments to have January 26 declared **Australia Day**.

AUSTRALIAN PATRIOTIC ASSOCIATION (APA) The APA was a political pressure group made up mostly of **Emancipists** in **New South Wales**, which was formed in 1835 to press the British government for reform of the colony's **legislative council**. This was largely achieved by a law of 1842 and the APA was disbanded in 1843.

AUSTRALIAN PLATE (*See* Indo-Australian Plate)

AUSTRALIAN RULES Australian Rules is a form of football that was invented in **Melbourne**, Victoria, in 1858. Originally based in working-class suburbs in Melbourne after which the teams were named, the game spread to other parts of Australia and became the dominant form of football except in **New South Wales** and **Queensland**. A dispute in New South Wales between the traditional rugby clubs and the Super League owned by **Rupert Murdoch** between 1995 and 1997 has enabled Australian Rules to become a significant spectator sport in New South Wales for the first time. Grand final matches in Melbourne draw Australia's largest sports crowds. (*See also* Sport)

AUSTRALIAN SECURITY INTELLIGENCE ORGANISATION (ASIO) ASIO is Australia's counter-spy agency. Modeled on Britain's MI5, it was set up by the federal **Chifley** government in 1949. It first came to public attention as a result of its role in the **Petrov Affair** in 1954, an event that brought on a major split in the **Australian Labor Party**, which viewed ASIO with suspicion thereafter. In 1974-77 and 1983 ASIO was investigated by Justice R. M. Hope (1919-). In 1985 legislation was passed to make ASIO more accountable to the federal parliament. With the end of the Cold War, ASIO has devoted more of its efforts to terrorism and industrial espionage.

AUSTRALIAN WOMEN'S WEEKLY **(AWW)** The AWW is Australia's largest and best-known women's magazine. It first appeared on June 10, 1933, and was founded by a newspaper director, Frank Packer (1906-1974) and a former **Australian Labor Party** federal treasurer Edward Granville Theodore (1884-1950). Although firmly focused on women and the domestic scene, the AWW also covered other issues of general interest and gained and held a male readership as well. By 1939 it was selling 400,000 copies a week. It was particularly popular among Australian soldiers during **World War II**, as evidenced by the fact that the Australian War Memorial Library is the only library to hold a full set of the AWW. In August 1975 the format of the AWW was reduced from a tabloid to magazine size and in January 1983 it was issued on a monthly basis while retaining its title. In January 1998 the AWW sold one million copies a month. (*See also* Press)

AUSTRALIAN WORKERS' UNION (AWU) From the 1900s to 1969, the AWU was the largest **labor union** in Australia. The AWU began as a sheep shearers' union in 1886. It grew by amalgamating with other unions, first with the rural laborers' union in 1894 and then with unions of semi-skilled workers in rural, general laboring, and **mining** between 1912 and 1917. By 1914, the AWU had 70,000 members. The AWU has been a powerful but conservative force in the labor movement and in the **Australian Labor Party**, particularly in **Queensland** and **New South Wales**. In the 1950s the AWU had about 200,000 members. Structural changes in industries and occupations, as well as internal disputes, have reduced the AWU membership since 1970 from 160,000 to 145,500 by 1997.

AWARDS Awards are legal documents issued by **industrial tribunals**, which contain details of pay and conditions of employment. They are the main way in which **labor unions** seek to set wages and conditions in the **labor force**. They are issued by either the federal industrial tribunal or by industrial tribunals operating under state laws. Since June 1986 occupational superannuation has been introduced into federal awards.

Between 1954 and 1990 the proportion of employees covered by awards has fallen from 92 to 80 percent. During the 1990s conservative governments have sought to eliminate awards and replaced them with enterprise agreements. Official surveys of labor relations at the workplace have found that between 1990 and 1995 the number of workplaces with only federal awards increased from 21 to 32 percent, that those with only state awards fell from 51 to 45 percent, and that those with both federal and state wards fell from 22 to 18 percent. The decline in state awards was highest in **Victoria** where state award incidence fell from 47 to 20 percent.

AYERS' ROCK Ayers' Rock is a huge sandstone rock in the south west of the **Northern Territory**. Discovered by Ernest Giles (1835-1897) in 1872 and named after the South Australian politician Henry Ayers (1821-1897), Ayers' Rock is 2.5 kilometers long by 1.5 kilometers wide, nine kilometers in circumference and 335 meters high. It is an important tourist attraction and is sacred to the Pitjantjantjan **Aborigines**. In 1986 Ayers' Rock and its surroundings were entered in the World Heritage List.

B

BANK OF NEW SOUTH WALES The Bank of New South Wales was Australia's first private bank. It opened in **Sydney** in April 1817 with the support of the governor, **Lachlan Macquarie**. After early difficulties, the Bank's future was assured by the growth of the **sheep and wool** industry from the 1830s. The Bank opened branches in **Brisbane** (1850), London (1853), **Perth** (1854), and **New Zealand** (1861). By adopting a careful lending policy toward the suburban land speculation of the 1880s the Bank was able to continue trading during the severe depression of the early 1890s and saw many of its competitors collapse in the crash of 1893. By 1900 the Bank was the largest in Australia. It absorbed the Western Australian Bank in 1927 and the Commercial Bank of Australia in 1981. It also maintained a significant presence in the south-west Pacific. In October 1982 the Bank was renamed Westpac. Unwise lending decisions in the late 1980s resulted in Westpac making a loss of $1.6 billion.

BANKS, JOSEPH (1743-1820) Banks was England's leading naturalist in the late eighteenth century and an important figure in the British colonization of eastern Australia. He accompanied **James Cook** on his journey around the world between 1768 and 1771. He was greatly impressed by the number of new plant and animal species he found in Australia, and it was at his urging that Cook's original Australian landfall was called Botany Bay. Back in England, he advocated that the British use Botany Bay as a place to send **convicts** from 1779. After the establishment of **Sydney** in 1788 he continued to take a close interest in the colony. He recommended William Bligh for governor and supported the exploration of the Australian coastline by **Matthew Flinders**.

BARTON EDMOND (1849-1929) Barton was Australia's first **prime minister** between January 1, 1901 and September 24, 1903. He was born and educated in **Sydney** where he qualified as a lawyer. In 1879 he was elected to the legislative assembly of **New South Wales** and held various positions in the colonial parliament until 1898. From the late 1880s he was the leading figure in New South Wales for the **federation** of the Australian colonies. He set up the Australasian Federation League to campaign for this objective. He led a delegation to London to explain the draft constitution that had been agreed to. He was elected to the new federal parliament and served as prime minister and minister for external affairs from 1901 to 1903. His administration was a conservative one. Barton was a supporter of **protection** and at the end of his term was appointed as a judge of the **High Court of Australia** where he remained until his death.

BARWICK, GARFIELD EDWARD JOHN (1903-1997) Lawyer and conservative politician, Barwick was born in Stanmore, an inner suburb of **Sydney**. He qualified as a lawyer from Sydney University in 1927 and became a barrister in 1941. In the late 1940s he was the leading counsel for the banks that were opposing the nationalization policies of the federal **Australian Labor Party** government led by **Ben Chifley**. Barwick was elected to the **house of representatives** in 1958 for the **Liberal Party of Australia**. He served as attorney-general from 1958 to 1961 and as minister for external affairs from 1961 to 1964 when he was appointed chief justice of the **High Court of Australia**. His judgments took a restricted view of the powers of the federal government, particularly with regard to taxation. He played a controversial role in the dismissal of the **Whitlam** government by giving an opinion to the **governor-general**, John Kerr, that it was within his power to sack the government.

BASIC WAGE The basic wage was a form of minimum wage introduced into Australian labor relations by the **Harvester Judgment** in 1907. The basic wage was general in the federal and state decisions of **industrial tribunals** by the 1920s. Allowances for skill (called "margins") and adjustments for inflation were also added to the wage. The basic wage was reduced by 10 percent in 1931 because of the Depression, but was largely restored to its previous level by 1934. The basic wage was theoretically based on a man providing for a wife and four children. The basic wage for women was set at 54 percent that of men in the 1920s and 75 percent in 1950. Regular cost of living adjustments stopped in 1953, a move that led to pressure by **labor unions** for wage increases over those provided for in **awards**. In 1967 the basic wage was replaced by the "total" wage, which absorbed margins into the basic wage.

BASS, GEORGE (1771-1803) With **Matthew Flinders**, George Bass was one of the outstanding explorers of Australia's coastline. Born in in Aswarby, Lincolnshire, England, and qualified as a ship's surgeon's mate in 1789. He and Flinders arrived in Sydney in 1795. Together they sailed around **Tasmania** proving it to be an island in 1798. The strait between Tasmania and mainland Australia was named after Bass. In February 1803 Bass disappeared on a trading venture to South America.

"BATTLE OF BRISBANE" The "battle of Brisbane" was a series of riots between Australian and U.S. military personnel on November 26, 1942, during **World War II**. At the root of the riots was Australian resentment over the superior pay, conditions, and facilities enjoyed by the American troops. One Australian died in the rioting and some others were injured. The riots were a notable exception to the otherwise excellent relations between Australians and Americans at the time. (*See also* United States of America)

BEER Beer has always been Australia's main alcoholic drink despite the rise in **wine** consumption over the past 30 years. Beer was brewed in **Sydney** as early as 1796 and officially promoted from 1803 by the early colonial governors as a wholesome substitute for the spirits then widely consumed and even used as a form of **currency** before 1817. During the nineteenth century most urban centers of moderate size had their own brewery, but from the early twentieth century, production was increasingly concentrated in the capital cities.

In 1938-39 beer consumption per head in Australia was 51.4 liters; by 1955 this had risen to 110.6 liters and stayed at about this level until 1967, since which time it rose slowly to peak at 129.3 liters in 1981. Beer consumption per head had fallen to 95.4 liters in 1995, a trend that encouraged Australian brewers to turn to overseas markets such as **Britain** and the **United States** for their product. An official survey conducted in May 1998 found that 31 percent of Australians over 18 had drunk beer in the previous week compared to 37 percent who had drunk some form of **wine**.

BIGGE REPORTS The Bigge Reports were three reports made on behalf of the British colonial office by John Thomas Bigge (1780-1843) into the administration, legal system and economy of the Australian colonies of **New South Wales** and Van Diemen's Land (**Tasmania**), which were published in 1822-23. Bigge, a lawyer, arrived in Australia in September 1819 and left in February 1821. The reports were critical of the administration of **Lachlan Macquarie**, particularly of his expenditure of public money and the relative leniency of his treatment of **convicts** and **emancipists**. The tenor of the reports was in favor of harsher treatment of convicts and the encouragement of a private sector **economy** supported by an extended **assignment system**.

BLACKBIRDING (*See* Kanakas)

BLIGH, WILLIAM (*See* "Rum Rebellion")

BOAT PEOPLE After the Communist victory in South **Vietnam** in 1975, many fled the country by boat. Of these 2,011 arrived in Australia between 1977 and 1981. Although they were officially accepted as refugees, only 5 percent of the Vietnamese born in Australia in 1981 came as "boat people." Since that time, the term has become a general one for any group who illegally comes to Australia by boat. Because of Australia's long coastline, it is vulnerable to such actions. From 1989 to September 1998, 3,050 people have come to Australia as boat people, of whom 672 have been granted entry to Australia. The others have been detained and deported. Although the great majority of this group of boat people come from south-east Asia, they include some from the Middle East and Europe. (*See also* Chinese, Immigration)

BODYLINE TOUR The "Bodyline" tour was a contentious **cricket** series conducted by the English team when it toured Australia in 1932-33. The word "bodyline"—called "fast leg theory" in English cricket—referred to a technique of bowling the ball in which the target became the batsman's body rather than the wicket. The tour aroused strong feelings in Australia, and the English team was accused of unsportmanlike behavior. The tour aroused especially strong popular feelings because it occurred in the aftermath of severe deflationary economic policies in Australia that had been carried out because of pressure from the Bank of England. The bowling of the English team injured some players, led to its public condemnation, and almost caused a diplomatic incident. The tactics were said to have been introduced to reduce the scores of Australia's greatest batsman, Donald George Bradman (1908-). The English team won the series, but in 1935 the Marylebone Cricket Club in England, the body that determines the game's rules, outlawed bodyline bowling. In the mid-1980s the tour was the subject of a mini-series on Australian television, *Bodyline*.

BOER WAR Australia avidly supported the British side in its war with the Boers between 1899 and 1902. In all, 16,500 Australians fought on the British side, of whom 588 were killed. The *Bulletin* was one of the few Australian newspapers to criticize the war and suffer a substantial loss of support for doing so. The Australian film *Breaker Morant* (1980) was based on an historical event during this war.

BOOMERANG Boomerang is the name of a curved, wooden throwing missile or club used by **Aborigines** for hunting, fighting, or recreation. The oldest boomerangs found are about 10,000 to 8,000 years old. The best-known type of boomerang can be thrown in such a way as to return to the thrower. Contrary to popular belief, the boomerang is not unique to Australia; similar tools have been found in ancient Egypt, Denmark, and Arizona. The word "boomerang" first appeared in print in 1825.

During **World War II**, the word was used as a title for the only fighter airplane designed and built in Australia. The first Boomerangs were delivered to the Royal Australian Air Force in

August 1942 but proved to be too slow to be used as fighters. Nevertheless, they were successful support aircraft for the Australian Army during the fighting against the Japanese in New Guinea in 1943-44. In all, 250 Boomerangs were built.

"BRADDON'S BLOT"   Also called the Braddon clause, Braddon's blot referred to section 87 of the **Australian Constitution**, which governed financial arrangements between the federal and state governments from 1901 to 1910. Named after its advocate, Edward Braddon (1829-1904), the **premier** of **Tasmania** between 1894 and 1899, the clause forced the federal government to retain no more than 25 percent of the net revenue from customs and excise for its own expenditure and pay the remainder to the **states** or use the money to pay the interest on certain states' debts for which the federal government had assumed responsibility. The main purpose of section 87 was to limit the growth of the financial power of the then new federal government and ensure that trade between the states was conducted on a uniform tariff. The growth of federal **defense** and **social security** expenditure from the late 1900s rendered Braddon's blot obsolete. It was replaced in 1910 by an agreement under which the federal government made annual payments of 25 shillings ($2.50) to the states per head of population. (*See also* Commonwealth-State Relations)

BRAGG, WILLIAM HENRY (1862-1942) and **BRAGG, WILLIAM LAWRENCE (1890-1971)**   The Braggs were a father and son scientific team who were jointly awarded the Nobel prize for Physics in 1915. William Henry Bragg was born in England and educated at Cambridge University, finishing third in his class in mathematics. In 1886 he accepted a professorship at the University of **Adelaide**, South Australia, which he held until 1908. In the early 1900s he became interested in the recent discoveries into atomic structure and radioactivity and began conducting research into X-rays. He X-rayed his son's broken arm thereby taking the first diagnostic X-ray.

His son, William Lawrence Bragg, was born in Adelaide and graduated from the University of Adelaide in mathematics and physics at the age of 18. In 1908 the Braggs went to England, the father to a professorship in physics at the University of Leeds and the son to further his study at Cambridge University. They continued to collaborate, and results of their research into X-ray earned them their joint Nobel prize. William Lawrence Bragg was only 25 when he won the prize; he was knighted in 1941. His father had been knighted in 1920.

BRISBANE   Brisbane is the capital of the state of **Queensland**. It is located in the south-eastern corner of the state on the Brisbane River on Moreton Bay, which was explored by **Matthew Flinders** in 1802, but no further explorations took place until the late 1820s. In 1824 the governor of New South Wales, Thomas Brisbane (1773-1860), after whom the city was named, ordered the establishment of a penal colony on the site of the present city, which housed 200 in 1840. In 1842 Brisbane was declared a free town and the first land sales were made. In 1859 Brisbane became the capital of the colony of Queensland after its separation from New South Wales.

Population growth was slow. Between 1861 and 1881 Brisbane's population increased from 6,000 to 31,000, but by 1891 it had grown to 87,000, or a quarter of the colony's population. By 1921 Brisbane had 210,000 people, and from 1954 to 1981 it had more than doubled from 502,300 to 1,096,200. In 1996 Brisbane had a population of 1,488,900.

In 1925 its various local government bodies were amalgamated into one body, the City of Greater Brisbane, the only Australian capital city where this has occurred. Since 1947 Brisbane has been Australia's third largest city. It has two universities: the University of Queensland, founded in 1909 and Griffith University founded in 1975. During **World War II** Brisbane was the headquarters of General Douglas MacArthur and a base for American submarines. Brisbane's lower-lying suburbs are prone to floods (1893, 1974). (*See also* Queensland)

BRITAIN   From 1788 to about 1960 Great Britain was the most influential country in the history of Australia. Britain founded Australia's first permanent European settlements in various spots around the Australian coastline from 1788 into the 1820s to ward off suspected French territorial claims. Britain used its **convicts** to provide the labor to build the foundations of Australia and after 1820 Australia became an increasingly important object of British investment. With the scaling down of the convict system and the growth of free **immigration** from the 1830s, Britain continued to be easily the largest single source of Australia's people.

But although Australia began as an extension of Britain and its society, its pattern of political and social development began to diverge from Britain's after the 1850s. The various Australian colonies were granted their own written constitutions and, when they federated in 1901, the **Australian Constitution** they were granted by the British parliament was also written in contrast to Britain's unwritten constitution. The comparative wealth of the colonies and their freedom from institutional restrictions on democracy, which prevailed in Britain, made the Australian colonies fertile ground for the success of reformist British ideas such as the **secret ballot**. Australia was a "melting pot" for Britons whether English, Welsh, Scots, or **Irish**. The Irish alone, through their **Catholicism**, retained a separateness in some areas, but they have always participated fully in the political process. The **labor unions** in the Australian colonies created a "labor" party to further their interests in 1891, and by 1914 had formed governments at the federal and state levels, well in advance of the British Labour Party.

Britain provided the model for Australia in law, education, the arts, and technology. Feelings towards Britain were very close until the 1930s when they were soured by the visit of Sir Otto Niemeyer of the Bank of England, who advised deflationary policies for Australia and a reduction in the standard of living (1930) and the **"bodyline" cricket** tour (1932-33), during which a number of Australian players were injured by the methods used by the visiting English team.

At the government level, relations between Britain and Australia remained very close until the 1960s. Australia and Britain were allies in all conflicts for over a century from 1850 to 1960. The **Vietnam** war was the first war in which Australian troops did not fight with British forces. Australia was particularly valuable to Britain as a place where nuclear weapons and missiles could be tested. From 1952 to 1963, 12 nuclear weapons were exploded in Australia as well as minor trials. Yet apart from emigration, Australia was marginal from a British perspective. It was not until 1958 that Australia was visited by a serving British prime minister, Harold Macmillan, despite a visit by Queen Elizabeth II four years earlier.

The Australian **economy** supplied **wheat** and **sheep and wool** to Britain in return for acting as a largely reserved market for British goods. This imperial system broke down in the post-1945 period. **Japan** overtook Britain as Australia's largest trading partner in the

1960s and in 1973 Britain joined the European Economic Community. The last constitutional links between Australia and Britain were severed in 1986 when appeals by Australians to the privy council were stopped, although constitutionally the British monarch also remains monarch of Australia, a state of affairs which could be ended if **republicanism** finds electoral support. Nevertheless, despite their separate paths, Australia and Britain retain many social, and cultural links, and even in 1996 the largest single group among Australia's foreign-born were the British (28.8 percent).

BROKEN HILL PROPRIETARY COMPANY LIMITED (BHP)
BHP is Australia's largest company and has been for most of the twentieth century. It was originally formed in 1885 to mine silver, lead, and zinc at Broken Hill in the far west of **New South Wales**. Faced with declining silver-lead deposits at its Broken Hill mines, BHP diversified into steel making, setting up a works at **Newcastle**, modeled on American lines in 1912-15. In 1935, BHP took over the other steelworks at **Wollongong** and became the national producer. BHP also bought interests in **coal** mining and shipping.

After 1960, the company moved into oil and natural gas production as well as **iron ore**, **gold**, and manganese mining. In 1983, BHP bought the American mining company Utah and established oil exploration rights in the South China Sea. The world depression in steel making in 1982-83 severely reduced the company's workforce at Newcastle, Wollongong, and Whyalla (South Australia). In April 1997 BHP announced that it would close its basic steel making operations at Newcastle in 1999. In December 1997 BHP considered that it would probably float its entire steel making division as a separate company. In 1997 BHP had a share market valuation of $35.8 billion. (*See also* Iron and Steel; Essington Lewis,

BRUCE, STANLEY MELBOURNE (1883-1967) Australian **prime minister**, Bruce was born in **Melbourne**, **Victoria**, but spent his formative years in **Britain**, where he studied law at Cambridge and managed an importing business. He fought with the British at **Gallipoli** and was awarded the Military Cross and the French Cross of War with Palm. He was elected to the **house of representatives** in 1918 at a by-election for the Victorian seat of Flinders.

He was prime minister from February 9, 1923, to October 22, 1929, when he led a conservative coalition of the **Nationalist Party** and the **Country Party**. As prime minister he vigorously promoted Australia's economic development and large-scale British **immigration**. His government also conducted many important economic and social investigations including sending a **labor delegation** to the **United States**. After the defeat of his government in the 1929 elections (at which Bruce became the first Australian prime minister to lose his seat), Bruce returned to federal politics in 1932 and from 1933 to 1945 was Australia's High Commissioner in London. From 1946 to 1951 he was chairman of the World Food Council of the United Nations Food and Agriculture Organization. In 1947 he was awarded the title Viscount Bruce of Melbourne.

BUDDHISM Buddhism was largely introduced into Australia by the **Chinese**. Its presence was first recorded by the census in **Victoria** in 1854, which found there were 2,677 Buddhists. Although most of the censuses in the Australian colonies enumerated Buddhists by 1891, the statistics they collected vary wildly and are of doubtful value. Between 1911 and 1947 the national census recorded a fall in the number of Buddhists from 11,964 to 926. The census did not identify Buddhists again until 1981 when it found that there were 35,973 Buddhists in Australia. Most of these Buddhists came from south-east Asia, particularly Vietnam. Between 1986 and 1996 the number of Buddhists increased from 80,383 to 199,812. (*See also* Religion)

BULLETIN Nationally known journal (and later magazine) produced in **Sydney**, **New South Wales**, from 1880, the *Bulletin* was important for promoting Australian nationalism and the arts. At first politically radical and anti-war, it became conservative after the **Boer War** (1900-02) and has remained so. Since the early 1980s, the *Bulletin* has incorporated the international magazine *Newsweek*. (*See also* Jules François Archibald; Henry Lawson; Press)

"BUNYIP ARISTOCRACY" In **Aboriginal** legend, a bunyip is a monster that lives near water. The term "bunyip aristocracy" was coined by Daniel Henry Deniehy (1828-1865) in 1853 to kill off a proposal to create an upper house in parliament made up of hereditary baronets in **New South Wales** along the lines of the British House of Lords. The idea was said to have originated with the colonial politician William Charles Wentworth (c.1792-1872) and was intended to bring greater stability to politics and society threatened with upsurge in democracy brought by the **gold rushes**. The proposal failed but the principle of an upper house acting as a house of review of legislation from the lower house was incorporated in the constitutions of the colonies (**states** after 1901) in the *Australian Colonies Government Act* (1850). **Queensland** was the only state to abolish its upper house (1922). (*See also* House of Representatives; Legislative Council; Legislative Assembly; Senate)

BURKE AND WILLS EXPEDITION The purpose of the Burke and Wills expedition was to make the first crossing of Australia from south to north. Well equipped and led by Robert O'Hara Burke (1821-1861) and William John Wills (1834-1861), the expedition started out from **Melbourne** in August 1860 and reached the Gulf of Carpentaria in northern Australia in February 1861. But after this triumph the expedition became a disaster though poor judgment, inadequate planning, and lack of survival skills needed in a harsh, dry environment. Seven of the party died, including its two leaders.

BURNET, FRANK MACFARLANE (1899-1985) One of Australia's greatest medical researchers, Macfarlane Burnet was born in the country town of Traralgon, **Victoria**. He completed his medical degree at the University of Melbourne in 1923 and his Ph.D. at the University of London in 1927. With another Australian scientist Jean Macnamara (1899-1968), he discovered that there were at least two viruses that caused poliomyelitis. In 1949 he suggested that the human ability to form antibodies against disease might not be inborn, and that resistance to disease might be developed very early in life through inoculation. In 1951 Sir Peter Medawar proved this was the case. Burnet was knighted in 1951 and in 1960, he and Medawar shared the Nobel prize in Medicine and Physiology.

BUSH-FIRES Bush-fires are Australia's most serious, recurrent natural threat to human life. A combination of scrubby woodlands and hot, dry summers—such as exist in California and the south of France—make much of south-eastern and south-western Australia especially prone to bush-fires. The risk is greatest from late

December to mid-February. Bush-fires have always been an integral part of the natural Australian habitat. Charcoal fragments in eucalypt fossils are known from 80 million years ago, and there was a significant increase in the presence of charcoal between 250,000 and 200,000 years ago, which indicated that bush-fires were a feature of the Australian environment long before the coming of the **Aborigines** who used man-made bush-fires as a hunting technique. A number of plant species have become adapted to regular burning.

Major bush-fires have occurred on February 6, 1851 ("Black Thursday"); January 13, 1939 ("Black Friday") both in Victoria; in 1967 (February 7); 1983 (February 16); and in January 1994. The persistent intrusion of post-1945 suburban expansion into bush land areas has brought with it a higher risk of the destruction of life and property. The fires in **Tasmania** on February 7, 1967, claimed 20 lives. The most serious fires in recent history occurred on February 16, 1983, in Victoria and **South Australia**; together these fires killed 37 people and destroyed 9,200 houses. In January 1994 the **Sydney** region was the scene of a series of large bush-fires, some of which were deliberately lit. (*See also* Drought)

BUSHRANGERS Bushrangers were outlaws who operated in south-eastern Australia and **Tasmania** between 1790 and 1900. The word is probably American in origin. The first bushrangers were former **convicts**, but with the greater opportunities for robbery opened up by the gold rushes, there was an upsurge in their activities. The spread of payments by checks probably contributed more to their disappearance than the well-publicized police actions of colonial governments. The most famous bushranger was **Ned Kelly**, who was hanged in 1880. Although the actual numbers of bushrangers operating at any one time was never large (less than 100), they grew in reputation and mythic stature after 1900 as rebels against unjust authority. The artist **Sidney Nolan** used Ned Kelly as an icon for a significant series of paintings.

BUSINESS COUNCIL OF AUSTRALIA (BCA) The BCA is an influential organization made up of representatives of Australia's 80 largest companies. It was founded in September 1983 from the merger of the Business Round Table (formed in 1979 as a senior executives' group, and the Australian Industries Development Association (which was originally set up in 1919 as the Australian Industries Protection League) and has an annual budget of $3 million. Unlike other **employer associations**, the BCA is not concerned with direct negotiations with **labor unions**, but is solely concerned with developing policies and directions for the economy and industrial relations.

BUTLIN, NOEL GEORGE (1921-1991) Australia's foremost economic historian, Butlin was born in Maitland, **New South Wales**, and completed his training in economics at the University of Sydney in 1942. After service with the Australian High Commission in London (1942-44) and the United Nations Food and Agricultural Organization in Washington D.C. (1944-45), he held a lectureship in economic history at the University of Sydney from 1946 to 1949 and was a Rockefeller Fellow at Harvard University from 1949 to 1951. He returned to Australian and joined the staff of the **Australian National University** where he was professor of economic history from 1962 to 1986. He was also Irving Fisher Professor of Economics at Yale University (1967-68) and professor of Australian Studies at Harvard University from 1979-80. Butlin's many achievements included the creation of a Chair of Economic History at the Australian National University, the setting up of a national archives of the records of employers and **labor unions**, the compilation of the first historical estimates for gross domestic product in Australia from 1861 to 1939, and the writing of two seminal publications, *Investment in Australian Economic Development, 1861-1900* (1964) and *Our Original Aggression* (1983), a work which argued that the number of **Aborigines** at the time of the Europeans arrival in 1788 was far higher than previously thought.

C

CAIRNS The largest urban center on the coast of north **Queensland**, the bay on which Cairns is built was visited by **James Cook** in 1770, but European settlement was not begun until 1873. Named in honor of the governor of Queensland, the early **economy** of Cairns was based on sugar and **gold** mining in the hinterland. It was linked to **Brisbane** by the **railroad** in 1923. During **World War II** it was an airfield and base for commando raids on Japanese-held territory, most notably the raid by the *Krait*, a former Japanese fishing boat that served in Australia's secret Z forces, on Singapore in 1942. The population was 3,600 in 1901, 12,000 in 1933, and 21,000 in

1954. The economy continued to be based on agriculture, fishing, **coal** mining, and its naval base (1974). Since 1981 its population has more than doubled from 46,600 to 121,900 in 1996. An international airport was opened in 1984 and Cairns has become an important center for **tourism**, attracting much interest and investment from **Japan**.

CAIRNS GROUP OF FAIR TRADERS IN AGRICULTURE The Cairns Group of Fair Traders in Agriculture was formed in **Cairns** at the initiative of Australia from senior ministers of 14 countries between August 25-27, 1986. The Group consisted of Argentina, Australia, Brazil, Canada, Chile, Colombia, Fiji, Hungary, Indonesia, Malaysia, **New Zealand**, Philippines, Thailand, and Uruguay. In 1985 these countries accounted for 26 percent of world agricultural exports. The purpose of the Cairns Group was to prepare common strategies against the adverse effects of the European Economic Community's Common Agricultural Policy and the subsidized agricultural policies of the **United States** in the context of the Uruguay Round of negotiations over the General Agreement on Tariffs and Trade. A ministerial meeting of the Cairns Group was held in Rio de Janeiro in June 1997. In February 1998 Hungary withdrew from the Cairns Group and was replaced by **South Africa**. (*See also* Protection)

CANBERRA Canberra is the national capital of Australia, the Australian counterpart of centers such as Washington D.C. and Ottawa. Its site within the borders of the **Australian Capital Territory** (ACT) was agreed upon between the federal and **New South Wales** governments in 1909. The ACT came under Commonwealth sovereignty in 1911. The name Canberra comes from an **Aboriginal** word meaning "meeting place."

An international competition for the design of Canberra was won by the Chicago architect Walter Burley Griffin (1876-1937) using principles drawn from L'Enfant's design for Washington, D.C. (1791). But Griffin's plan was dropped in favor of one prepared by a federal bureaucratic board. Griffin's ideas were seen as too costly and ambitious for what was envisaged as a small town. Griffin was appointed as part-time director of design and construction in 1913 and held the post until 1920. Although revised four times by 1925, Griffin's plan did much to influence Canberra's modern layout. His triangular layout of the center survived in the form of the new

Parliament House (opened in 1988) on Capital Hill, which provided the missing part of Griffin's original triangle. The other points were the Australian War Memorial (built between 1934 and 1941) and the shopping center of Civic (1920s). The artificial lake he planned was completed in 1964 and named in his honor.

In 1927 the federal parliament was moved from **Melbourne** to Canberra. The population was slowly built up from Melbourne with the transfer of federal government employees to the new town. Depression and war slowed growth from 2,000 in 1921 to 15,150 in 1947. However, the rise in the power of the federal government after 1942 proved a strong impetus for growth. As well, the creation of the Australian National University (formed by the amalgamation with Canberra University College in 1960) added to the forces of growth. Between 1961 and 1971 Canberra's population grew from 56,400 to 142,900 and by 1981 to 226,450, making it Australia's largest inland city. In 1996 Canberra had a population of 298,800.

Major planned suburban developments were started in the south at Woden (1962) and in the west at Belconnen (1966). Canberra became the home for the Royal Australian Mint (1965), the Australian National Library (present building opened in 1968), the **High Court of Australia** (1980), and the Australian National Gallery (1982). Canberra is unique among Australia's large cities in being fully planned (land can only be leased, not owned) and having self-government imposed upon it by the federal government in 1985. Since 1980 there has been much suburban expansion south in the Tuggeranong valley and north-west at Gunghalin. Of the 15,000 federal jobs cut by the government in 1996, a third occurred in Canberra.

CAREY, PETER [PHILLIP] (1943-) Leading contemporary Australian novelist, Carey was born in Bacchus Marsh, **Victoria**, and educated at Melbourne Grammar School. He made a career in advertising before becoming a writer. His best-known novels are *Bliss* (1981), *Illywacker* (1985), and *Oscar and Lucinda* (1988). This last work won Britain's Booker McConnell prize for fiction in 1988. A film based on *Bliss* won best film at the Australian Film Industry awards in 1981. A film version of *Oscar and Lucinda* was made in 1997. Carey lives in New York City.

CASEY, RICHARD GARDINER (1890-1976) A leading conservative federal politician, Casey was born in **Brisbane**,

Queensland, and educated at Melbourne and Cambridge University where he completed a degree in mechanical sciences. He served in the army at **Gallipoli** and on the Western Front in France during **World War I**. He was elected to the federal parliament in 1931 as **United Australia Party** member for Corio, **Victoria**. Casey served as assistant treasurer (1933), treasurer (1935), and minister for supply and development (to 1940). He failed in his bid to become **prime minister** in 1939, losing to **Robert Gordon Menzies**. He went to Washington to open Australia's first diplomatic legation to the **United States** (1940).

After **World War II** Casey returned to Australia and was re-elected to the **house of representatives** in the landslide win of the **Liberal Party of Australia** in 1949. He was minister for national development until 1951 when he was made minister for external affairs (1951-60). In this capacity he opened up good relations between Australia and south-east Asia, thereby leading Australia away from the insularity of the **White Australia Policy**. Casey retired from politics in 1960 when he was made Baron Casey of Berwick and of the City of Westminster, but went on to serve as **governor-general** from 1965 to 1969.

CASTLE HILL REBELLION   The Castle Hill Rebellion was a uprising by **convicts** that occurred north of Parramatta, **Sydney** in March 1804. Many of the convicts were **Irish**. The uprising was suppressed by the military; nine were killed or wounded in the fighting and eight others were hanged later. Others were flogged or sent to places of secondary punishment such as **Norfolk Island**.

CATHOLICISM   Until the migration of large numbers of southern Europeans to Australia in the 1940s, Australian Catholicism was largely based on the **Irish**-born or their descendants. The first Irish **convicts** arrived in 1791 and the first Mass authorized by the authorities was celebrated in 1803. But it was not until 1820 that Fathers John Joseph Therry (1790-1864) and Philip Conolly (1786-1839) were appointed priests to the Catholic laity because of opposition from the authorities and fears of an uprising by the Irish convicts such as occurred in the **Castle Hill Rebellion** in 1804. By 1828, 31 percent of the European population of 36,500 were Catholics. Therry tried to win religious freedom and greater social equality for Catholics. The first bishop, John Bede Polding (1794-

1877), was appointed in 1835. In 1836 the *Church Act* gave government funding for the major religions.

The 1860s finally saw the appointment of Irish bishops for Australia, and from that period until the 1960s the Australian Catholic church was shaped by Irish ecclesiastical politics. Catholics have been (and are) an important factor in Australian political and social life. Traditionally, Catholics were the poorer members of society. Cardinal Patrick Moran (1830-1911), the archbishop of Sydney from 1884 to 1911, supported the participation of Catholics in **labor unions** and the **Australian Labor Party** (ALP), which had many Catholic members and members of parliament.

In the bitter disputes over **conscription** in 1916-17, the Catholic community was one of the main opposition groups. Archbishop **Daniel Mannix** in **Melbourne** was one of the leaders of the anti-conscription campaigns. In 1937 the Catholic bishops set up "Catholic Action," whose aim was to promote Catholic social values among labor unions. This developed into an organization that fought communist influence in the unions and helped to bring about a split in the ALP (the effects of which were worst in **Victoria** and **Queensland**) and the formation of the **Democratic Labor Party** in 1956. Since the 1950s **immigration** from southern Europe has boosted the number of Catholics in Australia, and since 1981 Catholics have outnumbered the **Church of England** as Australia's largest single **religion** for the first time. In January 1995 Mary MacKillop (1842-1907) was made Australia's first saint by Pope John Paul during a visit to Australia. In 1996, 27 percent of Australians were Catholics.

CENSORSHIP Official censorship of printed works has been a feature of Australian history since 1803 when the **New South Wales** governor, Philip Gidley King (1758-1808), allowed the publication of the *Sydney Gazette* provided its contents were first read by a government official. This practice continued to 1824, after which the freedom of the **press** was accepted by governments. In 1901 the new federal government assumed a censorship role over imported publications and films under section 51(i) of the **Australian Constitution**, which gave it control over the regulation of trade and commerce with other countries and between **states**. Excluding wartime censorship, the states retained censorship powers over material produced within their own borders. Censored material included anything that was considered to be obscene, seditious, or blasphemous.

The censorship power has often been used by the federal government. For example, the original version of the film *King Kong* (1933) was censored for Australian audiences. By the early 1960s censorship began to come under sustained criticism for its inconsistency and restrictions on political and artistic liberty, especially with regard to "obscene" material. Many works freely available in Britain were either banned or censored in Australia. Since 1968 censorship has been substantially liberalized, although a tendency back to stricter censorship, particularly of **films**, has been evident in recent years.

CENSUS   The Australian census of **population** and housing grew out of official "musters" or counts of the **convicts**. In 1828 the **New South Wales** government produced a list of names of residents with some personal details and published a summary table. The next New South Wales census was held in 1833 and regular censuses were made every five years from 1836 to 1861. The other colonies began holding censuses in the 1840s. From 1881 the census was held simultaneously in the colonies in line with other parts of the British Empire.

After the creation of a federal government in 1901, census taking became a national responsibility under section 51(xi) of the **Australian Constitution**. The first nationally organized census of population and housing was held in 1911. Other censuses followed in 1921, 1933, 1947, and 1954. After 1961 the census was held every five years; the latest census was held on August 6, 1996. Unlike the American census, the Australian census has always included a question about **religion** and the individual returns are destroyed after processing.

CENTRAL COAST   The Central Coast is Australia's most recently designated major urban center. Located directly north of **Sydney**, the Central Coast consists of a series of settlements which have merged because of rapid **urbanization**. The main settlements are Gosford, Woy Woy, Terrigal, The Entrance, and Wyong. Although parts of the region were explored by sea as early as 1789 and it was settled by Europeans from 1794, poor communications and a limited economic base restricted population growth until the 1960s.

In 1947 the combined populations of its three largest towns—Gosford, Woy Woy, and Wyong—was only 7,800.

With the electrification of the **railroad** between Gosford and the building of a freeway to Sydney in the 1960s, the Central Coast became an attractive center for commuting workers while remaining an attractive area for **tourism** as well as for retirement. In 1986 the region was officially designated a major urban center for **census** purposes, that is it had a resident population of more than 100,000. Using this definition, the population of the Central Coast has doubled in the past 20 years from 101,800 in 1976 to 227,700 in 1996. The Central Coast and the **Gold Coast** are the two leading examples of this type of urban development in Australia.

CHANAK CRISIS The Chanak Crisis was an international crisis in 1922 which nearly led to a war between **Britain** and Turkey. Named after Chanak, the site of a British garrison, on the southern part of the **Gallipoli** peninsula, the crisis arose through military action by the Turks. Lloyd George, the British prime minister, wanted the dominions, including Australia, to send troops. **William Morris Hughes**, the Australian **prime minister**, agreed to send troops, but without consultation of the Australian parliament. He was censured by the parliament for this failure, and although the crisis passed, there was criticism of the lack of consultation; in 1924 a political liaison office was set up in London. The incident showed that Australian military support for Britain could no longer simply be assumed.

CHIEF MINISTER The term for leader of government in the **Northern Territory** and the **Australian Capital Territory** in contrast to **premier**. The office is a recent one in Australian political history, dating from the granting of self-government in these two territories, 1978 in the Northern Territory and 1989 in the Australian Capital Territory. Because the federal government can overturn the laws of the these territories under the **Australian Constitution**, the powers of chief ministers are inferior to those of premiers.

CHIFLEY, [JOSEPH] BEN [BENEDICT] (1885-1951) Australian **prime minister**, Ben Chifley was born in Bathurst, **New South Wales**. He became a locomotive engine driver in 1914 and was elected to the **house of representatives** in New South Wales in

1928 for the **Australian Labor Party**. From March to December 1931 he was minister for **defense** in the Scullin government. He lost his seat in the conservative landslide of December 1931 and did not regain it until 1940. He served as treasurer in the wartime administration of **John Curtin** and took over as prime minister July 13, 1945, and held office until December 19, 1949.

His administration improved **social security**, established a domestic government-run airline (1946), bought the international airline **Qantas** for the government, initiated the first large-scale **immigration** scheme for non-British European immigrants (1947), and began the **Snowy Mountains Hydro-Electric Scheme**. He lost office in the 1949 elections to **Robert Gordon Menzies** because he continued wartime rationing of petrol, because of his plan to nationalize the banks, and because he was blamed for the effects of the 1949 coal strike, which occurred during the winter.

CHILDE, VERE GORDON (1882-1957) Influential Marxist prehistorian and archaeologist, Childe was born in **Sydney** and educated at the universities of Sydney and Oxford. Between 1919 and 1921 he worked as private secretary to John Storey (1869-1921), **Australian Labor Party premier** of **New South Wales**. He then joined the staff of the University of Queensland, but its governing body soon dismissed him believing him to be too radical, despite his academic brilliance. This experience was the backdrop to Childe's first book, *How Labour Governs: A Study of Workers' Representation in Australia*, which was published in 1923. Childe left Australia and by 1927 had become professor of archaeology at Edinburgh, a post he held until 1946 when he moved to the University of London. He wrote scholarly and popular works on European archaeology, notably *The Dawn of European Civilization* (1925) and *Man Makes Himself* (1936). He returned to Australia in April 1957, but it was not a happy homecoming. He fell to his death in the Blue Mountains, near Sydney, in October 1957 and is generally thought to have committed suicide.

CHINESE The Chinese were the largest non-European immigrant group in nineteenth-century Australia and the focus of the most racial prejudice later expressed through the **White Australia Policy**. Although some Chinese arrived in Australia before 1850, it was the gold rushes of the next 10 years that attracted large numbers; between 1854 and 1857 the number of Chinese in

Victoria rose from 2,341 to 25,421. By 1861 there were 38,742 Chinese in Australia, accounting for 3.3 percent of the total population. Most of the Chinese came as indentured laborers from southern China. Nearly all were male and uneducated.

The Chinese were seen by most Europeans as aliens and as effective competitors on the gold diggings. They were the victims of riots, notably at Lambing Flat near Young, **New South Wales** (1860-61), and on the gold-fields of **Queensland** (1877). The Australian colonies introduced restrictions on Chinese immigration: Victoria (1855), New South Wales (1861), Queensland (1877), **South Australia** (1881), **Western Australia** (1886), and **Tasmania** (1887). The **labor unions** were particularly strong in their opposition to Chinese **immigration** and found it a useful way of gaining community support.

With the decline of gold mining, many Chinese moved to the towns to take up market gardening or to provide services for Europeans. In the **Northern Territory** they were more able to establish themselves as important citizens. Because nearly all the pre-1900 Chinese immigrants were male, intermarriage was common. From 1901 to 1947 the number of Chinese-born fell from 29,907 to 6,404. In the post-war period, the number of Chinese in Australia has increased steadily, particularly with immigration from **Vietnam** and other parts of Asia. At the 1996 **census**, there were at least 200,000 Australians of Chinese birth, from the Peoples' Republic (111,000), Hong Kong (68,400), Taiwan (19,600), and Macau (1,900). The census also revealed that 324,000 Australians spoke a Chinese language at home.

CHISHOLM, CAROLINE (1808-1877)   English philanthropist and promoter of female immigrant welfare, Chisholm was born in Northampton, England, and arrived in Australia in 1840 with her husband. She was greatly moved by the plight of female immigrants who were unemployed and liable to become prostitutes. She lobbied governments to help them and ran a home for female immigrants. She promoted family life as a means of "civilizing" Australia's frontier society. She was personally responsible for finding jobs for 11,000 people. In Britain her efforts led to the Family Colonization Loan Society to conduct family **immigration** to Australia. She became known as the "emigrant's friend" and from 1967 to 1992 she was commemorated on the reverse of the Australian $5 note.

CHURCH OF ENGLAND   The Church of England, or Anglican Church (Episcopal in the **United States**), has been nearly always the largest single Christian denomination in Australia since European settlement began in 1788. Between 1861 and 1947, about 40 percent of Australians, nominally at least, claimed to be members of the church at the population **census**. With the exception of the 1820s and early 1830s, the Church of England has never been the officially favored or "established" church as it was in England. Links between the parent British church and its Australian colonial churches were very strong, and the two only became legally distinct in 1962.

Because **Britain** was the major source of **immigration** to Australia, the number of adherents to the Church of England was maintained at a high level. When the Australian colonies formed a **federation** in 1901, the **Australian Constitution** was careful to specifically forbid the national government from making any **religion** the official religion or interfering with religious toleration (section 116).   The main competitor to the Church of England— officially renamed the Anglican Church of Australia in 1981—has been **Catholicism**. In 1992 the first women Anglican priests were ordained in **New South Wales**. Between 1901 and 1996, the proportion of Australians who claimed to be adherents of the Church of England fell from 39 to 22 percent.

CITIZENSHIP AND NATURALIZATION   There was no specific, legal provision for Australian citizenship until after **Australia Day**, January 26, 1949, when the *Nationality and Citizenship Act* of 1948 came into effect. Before that date, citizenship was derived from being a British subject, a status gained by birth or descent from someone born in **Britain**. Naturalization was a legal process whereby "aliens" (that is non-British subjects) were admitted to the rights and privileges of being a British subject. Because the great majority of immigrants to Australia before 1945 were British-born, and therefore British subjects whose civil status was, for all intents and purposes, uniform throughout the British empire, citizenship was largely only an issue for aliens.

The first aliens naturalized in Australia were two Americans for whom special legislation was passed in 1825. Between 1847 and 1870 all the Australian colonies enacted naturalization laws within the framework of British legislation even though the requirements for naturalization differed between the colonies. Naturalization procedures reflected growing racist sentiment which later became formalized in the **White Australia Policy**. This was shown by the restrictive conditions required for the **Chinese** by the 1880s. Nevertheless, the Chinese were the most prominent group which gained naturalization before 1890. In **New South Wales** 1,801 persons were naturalized between 1878 and 1888, of whom 774 were Chinese, 466 were **Germans**, and only 5 were Americans. In **Victoria**, 4,254 persons were naturalized between 1871 and 1887 of whom 2,969 were Chinese.

After **federation** in 1901, the colonies transferred their powers over "naturalization and aliens" to the federal government under section 51(xix) of the **Australian Constitution**. In 1903 the government enacted a *Naturalization Act* which denied naturalization to natives of Africa, Asia, and the Pacific Islands with the exception of **New Zealand**. In 1920 the government enacted another *Naturalization Act* based on a British law passed in 1914. Although the 1920 law removed the overt racial discrimination of its predecessor, it gave the **governor-general** the power to refuse naturalization. The 1920 law also recognized the status of any person naturalized elsewhere in the British empire.

The impetus for changing the citizenship law came from Canada, whose government wanted to establish its own nationality legislation, but was unable to do so within the framework of the common code of the British Empire; Canada enacted its citizenship law in 1946. To accommodate Canada and also retain India within the British Commonwealth, discussions were held in London in 1947 among representatives of the countries of the British Commonwealth. It was agreed that self-governing countries within the Commonwealth could enact citizenship laws which would define citizenship for their particular countries; the concept of British subject was retained. In Australia, the 1920 law was replaced by the *Nationality and Citizenship Act* in 1948 (which was renamed the *Australian Citizenship Act* in 1973); it transferred most of the previous powers given to the governor-general to the minister of the day responsible for its administration and created the status of Australian citizenship for the first time. Since the Australian citizenship legislation came into effect in 1949, 3.2 million persons have become Australian citizens up to July 1998. Australian citizenship confers rights and privileges, such as the ability to vote in elections, and obligations, such as jury service.

In January 1994 a new pledge of commitment as a citizen of the Commonwealth of Australia replaced the former oath of allegiance. The pledge reads:

> *From this time forward,* under God,
> *I pledge my loyalty to Australia and its people,*
> *whose democratic beliefs I share,*
> *whose rights and liberties I respect, and*
> *whose laws I will uphold and obey.*

The new citizen has the choice of making the pledge with or without the words "under God."

Both the 1996 (and earlier **censuses**) showed that many immigrants had not taken out Australian citizenship. The total take-up rate of citizenship among the foreign-born was 73.2 percent, but this varied greatly between the former countries of origin. The highest rates were: Greece (97.3 percent), **Papua New Guinea** (91.3 percent), and **Vietnam** (93.4 percent). The lowest rates were: United States (57.3 percent), **New Zealand** (35.1 percent), and **Japan** (25.3 percent). The rate for **Britain** was 62.2 percent, which is regarded as low. (*See also* Immigration; Table 13, Statistical Appendix)

CLARK, [CHARLES] MANNING [HOPE] (1915-1991) Historian, Clark was born in **Melbourne** and was the son of a clergyman. He was educated at Melbourne Grammar School and the Universities of Melbourne and Oxford. He became a university teacher at the University of Melbourne in 1946 and from 1949 to 1975 was foundation professor of Australian history of the undergraduate part of the Australian National University. His collections of source books on Australian history—*Select Documents in Australian History* (1950, 1955) and *Sources of Australian History* (1957)—which mainly cover the nineteenth century, were pioneering works and won Clark a high reputation. His *History of Australia* was published in six volumes between 1962 and 1987 and deals with Australian history up to 1935. This is a controversial history—and Clark was a controversial figure because of his anti-establishment views—which explores the past from a Christian-moral point of view. It is nevertheless important because of its attempt to break away from the more traditional approach of viewing Australian history largely through an economic lens and a contrast to the austere approach of **Noel George Butlin**.

COAL   Australia has been one of the world's largest coal exporters since 1984. In 1987 the U.S. Bureau of Mines estimated that Australia produced 4.4 percent of the world's black coal. Coal was first discovered at **Newcastle, New South Wales**, in 1797, and significant **mining** began in the late 1820s. Black coal was also found in **Queensland** in 1826 and mining began in 1846. These two **states** account for the bulk of Australia's coal exports. In **Victoria** "brown" coal or lignite was being mined by the 1890s, but it was not until 1918 that the state government opened a large-scale mining project for use in generating electricity.

From about 1860 to 1924 Australia developed a thriving export trade for New South Wales coal to countries bordering the Pacific Ocean, but the trade declined largely because Australian coal became too expensive compared with its competitors. Exports did not become an important feature of the industry again until 1953, when most of the exports went to **Japan**. New South Wales coal is usually mined underground, but most Queensland coal comes from open cut mining. Coal mining has long been a battleground between employers and **labor unions**, particularly in New South Wales where there were major **labor disputes** in 1909-10, 1916, 1929-30, and 1949. In 1997-98 Australia produced 218.9 million tonnes of black coal and coal of all kinds accounted for 10.9 percent of merchandise export earnings.

COBB AND CO   Cobb and Co operated the largest horse-drawn coach service in eastern Australia from 1853 to 1924. The firm was founded by four Americans, Freeman Cobb (1830-1878), John Murray Peck (1830-1903), who had worked for Wells Fargo, James Swanton, and John B. Lamber. Using American coaches and organizational methods, Cobb and Co was renown for its reliability. By 1890 it operated 6,400 kilometers of coach routes but increasingly proved unable to compete with the **railroads**. The company shifted its operations into motor coaches and ran its last horse-drawn coach in 1924. The firm's exploits were celebrated by Henry Lawson in his poem *The Lights of Cobb and Co*. (*See also* United States of America)

COGHLAN, TIMOTHY AUGUSTINE (1855-1926) Statistician and historian, Coghlan was born in **Sydney** to **Irish** parents. Coghlan became the colonial statistician of **New South Wales** in 1886, a post he held until 1905 when he became agent-general in London. His appointment as statistician was a surprise given his Australian birth as such appointments were generally given to the British-born and educated. Before his appointment he was assistant engineer with the harbors and rivers department. As a statistician, he achieved acclaim both in Australia and internationally; in 1893 he was made a Fellow of the Royal Statistical Society in London.

Coghlan not only re-organized the statistical collections of New South Wales, he systematically extended the collections and communicated their results in appealing publications with text and tables, notably in the yearbook *The Wealth and Progress of New South Wales*, which was first published in 1887. He tried to measure every kind of significant activity whether it was **urbanization** or the growth of the **labor unions**. In 1890 he published the first issue of *A Statistical Account of the Seven Colonies of Australasia* which included **New Zealand**, and was the first publication of its kind and the forerunner to the *Official Year Book of the Commonwealth of Australia*, which was first published by the federal government in 1908.

Because of his accuracy and his inside knowledge of political affairs, his publications remain an important source for their study in Australia. His great work was *Labour and Industry in Australia from the First Settlement in 1788 to the Establishment of the Commonwealth in 1901*, published as four volumes in 1918 by Oxford University Press, which continues to be an indispensable source for economic, political, and labor history in the last half of the nineteenth century. Coghlan was knighted in 1914.

COLES   A variety chain store group originally established in the **Melbourne** suburb of Collingwood by George James Coles (1885-1977) in 1914. Coles expanded considerably after 1945 to become one of Australia's leading retailers and companies. In 1985 Coles merged with another major Victorian retailer, Myer, to form the Coles-Myer group. In 1994-95 the group acquired the American-owned K-Mart stores. In 1997 Coles-Myer employed 148,000 staff, sold 28 percent of Australia's groceries, and had a stock market valuation of $5.7 billion. (*See also* Wholesale and Retail Trade)

COLONIAL/STATE GOVERNORS   Unlike their American counterparts before 1776, the early colonial governors of Australia exercised real political power. As representatives of the British monarch, they were either naval captains or military officers and used to giving orders. Captain Arthur Phillip (1738-1814), the first governor of **New South Wales** from 1788 to 1792, had a commission that gave him the power to grant land, pardon **convicts**, regulate the **economy**, appoint officials and hear judicial appeals. In 1808, the New South Wales governor, William Bligh, was removed in the **"Rum Rebellion."**

After 1823, the autocratic powers of the New South Wales governors were gradually reduced when a **Legislative Council** was created. In the mid-1850s most of the Australian colonies were granted self-government over their domestic affairs and their governors' powers were sharply limited, although they retained the right to summon and dismiss parliament and the power to appoint and dismiss ministers. By and large, however, the governors carried out the wishes of the government, and this convention was formalized in 1892 on instructions from Queen Victoria.

With the creation of the office of **governor-general** by the **Australian Constitution** in 1901, the colonial governors became state governors and, by implication, had their status reduced. Although they were generally figureheads, they have on occasion proved that they could exercise power in their own right if they considered the law was being broken or the government's advice was contrary to the public interest. For example, they have declined to agree to recommendations by governments to hold elections (**Tasmania** in 1923 and **Victoria** in 1952). However, the most spectacular use of their power occurred in New South Wales on May 13, 1932, when the governor, Philip Woolcott Game (1876-1961), dismissed the **Australian Labor Party** government of **Jack Lang** for breaking the terms of the 1927 financial agreement between the federal and the state governments.

COLONIES All the present **states** of Australia began as British colonies. **New South Wales**, the first Australian colony, was established in 1788. **Tasmania** was created as a separate colony in 1825, **Western Australia** in 1829, **South Australia** in 1836, **Victoria** in 1851, and **Queensland** in 1859. With the introduction of the **Australian Constitution** in 1901, all these colonies became states.

COMMONWEALTH BANK The Commonwealth Bank was begun by the federal **Australian Labor Party** government of **Andrew Fisher** as the Commonwealth Savings Bank in 1912. It opened a trading department in 1913, which was made into a separate bank in 1953. The purpose of the Bank was to strengthen federal control of the banking industry following the bank crashes in 1893. In the early 1930s the Bank functioned as a central bank, but under non-Labor governments, the Bank operated much like any other large bank. In 1959 federal legislation was passed to set up the Commonwealth Banking Corporation and the Reserve Bank, which was to act as the central bank of Australia. The Commonwealth Bank was completely privatized between 1994 and 1996 by the Labor government of **Paul Keating**. In 1997 the Bank had a share market valuation of $10.9 billion.

COMMONWEALTH SCIENTIFIC AND INDUSTRIAL RESEARCH ORGANISATION (CSIRO) The CSIRO is Australia's leading government science organization. Founded in 1920 to conduct research that would help rural industry, the CSIRO was given its present title in 1949. Its headquarters are in **Melbourne**. In 1936 the role of the CSIRO was widened to include secondary industry. Its charter for research was broadened again in 1978. In 1986 a 10-member board was established to determine the policy and administration of the CSIRO. In 1997 the CSIRO employed 6,709 staff (compared to 7,347 in 1987), of whom 43 percent were directly engaged in scientific research.

COMMONWEALTH-STATE RELATIONS With the **federation** of the Australian colonies in 1901, Australia gained a new federal government (named the Commonwealth of Australia), which gradually took more power from the **states** (the former **colonies**) than had been originally intended. This occurred mainly through the transfer of taxation powers to the Commonwealth government. In the interests of uniformity, the states had surrendered customs duties to the Commonwealth in the 1900s. Australia's participation in two world wars and the resultant need for national action as well as economic planning also strengthened the Commonwealth's power compared with the states. In theory, the **senate** was supposed to guard the interests of the states, but in reality the rise of **political parties**, owing an allegiance to a party rather than to a state, to made it ineffective in this role.

The greatest single shift of power came in 1942 when the Commonwealth gained (and held) the power over income tax. Differences between the Commonwealth and the states over their powers and the allocation of resources often require delicate negotiations or even resort to the **High Court of Australia**. (*See also* Australian Constitution, Braddon's Blot, Western Australia)

COMMUNIST PARTY OF AUSTRALIA (CPA)   The CPA was formed in **Sydney** on October 30, 1920, from members of various left-wing political groups. From the beginning, the CPA was prone to factional disputes based on doctrinal differences. In 1922, the Soviet Comintern recognized the labor union-based organization as the official Communist Party, which led to the collapse of the ultra-Marxist Australian Socialist Party.

In 1929 the new leadership of the CPA applied the Comintern's strategy of confrontation in Australia, a policy that attracted many members during the struggles of the unemployed during the Depression, especially through its front organization, the Unemployed Workers' Movement, which claimed 30,000 members in the early 1930s. In 1934 the Comintern encouraged the CPA to adopt a "united front" with the **Australian Labor Party**. The CPA was banned from mid-1940 to late 1941 under wartime regulations. Membership was at its height in 1943 when the CPA claimed 24,000 members.

Although strong in certain labor unions (notably the coal miners' and the waterfront workers' unions), CPA influence declined in the late 1940s especially after the defeat of the 1949 coal miners' strike in **New South Wales**. In 1951 a federal referendum to ban the CPA was only narrowly defeated, with 49.4 percent of the electorate voting in favor of the ban. After 1951 the CPA was further weakened by loss of membership and factional disputes based on events in world communism. Following the Soviet invasion of Hungary in 1956, membership fell to 5,500. In 1963 a pro-Chinese faction (calling itself the Communist Party of Australia) split from the CPA, followed by a pro-Soviet faction (the Socialist Party of Australia) in 1968; there was also a faction made up of the followers of Leon Trotsky, the Socialist Workers' Party. By 1984 the original CPA had only 1,300 members and in late 1989 the CPA dissolved itself. It was revived in October 1996 in Sydney as the Communist Party of Australia, but remains a marginal political party. (*See also* Democratic Labor Party; New Guard)

COMPULSORY VOTING Compulsory voting, that is, a legal requirement on threat of fine to vote in state and federal elections, makes Australia unique among English-speaking democracies in the use of the **franchise**. It was introduced first in **Queensland** in 1915 and then spread to the other **states** and was adopted for federal elections in 1924. The introduction of compulsory voting in federal elections raised voter turnout from 59 percent in 1922 to 91 percent in 1924. Voting for the constitutional convention on whether Australia should become a republic in November to December 1997 was exceptional in being voluntary; voter turnout was 46.6 percent of those eligible to vote. (*See also* Secret Ballot)

CONCILIATION AND ARBITRATION In Australia, conciliation and arbitration refers to the formal process for settling **labor disputes** by industrial tribunals. In this process, conciliation means that an industrial tribunal tries to help the employer and **labor unions** in dispute to reach a mutually agreed settlement. If this fails, the tribunal might resort to arbitration, that is imposing a settlement on the parties in dispute. Conciliation and arbitration had been advocated as a means of settling labor disputes by labor unions in Britain as early as 1845 and from the 1860s, but only on a voluntary basis and without government intervention. The failure of voluntary conciliation and arbitration in **Britain** and the **United States**, together with the severity of their labor disputes of the early 1890s, led the Australian colonies to opt for compulsory conciliation and arbitration administered by government-appointed industrial tribunals. Legislation to establish industrial tribunals to regulate disputes, wages, and conditions was introduced in 1896 in **Victoria**, 1900 in **Western Australia** and **South Australia**, 1901 in **New South Wales**, and 1912 in **Queensland**.

In 1904 a federal **industrial tribunal**, the Court of Conciliation and Arbitration, was established under section 51(xxxv) of the **Australian Constitution** to deal with interstate labor disputes, but soon become a party to disputes confined to one **state**. Labor unions could register as organizations under these conciliation and arbitration laws and legally compel those employers with whom they were in dispute to come before a state or the federal industrial tribunal to argue their case.

Up to 1921 the bulk of the court's work took the form of conciliation not arbitration. This was indicated by the number of industrial agreements it made—1,488—as opposed to only 190

awards. Industrial agreements (that is voluntary agreements between a labor union and an employer) were the product of conciliation, whereas awards were the product of arbitration. From 1922 the court tended to prefer arbitration rather than conciliation as means of settling disputes. Despite the many changes to the labor relations system since the 1920s, particularly the move to a more enterprise-based system since the late 1980s, conciliation and arbitration continued to be used for resolving those labor disputes which come before industrial tribunals.

CONFEDERATION OF AUSTRALIAN INDUSTRY (CAI)   The CAI was formed in December 1977 as the peak employer organization to counter the influence of the peak labor union organization, the **Australian Council of Trade Unions** and to be a national voice for employers. In the mid-1980s the CAI had 38 employer groups as members representing 100,000 employers. The influence of the CAI has suffered with the withdrawal of most of the large employer organizations, particularly the **Australian Chamber of Manufactures**, which accounted for a quarter of the CAI's annual budget of $2 million in 1989. Since late 1990 several large employer organizations have rejoined the CAI. On September 1, 1992, the Confederation of Australian Industry amalgamated with the Australian Chamber of Commerce to form the Australian Chamber of Commerce and Industry. (*See also* Employers' Associations)

CONSCRIPTION   Conscription for military service within Australia began in 1911 and was applied to all males aged 12 to 26. Even though it made no provision for conscientious objectors, the scheme had widespread support as a means of giving urban youth something to do. This scheme was suspended in 1929. During **World War I** the federal government of **William Morris Hughes**, acting on British advice, attempted to introduce conscription by **referendum**, but was beaten twice (1916, 1917) in campaigns of unusual bitterness. In the turmoil of the 1916 campaign against conscription, the **Australian Labor Party** split between those in favor (who were usually the older and British-born) and those against (who were generally younger and Australian-born).

On the outbreak of **World War II**, the federal government of **Robert Gordon Menzies** introduced conscription for all unmarried

21-year-old men for three months. In 1943 the federal ALP government of **John Curtin**, who had opposed conscription during World War I, approved sending conscripts outside Australia for the war in the south-west Pacific.

A conscription scheme operated from 1951 to 1960, but was greatly increased in 1965 when the "National Service" scheme was introduced. It required two years' service of those selected by ballot based on birthdays. In all, 63,735 national servicemen were conscripted into the army from 1965 to 1972. Of these, 19,450 fought in **Vietnam**, where 1,795 became casualties and 200 died. At first this conscription scheme was popular, but opposition to it and to the Vietnam war grew after 1968. National Service was abolished by the Labor government of **Gough Whitlam** on December 5, 1972.

CONSTITUTION (*See* Australian Constitution)

CONVICTS Eastern Australia was known from the explorations of **James Cook** in 1770 to have a temperate climate, and it was chosen as the new destination for convicts in 1786. From the first settlement at **Sydney** in 1788 until 1820, convicts made up most of Australia's European population. A total of 162,000 convicts were transported to Australia from 1788 to 1860 (137,000 men and 25,000 women). Most were sent to **New South Wales**, Van Diemen's Land (**Tasmania** after 1856), and **Western Australia**. The last convicts arrived in Western Australia in 1868.

Nearly all the convicts were young people from the cities convicted more than once of some form of theft. Only about 1,000 could be called political prisoners. The treatment they received varied enormously depending upon their time of arrival (those who came after 1820 tended to receive harsher treatment), who they had to work for, and whether or not they were convicted of new crimes in Australia. Those who were convicted of crimes within Australia suffered the most and could be sent to prisons like Port Arthur in Tasmania or **Norfolk Island** where they lived and died under conditions of calculated brutality. The standard punishment for convicts was flogging.

But most convicts on their arrival were placed ("assigned") with a settler to work as a laborer. With good behavior, a convict could get a conditional pardon ("ticket of leave"), which meant freedom in Australia, but not permission to return to **Britain**. Debate about the effect of the convict system began in the 1830s and has continued to the present. Some convicts prospered in Australia, such as the Sydney merchant Simeon Lord (1771-1840). Others were savagely ill-treated without justice or cause. Yet the convicts provided an essential workforce for the infant settlements of eastern Australia. (*See also* Emancipists)

COOK, JAMES (1728-1779) Britain's greatest navigator, Cook's claim to importance in Australian history lies in his exploration of the eastern coast of Australia, which he first saw on April 19, 1770 (modern Cape Howe). He reached Botany Bay (**Sydney**) on April 29, 1770, and thereafter sailed up the coast. The voyage nearly ended disastrously in July when his ship, the *Endeavour*, struck part of the **Great Barrier Reef**. After making repairs near modern Cooktown, **Queensland**, he sailed to Cape York (the northernmost part of the Australian mainland) where he took possession of the east coast of Australian for **Britain** (August 22, 1770). He reached Britain via Torres Strait in June 1771. Cook's voyage led eventually to the selection of Botany Bay as Britain's base in the south-west Pacific (1786), a step which began the British occupation of Australia. (*See also* First Fleet)

COOK, JOSEPH (1860-1947) Australian **prime minister**, Cook was born in Silverdale, Staffordshire, England. He left school at the age of nine to work as a coal miner and became an active **labor union** member. He emigrated to **New South Wales** in 1885. In 1891 he was elected to parliament as one of the first members of the newly formed Political Labour League, later called the **Australian Labor Party (**ALP), but quit after refusing to sign the party's "pledge" or undertaking that he would abide by majority decisions of its parliamentary party. In 1894 he was re-elected as an independent "labor" politician. In 1901 he moved into federal politics where he remained until 1921; in this period, Cook was an important figure in conservative politics.

In 1908 Cook became leader of the Free Traders' Party and was minister for defense in the **"Fusion" Liberal Party** government led by **Alfred Deakin** in 1909-10. In this capacity he was largely responsible for the introduction of **conscription** and other significant changes including the setting up of **Duntroon** military college. In 1913 he led the Liberal Party to victory at the national elections, but failed to win control of the upper house, the **senate**. Cook was prime minister between June 24, 1913, and September 17, 1914. His government was defeated by the ALP in the 1914 election. Following the split in the ALP over conscription in 1916 and the formation of the **Nationalist Party**, Cook became its deputy leader. His last official post was Australian High Commissioner in London, which he held from 1921 to 1927.

COOMBS, "NUGGET" [HERBERT COLE] (1906-1997) The leading federal bureaucrat from **World War II** to the early 1970s, and campaigner for rights for **Aborigines**, Nugget Coombs was born in Kalamundra, a small town east of **Perth**, and completed his education at the University of Western Australia. His nickname, "Nugget," referred to his short, stocky build. In the 1920s he was a secondary schoolteacher in rural **Western Australia**, where he first acquired an interest in the social and economic improvement of Aborigines. In 1931 he won a Harkness scholarship to study at Cambridge, but transferred his doctoral studies to the London School of Economics because it was cheaper and completed them in 1933. The experience of poverty in London during the Depression heightened his concern for social issues.

In 1935 Coombs joined the **Commonwealth Bank** as an economist and in 1936 eagerly embraced J. M. Keynes' *General Theory of Employment, Interest, and Money,* although he did not agree with everything that Keynes advocated. In 1939 Coombs joined the federal treasury in **Canberra**. In 1942 he became national director of rationing and a member of the board of the Commonwealth Bank. From 1943 to 1949 he was director-general of the federal department of postwar reconstruction. In 1948 he was made governor of the Commonwealth Bank, a post he held until 1960.

Coombs survived the defeat of the **Australian Labor Party** in the national elections of December 1949 and served a variety of coalition **Liberal/Country** Party governments with equal distinction. In 1968 he became chairman of the Council for Aboriginal Affairs, a body set up to remove discrimination against Aborigines following a successful **referendum** on the subject in 1967. His last significant official contribution was to chair a royal commission into Australian government administration in 1976. Otherwise, Coombs took an active interest in the arts and the environment. In 1981 he published his memoirs, entitled *Trial Balance*.

CORAL SEA, BATTLE OF   The Coral Sea lies to the north-east of the Australian mainland. Between May 4-8, 1942, it was the scene of a wide-ranging naval battle between U.S. and Japanese forces during **World War II**. Although American naval losses exceeded those of the Japanese, the effective loss of two aircraft carriers hampered the Japanese at the critical Battle of Midway soon afterwards. It was the first major battle in which Americans and Australians were allies. Australia provided aircraft and ships during the battle. The purpose of the Japanese offensive was not the invasion of Australia, as often thought, but the conquest of **Papua New Guinea**, Fiji, and Samoa, a move which would have cut Australia off as a base for military operations against the Japanese.

CORNFORTH, JOHN WARCUP (1917-) Leading organic chemist, Cornforth was born in **Sydney** and educated at the University of Sydney. Despite becoming deaf in 1934, he won a scholarship to Oxford in 1939 where he conducted research into the synthesis of steriods. In 1946 he joined the British Medical Research Council. In 1975 he shared the Nobel prize for Chemistry with Vladimir Prelog for his research into the stereochemistry of enzymes. He was knighted in 1977.

COUNTRY/NATIONAL PARTY OF AUSTRALIA   The Country Party has been the third largest political party in Australia since 1920. (It was renamed the National Party at the national level in 1982.) The party grew out of rural discontent based on **drought** (1914-15), loss of population to the towns, and a widespread feeling that governments, and their institutions, neglected the rural dweller. Since 1923, no conservative national government has been able to rule without the participation of the Country Party.

As a party, the Country Party representatives in either federal or state parliament were conservative on social issues but united in their desire to secure a greater share of government money for rural interests. Their highest priority has been for expenditure on roads, railways, dams and other services. They have historically been supporters of low tariffs and government bodies to regulate the production and marketing of rural goods.

The Country Party has been led by able politicians such as **Earle Page** (leader from 1921 to 1939) and **John McEwen** (leader from 1958 to 1971). It has been strongest in north-eastern **New South Wales** and **Queensland** where Jo [Johannes] Bjelke-Petersen (1911-) became **premier** in 1968 and achieved the unique distinction of ruling without the **Liberal Party** from 1983 to 1987. Since the late 1980s the image of the National Party has suffered from allegations of corrupt administration, which has led to legal inquiries and some convictions in Queensland. Nevertheless, the National Party has the most members (100,000 in 1994 compared to 130,000 in 1990) of any Australian political party. In the **Northern Territory**, the Country/National and Liberal parties have contested elections as a single conservative party since 1974. Negotiations to merge the two parties have also been held in Queensland, but these failed. Like the Liberal Party, the National Party is a member of the Pacific Democrat Union which was formed in 1982.

In the national elections on October 3, 1998, the National Party attracted only 5.3 percent of the vote for the **house of representatives** (compared to 8.2 percent in 1996) and 1.9 percent for the **senate** (compared to 2.9 percent in 1996). The reduction in the party's vote was largely because of competition from the **One Nation Party** for the rural vote. Since 1990 the leader of the National Party has been Tim Fischer (1946-). (*See also* United Australia Party)

COUNTRY WOMEN'S ASSOCIATION (CWA) The CWA is the oldest and largest organization for **women** in Australia. Drawing on similar organizations in Canada from the 1890s and **Britain** (1913), the CWA was formed first in **New South Wales** in 1922 and then in other **states**. Its aims were the improvement of the lives of rural women and children. The CWA is non-political and non-sectarian. By 1954 it had 110,000 members and 2,000 branches in the capital cities as well as country areas. It has been responsible for setting up rest rooms and baby health centers in many country towns. The CWA is a member of the Associated Country Women of the World. By 1983 the membership of the CWA had fallen to 55,000.

CRICKET The English game of cricket is one of Australia's most popular summer sports. The first known cricket match was played in **Sydney** in 1803, and by 1851 the first match was played between **Victoria** and **Tasmania**. The tradition of intercolonial matches was formalized in the annual **Sheffield Shield** competitions. English cricket teams began visiting Australia in 1862 and the first "test" match was played in **Melbourne, Victoria**, in 1877. After Australia's victory in the 1882 test the London *Times* carried a mock obituary of the death of English cricket saying that after its cremation its "ashes" would be taken to Australia. Thereafter the "ashes" became the symbolic prize of victors of test matches while a real urn containing the ashes of a cricket stump remained permanently at Lord's Cricket Ground, England.

The regular contests between Australia and England provided a focus for Australian **nationalism**, which was powerfully demonstrated during the **"bodyline"** tour of the English team in 1932-33. Since 1945 there have been regular cricket matches between Australia and India, Pakistan, the West Indies, and **New Zealand**. In 1996 an estimated 200,000 Australians were regular cricket players and millions more watch the game during the summer on **television**.

CURRENCY Because the **First Fleet** brought little coinage with it, the early British settlement at **Sydney** had to use foodstuffs and rum as currency. Some currency, notably Spanish dollars, came in the course of trade, but these were quickly traded for other goods the colony needed. The colony suffered from a severe shortage of currency until 1813 when the governor, **Lachlan Macquarie**, issued 40,000 Spanish dollars for circulation. Following British colonial practices in the eastern Caribbean and Guyana between 1765 and 1811, the centers of the dollars were cut out. The outer ring or "holey dollar" and the inner disk or "dump" were counter stamped with new and higher values so as to keep them within the colony. These coins remained legal tender until 1829 when they were replaced by British coinage. As in **Britain**, shopkeepers issued their own small change called traders' tokens. With the **gold** rushes after 1851, the Australian colonies set up mints to issue gold coins in Sydney (1855), Melbourne (1872), and Perth (1899).

Under the **Australian Constitution**, the federal government was authorized to make laws with respect to "currency, coinage, and legal tender" (section 51xii) and the states were forbidden to issue gold and silver coins (section 115). The first Australian coins were issued by the federal government in 1910 and the first paper currency in 1913. Pounds, shillings, and pence were the basis of Australian currency until February 14, 1966, when the conversion was made to decimal currency based on dollars and cents. Most of Australia's currency is produced at the Royal Australian Mint in **Canberra**.

For international **trade**, the value of Australia's currency against the British pound hardly varied between 1851 and 1930, but because of Australia's disastrous trade performance during the Depression, the exchange rate with Britain was reduced by 30 percent in February 1931 and fixed at 25 percent below sterling in December 1931 at which level it remained until 1967. Since 1971 Australia's exchange rate has been quoted in U.S. dollars not pounds sterling. There have been devaluations in Australia's currency in response to poor economic performance, notably in 1974 (13.6 percent), 1976 (17.5 percent), and 1983 (10 percent). Since December 1983, the value of the dollar has been allowed to "float" in response to market conditions rather than by government action. Since 1982 the value of the Australian dollar fell below parity with the U.S. dollar for the first time. In 1997-98 the average value of the Australian dollar was $0.61 (U.S.) and £0.37.

CURTIN, JOHN JOSEPH (1885-1945)   Australian **prime minister**, Curtin was born in Creswick, Victoria. He worked as a printer and a clerk before joining the Victorian Socialist Party in about 1906. In 1916 he was briefly jailed for his opposition to **conscription**. In 1917 he moved to **Western Australia** where he became editor of the *Westralian Worker*. He was elected member to the **house of representatives** for the electorate of Fremantle in 1928, defeated in 1931, but regained the seat in 1934. He became leader of the federal **Australian Labor Party** parliamentary party in 1935. On October 7, 1941, Curtin became prime minister after the failure of the previous conservative government led by **Robert Gordon Menzies** to hold its majority in the house of representatives. As wartime prime minister until 1945, Curtin made two important decisions. First, he recalled Australian forces committed to the Middle East back to Australia (1941) and refused Churchill's attempt to have them sent to Burma. Second, he appealed to the **United States** for help (1942). The strain of the war contributed to his comparatively early death at 60 on July 5, 1945. In recent years Curtin's wartime decision-making has been criticized for being too influenced by the American Allied commander-in-chief General Douglas MacArthur and the Australian senior army officers.

D

DART, RAYMOND ARTHUR (1893-1988) Anatomist and paleo-anthropologist, Dart was born in **Brisbane** where he attended **Queensland** University and then the University of **Sydney**. After holding university positions in **Britain** and the **United States**, he was appointed professor of anatomy at Witwatersrand University in Johannesburg in 1928 where he remained until 1958. In this position, he made important discoveries concerning human evolution and the evolutionary break between humans and apes, particularly the idea that the ability to walk on two legs preceded the increase in brain capacity and the reduction in the size of the jaw. The work he pioneered supported Darwin's suggestion that humans first evolved in Africa.

DARWIN Darwin is the administrative center and largest town of the **Northern Territory**. To discourage the Dutch from making territorial claims to northern Australia, the British set up military settlements in the region at Melville Island (1824), at Raffles Bay (1827), and at Port Essington (1838). The harbor of the present town was discovered in 1839 by the crew of the British ship *Beagle* and named in honor of Charles Darwin who had been a naturalist on an earlier voyage of the ship. The site was planned in 1869 and the town was called Palmerston, in honor of the British prime minister, until 1911. Darwin's population size reflected the uncertain economic development of the region. From a population of 780 in 1874, it grew to 4,900 by 1891 and then fell to 944 in 1911.

But Darwin was strategically important; it was the terminus of the **Overland Telegraph** and possessed one of the best harbors on Australia's northern coast. It was also the primary airport for aircraft entering northern Australia. During **World War II** Darwin was bombed 63 times by the Japanese, the first raid on February 19, 1942, killed 243 (about half of whom were American servicemen), wounded over 300, and sank or damaged 21 ships. The town was last attacked on November 12, 1943.

Darwin was rebuilt and became a city in 1959. Between 1961 and 1971 the population rose from 12,000 to 38,900. On December

24-25, 1974, the town was devastated by a cyclone, which killed 66. All but 12,000 of Darwin's 40,000 residents had to be evacuated south. In 1996 Darwin had a population of 78,400. (*See also* Northern Territory)

DEAKIN, ALFRED (1856-1919) Australian **prime minister**, Deakin was born in Collingwood, a suburb of **Melbourne**. He became a lawyer and entered politics as a Liberal in 1879 for the Melbourne electorate of West Bourke. He held various ministries in the Victorian colonial government and introduced Australia's first law to regulate working conditions in factories in 1886. In 1887 Deakin attended the first colonial conference in London where he urged (for the first time) that the Australian **colonies** be given a greater say in imperial policy, especially in **defense**. In the 1890s he promoted the **federation** of the Australian colonies. He was attorney-general in the first federal government headed by **Edmund Barton**. In his first term as prime minister from September 24, 1903, to April 27, 1904, he shaped the **White Australia Policy** and introduced the *Conciliation and Arbitration Act* (1904). In his second term as prime minister from July 5, 1905, to November 13, 1908, ruling with the support of the **Australian Labor Party**, Deakin brought in a series of laws such as the *Invalid and Old Age Pension Act* (1908), which earned Australia an international reputation in social reform. He served a third term as prime minister from June 2, 1909, to April 29, 1910, after he successfully created a merger of the conservative parties into the **"Fusion" Liberal Party**. Deakin University in **Geelong**, Victoria, which was opened in 1978, was named in his honor.

DEFENSE For much of its history Australian defense policy was one of ultimate reliance on the support of either **Britain** or the **United States** in return for whatever assistance Australia could offer. Australia's governments saw Australia as a small, vulnerable country surrounded by populous Asian neighbors who might be tempted to invade it for its resources and living space. Reliance on a superior power was therefore unavoidable.

Between 1788 and 1870 British military units were stationed in Australia, largely to support the civil administration in guarding and controlling the **convicts**, but also to provide a defense force should any other European power be tempted to establish a foothold in

Australia. In the early years of European settlement, **France** was the country which aroused most suspicion in this regard. Australia's isolation aroused fears from even the most unlikely of enemies, such as the Russian Empire in 1859, 1877, and 1885. The vulnerability of Australia to naval incursions by other countries was demonstrated by the *Shenandoah* **Incident** in 1865.

The entry of the Germans into the Pacific, specifically over the German ambitions with respect to **Papua New Guinea**, which was rightly seen as a possible invasion point to Australia, heightened official concern about defense policy. Up to this time, the eastern half of the island of New Guinea had not been claimed by any European power. The **Queensland** government attempted to annex this territory in 1883, but this move was disallowed by the British government. In 1884 the German government took over the north-eastern part of New Guinea as well as the offshore islands (Admiralty Islands, New Ireland, and New Britain). In 1885 the British took over the remaining unclaimed land to the south (Papua). In 1906 Papua was transferred to Australian control.

After **federation**, the new federal government was given the sole right to make laws for the "naval and military defence of the Commonwealth" under section 51(vi) of the **Australian Constitution**. It was envisaged that this power would be supported by British military forces. In return, Australia had provided men for supporting British campaigns in the Crimea (1854-56), during the conflict with the Maoris in **New Zealand** (1860), and sent contingents to fight in the Sudan (1885), in South Africa against the Boers (1899-1902), and in China against the Boxers (1900). The contributions made by Australia in these conflicts and most impressively during **World War I** were made largely in the spirit of imperial cooperation and popular sentiment rather than any cold calculation of gains. However, there was an expectation that Britain would come to Australia's military aid if the occasion demanded it.

The victory of **Japan** over the Russian Empire in the war of 1904-5 was a turning point in Australian defense thinking. From that time on to **World War II**, there was an expectation that Australia had most to fear from Japan as an invader. Thus the purpose of encouraging the visit of the **Great White Fleet** in 1908 was not to turn to the United States for assistance, but to prod the British into making a greater effort to defend Australia following Japan's victory. This feeling began to grow after Japan's invasion of Manchuria in 1931.

After World War I, Australia, as one of the victorious Allies, took over Germany's colonies in the Pacific, but Japan (also as one of the victorious Allies) took over the German's other Pacific Islands (the Mariana Islands, Caroline Islands, and Marshall Islands) under the Treaty of Versailles (1919). In the Pacific Ocean, Australia and Japan were now neighbors. In 1937 the Australian government attempted to created a non-aggression pact in the Pacific, but failed because of the preoccupation of the Imperial Conference with the threat posed by Hitler.

Japan's quick conquest of south-east Asia, especially the surrender of the key naval base of Singapore on February 15, 1942, caused a general loss of faith in the British as protectors of Australia's interest. The British were not abandoned as protectors as sometimes suggested, but it was felt that they needed to be supplemented by the United States. For example, between 1952 and 1963 Australia provided the location for a series of British atomic tests as well as a testing range for British rockets at Woomera in **South Australia**. World War II shattered popular illusions about the ability of British to defend Australia.

The participation of Australia in forces during conflicts in Malaya (1950-60) and against the Indonesians in their confrontation with Malaya and Borneo (1964-66) was done to preserve regional stability (and hence Australia's defense) rather than as an insurance policy for defense favors. On the other hand, Australia's participation in America's war with **Vietnam** (1962-72) was made to impress on the United States Australia's reliability as an ally under the **Anzus Treaty** (1951). However, military American bases in Australia, which operated since 1962, have been criticized on the grounds that they compromise Australia's sovereignty.

In the 1990s Australia's defense priorities are to maintain the American alliance (largely through the continued hosting of its bases which are known to be very important to the military communications system of the United States) and to ensure the political stability of its immediate neighbors, **Papua New Guinea** and **Indonesia**. In June 1997 Australia had a defense force of almost 57,200 of whom 25,900 were in the army, 16,600 were in the **Royal Australian Air Force**, and 14,700 were in the **Royal Australian Navy**. In addition, there were 23,700 in the defense reserves. (*See also* Australian Imperial Force)

DEMOCRATIC LABOR PARTY (DLP) The DLP was a political party formed in 1957 from anticommunist groups that had previously been part of the **Australian Labor Party** (ALP). Although it had support in other **states**, the power base of the DLP was always **Victoria** where it had about 12,000 of its national total of about 18,000 members in the late 1950s. It drew most of its support from sections of the Catholic community. It was at its strongest from the late 1950s to 1970 when it was able to use the preferential voting system to direct votes away from the ALP. The DLP prevented the ALP from becoming the national government until December 1972. It ended ALP rule at the state level in Victoria in 1955 and in **Queensland** in 1957. There was no ALP government in Victoria until 1982 and in Queensland until 1989. The DLP stood for strong opposition to communism, support for the armed services, and was conservative on social and moral issues. The DLP exerted most of its power through the **senate**, but there has been no DLP senator since 1974. (*See also* Catholicism; Herbert Vere Evatt; Daniel Mannix; Petrov Affair)

DENNIS, C[LARENCE MICHAEL] J[AMES] (1876-1938) Journalist and popular poet, C. J. Dennis was born in Auburn, **South Australia**, and contributed to various newspapers, including the *Bulletin*. He is best known for his doggerel verse which captured the argot of Australian urban working class. His best-known and immensely popular work was *The Songs of a Sentimental Bloke*, which was published in 1915 and made into one of the best of the early Australian silent films in 1919.

DIAMONDS Diamonds are Australia's latest major mining industry. They were first extracted in 1982 in **Western Australia** and by 1994 Australia had become the world's largest supplier of diamonds, accounting nearly 40 percent of global output. Production began in 1985-86 at the Argyle Diamond Mine in northern Western Australia. In 1997-98 Australia produced 42.3 mega carats of diamonds. Large diamond deposits have also been found off the coast of northern Australia in Joseph Bonaparte Gulf.

DICTATION TEST The Dictation Test was used by the federal government of Australia from 1902 to 1958 as a way of excluding groups or individuals from immigrating to Australia and to enforce the **White Australia Policy**. Using the example of Natal (1897), intending immigrants could be given a dictation test in any European language, preferably one which they did not know. The most celebrated case of the application of the Test was on the well-known anti-fascist German-writing Czech reporter and linguist Egon Erwin Kisch (1885-1948) who failed the Test in Gaelic (1934). Kisch successfully won a court case on the grounds that Gaelic was no longer a living language.

DIVORCE Australian divorce law was based on the English *Divorce Act* of 1857, which allowed the higher civil courts to dissolve marriages. The Australian colonies enacted their first divorce laws in 1860 (**Tasmania**), 1861 (**Victoria**), 1863 (**Western Australia**), 1864 (**Queensland**), 1867 (**South Australia**), and 1873 (**New South Wales**). The cost of divorce and its social stigma kept the number of divorces low. Between 1871 and 1900 only 4,570 people were divorced. After 1900 the rate of divorces per 10,000 population aged 15 and over rose slowly from 1.4 in the 1900s to 3.7 in the 1930s. From the late 1940s to the early 1970s the average divorce rate was 11 per 10,000 population aged 15 and over.

Although divorce was included as a federal power in the **Australian Constitution** (section 58xxii), it was not until 1975 that the **Whitlam** government passed the *Family Law Act* which substantially liberalized the grounds for divorce and provided a comprehensive national law to replace the various state laws. The liberalization of the law as well as wider economic and social changes has raised the incidence of divorce. By 1981 the divorce rate per 10,000 population over 15 had risen to 39 (or nearly four times what it had been in the 1960s and early 1970s), and has averaged at about 35 between 1991 and 1997. (*See also* Women)

DOHERTY, PETER CHARLES (1940-) Scientist and joint Nobel prize winner, Doherty was born in Oxley, a suburb of **Brisbane**. He studied veterinary science at the University of Queensland and completed a doctorate at the Moredun Research Institute at the University of Edinburgh on experimental pathology and a virus infection of a sheep's brain. He returned to Australia to conduct postgraduate research at the John Curtin School of Medical Research at the Australian National University between 1972 and 1975. It was in this period that he, and his colleague, Rolf Zinkernagel, did the research into immunology which resulted in their shared Nobel prize for Medicine and Physiology in 1996. Doherty is presently based at St. Jude Children's Hospital in Memphis, Tennessee, where he is chairman of the department of immunology.

DROUGHT Because of its highly variable as well as low average rainfall, severe droughts have been a recurrent feature of Australian history. Their effect on **sheep and wool** and **wheat** production and the **economy** generally have been extensive. Widespread droughts occurred in 1864-66, 1895-1903, 1911-16, 1938-45, 1954-55, 1964-66, and 1978-83, but as well, there were many other droughts that were just as severe but affected single states or regions (for example, the 1933-38 drought in **Western Australia**). The 1895-1903 drought may have been the worst of all; it reduced the number of sheep from 100 to 54 million and it was not until 1926 that the figure of 100 million sheep was again reached. The 1978-83 drought reduced the value of rural output by 18 percent. (*See also* Agriculture)

DUNTROON Duntroon is the popular name for the Royal Military College, an establishment for military officer training and the Australian equivalent of institutions such as West Point and Sandhurst. It is located in **Canberra**. Duntroon was established following a report by the British field marshal, Lord Kitchner after an official visit to Australia in 1910. Duntroon also provided officer training to cadets from **New Zealand**. The college had a difficult time during the 1920s and early 1930s when government expenditure on **defense** was cut severely; the college was relocated to **Sydney** between 1931 and 1934 and was not reopened at Duntroon until 1937. Since then Duntroon grew in response to the demands of **World War II** and subsequent Australian participation in wars in **Korea** and **Vietnam**. In 1967 Duntroon became an affiliated institution with the University of New South Wales in Sydney.

E

ECCLES, JOHN CAREW (1903-1997) Eminent Australian neurophysiologist, Eccles was born in **Melbourne**. After graduating from Melbourne University in 1925, he won a Rhodes scholarship to

Oxford. He was awarded a Ph.D. from Oxford in 1929. For his research into the chemistry of transmissions across the synapses in the nervous system, he shared the Nobel prize for Medicine and Physiology in 1963 with A. L. Hodgkin and A. F. Huxley. Eccles returned to Australia in 1937. After a professorship in **New Zealand**, he was made a professor at the John Curtin School of Medical Research at the Australian National University in Canberra in 1951. Knighted in 1958, Eccles left Australia in 1966 for the Institute for Biomedical Research in Chicago to continue research and avoid compulsory retirement at 65. (*See also* Frank Macfarlane Burnet)

ECONOMY For much of its history, the Australian economy served as a supplier of raw primary products for **Britain**. Domestic **manufacturing** was relatively small before the 1930s, and Australia imported most of its finished goods from Britain. Like the U.S. economy, the Australian economy received considerable British investment before 1914. In 1911 Britain had 380 million pounds invested in Australia and **New Zealand** compared to 688 million pounds in the **United States**. Britain continued to be the largest single investor in Australia until the 1980s.

By 1986 the United States had overtaken Britain as the largest foreign investor in Australia. The scale of foreign investment aroused much debate in Australia in the late 1960s and through to the 1970s, but has since been more accepted as a necessary part of economic development because of the increase in skills and technology. Official surveys of workplaces in 1990 and 1995 found that the proportion that were wholly Australian owned fell from 73 to 72 percent.

Agriculture was the largest single contributing industry to Australia's gross domestic product until the 1950s. It was largely based on **sheep and wool** and **wheat** production. Its fortunes have been heavily dependent upon on the climate, particularly long periods of **drought**.

Unlike the United States, **mining** continued to play a significant role in the Australian economy after 1920. Between 1921 and 1961 mining (largely **gold**) contributed less than 3 percent of Australia's gross domestic product, but since the 1960s other minerals have been found in large quantities to the extent that Australia once more became an important supplier to the world market. Between 1960-61 and 1997-98, the share of mining to gross domestic product rose from 1.8 to 4.3 percent.

Manufacturing contributed only 20.3 percent of Australia's gross domestic product in 1939. It was largely based in the capital cities and the heavy industrial centers of **Newcastle** and **Wollongong**. Along with the growth of domestic demand after 1945, manufacturing was boosted by tariff **protection**. Between 1950-51 and 1970-71 manufacturing increased its share of gross domestic product from 24.4 to 27.4 percent, but thereafter its share of manufacturing in Australia's gross domestic product has fallen. Between 1980-81 and 1997-98 it fell from 20.7 to 13.2 percent as a result of the gradual reduction of protection and because of shifts in domestic and global demand.

The **services** sector of the economy—that is that part of the economy not made up of primary production (agriculture and mining) and manufacturing—has always been an important, if generally overlooked, part of the Australian economy. Between 1921 and 1960-61, the services sector contributed 54 percent of gross domestic product, and its share has been rising ever since in line with the maturing of the Australian economy. Between 1970-711 and 19997-98 the contribution made by the services sector to gross domestic product rose from 61.7 to 78.8 percent.

The trends so far described have occurred less in response to the demand of Australia's domestic population, which has always been relatively small, but rather more in response to changes in the world economy. Unlike the United States with its large domestic population, the Australian economy has always had a fairly high exposure to international **trade**. This has made it especially vulnerable to depressions, most notably in the 1890s, the early 1920s, and much of the 1930s, as well as the recession of the early 1990s.

In addition, the small domestic market has forced Australia to be fairly reliant on foreign investment. Until 1914 almost all of the foreign investment in Australia came from Britain. Investment from the United States grew considerably after **World War II**. In the 1960s the scale of foreign ownership of the Australian economy had become a political issue, along with difficulty in measuring that investment directly from official statistics. Such investment, although criticized, also resulted in important transfers of new technology and ideas.

The rate of economic growth in Australia as been variable. High growth rates were achieved between 1860 and 1890 which were channeled into **urbanization** and led to Australia having one of the highest levels of income in the world by the end of the period. Between 1861 and 1891, gross domestic product more than trebled from $113 million to $365 million, but this expansion was abruptly ended by a financial crisis in 1893 and a massive drought between 1895 and 1903. For much of the period between 1901 and 1951 economic growth was relatively slow. By 1920-21 gross domestic product had reached $1.38 billion. It fell to $1.29 billion by 1931 and to $1.21 billion in 1932. Recovery was slow and it was not until 1936-37 that Australia's gross domestic product was comparable with what it had been in 1928-29. A sustained rise in gross domestic product was marked from the late 1940s. Official concern about Australia's relatively poor economic performance compared to the United States, West Germany, and Japan began to be expressed in the 1950s. As indicated, this was a reflection of Australia's reliance on raw, unprocessed goods for its exports, its distance from major markets, and its small domestic population.

These changes in Australia's relative economic standing can be seen by examining the exchange rate. Between 1901 and 1961 the value of the Australian dollar against the U.S. dollar—the Australian exchange rate has been officially quoted against the U.S. dollar since 1971—fell from $2.41 to $1.14, reached parity with it for the first time in 1982, and has generally tended to fall ever since. The onset of the Asian financial crisis from July 1997 has also depressed the value of the Australian dollar to an average of only $0.61U.S. for 1997-98.

Retail price movements in Australia since 1851 have been comparable with most other Western economies. In the last half of the nineteenth century, prices tended to decline. Before the late 1960s, inflation was only a significant feature of the economy between 1914 and 1921 and in the early 1950s, that is during and after **World War I** and during the Korean war (1950-53), periods when price controls were inadequate; in contrast, price controls during **World War II** were far more effective although they rose relatively sharply between 1946 and 1950 and contributed to **labor disputes**. As in other countries, inflation was a feature of the Australian economy in the 1970s through to the mid-1980s. In contrast, and again like most Western countries, the 1990s have been characterized by very low increases in prices.

Australian gross domestic product per head in U.S. dollars was comparable with the United States in the late nineteenth century, but declined thereafter. In 1996 gross domestic product per head was $21,470 (U.S.) in Australia compared to $28,422 in the United States. (*See also* Currency; Labor Force; Trade; Tables 23 to 28 in Appendix 3)

EDUCATION The first school in **New South Wales** was established in 1789 and by 1797 there were six, all under the control of the **Church of England**. In 1800 the governor, Philip Gidley King (1758-1808), taxed imports to form a fund to assist education. In 1806 a separate education system for Catholics was begun. Until 1848 all education in New South Wales was run by religious bodies. After that date, a non-denominational government-run system was set up. By the 1870s the system of schooling in the **colonies** was a hybrid of state, religious, and various private schools based on the "public" schools of **Britain**. That the colonies needed a good educational system was evident from the literacy statistics. In 1857 28 percent of persons marrying in New South Wales could not sign the marriage register; by 1872 this figure had fallen to 14 percent, but it was only after 1884 that it fell below 5 percent.

Proportionally fewer children attended schools in Australia than in the **United States**. Between 1830 and 1887 school enrollments as a percentage of the total population rose from 6 to 14 percent in Australia compared with 15 to 22 percent in the United States. In 1928 school enrollments were 16 percent of the population compared with 24 percent in the United States.

The great divide in the Australian school system was between Catholic and non-Catholic schools. From the 1870s colonial governments took over the primary education system and withdrew financial aid to religious schools, a move that aroused great antagonism from the Catholic community, which responded by developing its own educational system. The cost of maintaining this system without government support remained an unresolved political issue until 1964 when the **Liberal Party** government of **Robert Menzies** provided federal funds for scholarships and school buildings regardless of whether they were government or non-government schools. In 1973 the issue of "state aid" was largely resolved by the **Australian Labor Party** government of **Gough Whitlam**, which expanded federal funding to non-government schools on a "needs" basis.

The condition of Australian education varied according to the condition of the **economy**. In 1935 a report prepared with assistance from the Carnegie Corporation of New York by Ralph Munn, the director of the Carnegie Library, Pittsburgh, and an Australian librarian, Ernest Roland Pitt (1877-1957), found that since 1914 Australia had fallen behind most other English-speaking countries in the provision of free public libraries and was, in fact, worse off than in 1880. The lack of libraries limited the opportunities for the public to educate and inform themselves.

Education was seen in narrow terms, with most leaving school at the minimum age of 15. Indeed in **Victoria**, until 1943, 14 years was the minimum school age. In 1938 only 25 percent of teenagers between 15 and a half and 16 and a half were at school. Some teenagers entered apprenticeships after school, which provided a combination of technical training and employment, but this was a limited system until the 1950s. In 1933 there were only 26,369 apprentices in training or 4 percent of those aged 15 to 19. Even by 1947 there were only 26,307 apprentices in training.

Technical education like the rest of the education system reflected the condition of the economy. Enrollments in technical education rose from 42,940 in 1910 to 95,600 in 1930, but fell to 68,300 by 1934 and even by 1945 had only reached 110,840. With the expansion of **manufacturing** from the 1950s to the early 1970s, apprenticeship and technical education grew. By 1983 there were 151,100 apprentices in training, 91.1 percent of whom were males. In 1996 there were 126,300 apprentices in training, of whom 88.2 percent were males.

Other important developments in Australian education since 1945 have been the setting up of the **School of the Air**, the Wyndham Report into secondary education in New South Wales (1958), the entry of the federal government as a provider of funds (1964, 1973), the growth of colleges of advanced education since 1965 (following the Martin Report, which recommended increasing the amount and range of tertiary education), and the rising proportion of teenagers remaining at school after the minimum leaving age since 1980. Nevertheless in 1985 only 78 percent of 16- to 17-year-olds in Australia were enrolled in some form of educational institution compared with 92 percent in the United States.

In May 1996 an official survey found that of 12 million Australians aged 15 to 64, 34.7 percent had not completed the highest level of schooling and that 52.5 percent had no post-school qualifications. Since the mid-1990s literacy standards have been an important topic in political debates and were the topic for an official survey in 1996. (*See also* Catholicism, Universities)

EIGHT HOUR DAY (*See* Labour Day)

EMANCIPISTS Emancipists were British **convicts** who had been "emancipated" that is, they had either been pardoned or served out the terms of punishment in Australia. The term dates from 1822 and was part of the political vocabulary in eastern Australia until about 1870. Emancipists sought the restoration of full civil rights such as sitting on juries.

EMIGRATION Because of its traditional concern with **immigration**, emigration is a relatively neglected topic in the history of Australia's **population**. This is because for most of its history, Australia has been a net gainer from migration, not a loser. Yet, apart from wartime, there have been periods when the number of people leaving Australia has exceeded those arriving. This occurred when the economy was depressed (1892 to 1893, 1899 to 1900, 1902 to 1906, 1930 to 1932) or in unusual circumstances, notably the departure of Australian war brides to the **United States** in 1946.

The effect of emigration has been the creation of a significant Australian expatriate population which has been a significant, if largely overlooked, feature of its history in the twentieth history. Since 1901 the expatriate population of Australia has, on average, been the equivalent of about 2 percent of the Australian-born living in Australia. The most popular countries for expatriate Australians have been **New Zealand**, **Britain**, and the United States. The reasons for the country preferences of Australian expatriates have been varied. There have been times when the New Zealand economy had been seen as offering more opportunities than Australia and hence it has attracted more Australians as settlers. Other countries, notably **South Africa**, have attracted Australians because it was part of the imperial trade route between Britain and Australia and because the two societies shared some important similarities, such as being English-speaking and being based on **agriculture** and **mining**. **Papua New Guinea**, as an Australian territory, had an important expatriate population of administrators and missionaries from the 1940s to the 1980s; there were 28,542 Australian-born in Papua

New Guinea in 1971 (compared to 4,200 in 1947), but that number had fallen to 5,168 by 1990.

New Zealand aside, Britain has been the most popular country with expatriate Australians. There were three main reasons for its popularity. First, kinship links with Britain were very close as might be expected in a society primarily made up of British immigrants and some of those who prospered in Australia retired to Britain. Second, the cultural ties between Australia and Britain were extremely strong and acted as a powerful magnet for educated Australians such as **Patrick White**. The third reason, and closely allied to the second, was the lack of opportunity in Australia throughout much of its history for its talented scientists, writers, and artists. Australian **universities** offered little scope for research before the late 1950s. Notable expatriate Australians of recent years in Britain have been the author and feminist Germaine Greer (1939-) and the author and broadcaster Clive (Vivian Leopold) James (1939-).

Australians have generally been far less attracted to the United States before the 1940s. The volume of Australian emigration to the United States increased after 1945 because of war brides and Australia's closer defense ties. Carnegie scholarships also attracted some, but otherwise the main appeal of the United States was its superior economic opportunities. Leading Australian expatriates in the United States have been the leader of the San Francisco longshoremen Harry Bridges (1901-1990), the media tycoon **Rupert Murdoch**, the academic Jill Ker Conway (1934-), the art critic and non-fiction writer **Robert Hughes**, authors such as Shirley Hazzard (1931-), and **Peter Carey** (1943-), the golfer Greg Norman (1955-), and the astronaut Andy Thomas (1952-).

Recent studies of Australian emigration suggest that the grounds for leaving are varied and complicated and are often based on social reasons rather than economic ones. Changes to portability of pensions between countries since 1973 have also influenced emigration patterns. In the case of New Zealand, the economic association is particularly strong with a number of studies showing that permanent movements between Australia and New Zealand are dependent on differences between relative real incomes and employment opportunities in the two countries. (*See also* Immigration; Grainger, George Percy; Melba, Nellie; Sutherland, Joan; Population)

EMPLOYERS' ASSOCIATIONS   Australia employers' associations have many objectives. Some are professional bodies; some are concerned with ethics and status; and some are concerned with marketing. Associations representing the interests of employers date from 1825 when the Sydney Chamber of Commerce was formed. Before 1860 employers' associations were aimed largely at promoting their particular trade interests. They became concerned about labor relations only after 1870 with the growth of industrial legislation and **labor unions**. The creation of an employers' group by the five largest coal producers in the **Newcastle** district of **New South Wales** in 1872 was an early example of this process. Chambers of Manufactures were formed in **South Australia** (1869), **Victoria** (1877) and New South Wales (1885), but it was not until 1890 that the first national employers' association, the Master Builders' Federation of Australia, was created.

In 1903 the various state Chambers of Manufactures formed a federal body. They were followed by the state employers' federations in 1905. Most employers' associations disagreed with the compulsory **conciliation and arbitration** system in the 1900s by which **labor disputes** had to be referred to government-run **industrial tribunals**, but after about 1920 they accepted the system. Until the 1970s employers' associations were largely state-based and relatively ineffective as national associations.

In contrast to the labor unions, there was little official interest in the membership of employers' associations. National membership figures were only published between 1922 and 1939. Between 1922 and 1939 the total membership of these associations rose from 51,706 to 177,090.

In 1977 the first national umbrella employers' association, the **Confederation of Australian Industry**, was formed as a counterpart to the **Australian Council of Trade Unions**, but by 1990 most major employer organizations had withdrawn from the Confederation, which reduced its effectiveness. By 1990 there were 418 employers' associations that had some role in labor relations, but the three most effective were the **Metal Trades Industry Association** (MTIA), the **Australian Chamber of Manufactures** (ACM), and the **Business Council of Australia**. In May 1998 the MTIA and the ACM announced that they would merge to form the Australian Industry Group.

Official surveys of workplace labor relations have found that between 1990 and 1995 the proportion of private sector workplaces whose employers were members of an employer's association fell from 82 to 74 percent.

ENVIRONMENT   The Australian environment has been greatly modified by natural and human forces over the past 10 million years. Even 50 million years ago when it was still fairly close to **Antarctica**, the climate of Australia was warm and wet, but once it had drifted into its present latitude, much of the land began to dry out. Excavations at the Alcoota cattle ranch in the southern part of the **Northern Territory** since 1984 have revealed a large concentration of fossil remains of larger versions of the earliest fauna (including 18 previously unknown species) that are believed to have perished during a massive **drought** about eight million years ago.

The first humans in Australia were the **Aborigines**. The date of their coming has been progressively extended by research. It is thought that they came between 80,000 and 60,000 years ago, but some have argued it may have been as much as 100,000 years ago. Aborigines modified the environment in various ways. As in other continents, they seem to have been largely responsible for the killing of the megafauna, that is the large versions of the fauna that are known today. They introduced the dingo (a domesticated dog) to Australia as an adjunct to hunting. They used controlled burning as part of their hunting practices.

At the time of the European arrival in 1788, the Australian landscape was far more extensively wooded than today. A third of the surface area was either forest (10 percent) or woodlands (23 percent). Compared to the Aborigines, the environmental impact of the Europeans was massive and general. The extensive clearing of the land for **agriculture** and the unwillingness of generations of settlers to accept that the arid nature of much of the Australian landscape was a permanent feature, quickly degraded the environment. By 1920 agricultural or pastoral activities covered half the area of Australia.

Imported fauna wreaked disaster for native fauna which often had few natural predators other than the Aborigines. Rabbits were introduced as game in 1859 and quickly became a major pest for agriculture and remained so until successful biological controls were introduced in the 1950s. Foxes were also introduced as game and contributed to the annihilation of the smaller fauna as did feral animals such as dogs and cats. In 1990 it was estimated that since the arrival of the Europeans, 97 plant species have become extinct and a further 3,329 species were either rare or endangered. In addition, 20 species of mammals and ten species of birds have become extinct.

Concern about the environment was slow to develop. Australia was regarded as being like the **United States**, a land of unlimited potential. Individuals who spoke out against this view, notably **Griffith Taylor**, were harshly criticized. In particular, the obvious proneness of the environment to drought was ignored. Neither were the native fauna particularly valued in their own right. In 1927 the **Queensland** government permitted the shooting of koalas for pelts and about 60,000 were killed. In the 1930s concerns were first raised about the impact of erosion caused by felling too many trees and overstocking, but it was not until the early 1970s that political groups supporting conservation of the environment began in Australia. These had two main sources: community opposition to redevelopment projects in the older, inner areas of **Melbourne** and **Sydney**, and opposition to the damming of the Franklin River to create Lake Pedder in **Tasmania** to provide hydro-electricity. The oldest environmental lobby group, the Australian Conservation Foundation, was established in 1966.

The federal **Whitlam** government set up the "national estate" in 1975 to register those parts of the natural or cultural environment of aesthetic, historic, social, or scientific importance. By 1980 some 5,843 parks, reservations, buildings, and shipwrecks had been included on the register, but support for the environment fell among the major political parties, which have tended to be more attracted to using the environment for economic gain. Nevertheless, in 1982 the **Fraser** government refused to support the Tasmanian government in building a dam on the Franklin River and won its case in the **High Court of Australia**.

A national study conducted in 1975-78 of Australia's non-arid land (that is, only 30 percent of its total area), found that two-thirds had been degraded by either soil erosion or salinity. Further, 2,000 species of plants (a tenth of the total) are at risk of becoming extinct. Nineteen vertebrate animals are believed to have died out with a further 74 animals at risk. Since this survey, there has been greater official recognition of environmental problems and resolve to address them by measures such a massive tree-planting program.

Support for environmental or "green" policies is highest among young and better-educated voters. In contrast to the declining membership of the major political parties, support for "green" political groups grew in the 1980s. The Wilderness Society's membership grew from 2,300 in 1980 to 14,000 in 1990, and Greenpeace (established in Australia in 1977) claimed 96,100 subscribers in 1992 compared with 20,000 in 1989. The Australian Conservation Foundation claimed 20,000 members in 1992. Since 1992 environmental concerns have tended to slip with the main political parties (the **Liberal Party of Australia** and the **Australian Labor Party**), which are more interested in the promotion of economic growth. The **Australian Democrats** are the leading political party supporting better environmental policies. (*See also* Green Bans; Fleay, David Howells; Kangaroos and Wallabies; May, Robert Mccredie; Whaling and Sealing)

EUREKA STOCKADE The Eureka Stockade was an armed clash between police, military forces, and **gold** miners camped at the Eureka Stockade, Ballarat, **Victoria**, on December 3, 1854. The incident resulted in the deaths of 30 miners and 5 soldiers died. Between 50 and 60 miners and 12 soldiers were wounded. The incident was caused by the miners objecting to the high cost of the mining licenses imposed by the government. The Eureka Stockade forced the government to listen to public opinion and marked the end of an autocratic style of government. Some of the miners' leaders were ex-Chartists; one of them, Peter Lalor (1827-1889), was later elected to the Victorian parliament and served as speaker of the **legislative assembly** from 1880 to 1887.

EVATT, HERBERT VERE (1894-1965) **Australian Labor Party** (ALP) leader, lawyer, and author, Evatt was born in East Maitland, **New South Wales**. After outstanding academic achievement, he entered the legal profession in 1918. He was elected to the Sydney state electorate of Balmain in 1925 and held that position until 1930 when he was nominated as a judge of the **High Court of Australia**, where he remained until 1940 when he was elected to the house of representatives. In October 1941 Evatt became minister for external affairs and attorney-general, positions he held until the defeat of the **Chifley** government in December 1949. Under his leadership Australia practiced a far more independent foreign relations policy. Evatt served as president of the general assembly of the United Nations in 1948-49.

From 1950 to 1960 he was leader of the federal parliamentary ALP and became a controversial and increasingly unsuccessful figure. In November 1951 he led a successful campaign against the Menzies referendum to ban the **Communist Party,** but his failure to rebut fully claims that some of his staff were associated with Soviet spying during the **Petrov Affair** in 1954 added to growing divisions in the ALP, which led to the formation of the **Democratic Labor Party**. Evatt's last public position was as chief justice of the Supreme Court of New South Wales (1960-62).

EXPLORATION Sea and land exploration were important activities in Australian history. Sea exploration proceeded relatively quickly after the foundation of **Sydney** in 1788. In 1798 **George Bass** and **Matthew Flinders** sailed round **Tasmania** and proved it was an island. In 1801-3, Flinders carried out a remarkable survey voyage around the Australian mainland.

In contrast, land exploration was slow, difficult, and expensive because of the lack of navigable rivers leading to the interior. In 1813 Gregory Blaxland (1778-1853), William Charles Wentworth (c.1792-1872), and Lieutenant William Lawson (1774-1850) discovered a passage over the rugged Blue Mountains, thereby opening up the interior for **agriculture**, **sheep and wool**, or cattle raising. In 1830 **Charles Sturt** followed the Murray River to the sea and disproved the idea that it flowed into an inland sea. In 1836 **Thomas Mitchell** explored the interior river systems and western **Victoria**. There were two epic overland journeys made in the 1840s: the first in 1841 by **Edward John Eyre** who crossed the desert Nullabor Plain from east to west and, the second in 1844-45 by **Ludwig Leichhardt** from Sydney to Port Essington in the **Northern Territory**.

The first crossing of the Australian mainland from south to north was made by **John McDouall Stuart** in 1862; an attempt by Robert Burke (1821-1861) and William Wills (1834-1861) nearly succeeded, but ended in their deaths. Although the purpose of these journeys was mainly inspired by the hope of expanding the colonies' economic resources, they were also motivated by the quest for scientific knowledge. The last major land explorer was John Forrest (1847-1918) who explored much of the interior of **Western Australia** between 1870 and 1879. Thereafter land exploration proceeded on a lesser scale and was largely complete by 1900. (*See also* Burke and Wills Expedition)

EYRE, EDWARD JOHN (1815-1901) Born in Hornsea, Yorkshire, England, Eyre arrived in Australia in 1833. His chief contribution to Australian history was as a land explorer. In 1840 he discovered what is now known as Lake Eyre, a huge dry salt lake in the center of Australia. He then made an epic journey of exploration from **Adelaide** in **South Australia** to Albany in **Western Australia** from 1840 to 1841. In the desert conditions, two of his four companions died. Eyre Peninsula in South Australia is named after him. In 1865, while governor-in-chief of Jamaica, he used martial law powers to crush a riot at a cost of 600 lives. Eyre was recalled to England. A royal commission of inquiry found he had acted with undue harshness. (*See also* Exploration)

F

FACTIONS There have always been factions in Australia's political parties, that is, groups that center upon an individual or who support particular sets of views; "right" for conservative, "moderate" or "left" for radical. In the nineteenth century, before the rise of modern **political parties**, politics was based on separate "factions" more attached to leading personalities—such as **Henry Parkes**— rather than principles or ideologies.

Since the 1950s, the term "faction" has taken on a different meaning, usually in connection with explaining shifts in the balance of power *within* the **Australian Labor Party** (ALP). In the federal parliamentary ALP, factions were the basis of the **Hawke** and **Keating** governments from 1983 to 1996. The ALP has always had conservative and radical elements, but they have previously not been rigorously organized before February 1984. Those parliamentarians who were neither on the "Right" nor "Left" formed their own faction, the "Center Left." In June 1991 it was estimated that of then 110 federal ALP parliamentarians, 46 belonged to the "Right," 32 to the "Left," 20 to the "Center Left," and 12 were not aligned with any faction. Factions are fundamental in the ALP in the **states**. From the 1940s the **New South Wales** Branch of the ALP has been on the "right" and the Victorian Branch on the "left." (Similar divisions of "right" and "left" are also a feature of Australia's **labor unions**.)

In the **Liberal Party** in the 1980s factions were far less clearly drawn although a common distinction has been between "dries" and "wets" based on greater (or lesser) support for free market policies and greater (or lesser) government regulation of the economy. The most significant faction within the **Howard** government, which was elected in 1996, is the **Lyons Forum**. (*See also* New Right)

FADDEN, ARTHUR WILLIAM (1895-1973) Country Party leader and **prime minister**, Fadden was born in Ingham, **Queensland**. After finishing high school at Mackay, Queensland, he served as clerk and then town clerk of Mackay City Council. He became a chartered accountant first in **Townsville** and then in **Brisbane**. He was elected to the **house of representatives** in 1936 for the electorate of the Darling Downs in Queensland and became leader of the parliamentary Country Party in March 1941. He acted as prime minister while **Robert Gordon Menzies** was in Britain and occupied the office after Menzies resigned between August 29 and October 7, 1941. He was treasurer from October 1940 to October 1941. Fadden led the Country Party until his retirement from federal politics in 1958.

FEDERATED MISCELLANEOUS WORKERS' UNION (FMWU) The FMWU is a **labor union** whose members are mainly in service occupations, such as cleaning and in certain areas of **manufacturing**. As a rule, it recruits employees in occupations that are not recruited by other unions. Founded in September 1915, the FMWU has grown by 50 amalgamations with other unions. By 1969 it had 73,000 members. In November 1990 the FMWU (with 135,000 members) announced it would merge with the 115,000 strong Federated Liquor and Allied Industries Employees' Union to create Australia's largest labor union. Between 1984 and 1990 the federal secretary of the FMWU was Martin Ferguson (1953-), who was president of the **Australian Council of Trade Unions** from 1990 to 1995. In 1997 the FMWU had 160,300 members compared to 201,700 in 1995.

FEDERATION Until January 1, 1901, Australia had no national government. Issues relating to Australia as a whole, such as foreign relations, were handled by **Britain**. The individual **colonies** governed themselves with their own written constitutions, which had been approved by Britain in the 1850s. Large distances between the major centers of population discouraged the colonies from viewing Australia as a nation, and until the twentieth century, most Australians tended to think of themselves first as being part of their colony and only second as being Australians.

After 1860, the various colonial governments began to take a broader view and to develop mechanisms for greater cooperation among themselves. A series of inter-colonial conferences were held from 1860 to 1880, and a Federal Council was formed in 1883, but **New South Wales** refused to join. With 72 percent of Australia's population in 1881, the attitudes of New South Wales and **Victoria** toward federation were critical for its success. But these two colonies were divided over economic policy. New South Wales favored **free trade** and Victoria favored **protection** for manufacturing.

In 1890 the colonies agreed to establish a federation. They used the **United States** Constitution as their model because it seemed to give greater protection to the rights of states. After three conferences (1891, 1895, 1896-97) to discuss details, a draft **Australian Constitution** was submitted to the voters. This draft underwent further revisions after it gained only a slender majority of support in New South Wales compared with Victoria, **South Australia**, and **Tasmania**. The new draft Constitution was agreed on by the voters in New South Wales, **Queensland**, and **Western Australia**. After some amendments in Britain, the Australian Constitution was enacted by the British parliament in 1900. Federation was never a mass political movement, but once it had been achieved, it created a new political framework for Australia in the twentieth century. (*See also* Commonwealth-State Relations; Deakin, Alfred; Parkes, Henry; Reid, George Houston)

FERTILITY   Fertility is the rate at which women produce children and an important feature of the analysis of **population**. The fertility rate can be calculated in a number of ways of which the simplest is the crude birthrate (the number of births per thousand population). A crude birthrate of 30 or more is indicative of high fertility. In most Western European societies fertility began to fall markedly at various times after 1830. In Australia the transition to lower fertility (that is, the crude birthrate fell below 30) came in the 1890s, largely in response to acute economic depression and also to the greater use by married couples of condoms, which came into use in the 1880s. The decline in fertility caused official concern and led to the appointment of a royal commission of inquiry in 1903 in **New South Wales**. The reasons for the failure of the birthrate to recover to its pre-1890s levels are complicated, but the result of the fertility decline was a permanent reduction in the size of families. Women born in 1903-8 had an average of 2.6 children in their lifetime, whereas women born in 1851-56 had produced an average of 6.3 children in their lifetime.

During the twentieth century, the general fertility rate—the number of births per thousand women aged 15 to 44—declined from 117 in 1900-2 to 71 in 1932-34. It recovered to 112 in 1960-62 and then fell steadily to reach 63 in 1995-97. (*See also* Table 15 of Appendix 3)

FILMS The Australian film industry is one of the oldest in the world. It began in 1896 when some footage was taken of **Sydney** and the holding of the **Melbourne Cup** horse race. The Salvation Army made two films in this period: *Early Christian Martyrs* (1899) and *Soldiers of the Cross* (1900), the latter of which lasted two hours and was one of the world's first feature films; sadly, no print of this film has survived. Between 1906 and 1920, a local film industry emerged that produced films based on Australian history or popular works of fiction. The best known of these films were *The Story of the Kelly Gang* (1906), *The Sentimental Bloke* (1919), and *On Our Selection* (1920). The Australian film industry suffered severely from competition with Hollywood. Between 1914 and 1923, the proportion of American films shown in Australia rose from about half to over 90 percent. Although the industry struggled to survive thereafter, some important feature films were produced, notably *The Squatter's Daughter* (1933), *Forty Thousand Horsemen* (1941), *The Rats of Tobruk* (1944), *Jedda* (1955), and *The Sundowners* (1960). In 1943 Damien Parer (1912-1944) won an Oscar for his film *Kokoda Frontline*, the first time that an Australian filmmaker had been so honored.

In 1958 the Australian Film Institute was formed in **Melbourne** and began to issue its annual awards, but it was not until the 1970s that the Australian film industry really revived, partly in response to a greater sense of **nationalism**. For the first time Australian films and Australian actors and actresses began to receive international attention. Of the 200 feature films made between 1970 and 1985, the best known included *Picnic at Hanging Rock* (1975), *Sunday Too Far Away* (1975), *My Brilliant Career* (1979), *Mad Max* (1979), *Breaker Morant* (1980), *Gallipoli* (1981), and *Crocodile Dundee* (1986), the latter being Australia's most commercially successful film to date. Since the late 1980s the Australian film industry has again been depressed causing many of its most capable producers and actors to go to the **United States**, for example, Peter Weir (1944-), who directed *Gallipoli* and who was nominated for an Academy Award for Best Director for his American film *Witness*. In March 1997 Geoffrey Rush won an Oscar for his role as the Australian pianist David Helfgott in *Shine*.

FIRST FLEET   This name was given to the 11 ships carrying the first Europeans to settle in Australia. The fleet left England on May 17, 1787, and arrived at Botany Bay, **New South Wales**, on January 18-20, 1788. Remarkable for the time, only 40 died on the long journey, a tribute to the discipline and dietary precautions of the captain, **Arthur Phillip**. On board were officials, 212 soldiers and their families and 579 **convicts**. Phillip decided that Botany Bay was not a suitable site for the new colony and moved north to Sydney Cove, Port Jackson, where he hoisted the British flag on January 26, 1788 (now **Australia Day**). In 1968 the 1788-1820 Association was formed in **Sydney**, made up of individuals claiming descent from those who came on the First Fleet or subsequent voyages up to 1820; in 1988 this Pioneers' Association claimed 800 members. (*See also* James Cook)

FISHER, ANDREW (1862-1928)   Coal miner and **Australian Labor Party** (ALP) leader, Fisher was born in Crosshouse, Ayrshire, Scotland. He began work as a coal miner at the age of 10 and was elected secretary of the Ayrshire Miners' Union in 1879; he was an admirer of Keir Hardie, the Scottish socialist who advocated the formation of a separate political party for the working class. In 1881 Fisher was blacklisted for taking part in a 10-week-long coal miners' strike.

Fisher emigrated to **Queensland** in 1885 where he again worked as a coal miner, read works on social science and economics, and became an active member of the Amalgamated Miners' Association, which provided him with a base for entry into politics. In 1893 he was elected to the **legislative assembly** of **Queensland** for the **Australian Labor Party** (ALP) and served in the brief ministry of Andrew Dawson (1863-1910) in 1899, the first ALP government in Australia and the first government based on **labor unions** in the world. In 1901 Fisher moved from state to federal politics and in 1907 became minister for trade and customs in the ALP government of **John Christian Watson**.

He was elected leader of the parliamentary ALP in 1904 and served three terms as **prime minister** and treasurer (November 13, 1908, to June 2, 1909, April 29, 1910, to June 24, 1913, and September 17, 1914, to October 27, 1915). At the elections on April 13, 1910, the ALP won a majority in both the **house of representatives** and the **senate** which enabled Fisher's administration to introduce many important reforms including a graduated land tax (1910), the establishment of a government-owned bank (the **Commonwealth Bank**) (1911), and a maternity allowance (1912). His administration also sought, unsuccessfully, through **referendums** to give the federal government the power to make laws with respect to monopolies (1911); trade, commerce, and corporations (1913); and trusts and the nationalization of monopolies (1913). Fisher retired from politics in October 1915 in favor of **William Morris Hughes**.

FLEAY, DAVID [HOWELLS] (1907-1993) Zoologist, and pioneer conservationist, Fleay was born in Ballarat, **Victoria**, and educated at Ballarat Grammar School and the University of Melbourne. He worked as a teacher from 1927 until 1934 when he joined staff of the Melbourne Zoological Gardens and set up an Australian section. Between 1937 and 1951 he created a wildlife sanctuary at Healesville, a town northwest of **Melbourne**, where he successfully bred the first platypus in captivity in 1943. From 1951 he established a wildlife sanctuary on the **Gold Coast, Queensland** and remained its director for the rest of his life, resisting attempts to sell the land for residential development. This sanctuary is now an important tourist attraction. Fleay made two important contributions to Australian zoology. First, he pioneered the breeding of endangered native fauna in captivity. Second, he published popular as well as scientific work about Australia's wildlife, thereby helping to build a consciousness about the **environment**.

FLINDERS, MATTHEW (1774-1814) Navigator and hydrographer, Flinders was born in Dorington, Lincolnshire, England, and joined the navy in 1789. He came to Australia in 1795. During the voyage, he became close friends with **George Bass**. In 1798-99 he and Bass sailed around **Tasmania**, proving it to be an island. On his return to England, Flinders was promoted to captain and ordered to chart the unknown parts of the Australian coastline, which he carried out between 1801 and 1803. Unfortunately, he was able to survey only

about half the coast—from the south-western corner to the western
shore of the Gulf of Carpentaria in the **Northern Territory**—
because of the poor condition of his ship. However, he did complete
the first voyage around the Australian mainland.

On his journey back to England, Flinders was forced to stop at
Mauritius, then under French control, where he and his crew were
arrested because England was at war with **France** under Napoleon.
Although Napoleon ordered Flinders to be released in 1807, it took
three years for the order to be carried out. Flinders was kept prisoner
for seven years, during which time he wrote *A Voyage to Terra
Australis*, a book that popularized the name "Australia" and was
published the day before he died.

FLOREY, HOWARD WALTER (1898-1968)   Florey was the
scientist most responsible for the development of penicillin, the anti-
bacterial medicine, which was first used on wounded Allied soldiers
in Tunisia and Sicily in 1943. It was first used on Australian soldiers
in **Papua New Guinea** in early 1943. Born in **Adelaide**, South
Australia, Florey completed a medical degree at the University of
Adelaide in 1921 and his doctorate at Cambridge, England, in 1927.
In 1935 he became professor of pathology at Oxford where together
with Ernest Boris Chain (1906-1979), a German-born scientist
whom Florey had invited to Cambridge, he developed penicillin,
which Alexander Fleming (1881-1955) had accidentally discovered
in 1928. For his work, Florey shared the 1945 Nobel prize for
Medicine and Physiology with Chain and Fleming. Florey was
knighted in 1944 and in 1960 was elected president of the British
Royal Society, the first Australian to occupy the position.

FORDE, FRANCIS MICHAEL (1890-1983)   Australian **prime
minister**, Forde was born in Mitchell, **Queensland** to Irish-Catholic
parents. He was elected to the Queensland parliament for the
Australian Labor Party (ALP) in 1917 and represented a
Queensland electorate in the **house of representatives** between
1922 and 1946. He was deputy prime minister in the government of
John Curtin between 1941 and 1946. After the death of Curtin, he
was prime minister between July 6 and July 13, 1945, a period of
eight days making his time in office the shortest of any Australian
prime minister. He was replaced by **Ben Chifley**. Forde was high
commissioner to Canada from 1946 to 1953 and re-entered

Queensland state politics on his return where he remained until 1957.

FRANCE   French navigators played an important part in the exploration of the coast of Australia in the eighteenth century. The most notable voyages were made by Jean-François de Galoup La Pérouse (1741-c.1788), who visited the new British colony at Botany Bay in 1788, and Thomas Nicolas Baudin (1754-1803) in 1801-3. Although the main interest of these explorers was scientific, their activities aroused concern by the British government that France intended to annex parts of Australia. To forestall the French, British outposts were established in the **Northern Territory**, **Victoria**, and **Western Australia** between 1824 and 1826. Finally, in 1829 Britain claimed all of Australia. In fact, the French Revolution and the European interests of Napoleon made it difficult for the French to make good any claims they might have had on Australian territory. The French did not assert themselves in the south-west Pacific again until 1843 when they established a protectorate over Tahiti and again in 1853 when they annexed the island of New Caledonia. In this period there was considerable French interest in Australia as a penal colony.

During **World War I** most of Australia's army fought in France and Flanders; 132,340 were battle casualties of whom 45,033 were killed or died of wounds between April 1915 and November 1918. During **World War II** Australian troops helped to defeat the Vichy French forces in Syria (June-July 1941).

Australia has never been a popular country for emigration from France. Between 1861 and 1891 the number of French-born rose from 2,208 to 4,285, but fell to 2,217 by 1947, and did not surpass its 1891 level until 1954. In 1996 there were 16,064 French-born living in Australia compared to 14,870 in 1986.

France made a generous contribution to Australia's bicentennial celebrations in 1988. Australia has been at the forefront of protests against France's policy of testing nuclear weapons in the south Pacific in 1994-95. In 1997-98 France accounted for 1 percent of Australia's exports and supplied 2.2 percent of Australia's imports. On July 4, 1998 four survivors of the **Australian Imperial Force** who had fought in France during **World War I** were awarded the *Légion d'honneur* in Villiers Bretonneux.

FRANCHISE In spite of its unpromising beginnings as a British penal colony, Australia became a proving ground for liberal democracy in the last half of the nineteenth century. The first franchise laws for the **legislative councils** came into force in 1843 and 1850. They gave men the vote, subject to a significant property qualification. The vote was given to virtually all males over 21 in elections to the lower houses (**legislative assembly**) of the various colonies, beginning with **South Australia** (1856), **Victoria** (1857), **New South Wales** (1858), **Queensland** (1859), and then **Western Australia** (1893) and **Tasmania** (1896). The **secret ballot** was another important advance in the nineteenth century, being first introduced in South Australia and Victoria in 1856.

The vote for **women** was first introduced in South Australia in 1894, in federal elections and New South Wales in 1902, in Tasmania in 1903, in Queensland in 1905, in Western Australia in 1907, and in Victoria in 1908.

In 1911 it became compulsory for voters to enroll on the federal electoral rolls. Preferential voting was first introduced for the federal **house of representatives** in 1918 and in a general federal election in 1919. Under this system, the votes of unsuccessful candidates are distributed to the candidates of other parties according to the preference of the voter. **Compulsory voting** was first used in Queensland in 1915 and was nationwide by 1939. Plural voting, that is the ability to vote more than once for those with a certain level of property, was eliminated between 1894 and 1907. There were important exceptions to this progress. The franchise for elections to the upper houses of state legislatures (legislative councils) remained restrictive until after 1945. Similarly, the franchise for local government elections was also restricted in various ways until the 1920s. In 1962 **Aborigines** were allowed to vote in federal elections and referendums. The age of eligibility for the franchise was reduced from 21 to 18 in 1973. (*See also* Compulsory Voting; Referendum; Secret Ballot)

FRASER, [JOHN] MALCOLM (1930-) Australian **prime minister**, Fraser was born in **Melbourne** and educated at Melbourne Grammar School and at Oxford University where he studied politics, philosophy, and economics. In 1955 he was elected to the **house of representatives** for the western rural Victorian electorate of Wannon for the **Liberal Party**. He was minister for the army (1966-68), education and science (1968-69), and for **defense** (1969-71), during which time he was a strong supporter of Australia's participation in the **Vietnam** war. While the federal parliamentary Liberal Party was in opposition, he emerged as leader in March 1975. As leader, Fraser used the opposition's majority in the **senate** to block supply (that is, the supply of money) to the **Whitlam** government. When the government resisted, the **governor-general**, Sir John Kerr (1914-1991), dismissed the Whitlam government and appointed Fraser as caretaker prime minister (November 11, 1975).

Fraser easily won the elections on December 13, 1975. The policy of his government was to reduce government expenditure, stimulate private-sector growth, and fight inflation. His government's success in these areas was mixed. Although Fraser won the 1977 election by a large margin, his win in 1980 was narrow and resulted in the coalition losing control of the senate. The onset of a severe **drought** in 1982 harmed the **economy** and increased unemployment. Fraser lost the elections on March 5, 1983, and later in the year resigned from parliament. Always an outspoken opponent of apartheid in **South Africa**, Fraser was nominated by the **Hawke** government as its representative on an Eminent Persons Group to visit South Africa and report on its racial policies (1985).

FREE SELECTION Free selection was the name of a policy of Australian colonial governments in the 1860s to increase the number of farmers on lands illegally occupied by sheep and cattle raisers through **squatting**. It was an important feature of Australian **land settlement** in the 1830s and 1840s. Under laws passed between 1859 and 1872, men and single women over 18 could "select" up to 320 acres (130 hectares) that had not been legally disposed of by the government. Generally, the laws failed because of successful resistance by the squatters who either "selected" the best lands or sources of water for themselves or used nominees to do it for them. Often, too, the selectors failed because they did not have enough capital for farming. But some free settlers did make good, for example, in **South Australia**.

FREE TRADE During the last half of the nineteenth century, the major ideological division between the Australian colonies was over tariff policy, that is the level of charges governments should impose on goods and services which crossed their borders. Colonies which were able to raise much of their revenue from land sales, such as **New South Wales**, favored "free trade," that is, no or minimal government imposts on the movement of goods and services, whereas a colony like **Victoria** lacking such lands was forced to rely on relatively high levels of government imposts and adopted a policy of **protection**. Within New South Wales, free trade was a gathering point for political conservatives; in contrast, the **labor unions** supported protection. Supporters of free trade also drew on the example of **Britain**, where it was an article of faith in the nineteenth century and up to 1914. After the Australian colonies federated in 1901, a Free Trade Party was formed which was one of the constituents of the **"Fusion" Liberal Party** in 1909.

"FUSION" LIBERAL PARTY The "Fusion" Liberal Party was the main conservative political party from 1909 to 1916. It was formed in May 1909 when **Alfred Deakin** joined or "fused" his Protectionist Party with the Anti-Socialists led by **Joseph Cook** and the Liberal or "Corner" Party led by John Forrest (1847-1918). The "Fusion" Liberal Party became the federal government under Deakin in 1909-10 and under **Joseph Cook** in 1913-14, by which time they had become known as the Liberal Party. The Liberal Party merged with the pro-conscriptionist members of the federal **Australian Labor Party** government of **William Morris Hughes** in February 1917 to form the **Nationalist Party**. (*See also* Political Parties)

G

GALLIPOLI Gallipoli is a rugged peninsula on the north-western coast of Turkey (there is also a small town on the peninsula called Gallipoli). Between the eastern side of Gallipoli and the coast is the Dardanelles, a narrow strait linking the Aegean Sea with the Sea of Marmara and the Black Sea. During **World War I**, the Russian government asked the British to attack Turkey to divert Turkish attacks from Russia. Gallipoli was chosen as the site for a full-scale amphibious assault on Turkey. It was also hoped that the sea lines would be opened up to get more Allied assistance to Russia. After the failure of a naval attack in March 1915, it was decided to attack the western side of the Gallipoli peninsula. The fighting, from the disastrous landing to the highly successful evacuation, lasted from April 25, 1915, to January 8, 1916, and cost the Allies about 214,000 casualties out of a total of 480,00 men committed. The Turks suffered a similar level of casualties. Australians played a significant role in the fighting: They suffered 27,859 casualties

(8,418 killed and 19,441 wounded). In Australia the efforts of the soldiers were venerated and the day of the first landing was hailed as marking Australia's birth as a nation.

Although generally judged to have been a disaster as a military operation, studies by U.S. marine and naval officers at Quantico, Virginia, indicated that such amphibious operations could succeed if they were well organized. Their ideas were the basis for U.S. doctrines of amphibious operations in the Pacific during **World War II**, operations that preserved Australia from Japanese invasion.

One of Australia's leading filmmakers Peter Weir (1944-) made a film about the Australian landing and fighting on Gallipoli (called *Gallipoli*) in 1981. In April 1985 the Turkish government agreed to officially name the Australian's landing place at Gallipoli, Anzac Cove. In April 1990 the **prime minister**, **Bob Hawke** led a delegation of Australian survivors to Gallipoli to commemorate the seventy-fifth anniversary of the landing. The last Australian survivor of the original landing on April 25, 1915, died in December 1997, aged 101, leaving eight survivors from the original Australian force of 60,000. (*See also* Anzac)

GEELONG Geelong is the second largest city in the state of **Victoria**. Its name comes from an **Aboriginal** word. The district was first explored by sea in 1802 and by land in 1824. The first European settlers arrived in 1837 and the town was legally incorporated in 1849. Population growth was fairly slow until the 1940s. By 1891 Geelong had 17,500 people and even by 1933 had only 39,200. But by 1954 the city had 72,300 people and it has continued to grow. In 1996 Geelong had an estimated population of 146,200.

Geelong is important as an agricultural and industrial center. The first woolen mill in Victoria was set up at Geelong in 1912, a paper mill was founded in 1922, and a rayon spinning factory in 1952. In 1963 Alcoa began an aluminum smelter in the area. In 1971 Deakin University was founded at Geelong. During the 1960s major improvements were made to the harbor, which aided its growth. Since the late 1980s Geelong has suffered from the decline in **manufacturing** employment and the depressed condition of the state **economy**.

GERMANS From 1871 to 1921 the German-born were the largest non-British immigrant group in Australia. Their most important settlements were in **South Australia** and **Queensland**. The first

German immigrants were 517 Old Lutherans from Klepsk in present day Poland who came to South Australia in 1838 to practice their religion without government persecution. The Germans made up between 7 and 10 percent of the South Australian population before 1914. About 80 percent were settled on the land. The first German immigrants to Queensland came in 1854 and settled in the south-east on the Darling Downs. In 1901 there were 38,552 German immigrants in Australia, of whom 6,672 lived in South Australia, 13,233 in Queensland, 8,676 in **Victoria**, and 7,647 in **New South Wales**.

During **World War I** the German-born were subject to official harassment. In South Australia the teaching of German at school was prohibited in 1917. The names of many German towns were also Anglicized. From a peak level of 45,320 in 1891, the number of German-born declined to 14,583 by 1947. Post-war immigration has lifted their numbers to a peak of 114,810 in 1986. However, in terms of ancestry, the German **immigration** has been much more important. In the 1986 census, 436,667 Australians claimed some German ancestry. In 1996 there were 110,331 German-born in Australia.

GIBBS, [CECILIA] MAY (1877-1969)   Artist and writer, May Gibbs was born in Cheam Fields, Surrey, England, and emigrated to **South Australia** in 1881 with her mother and brothers to join her father. She studied art in England between 1901 and 1904. She is best known for her best-selling illustrated children's stories *Gumnut Babies* (1916) and *Snugglepot and Cuddlepie* (which sold 17,000 copies on its first release in 1918) based on accurate and sympathetic observations of Australian animals and their bush setting. They are among the classic works of Australian children's literature. (*See also* Literature)

GINGER MEGGS   *Ginger Meggs* is the Australian cartoon character created by James Charles Bancks (1889-1952) in 1921. *Ginger* is a boy about 10 years old living in the suburbs. His adventures in life include the occasional battle with a teenaged bully and regular ones with his stupid parents. Syndicated nationally and then in other countries, *Ginger Meggs* has appeared in book, play, and film (1982) form. The character of *Ginger Meggs* is important for his suburban setting rather than the rural one favored by many other Australian authors.

GOLD   Although traces of gold were found in Australia in 1823, the first commercial find was not made until 1851 when Edward Hargraves (1816-1891) announced his find at Ophir in **New South Wales** and began a gold rush. Major finds of gold were also made in **Victoria** in 1851, which accounted for a third of world gold production between 1851 and 1860. There were other gold rushes in **Queensland** (1867) and **Western Australia** (1893).

News of the discovery of gold drew in thousands of hopeful immigrants. Between 1851 and 1861, Australia's **population** grew from 405,400 to 1,145,600, of which 79 percent came from **immigration**. A tiny few struck it rich, but the great majority did not and they put pressure on colonial governments to open up land occupied by sheep and cattle raisers by **squatting** for farming through a policy of **closer settlement**. Those who opened shops to cater to the miners made the most money. Along with British immigrants, the gold fields attracted thousands of **Chinese** miners whose presence led to resentment, violence, and finally to laws restricting the immigration of Chinese altogether, thereby laying the foundations of the **White Australia Policy**.

In the 1980s gold once again became a significant Australian export; in 1996 Australia accounted about 11 percent of total world production. In 1997-98 Australia produced 317 tonnes of gold and gold accounted for 7.1 percent of Australia's merchandise exports. (*See also* Eureka Stockade, Victoria)

GOLD COAST   The Gold Coast has been one Australia's major urban centers since the 1970s and, with the **Central Coast**, represents an important feature of post-1960 **urbanization** in Australia, namely the emergence of large non-metropolitian urban areas based on **tourism**, commuters, and retirees. Located south of **Brisbane** and occupying the south-eastern coastal corner of **Queensland**, the Gold Coast covers Southport, Coolangatta, Surfers' Paradise, Palm Beach, and Burleigh Heads. It owes its growth to **tourism** based on its beaches. The core of the area began as Surfers' Paradise, a term coined by a real estate agent in the 1920s. Despite the opening of a coastal road in 1933, growth was slow and the population had reached only 12,500 by 1947. In 1959 the area became the City of Gold Coast. Its population in 1961 was 33,700, but at the height of the summer it rose to 135,000. By 1971 the resident population had doubled to 66,700 and nearly doubled again to 117,800 by 1981.

The southward growth of the Gold Coast has created a conterminous urban center with Tweed Heads, formerly a separate town just over the state border in **New South Wales**. Between 1961 and 1981 the population of Tweed Heads grew from 3,300 to 19,300. The Gold Coast has continued to experience high population and economic growth in the 1990s, raising the population to 279,400 by 1991. In 1994-95 the Gold Coast attracted about 1.2 million visitors from other parts of Australia. In 1996 the Gold Coast had a resident population of 334,800 of whom 17.1 percent were aged over 65 compared to 12.1 percent for all Australia. Between 1976 and 1997 the population of the Gold Coast-Tweed Heads as a major urban center grew from 105,800 to 311,900.

GORTON, JOHN [GREY] (1911-) Australian **prime minister**, Gorton was born in **Melbourne** and completed his education at Oxford University. He was a fighter pilot in the **Royal Australian Air Force** between 1940 and 1944 during which time he was badly wounded. In the landslide election of 1949 he was elected to the **senate** for Victoria for the **Liberal Party** and remained there until 1968 when he was elected to a seat in the **house of representatives** in 1968. He became prime minister on January 19, 1968. His period in office was marked by much in-fighting with the **Liberal Party**, which eventually brought about his removal on March 10, 1971, when he voted against himself in a ballot of no-confidence. His term as prime minister was notable for his identification with a rising sense of Australian **nationalism**. (*See also* MacMahon, William)

GOVERNOR-GENERAL Under section 2 of the **Australian Constitution**, the governor-general is the representative of the British monarch in Australia and, as such, is head of state. The office was created to carry out similar functions to those of a British monarch. Accordingly, the governor-general was given seemingly wide powers to operate and maintain the constitution and the laws passed under it. For any legislation passed by the Commonwealth parliament to become law, it has to be signed into law ("assented") by the governor-general. The governor-general also has power to appoint or dismiss senior officers of the federal bureaucracy and is commander-in-chief of the armed forces.

Relations between the governor-general and the new Australian federal government started awkwardly. Acting on advice from the British Colonial Office, the first governor-general, the Earl of

Hopetoun (1860-1908) tried to appoint Sir William Lyne (1844-1913), the premier of **New South Wales** and an opponent of **Federation**, as the first Australian **prime minister**. Unable to find sufficient supporters, Lyne failed to form a government and **Edmund Barton**, the leader of the Protectionist Party, became the first prime minister on January 1, 1901. The incident became known as the "Hopetoun Blunder."

With the growth of **political parties**, the role of the governor-general in forming governments soon became irrelevant and the office became largely ceremonial in character, although Sir Munro-Ferguson who was governor-general from 1914 to 1920 played an important part during **World War I** in organizing Australia's contribution to **Britain**.

Until January 1931, all governors-general were appointed from the British aristocracy. The office was regarded as poorly paid with little real power. The first Australian-born governor-general was **Isaac Isaacs**, who held the office from 1931 to 1936. The next Australian-born occupant was Sir William McKell (1891-1985), who served from 1947 to 1953. Since the appointment of **Richard Gardiner Casey** to the office in 1965, all governors-general have been Australian-born. They are usually appointed from former important members of the **Australian Labor Party** or **Liberal Party** or from senior members of the judiciary.

On November 11, 1975, the office of governor-general was thrown into high relief when its occupant, John Kerr (1974-77), a former Chief Justice of New South Wales, took the unprecedented steps of dismissing the **Whitlam** government after its Liberal-**Country Party** opponents in the **senate** refused to pass supply (that is, money legislation), and installing **Malcolm Fraser** as head of an interim government pending the calling of an election. Although Kerr's action was technically legal, it violated long-standing conventions and resulted in his being subjected to demonstrations whenever he appeared in public. His action, together with his sometimes unseemly public behavior, resulted in the discrediting of the office of governor-general. Since Kerr's departure in December 1977, his successors have had to work hard to restore the reputation and standing of the office. During the constitutional convention on whether Australia should become a republic in February 1998, the nature of the office of governor-general was central to the debates, particularly how it might be transformed into a future president of Australia. (*See also* Colonial/State Governors, Appendix 2)

GRAINGER, [GEORGE] PERCY (1882-1961) Musician Percy Grainger was born in Brighton, a suburb of Melbourne. His father was an engineer. Grainger showed early artistic promise and gave his first public performance as a pianist in 1894. In 1895 he left Australia with his mother to study piano in Franfurt-am-Main, Germany, and although he never returned to Australia to live, he remain strongly nationalistic at heart. Between 1900 and 1913 he established an international reputation in Europe as a pianist and composer. In 1908 he composed the tune he is best remembered for, *Country Gardens.* In September 1914 he emigrated to the **United States** and joined the U.S. Army as a bandsman in 1917; he did not see active service.

In the following year he became an American citizen, but continued to make return visits to Australia in 1924, 1926, 1934-35, and 1955-56. His 1934-35 visit was sponsored by the Australian Broadcasting Commission (the predecessor of the present **Australian Broadcasting Corporation**) and he used the income from this visit to establish a music museum in Melbourne which was opened in 1938. Gifted, generous, and eccentric, Grainger's importance as an musical innovator and pioneer, as opposed to his lifetime reputation as a composer of popular music, has been increasingly recognized.

GREAT BARRIER REEF The Great Barrier Reef is the largest single collection of coral reefs and islands in the world. It lies off the north-east coast of **Queensland** and is 1,250 nautical miles long. The reef is about half a million years old and has been created and destroyed about 12 times as a result of changes in sea levels. A major tourist attraction, the reef was declared a national park in 1976 and was entered in the World Heritage List in 1981. In 1996 1.5 million people visited the reef. (*See also* Tourism)

GREAT WHITE FLEET This was the term popularly applied to the visit of the **United States** Pacific fleet to Australia in 1908. The fleet, which came at the invitation of **Alfred Deakin**, was made up of 16 white-painted battleships. The fleet docked at **Sydney**, **Melbourne**, and Albany in **Western Australia** during its world tour and attracted huge crowds. The purpose of the visit was not to indicate that Australia had turned to the United States for **defense**, but to spur **Britain** into making a greater naval commitment to

Australia's defense following the victory of **Japan** over the Russian fleet in 1905.

GREEKS   Greek **immigration** to Australia was negligible before 1920. In 1921 there were only 3,664 Greek-born in Australia, but by 1947 there were 12,292. Large numbers came to Australia after 1950, with many settling in **Melbourne** and **Sydney**. In 1971 there were 160,200 Greeks in Australia, their highest level, and their numbers have been declining slowly ever since. At the 1986 census 293,020 Australians claimed some Greek ancestry. In 1996 there were 126,524 Greeks in Australia (compared to 146,00 in 1986) of whom 48.9 percent were living in **Victoria**.

GREEN BANS   Green bans were a form of **labor dispute** carried out by certain Australian **labor unions**. A ban is any type of restriction placed on how work is carried out. They can cover some or all of the work. "Green" bans were an application of this principle to the politics of protecting the **environment**. They took the form of prohibitions placed on the destruction or redevelopment of historic buildings, housing occupied by low-income earners, or parks, particularly in inner **Sydney** in 1971 and 1972, although others have occasionally happened since that time. The "green" bans of the 1970s were enforced by the militant Builders' Labourers' Federation. Green bans were important for leading to a federal government Committee of Inquiry into the National Estate in 1973 and in raising public consciousness about the need to protect the **environment** against the demands of developers.   (*See also* Australian Democrats)

GREGG, NORMAN [MCALISTER] (1892-1966)   Born in the **Sydney** suburb of Burwood, Gregg became an ophthalmic surgeon. He made a major contribution to medical research in Sydney in 1941 when he established the link between German measles, or rubella, in pregnant women and birth defects. There had been an epidemic of rubella in Australia in 1940-41. Gregg's discovery helped to found a new field of medical research, teratology, the study of birth defects. He was knighted for his work in 1953. He was invited to the **United States** in 1966 as the guest of honor of the American Medical Association, but was unable to attend. (*See also* Health and Medical Services)

H

HANSON, PAULINE (*See* One Nation Party)

HARVESTER JUDGMENT   The Harvester Judgment was the term given to a landmark decision handed down by Justice Henry Bourne Higgins (1851-1929) of the newly formed Commonwealth Court of Conciliation and Arbitration in 1907. The decision set a general "basic" or minimum wage for unskilled male adult employees of seven shillings ($1.40) a day. The decision was an extension of the federal *Excise Tariff Act* (1906), which provided that local employers could be exempt from excise duty if the Court of Conciliation and Arbitration decided that the wages paid by an employer were "fair and reasonable." Hugh Victor McKay (1865-1926), a prominent manufacturer of agricultural machinery, had claimed exemption under the *Act*. The Harvester Judgment linked wage levels to tariff **protection** and began the practice of using cost of living statistics by **labor unions** in their claims before **industrial tribunals** for higher wages. It also recognized that skilled workers should receive an additional wage or "margin." These two elements, the "basic" wage and the "margin," continued as features of the national wage fixation system until 1967.

HAWKE, "BOB" [ROBERT JAMES LEE] (1929-   )   Australian **prime minister**, Hawke was born in Bordertown, South Australia. He was educated at the universities of Western Australia and Oxford, which he attended as a Rhodes scholar. In 1958 he joined the **Australian Council of Trade Unions** (ACTU) as research officer and industrial advocate. Hawke was elected president of the ACTU in 1970 and held the position until 1980 when he was elected to the house of representatives for the Victorian working-class electorate of Wills for the **Australian Labor Party** (ALP). In February 1983 he became leader of the federal parliamentary ALP and with the ALP's victory at the elections on March 5, 1983, he became prime minister on March 11, 1983, and held the post until December 20, 1991.

Hawke's government encouraged greater communication between **labor unions** and employers, enacted the **Accord** between the ALP and the ACTU, deregulated the finance industry in 1985, reformed the conditions of federal government employees, and tried to make government business enterprises operate more like private enterprises. The deterioration of the **economy** after 1987, particularly the continuing adverse balance of **trade** and sharply rising foreign debt, was a major problem for his government. The recession, which afflicted the economy from September 1990 and throughout 1991, eroded Hawke's popularity in opinion polls and made it possible for his former treasurer, **Paul Keating** to successfully challenge Hawke for his position. On December 19, 1991, Hawke was voted out of the position of prime minister by federal ALP parliamentarians by 56 to 51 votes. He resigned from federal parliament on February 20, 1992.

HEALTH AND MEDICAL SERVICES European diseases and medical services arrived in Australia with the **First Fleet**. A naval surgeon was included in the staff of the fleet to attend to medical needs. Because of its isolation, the great bulk of Australia's **Aborigines** had no exposure to diseases such as smallpox, and the first epidemic among them broke out in April 1789. Smallpox is now thought to have been the long-executioner of the Aborigines in eastern Australia. A second epidemic among them in the 1830s has provided powerful evidence that their numbers before 1788 were considerably greater than previously thought because smallpox needs a minimum population of 250,000 to remain active. Unlike North America, there was no deliberate policy to spread the disease among indigenous people and the spread of the disease was largely through contact with escaped **convicts**.

For the early European settlers in Australia, the main health problem was having enough to eat as well as tending to the needs of convicts who arrived sick after the voyage from **Britain**. With the growth of a free society after 1820, Australia's mortality figures slowly began to move closer to those of Britain's. The frontier nature of much of the early settlement and its dominance by males (there were 206 males for every 100 females in 1841) contributed to high levels of mortality.

Urbanization, an early important feature of Australian society, also raised mortality because it resulted in the concentration of settlement before the provision of supplies of fresh water and sewerage services which mainly dated from the late 1880s. It is no accident that both the crude death rate and the infant mortality rate changed relatively little in Australia between 1870 and 1900; in this same period, the level of urbanization rose from 35.7 to 47.7 percent. Effective public health and pure food laws were also only enacted after 1890 as was legislation to register physicians and dentists. Political concern about community health was stimulated by the possible needs of **defense** from the 1900s. State governments began to conduct medical inspections of school children and to introduce baby clinics designed to educate mothers about the benefits of breast feeding and good hygiene. **World War I** showed that Australians had poor teeth with nearly 15,800 men being rejected for the **Australian Imperial Force** because of dental disease out of several hundred thousand who tried to enlist in the first 18 months of the war. The returning troops raised the incidence of venereal disease and led to the formation of public health groups such as the Father and Son Movement in the 1930s.

The contribution of medical services to improved health was secondary to that made by public health measures and rising living standards. It was only really with the introduction of sulfa drugs in the 1930s, penicillin in the 1940s, and later medicines that medical science began to made a significant contribution in its own right to increasing health and the length of life. Between 1881-91 and 1946-48, life expectancy at birth for males increased from 47 to 66 years and for females from 51 to 71 years, but this was largely because of a sharp decline in infant mortality; this rate fell from 110 infant deaths per thousand births to 28 per thousand births over this same period.

Health care was not specifically mentioned as a power for the federal government in the **Australian Constitution** which envisaged it remaining solely the preserve of state administrations with the notable exception of quarantine. Yet for many reasons, this division of powers could not endure. In 1912 the federal government introduced a payment for European mothers of five pounds after the birth of a child. Better communications meant that diseases were less easily contained. The Spanish influenza pandemic of 1919 killed 12,000 people across Australia despite the efforts of the federal government to quarantine infected vessels. In 1925 it appointed a royal commission into health which produced a detailed, national body of information on the subject for the first time.

The cost of medical care and its availability to the public have been contentious political issues in Australia since the 1920s. In 1927 the royal commission into national insurance recommended a compulsory system for health care insurance based on contributions from employees and employers. The idea perished during the Depression, but reappeared in 1938 before being overtaken by

World War II. Disagreements between the major political parties as well as with the Australian Medical Association have marked health care policy since 1950. A pharmaceutical benefits scheme was introduced by the federal government as was a pensioner medical service in 1951. On July 1, 1975, the **Whitlam** government introduced a universal medical scheme, Medibank, which was much reduced by the **Fraser** government in 1981 and then relaunched in a revised version as Medicare by the **Hawke** government. The coalition parties favor private health insurance. Rising health costs have been a major concern for all political parties since the 1970s and have led to many modifications of health programs.

For all the public money devoted to health care, it was not until 1977-78 that the first official household survey of the health status of Australians was undertaken. It has been conducted irregularly ever since and is based on the U.S. model.

Australia has made important contributions to health care through the work of its researchers, particularly in immunology. **Norman Gregg** established the link between German measles or rubella in pregnancy and birth defects in 1941, thereby being largely responsible for the founding of new field of medical research, teratology. **Howard Florey** was a joint winner of the Nobel prize for Medicine and Physiology in 1945 for his leading role in the development of penicillin. Other Nobel prize winners for Medicine and Physiology are **MacFarlane Burnet** (1960), **John Eccles** (1963), and **Charles Doherty** (1997).

Together with affluence, better health and medical services have continued to raise the life expectancy of Australians. Preliminary calculations for 1996 suggest that a male baby can expect to live to 75 years (compared to 71 years in 1981) and that a female baby can expect to live to 81 years (compared to 78 years in 1981). Apart from the health status of Aborigines, which remains well below the general standard of Australians, the main current health problems for health policy in Australia are inadequate immunization of children and the consequences of obesity and lack of exercise.

HELPMAN, ROBERT [MURRAY] (1909-1986)   Actor, ballet dancer, choreographer, and director, Helpman was born in Mount Gambier, a small town in **South Australia**. He made his debut as a dancer in 1923, joined Anna Pavlova's touring ballet company in 1929, and became the principal male dancer with the Sadler's Wells Ballet company in London in 1933. He danced with Margot Fonteyn and created his own ballets, *Comus* and *Hamlet* (1942), *Miracle in the Gorbals* (1944) and *Adam Zero* (1946). He also appeared in a number of notable British films, *Henry V*, *One of Our Aircraft is Missing*, and *Red Shoes*. In 1955 he returned to Australia and played a leading role in the emergence of modern ballet in Australia with production such as *The Display* (1964) and *The Merry Widow* (1974). He was named Australian of the Year in 1966 and knighted in 1968.

HERBERT, [ALFRED FRANCIS] XAVIER (1901-1984) Novelist, Herbert was born in Port Hedland, a remote coastal town in northern **Western Australia**. He qualified as a pharmacist from the University of Melbourne, but abandoned this career and turned to writing. To support himself he worked at a variety of rural jobs. His best-known works are *Capricornia* (1938), for which he won the Commonwealth Sesquicentenary Literary Prize, and *Poor Fellow, My Country* (1975). Pervading these works is a deep concern and resentment over the Europeans' treatment of the **Aborigines**. In 1963 he published his autobiography, *Disturbing Element*. He won the Miles Franklin award for *Poor Fellow, My Country* in 1975. (*See also* Literature)

HIGH COURT OF AUSTRALIA The High Court is the supreme court of Australia. The court was established under Chapter 3 of the **Australian Constitution** in 1903 under federal judiciary legislation using the U.S. Supreme Court as a model. As a body independent of parliament, the court has significant powers, particularly in the field of constitutional interpretation. Many of its cases have concerned certain parts of the Australian Constitution, such as section 92 (interstate trade) and section 51(xxxv) (the conciliation and arbitration power in **labor disputes** extending beyond a **state**). From 1920 most of its decisions have tended to favor the Commonwealth or federal government in disputes with the states, so the court has been an instrument of the extension of Commonwealth power in **Commonwealth-State relations**. It was possible to appeal against its decision to the English Privy Council, but this was removed by the **Whitlam** government in 1975; there were some exceptions, but these were removed too in 1986. Since 1980 the court has operated from new buildings in **Canberra**. The court enjoys an excellent international reputation. (*See also* Commonwealth-State Relations; Barwick, Garfield Edward John; Mabo Judgment; Wik Decision)

HOBART   Hobart is the capital city of the **state** of **Tasmania**. Named after the then British secretary of state for colonies, Hobart was founded by Lieutenant-Governor David Collins (1756-1810) in 1804 as the administrative center for what was then known as Van Diemen's Land. Although an active port, Hobart grew slowly reflecting the generally slow growth of the Tasmanian economy. By 1881 its population had reached only 27,100 and even by 1933 had reached only 60,400, making Hobart easily the smallest of Australia's capital cities. In 1996 Hobart had a population of 189,900 or 33.4 percent of the state's population.

Hobart gained a university in 1890. The annual Sydney to Hobart yacht race was first held in 1945 and begins from **Sydney** on December 26. Since the 1960s it has been a major event in Australian **sport**. To boost the local economy, the first legal casino was opened in Hobart in 1973. The eastern and western suburbs were linked by the Tasman Bridge in 1964; it was closed after being damaged by a ship in 1975 and not reopened until 1979. (*See also* Tasmania)

HOLT, HAROLD [EDWARD] (1908-1967)   Australian **prime minister**, Holt was born in **Sydney**, but educated in **Melbourne**. He graduated as a lawyer from Melbourne University and worked as a solicitor from 1933 to 1935 when he was elected to the **house of representatives** for the **United Australia Party** and from 1944 to his death for the **Liberal Party**. He became deputy leader of the party in 1956 and succeeded **Robert Menzies** as leader and prime minister on January 26, 1966.

Under Holt there was a marked growth in Australia's participation in the **Vietnam** war, over which he fought and won a highly successful federal election on November 26, 1966. His term in office was also notable for the first visit to Australia by a current American president, Lyndon Baines Johnson, to whom Holt publicly pledged full Australian support to the **United States** in the Vietnam war, using the line "All the Way with LBJ." On December 17, 1967 Holt went swimming off the coast of **Victoria**, and never returned. As his body was never recovered, he was presumed to have drowned. He was replaced as prime minister by **John McEwen**.

HOME OWNERSHIP   The high level of individual home ownership has been one of the most important features of Australian society in the twentieth century. It distinguished Australian society from

Britain, where home ownership rates were low until the 1970s. Unlike the U.S. census which collected statistics on home ownership from 1890, no Australian **census** asked about home ownership until 1911. Before 1911 the only sources for statistics on home ownership are the rate books maintained by municipal councils, which often have this information from about 1870, and the rate books of water and sewerage authorities which became available from the late 1880s. Because no systematic investigation has been made of these sources, the general level of home ownership in urban areas in Australia is not known for certain, but from what data are available, it is evident that by 1891 a high level of home ownership had been achieved, the product of the high level of economic growth enjoyed by the Australian **economy** between 1861 and 1891. Home ownership in **Melbourne** (59 percent) was considerably higher than in **Sydney** (28 percent) and this remained true in 1911. Outside of Sydney and Melbourne, home ownership rates of 40 percent or more were common. The municipal rate books for **Newcastle** and **Wollongong** show that home ownership made rapid progress between 1886 and 1890. The depression and **drought** of the 1890s and early 1900s halted the growth in home ownership.

When the first national figures on home ownership were collected at the census in 1911, 49 percent of Australia's homes were either owned or being bought by their occupiers. In the capital cities only 36 percent of homes were owner-occupied as opposed to an average of 57 percent outside the capitals. Since 1911 the difference between home ownership levels in the capital cities and elsewhere has become less marked.

Between 1921 and 1947 the general level of home ownership was remarkably stable at about 53 percent. It has been suggested that the high level of home ownership was an important source of social and political stability. In his *Australian Journey* (1939), Paul McGuire, an English visitor to Australia, attributed much of the country's social stability to the wide distribution of home ownership. "Revolutions," he wrote, "are seldom made by house-owners."

The Depression and **World War II** severely reduced home building in Australia. Between 1933 and 1947 the number of occupied homes only rose from 1.5 to 1.9 million, an annual rise of 1.7 percent, and caused a housing shortage in the main urban centers during the late 1940s. In the 1950s full employment, and assistance schemes for World War II veterans boosted home ownership levels to 69.9 percent by 1961. Home ownership reached a peak in 1971, when 70.6 percent of homes were owner-occupied, and then leveled off and declined because of Australia's economic difficulties in the early 1990s. In 1996 the national average home ownership level was 66.4 percent. Nevertheless, home ownership continues to be a general desire in Australia. (*See also* Wealth and Income; Tables 21 and 22 of Appendix 3)

HOUSE OF REPRESENTATIVES The lower chamber of the Australian federal parliament, the house of representatives was created by the **Australian Constitution** in 1901. Modeled on the U.S. House of Representatives, it is elected by a majority of voters, in contrast to the **senate**, which is elected on a state basis. The house of representatives initiates legislation and the **prime minister** of the day always holds a seat in it. In 1998 there were 148 seats in the house of representatives compared to 75 when it began in 1901.

HOWARD, JOHN WINSTON (1939-) Australian **prime minister**, Howard was born in Earlwood, a suburb of Sydney. He graduated from the University of Sydney as a lawyer in 1961. A lifelong supporter of the **Liberal Party**, he was elected to the **house of representatives** for the Sydney electorate of Bennelong in 1974 and held the shadow portfolio of consumer affairs and commerce. After the party's victory in the elections of December 13, 1975, Howard was made minister for business and consumer affairs from 1975 to 1977, minister of state for special trade negotiations in 1977, and treasurer from 1977 until March 1983 when the government of **Malcolm Fraser** was defeated. As treasurer, he cut government expenditure and attempted to reduce tax evasion. In 1982 he became deputy leader of the Liberal Party and was party leader from September 5, 1985, to May 9, 1989. Infighting in the Liberal Party and with elements of its coalition partner, the **National Party**, resulted in Howard losing the leadership. He was shadow minister for labor relations from 1990 to 1995.

On January 30, 1995, he was again elected leader of the Liberal Party and on March 2, 1996, led the party to a landslide victory at the national elections. He became prime minister on March 11, 1996. Following the mass murder of 35 people by a deranged gunman in **Tasmania** in April 1996, Howard personally led a campaign to outlaw semi-automatic and automatic firearms though coordinated legislation by the **states** and **territories**. His government has been notable for massive cuts in public expenditure, the creation of a budget surplus, the reduction in the number of federal government employees by 15,000, privatizing one-third of the government-owned telecommunications agency (Telstra) in October 1997, and generally trying to minimize the economic role of government and the power of **labor unions**. His government was returned to power with a reduced majority following the national elections on October 3, 1998, after a campaign largely fought on his advocacy of a goods and services tax of 10 percent.

HUGHES, ROBERT [STUDLEY FORREST] (1938-) Art critic and author, Hughes was born in **Sydney** and studied architecture at the University of Sydney. He studied and practiced painting in Europe before concentrating on writing about art. In 1966 he published *The Art of Australia*, but he was unhappy with its contents and had most of the first edition pulped and issued a revised version in 1970. In the same year he became the art critic for *Time* magazine and has become one of Australia's best-known expatriates. He now lives in New York. Hughes has also made a number of television documentaries since 1980, notably *The Shock of the New* and *American Visions*, which have been used as the basis for books with the same titles. In 1987 he published *The Fatal Shore*, which presents a detailed account of the early settlement of Australia and the treatment of its **convicts**. Although a highly successful work, his gloomy presentation of the period has not won the support of most scholars of the subject. Hughes is a supporter of **republicanism** for Australia.

HUGHES, WILLIAM MORRIS (1862-1952) Australian **prime minister**, Hughes was born in London to Welsh parents. He became a schoolteacher and spent some years teaching in Wales. He emigrated to Australia in 1884, where he eventually settled in **Sydney**. In 1894 he entered **New South Wales** politics for the **Australian Labor Party** (ALP) and in 1901 transferred to federal politics. He was also one of the founders of the Waterside Workers' Federation, the main labor union for waterfront workers. He was attorney-general in both **Fisher** governments in 1910-13 and 1914-15. As prime minister from October 27, 1915, to February 9, 1923, much of Hughes's ministry was devoted to organizing Australia's war effort. This included leading two exceptionally bitter campaigns in support of **conscription** in 1916 and 1917, which split the ALP.

In 1916 he switched sides and joined the conservatives to form the **Nationalist Party**. At war's end in 1918, he used the size of Australia's contribution to gain a separate place for Australia at the Versailles peace conference. His efforts resulted in Australia acquiring control of the former German territories in **Papua New Guinea**. Always a polemical figure, Hughes remained in federal politics until his death, having become the longest serving member of the **house of representatives** in Australian history.

As well as being a politician, Hughes was a capable writer. He wrote *The Case for Labor* (1910)—the earliest exposition of the philosophy of the ALP—*The Splendid Adventure* (1929), *Australia and the War Today* (1935), and two entertaining books of reminiscences, *Crusts and Crusades* (1947) and *Politicians and Potentates* (1950).

I

IMMIGRATION Like the Americas, Australia is a continent peopled by immigration. In 1920 the foreign-born made up 15.5 percent of Australia's population compared to 22.3 percent in Canada, 13.2 percent in the **United States** and 24 percent in Argentina. Since 1960 immigration has played a disproportionately greater role in shaping Australia and its people. By 1990 24.5 percent of Australians were foreign-born compared to 15.9 percent of Canadians and 7.9 percent of Americans

Immigration has been a central feature of Australia's history as a European society. It has been a major factor in the growth of population: between 1800 and 1997, more than a third of the total increase in the population from 5,200 to 18.5 million—35.2 percent—came from immigration, a total of 6.5 million. Because of the distance from Europe, Australia was not easily able to attract large numbers of immigrants. Governments therefore provided assistance for immigration: between 1831 and 1980, 3.3 million people were assisted to come to Australia.

A large share of the first European immigrants came as **convicts** (a total of 162,000 arrived from 1788 to 1860), but the first free immigrants arrived in 1793. In 1831 the **New South Wales** government introduced a policy of financing immigration from the sale of government lands. The first government-assisted immigrants (all single women) arrived in 1831. The **gold** rushes of the 1850s drew into Australia 587,000 immigrants, mostly Europeans, but including 38,000 **Chinese**. Fears of the Chinese as a threat to

European workers led to violence against them by the Europeans and eventually to the creation of the **White Australia Policy**. Thereafter, the flow of immigrants was regulated by the state of the **economy** and by government policy. If labor demand was high, the government assisted more immigrants; if not, it suspended assistance. Of the 746,800 immigrants to Australia between 1860 and 1900, half were government assisted. Most of these immigrants came between 1877 and 1889.

At the **federation** of the Australian **colonies** in 1901, 22.8 percent of the population of 3.8 million were overseas-born. Immigration became a responsibility of the new federal government, and national policies replaced those of the separate colonies. The federal government enforced policies to encourage British immigrants and exclude non-Europeans. The stream of immigration was strong in 1909 to 1913 and again just after **World War I** and until 1930. In the 1920s Australia and Britain had agreements to settle British immigrants on the land. Between 1920 and 1929, 221,200 British immigrants were assisted to come to Australia. Some of these British migrants were brought out as teenagers to work in rural areas. The first of these schemes, the Dreadnought Scheme, began in 1911 and was used to settle 7,000 young British migrants in Australia by 1930. It was succeeded by the Big Brother Movement which began in 1925, operated until the early 1930s and was revived in the late 1940s. In the 1940s unwanted British children from orphanages or simply poor families were also sent to Australia. The circumstances of their migration and their often poor treatment in Australia were widely publicized in the mid-1990s.

Among the non-British immigrants, the most important groups until 1921 were the **Germans** (22,400) and the Chinese (15,200). **World War II** and the threat of invasion by the Japanese in 1942 changed Australian government policy in favor of large-scale immigration. Although British immigrants were still preferred, other European immigrants were granted assistance. Between 1947 and 1971, immigrants changed the social landscape of Australia. Nearly 2.87 million people arrived in Australia of whom 39 percent came from Britain, 23 percent from South Europe, and 26 percent from the rest of Europe. As in the pre-1947 period, most of the immigrants settled in the major cities, mainly **Sydney** and **Melbourne**. At the 1996 **census** the highest concentrations of foreign-born were in Sydney (34.5 percent), followed by **Perth** (33.4 percent), Melbourne (31.1 percent), and **Adelaide** (25.6 percent).

The impact of immigration can also be measured by the proportion of the population who were "second generation" Australians, that is they were born in Australia, but had at least one parent who was foreign-born. In 1996, 27 percent of Australian-born were "second generation" Australians.

Since 1947, more than 570 000 people arrived in Australia under humanitarian programs, initially as displaced persons in the 1940s and 1950s, and more recently as refugees. The highest number of immigrants to arrive in any one year since World War II was 185,099, in 1969-70. The lowest number in any one year was 52, 752 in 1975-76. These years were years of high and low labor demand in Australia.

In 1997-98, 77,300 people came to Australia as settlers. Of these the largest groups were from Oceania (23 percent), Europe and the former Soviet Union (25.2 percent), north-east Asia (13.2 percent), south-east Asia (12.5 percent), Africa (excluding North Africa) (8.1 percent), the Middle East and North Africa (7.5 percent), and southern Asia (6.9 percent). Only 2.6 percent of settlers came from North America and 0.9 percent from the remainder of the Americas. The main countries represented in this migration were: **New Zealand** (19 percent), the United Kingdom (11.9 percent), China (5.6 percent), **South Africa** (5.5 percent), Hong Kong (4.1 percent), India (3.6 percent), Philippines (3.6 percent), **Vietnam** (3 percent), and **Indonesia** (2.5 percent).

Since the 1960s, the main shifts in immigration patterns have been an increase in the intake from Asia and the Middle East, greater efforts to match immigrants with the skills needed by the Australian economy, and more emphasis on refugees who, since 1980, are the only immigrants granted assisted passage. Since 1978 government policy has supported "multiculturalism" (that is, acceptance of immigrants' cultural diversity), whereas the previous policy dating from 1946 was one of assimilation to an Australian way of life derived from Britain.

In recent years the difficulties and disappointments of the Australian **economy** have led to a questioning of immigration as a national policy which assumed racist anti-Asian tones among a small minority of Australians. Immigration has been reduced—as it has on many previous occasions in the past—in response to the domestic demand for labor. In May 1997 the federal government reduced the intake level for non-humanitarian migration to 68,000 in 1997-98 compared to 82,560 in 1995-96. A poll taken in May 1997 found that although 64 percent of Australians thought that immigration was too high, 78 percent considered that multiculturalism was good for Australia. (*See also* Caroline Chisholm; Greeks; Irish; Italians; Jews; "New Australians;" One Nation Party; Population)

INDO-AUSTRALIAN PLATE One of the 18 tectonic plates which cover the surface of the world, the Indo-Australian plate includes India and parts of New Guinea and **New Zealand**. Earthquakes and volcanic activity occur to varying degrees on the borders of tectonic plates. Although most of Australia is geologically stable, earthquakes have been relatively frequent in some isolated centers. Until the extensive earthquake damage to inner **Newcastle** in December 1989, Australia's large population centers had been virtually free of earthquakes.

INDONESIA Australia's first recorded contact with the islands of Indonesia came when the Dutch explorer, Abel Tasman (c.1603-1659), based in Java, discovered **Tasmania** in 1642. Apart from Dutch explorers, the only contact between the indigenous people of the region and Australia was through the voyages of fishermen from Macassar (modern Makasar) in the southern Celebes to the northern Australia waters for trepang ("sea slugs") to sell to China where they were considered a great delicacy. They are thought to have begun making these voyages between 1675 and 1700, by which time the Dutch had replaced the English as the dominant colonial power in the region. In 1828 the Dutch annexed the western half of the island of New Guinea.

During **World War II** Indonesian nationalists declared Indonesia's independence from Dutch rule. In the ensuing struggle (1945-1949), Australian maritime **labor unions**, the Seamen's Union of Australia and the Waterside Workers' Federation, refused to load Dutch shipping, thereby greatly hampering Dutch efforts to suppress the uprising. The Australian government of **Ben Chifley** supported the struggle for Indonesian independence through diplomatic channels and also refused to assist the military efforts of the Dutch government to maintain its rule over Indonesia.

In 1959 Australia and Indonesia signed a trade agreement. In 1963 Indonesia annexed the western half of New Guinea and in 1975 invaded the former Portuguese colony of east Timor despite Australian protests. Indonesia is a recipient of Australian foreign aid ($108 million in 1996-97) and its island of Bali is a popular Australian tourist resort. Between 1986 and 1996 the number of Indonesians living in Australia increased from 25,000 to 44,157. In

January 1998 Australia agreed to provide $1.6 billion in financial assistance to Indonesia through the International Monetary Fund to help stabilize its currency crisis. (*See also* Papua New Guinea)

INDUSTRIAL TRIBUNALS   Industrial tribunals are bodies established under federal and state laws that decide the wages and conditions of employees or help to solve **labor disputes**. Industrial tribunals were set up in **Victoria** (1896), **Western Australia** and **South Australia** (1900), **New South Wales** (1901), and **Queensland** (1912). The federal industrial tribunal was established in 1904 and since the reforms of 1988 is known as the Australian Industrial Relations Commission. Although the state tribunals are independent bodies, since the mid-1970s there has been a growing degree of coordination between them and the federal tribunal in their decisions. During the 1990s conservative governments have sought to reduce the importance of industrial tribunals. (*See also* Accord; Awards; Harvester Judgment)

INGAMELLS, REX [REGINALD CHARLES] (1913-1955)   Poet, Ingamells was born in Ororro, **South Australia**. He published an anthology of poems, *Gumtops*, in 1935 and wrote an epic poem about the history of Australia called *The Great South Land* in 1951. However, his most lasting contribution to Australian poetry was his creation of the nationalist literary group, the **Jindyworobaks**, in 1938. (*See also* Literature)

INTERNMENT   In both world wars the Australian government interned individuals regarded as dangerous to national security. During **World War I** over 6,739 were interned, mainly **Germans**, of whom 5,276 were sent back to their countries of origin. During **World War II** internment was at its height in 1942, when 10,732 were held; 4,022 were Japanese, 3,836 were **Italians**, and 2,661 were Germans. By 1945 only 4,512 were interned. Some of the interned were Australians suspected of pro-Fascist views. (*See also* Australia First Movement)

IRISH   Although there were some Irish **convicts** on the **First Fleet** in 1788, the direct transportation of Irish convicts to Australia began in 1791. By 1868 when the convict system ended, 36,000, or 23 percent, of all the convicts sent to Australia were Irish. A quarter of the Irish convicts were female. The typical Irish convict was illiterate, of rural origin, and anti-English. Three hundred rebelled during the **Castle Hill Rebellion** in **Sydney** in 1804; 15 were killed, 9 were hanged, and 50 were sent north to **Newcastle** to work in the coal mines. A total of about 5,000 of the Irish convicts transported to Australia were participants in the political uprisings of 1798, 1848, and 1867.

The second way the Irish came to Australia was by free **immigration**. Between 1831 and 1914 about 300,000 Irish emigrated to Australia, the bulk of them to **New South Wales**, **Victoria**, and **Queensland**. Most of these immigrants were government assisted, most were Catholics and over half were female, in contrast to the male dominance of most of the other immigrant groups. Until the 1860s, only about half the Irish were literate, which, together with employment discrimination because of their **Catholicism**, meant that the Irish-born tended to work mainly as unskilled laborers or in other forms of menial work. As a group they were disadvantaged.

In 1911, 70 percent of the 141,300 Irish-born were Catholics, 14.1 percent were **Church of England** and 8.5 percent were **Methodists**. Yet it was the Catholic majority among them who attracted the most attention as they tended to remain outside the mainstream of Australian society. Because of their size, social cohesion, and economic disadvantage, Irish Catholics played a significant role in Australian political life, especially in the **Australian Labor Party** (ALP) after the party split over **conscription** in 1916. Between 1921 and 1951, the proportion of Irish Catholics among members of the federal parliamentary ALP increased from 33 to 40 percent. Six of Australia's 25 **prime ministers** have had Irish-Catholic backgrounds: **James Scullin**, **Joseph Lyons**, **John Curtin**, **Francis Forde**, **Ben Chifley**, and **Paul Keating**.

That most of the Irish-born Catholics and their descendants remained economically disadvantaged in the pre-1950 period was evident from the 1933 census, which showed that of male breadwinners earning 260 pounds or more (the highest income category), Catholics were the poorest of the major religions. Only 10.4 percent of Catholic male breadwinners were in this top income category compared with 13.6 percent of Church of England male breadwinners, 18.4 percent of **Presbyterians**, and 15.3 percent of Methodists. Catholic schools were used to encourage the brightest students to enter medicine or law to raise the proportion of Catholics in the professions and so raise the socio-economic status of Catholics generally.

The number of Irish-born increased from 177,405 in 1861 to 229,165 in 1891, its highest level, and fell to 45,066 in 1947, its lowest level. Post-1947 immigration lifted the number of Irish-born. At the 1986 census, 803,372 Australians—5.1 percent—claimed some Irish ancestry. In 1996 there were 74,477 Irish-born in Australia (compared to 67,738 in 1986); 69 percent of these immigrants came from the Republic of Ireland.

IRON AND STEEL The first attempt to smelt **iron ore** in Australia was made at Mittagong, southern **New South Wales**, from 1848 to 1850, but the venture failed and it was not until the 1870s that the industry began again. Production was limited; by 1884 only 22,260 tonnes of pig iron in all had been produced. From 1885 to 1916 the center of the industry was Lithgow, New South Wales; by 1906 total production amounted to 120,000 tonnes.

In 1915 the **Broken Hill Proprietary Company Limited** (BHP) opened an integrated steelworks at **Newcastle**, based on American technology and technical staff. By 1925 annual production at Newcastle had reached 326,000 tonnes of pig iron and 30,000 tonnes of steel. In 1930 Australian Iron and Steel opened a second steel plant using obsolete British technology at **Wollongong**, south of Sydney. The plant became a victim of the Depression and was bought by BHP in 1935. In 1941 BHP opened a pig iron plant at Whyalla, **South Australia**, and began producing steel there in 1950, although the industry remained centered upon Newcastle and Wollongong.

The iron and steel industry prospered during the 1950s and 1960s when BHP was credited with producing the world's cheapest steel, but in 1982-83 the industry underwent a crisis because of the depressed condition of the world steel market and the recession in the Australian economy caused by **drought**. In this period, BHP's steel capacity fell from 8.9 to 6.6 million tonnes and employment fell from 36,000 to 25,600. BHP appealed for federal government assistance, which was provided under the Steel Industry Plan (1984-87) in return for greater investment by BHP in steel making. The later recovery in the industry has been attributed by the Bureau of Industry Economics not to the plan but more to BHP's earlier cost-cutting measures, the fall in the value of the Australian dollar and the general recovery in the Australian economy. In 1997-98 iron and steel accounted for 2.1 percent of Australian exports by value.

During the 1990s the international competitiveness of the Australian iron and steel industry continued to decline and led to an announcement by BHP's management on April 29, 1997, that its steelworks at Newcastle would be closed in 1999 as well as two smaller mills in Sydney and **Geelong**. It also indicated that its mills at Whyalla in South Australia and Glenbrook in **New Zealand** would also be closed by 2007. The effect of these changes would be to concentrate the industry in Wollongong. (*See also* Manufacturing)

IRON ORE   Australia is one of the world's largest exporters of iron ore. Significant exports of iron ore were made in 1929 to Europe, the **United States**, and **Japan**; indeed Japan was Australia's main market for iron ore from 1933 to 1938. In its modern form, the industry began in 1960 when the federal government lifted its ban on the export of iron ore. The ban, which had been in force since July 1938, had been imposed to deny iron ore to Japan because of its war against China and because Australia's reserves of iron ore had previously been thought to be limited.

But in 1960 huge new deposits of high grade iron ore were discovered in the Pilbara region of north-west **Western Australia**. Most of the exports went to Japan's iron and steel industry. In 1997-98, Australia produced 161 million tonnes of iron ore (compared to 4 million in 1960 and 110 million tonnes in 1989-90), nearly all of which was exported. Although Australia's main market remains Japan, China and South **Korea** have also become important markets in recent years. In 1997-98 iron ore accounted for 4.3 percent of Australia's merchandise exports. (*See also* Iron and Steel; Mining; Wollongong)

ISLAM   Muslims were first identified in the **census** for **Victoria** in 1854; it enumerated 332 adherents. The majority of Muslims were from India or the Middle East. Between 1911 and 1947 the number of Muslims in Australia fell from 3,908 to 2,704. By 1971, when they were again separately identified in the census, their numbers had increased to 22,311 as a result of immigration from Muslim countries. Since 1981, when they overtook Judaism as Australia's largest non-Christian religion, the number of Muslims has grown to 109,523 in 1986 and to 200,886 in 1996. (*See also* Jews; Religion)

ITALIANS   The Italian-born have been the second largest group of non-British immigrants in Australia since 1933 when their numbers had reached 26,760 compared to 8,164 in 1921. Their main center of settlement in this period was on the sugar plantations of north **Queensland**. Large-scale Italian **immigration** to Australia began in 1951, with **Sydney** and **Melbourne** being their preferred areas of settlement. Between 1947 and 1971, the number of Italian-born rose from 33,635 to the postwar peak of 289,477. A total of 566,291 Australians claimed some Italian ancestry at the 1986 **census**. In 1996 there were 238,200 Italian-born in Australia, of whom 42 percent lived in **Victoria**. (*See also* Greeks)

J

JAPAN Australia's commercial relations with Japan began in 1865 with an import of some Australian coal. In 1872 some wool from **New South Wales** was exported to Japan in return for imports of cotton and silk. In 1878 a Japanese delegation came to Australia to arrange to buy wool at auction sales regularly. Some Japanese had already entered Australia before this date because the population census for 1871 records six Japanese living in Australia; before 1866 it was a capital crime to leave Japan. Between 1891 and 1901, the number of Japanese in Australia rose from 461 to 3,601 largely in response to the rise of the pearl fishing and sugar industries in **Queensland** which accounted for 63 percent all Japanese. Nearly all the Japanese were male. With the introduction of the **White Australia Policy**, their numbers declined steadily to 2,257 in 1933 and to 330 by 1947.

Although Australia was suspicious of Japan's military intentions towards the south-west Pacific region after its victory over the Russian Empire in 1905, Japanese ships provided an escort to Australian troops on their way to the Middle East during **World War I**. From the Japanese point of view, Australia was of importance as a potential supplier of raw materials from at least 1928. In that year Nobuturo Umeda approached the government of **Western Australia** about mining **iron ore** from Yampi Sound in the northern part of the state and shipping it to Japan. A company to do this was formed in 1935, but the venture was vetoed by the federal government.

The value of Australian exports (mainly wool, scrap iron and steel, and pig iron) to Japan slowly increased from $14.4 million in 1920 to $34.4 million in 1936, but declined to zero by 1942. An Australian trade commissioner was stationed in Tokyo in June 1935.

In the same year, a Japanese Goodwill Mission visited Australia. A change in Australia's policy on imports to encourage local manufacturing and exports of primary products led to a trade dispute with Japan and its restriction of Australian imports (June 15 to December 27, 1936). One of the main Australian exports had been iron ore, but this was prohibited after 1938 following protests from waterfront workers in **Wollongong**, who objected to its use to help Japan's war in China.

During **World War II**, 21,467 Australians were captured by the Japanese during their conquest of south-east Asia, of whom 7,602 died of disease, brutal treatment, or murder such as on Ambon in 1942 and on Borneo in 1945. Japanese aircraft bombed the Australian towns of **Darwin, Townsville**, and Broome (Western Australia). Japanese submarines sank 17 ships off the Australian coast and launched attacks on **Sydney** and **Newcastle**. Virtually all the Japanese-born were interned and most were deported at the end of the war. In 1945 Australia had 5,569 Japanese prisoners of war. Australian forces were part of the Allied Occupation of Japan. A total of 36,000 Australian soldiers and army nurses took part in the occupation and most were based at Hiroshima. Apart from the usual military tasks, such as weapons disposal and the repatriation of former soldiers, the members of the occupation were encouraged to promote democracy. Contact with the Japanese resulted in the formation of liaisons between Australian soldiers and Japanese women, but the federal government banned their admission into Australia until 1952 when about 200 Japanese "war brides" were admitted.

From 1950 significant **trade** began again between Australia and Japan with Australia assuming its present role as a supplier of raw materials, particularly **coal** and iron ore, for Japanese industry. In 1957 the two countries signed a most favored nation treaty, and by 1966 Japan had replaced **Britain** as Australia's largest trading partner. In 1976 Australia and Japan signed a treaty of friendship. Although the basis of the relationship continued to be Australia's supply of raw or semi-processed materials, there has been a marked growth in **tourism** to Australia by the Japanese in the late 1980s. Between 1986 and 1996 the number of Japanese in Australia rose from 11,200 to 23,000 of whom 15,600 lived in New South Wales and Queensland.

JEWS   Jews have been present in Australia since the beginning of European settlement in 1788. It is believed that between eight and

14 members of the **First Fleet** were Jews. Until the 1930s most Jews came to Australia as part of the stream of British immigration. By 1901 there were 15,239 Jews in Australia, the largest non-Christian denomination. In 1938-39 between 7,000 and 8,000 German Jews were admitted to Australia as refugees. Although a small minority, remarkable Australians have emerged from the Jewish community. **John Monash**, who was of German-Jewish parents, was Australia's ablest general during **World War I**. Two Jews have occupied the post of **governor-general**, Sir Isaac Isaacs (1855-1948), from 1931 to 1936, and Sir Zelman Cowen (1919-), from 1977 to 1982. Until 1981 Judaism was Australia's largest non-Christian religion, but has since been overtaken by **Islam**. In 1996 Judaism claimed 79,800 adherents with 88 percent of them living in **New South Wales** and **Victoria**. In 1996 only 0.4 percent of Australians were Jews. (*See also* Table 17 in Appendix 3)

JINDYWOROBAKS   The Jindyworobaks was an Australian nationalist literary movement formed in 1938 by a poet, **Rex C. Ingamells**. The term "jindyworobak" was taken from an **Aboriginal** language meaning to annex or to join. The movement drew inspiration from D. H. Lawrence, who visited Australia in 1922 and lived for a time near **Wollongong**, the Australian writer Percy Reginald Stephensen (1901-1965), and used the Aborigines and the Australian landscape as source material for art and **literature**. One of the poets of the movement was Ian Mudie (1911-1976). (*See also* Angry Penguins; Australia First Movement)

K

KANAKAS Kanakas was the term applied to the 60,000 Melanesian indentured laborers brought to Australia to work on cotton and sugar plantations in tropical **Queensland** from 1863 to 1904. The term comes from a Hawaiian word for man, and its first recorded use was in 1836 when it was claimed that Melanesians discharged from American and British **whaling** ships supplied half of the crews of Australian whalers. Between 1842 and 1847 Melanesians from Fiji were brought in as laborers in **New South Wales**, but the experiment failed. In 1863 the Sydney merchant, Captain Robert Towns (1794-1873) imported 67 Melanesians to grow cotton in Queensland to profit from the disruption to cotton supplies caused by the American Civil War, but with the ending of the war, the

Australian cotton industry was unable to compete with the resumption of American cotton exports.

In 1864 Louis Hope (1817-1894) used 54 Melanesians to found the sugar industry in Queensland, thus beginning the regular recruitment by contract of Melanesians from the New Hebrides, the Solomon Islands, and, later, New Guinea. By 1890 about 47,000 Melanesians had worked in Queensland at some time. The largest number at any one time was in 1891 when there were 10,037 (9,116 males and 921 females). It has been estimated that about a quarter of all the Kanakas who came to Australia were tricked or forced into coming.

The system drew criticism from those who saw the Melanesians as a threat to European living standards and by others who saw it as a form of slavery as evidenced by the high death rate on some ships. In 1901 the new federal government banned the importing of Kanakas after 1904 as part of the **White Australia Policy**. The law was amended in 1906 to allow the older Melanesians to remain. Of the 5,000 in Australia at the end of 1906, 3,642 were returned to Pacific islands and others were settled on Moa, an island in Torres Strait.

KANGAROOS AND WALLABIES   Kangaroos are Australia's best known large marsupials. They have strong tails, large powerful hind legs, and small fore-limbs. They move by hopping and are well adapted to grassy plains. The word "kangaroo" is Aboriginal and was first used in 1770; its present spelling dates from 1788. Wallabies are smaller versions of kangaroos. They were first described by the Dutch navigator François Pelsaert (c.1591-1630) in **Western Australia** in 1629. There are 17 families of kangaroos and wallabies, making up about 50 species in all.

Kangaroos have been part of the coat of arms of the federal government since 1908 and of **New South Wales** since 1906. They were depicted on the reverses of Australian pennies and half-pennies from 1939 to 1966. They also have been widely used as symbols of Australia such as on the aircraft used by **Qantas**.

The larger species of kangaroo are numerous and treated by farmers as a pest. The smaller kangaroo and wallaby species are under threat from urban development of native habitats. In 1980, 12 species of kangaroo and wallaby were classified as endangered. In 1990 it was estimated that there are least 18 million kangaroos of all species. The most common type is the Red kangaroo of which there are about 10.5 million, followed by the Eastern Gray (4.9 million), and the Western Gray (2.6 million). In March 1993 it became legal to sell and serve kangaroo meat for human consumption in New South Wales. (*See also* Environment)

KEATING, PAUL JOHN (1944-   ) Australian **prime minister**, of Irish-Catholic background Keating was born and educated in **Sydney**. He began his working life as a research officer with the Federated Municipal and Shire Council Employees' Union. He joined the **Australian Labor Party** (ALP) at 15 in 1959 and became president of the New South Wales Youth Council of the ALP in 1966. His political education included an association with the former **New South Wales** ALP **premier Jack Lang** as well as serving as president of the New South Wales branch of the ALP (1979-83). In 1969 he was elected to the **house of representatives** for the outer Sydney suburban electorate of Blaxland.

Keating served as minister for northern Australia in the **Whitlam** government for six weeks before it was dismissed in November 1975. While in opposition, he was shadow minister for minerals and energy (1976-80) and resources and energy (1980-83) until becoming spokesman on treasury matters on January 14, 1983. After the victory of the ALP in the federal elections on March 11, 1983, Keating became treasurer of the **Hawke** government and, with Hawke, its principal policymaker. He oversaw the progressive deregulation of the financial system, the floating of the Australian dollar, and reforms of the taxation system. His close association with the **Australian Council of Trade Unions** was important in maintaining the **Accord**.

Personal and policy differences between Keating and Hawke led Keating to resign as treasurer on June 3, 1991, after losing a challenge for the position of prime minister by 66 to 44 votes. A second challenge, on December 19, 1991, was won by Keating by 56 to 51 votes. Keating became prime minister on December 20, 1991. As prime minister Keating continued the previous policies of Hawke with their emphasis on maintaining close relations with the organized sections of the electorate, specifically large corporations, **labor unions**, and other interest groups such as the financial sector. These policies made him unpopular with the traditional supporters of the ALP. Remarkably, in the campaign for the elections on March 13, 1993, he retained office by campaigning hard against the proposed introduction of a general goods and service tax by the **Liberal Party**. Accused of being arrogant and aloof, his personal popularity continued to decline along with the lackluster performance of the Australian **economy**. Keating continued as prime minister until March 11, 1996, after the crushing defeat of the ALP on March 2, 1996. He resigned from federal parliament shortly afterward.

KELLY, "NED" [EDWARD] (1855-1880) Ned Kelly was Australia's most famous **bushranger**. He was born at Beveridge, **Victoria**, of **Irish** parents. His father, John ("Red") Kelly had been transported to Van Diemen's Land (**Tasmania**) in 1841 as a **convict**. Growing up in a criminal environment, Ned Kelly's life of crime began at the age of 14. He was arrested first in 1869, again in 1870 (when he spent some time with another bushranger, Harry Power), and was arrested a third time later in 1870 when he was convicted and jailed. Released in 1871, he was arrested a fourth time for cattle theft, beaten brutally by the police, and jailed for three years. In 1878 Kelly's mother was arrested and sentenced to three years' hard labor. Kelly's gang moved into large-scale cattle stealing and then bank robbery. In the course of the "Kelly outbreak," Kelly killed three troopers. Finally, the gang was captured at Glenrowan in north-central **Victoria**, and Kelly, who survived the bullets of the police by wearing body armor, was hanged.

Even in his lifetime, Ned Kelly became a legend and, after his death, a folk hero. As a symbol of defiance against brutal injustice, he has been of continual interest to artists. One of Australia's earliest feature **films** was made about him in 1906 and Mick Jagger played him in another film in 1970. The artist **Sidney Nolan** painted his notable *Ned Kelly* series between 1947-48.

KENEALLY, THOMAS MICHAEL (1935-) Novelist, Keneally was born in **Sydney**. He at first intended to become a priest, but left and worked as a schoolteacher. He published his first novel, *The Palace at Whitton*, in 1964 which he followed with *Bring Larks and Heroes* in 1967. He has won many literary awards, most notably the Booker McConnell fiction prize in 1982 for *Schindler's Ark*, which was later made into the film *Schindler's List* by Steven Spielberg. His novel, *The Chant of Jimmie Blacksmith* (1972) was made into a film in 1978. For his work, Keneally has received honorary degrees from Australian, Irish, and American universities. Along with his considerable literary output, Keneally is also well known for his leading role as a supporter of Australian **republicanism**. (*See also* Literature)

KINGSFORD SMITH, CHARLES [EDWARD] (1897-1935) One of Australia's greatest aviators, Kingsford Smith was born in **Brisbane, Queensland**. After service in the Australian Flying Corps during **World War I**, he set up his own aviation company in 1924. With Charles Ulm (1898-1934), he carried out a series of pioneering flights. In January 1927 he and Ulm set a new record for flying between **Perth** and **Sydney**. Between May 31 and June 9, 1928, he and Ulm made the first flight across the Pacific when they flew from Oakland, California, to Brisbane with stopovers at Honolulu and Suva, Fiji. Knighted in 1932, Kingsford Smith is believed to have crashed into the Bay of Bengal on his way to Britain.

KOREA Although there was a tiny amount of **trade** between Australia and Korea in the 1900s, and 153 Koreans were enumerated by the Australian **census** in 1901, modern relations did not begin until July 6, 1950, when the Australian government decided to send ground, air, and naval forces to Korea as a contribution to the United Nations forces resisting the invasion from communist North Korea (1950-53). Over 15,000 Australians took part in the war: 339 were killed and 1,216 were wounded. The war more than doubled Australian **sheep and wool** prices, largely as a result of American demand.

Since 1965 when the first trade agreement was signed between Australia and South Korea (the Republic of Korea), the two countries have become significant trading partners. In 1989 the Republic of Korea's president Roh Tae Woo visited Australia and **prime minister Hawke** made a reciprocal visit to the Republic of Korea. During the 1990s Australian-Korean relations continued to expand. There was Korean interest in the Australian **Accord** as a way of improving labor relations. The number of Koreans living in Australia has grown from 468 in 1971 to 4,701 in 1981 and to 20,997 in 1991. In 1996 there were 30,088 Koreans in Australia, including 21 from North Korea, and 72.8 percent of them live in **New South Wales**. In 1997-98 Korea accounted for 7.3 percent of Australian exports (compared to 4.3 percent in 1987-88) and 4.1 percent of Australian imports (compared to 2.5 percent in 1986-88). Korea is the third largest market for Australia's merchandise exports (mainly mining and agricultural products) after **Japan** and **New Zealand**.

L

LABOR DELEGATIONS On two occasions in the twentieth century the Australian government has sent delegations by representatives of the government, the **labor unions**, and the **employers' associations** to visit other countries and report on what lessons could be learned about their labor relations that might be applied to Australia. The first labor delegation visited the **United States** between February and August 1927. It conducted a comprehensive inquiry into American labor relations, the efficiency and methods of industrial production, unemployment, working conditions, welfare, and the employment of women. The representatives of the unions and the employers produced separate reports of their findings in their report to the federal parliament. A correspondent with the delegation, Hugh Grant Adam (1890-1950), the associate editor of the Melbourne *Herald*, published an account of his impressions entitled *An Australian Looks at America: Are Wages Really Higher?* in late 1927. The work of the delegation had no real influence on government policy and it was overtaken by the Depression.

The second government-sponsored labor delegation from Australia was made to Sweden, a country then considered to have important policy lessons for Australia. From this delegation, the **Australian Council of Trade Unions** produced a report *Australia Reconstructed* in 1987. Like its predecessor, this report failed to influence government policy.

LABOR DISPUTES Labor disputes, whether initiated by employers (lockouts) or **labor unions** (strikes), have always been a feature of the Australian **economy** and society. Strikes have been legal in Australia since 1825. Strikes occurred at least as early as 1829. They have been especially prominent in **coal** mining, the **sheep and wool** industry, and on the waterfront. Coal mining in **New South Wales** has accounted for an excessive number of labor disputes since 1860.

High levels of economic growth from the **gold** rushes from 1850 to 1890 and British **immigration** encouraged the rise of labor unions and often led to successful strikes for higher pay. However, the confidence of organized labor was severely dented by the failure of the **Maritime Strike** in 1890. Since 1890 major disputes occurred in 1912 (**Brisbane**), 1917 (**New South Wales** and **Victoria**), 1929, 1949 (coal mining), and 1974.

Statistics on labor disputes have been maintained by the federal government since 1913. They show that, in common with other Western economies, there was a high level of labor disputes in the inflationary period between 1913 and 1920. Strikes were also at a high level between 1926 and 1930. They declined along with the strength of the labor unions during the 1930s, but rebounded between 1946 and 1950. The other period of high strike activity was during the early 1970s, another period of high inflation. **Mining** has made a disproportionately large contribution to strikes in Australia, accounting for about a fifth of all working days lost through strikes between 1981 and 1996. Contrary to popular belief, wages are only the single largest cause of labor disputes during periods of high inflation. Since the early 1980s to the early 1990s the level of labor disputes has been historically low, which most commentators have attributed to the **Accord**, as well as to wider changes in the **economy** and the **labor force**.

Compared to other Western countries, Australia often seems a country with a particularly high level of labor disputes, but this impression is misleading. First, relatively more effort is put into the collection of these statistics in Australia than in many other countries with the result that many strikes go unrecorded elsewhere. Second, there are often legal barriers to strikes in other countries which do not generally apply in Australia. Third, despite International Labor Organisation recommendations on what labor disputes to collect, these are not always followed by member nations.

Official surveys of Australian workplaces in 1990 and 1995 found that the proportion that experienced no labor disputes in the previous 12 months rose from 72 to 78 percent. Of those workplaces that experienced labor disputes, the industries most affected were mining, education, and transportation and storage.

Because of the close links between the labor unions and the **Australian Labor Party**, particular labor disputes can easily assume a political aspect. The coal miners' strike in 1949 helped to bring down the **Chifley** government. The attempt by the **Howard** government to change work practices on the waterfront led to a lengthy labor dispute with the Maritime Union of Australia in early 1998. (*See also* Table 34 in Appendix 3)

LABOR FORCE The labor force refers to the labor component of the **economy**. Since 1891 about 60 percent of the population aged over 15 has been in the labor force. Up to the 1820s **convicts** were the core of the labor force in Australia, but by the 1840s the labor force was mainly free. **Agriculture** dominated the employed labor force up to the 1940s, accounting for about a quarter of the total. **Mining** employment exploded as a result of the **gold** rushes in the 1850s and employed 19.4 percent of the labor force in 1861, but from then on declined, falling to 11.4 percent in 1871, although in 1901 it accounted for 7.3 percent of the labor force.

Manufacturing employment lagged for much of the nineteenth century, being relatively small scale and geared to the demands of the domestic market. In 1901 it accounted for 11.7 percent of the employmed labor force, the same level as in 1881. Manufacturing employment was boosted by the demands of the two world wars. By 1941 it had overtaken agriculture as the largest employer with 24.9 percent of the employed labor force. By 1961, 28.2 percent of the employed labor force worked in manufacturing, but this level could not be sustained and by the end of the decade manufacturing employment had begun to decline because of its internal weaknesses, and from the 1970s because of the reduction in federal government **protection**.

Because of the relative weakness of manufacturing, employment in the **services** sector (the services sectors are all other economic sectors other than agriculture, mining, and manufacturing) was high. In 1901, 56.8 percent of the employed labor force worked in the services sector. Since 1961 this proportion has risen steadily. In August 1998 81.1 percent of the employed labor force worked in the services sector compared to 12.9 percent in manufacturing, 5 percent in agriculture, and 1 percent in mining.

These shifts in the industry distribution of the labor force have also changed the distribution of the status of the employed labor force, that is, the proportions who were employers, self-employed or employees. The decline of agriculture lowered the proportion of employers who made up about 11 percent of the labor force from 1891 to 1911 to half this figure in the post-1947 period. The proportion of the labor force who were self-employed was 15.8 percent in 1901, which grew to 17 percent in 1921, and slowly declined to 7.2 percent in 1971. But since 1971 the proportion of self-employed has risen in response to changed economic conditions, particularly redundancies and the growth of consultants. Employees have always been by far the largest single group within the Australian labor force, accounting for 80 percent of the labor force since 1947.

The Australian labor force was heavily male-dominated before the early 1930s. Between 1891 and 1933, women made up only 20 percent of the total. The growth of manufacturing and clerical employment brought with it a rise in female employment. Between 1947 and 1966 females increased their share in the labor force from 22.4 to 29.5 percent, but since that time women—particularly married women—have entered the labor force in far higher numbers. By 1986, 39.5 percent of the labor force was made up of women and by August 1998 this figure had risen to 43 percent.

Until 1947 the Australian labor force was dominated by blue-collar occupations. Between 1891 and 1947 the proportion of the labor force in these occupations fell from 81.2 to 67.3 percent and has continued to fall ever since. By August 1998 only 33.6 percent of Australians worked in blue-collar jobs. In contrast, the proportion of Australian workers in white-collar jobs has been continually rising over the past century; from 18.8 percent in 1891 to 67.2 percent in August 1998. Growth in white-collar jobs has been particularly marked since 1947. Of these white-collar jobs, about half can be classed as information or knowledge-based, in response to the growth in the maturity of the economy.

The growth of part-time employment has also been a feature of the Australian labor force since 1966. In August 1966 only 9.8 percent of the Australian labor force worked part-time (that is, less than 35 hours a week), but by August 1998 this had risen to 25.9 percent. In August 1966 24 percent of women worked part-time compared to 3.7 percent of men, but in August 1998, 43.6 percent of women were part-time workers compared to 12.1 percent of men.

Unemployment (those members of the labor force without work) has always been an aspect of the Australian labor force in depressed periods such as the 1840s, 1890s, and 1930s, in common with other Western economies. One consequence of high unemployment was that federal governments reduced assisted **immigration**. Between 1901 and 1928, the annual average unemployment rate was 4.8 percent, varying from a low of 3.3 percent in 1914 to a high of 9.4 percent in 1904. It reached its height at the worst part of the Depression in 1931-32 when it was 21 percent, but fell steadily from 1936; indeed the unemployment rate in the late 1930s was lower than in the 1920s, despite the reputation of the 1920s as a decade of prosperity. "Full" employment or the absence of large numbers of unemployed was a feature of the Australian labor force from 1942 to 1973. In this period, the average annual unemployment rate was 1.9 percent.

After 1973 unemployment reappeared as a social and economic issue. As with other countries, it was mainly a feature of young entrants to the labor force, but then it spread to older workers, particularly those retrenched from manufacturing. In the 1990s unemployment has grown among white-collar workers as a result of retrenchments in banking, insurance, and finance, and in government employment. In 1992-93, unemployment reached its post-1945 high of 11 percent, the highest rate since 1936 (11.7 percent), but has declined slowly since then. In August 1998 the unemployment rate was 7.9 percent (8.3 percent for men, 7.2 percent for women).

Before 1940 the **census** was the primary source of statistics about the labor force. Other sources included manufacturing and government employment statistics collected by the **states**. The introduction of payroll taxation in 1941 generated statistics which could be used to monitor employment, but the disadvantage with this source over time was its susceptibility to changes in the law about the size of firms liable to pay the tax. In 1960 the Commonwealth Bureau of Census and Statistics, the forerunner to the present Australian Bureau of Statistics, began a labor force survey based on the U.S. model. At first this survey was confined to the capital cities, but from August 1966 it was conducted on a national basis. Since February 1978 it has been conducted monthly and is the means for collecting a wide range of regular labor data as well as conducting supplementary surveys of particular topics of interest. (*See also* Tables 30 to 32 in Appendix 3)

LABOR PARTY (*See* Australian Labor Party)

LABOR UNIONS   Labor unions have long occupied an important place in Australian history. In 1891 about 23 percent of Australian employees were members of labor unions, the highest level in the world at that time. During the twentieth century the proportion of employees who were members of labor unions has generally been high until the 1980s. Unions also play a central political role in Australia. They have been the basis of the **Australian Labor Party** (ALP) since its foundation in 1891.

The first labor unions in Australia arose among shipwrights in 1829 but it was not until after the gold rushes in the 1850s that organized labor became more important. Before the 1880s most unions were formed by employees in a limited range of occupations, but in the 1880s there was an upsurge of "new" unionism, which embraced a wider range of occupations. By 1890 there were about 200,000 union members. Between 1878 and 1900 the seven colonies which then made up Australia passed laws that recognized labor unions. In 1879 the labor unions held their first inter-colonial congress in **Sydney**; subsequent congresses were held in 1884, 1886, 1888, 1889, 1891, and 1898.

Between August and December 1890, 50,000 workers took part in the great **Maritime Strike** over freedom of contract; the strikers suffered defeat. Between July and September 1894 the unions suffered a second major setback as a result of the wool shearers' strike in **Queensland**. The depression of the early 1890s, which was aggravated by a severe **drought**, retarded economic growth and caused union membership to fall to 97,000 (or about 9 percent of employees) in 1901.

The unions also used politics to improve their position. Following the introduction of public payment of a salary to members of parliament in **New South Wales** in 1889, the Sydney Trades and Labour Council resolved to support "labor" candidates, a decision which resulted in the election of 35 "labor" members to parliament at the 1891 election, an event which marked the birth of what later was called the Australian Labor Party. Assisted by the introduction of compulsory **conciliation and arbitration** as a means of settling **labor disputes**—a system which eased the process for unions to collectively bargain with employers by granting them legal recognition—union membership rose to 498,000 or 34 percent of employees in 1913, again giving Australia the highest density level of union membership in the world.

As in other countries, white-collar unions began to organize during the 1900s, but most union members continued to be predominantly male blue-collar employees. With the establishment of the **Federated Miscellaneous Workers' Union** in 1915, the structure of organized labor remained relatively unchanged until the late 1980s. Between 1920 and 1970 New South Wales accounted for about 40 percent of Australia's union members, **Victoria** for about 25 percent and Queensland for about 15 percent. Since 1980 the share of union members in New South Wales has fallen steadily from 37.0 percent in 1982 to 33.4 percent in 1996. This decline accounts for nearly half of the total decline in labor union membership in this period.

Australian labor unions have been a mixture of large and small organizations since the 1890s, but since the 1970s the number of unions with very small memberships has fallen markedly. Between 1913 and 1996 the proportion of unions with less than a thousand members fell from 80 to 47 percent. The number of labor unions has also declined from a peak of 432 in 1913 to 305 by 1970 and 205 by

1990. The proportion of union members in unions with less than 10,000 members fell from 15 to 6 percent between 1970 and 1996. From 1987 to 1996 the **Australian Council of Trade Unions** and the federal **Hawke** government have encouraged the amalgamation of unions, but the **Howard** government reversed this policy and has tried to promote the growth of smaller unions.

Since 1913 union membership rose and fell according to the state of the economy and the distribution of employment by industry. Unionism was strongest among blue-collar workers and skilled tradesmen. It was weakest among casual employees and white-collar workers. As a proportion of employees, unions reached their height in Australia in 1953 when 63 percent of employees were members. Between 1970 and 1997 the structure of union membership in Australia was changed by the rising proportion of women members (up from 24.4 to 40.4 percent) and the growth in government employment; its share of union membership rose from 23 to 42 percent.

In August 1997 an official household survey of the weekly earnings of employees found that there were 2,110,300 union members which represented 30.3 percent of employees. As in the previous surveys conducted from 1982, the largest divide in union penetration was between the public and private sectors. In 1997, 54.7 percent of public sector employees were union members compared to 23.3 percent in the private sector. (*See also* Australian Workers' Union; Hawke, Robert James Lee; Hughes, William Morris; Labour Day; Labor Disputes; Labor Force; Table 32 in Appendix 3)

LABOUR DAY Previously known as Eight Hour Day, this public holiday grew out of the campaign by **labor unions** in the 1850s for an eight-hour workday. Celebrated on the first Monday in March in **Western Australia** and **Tasmania**, the first Monday in May in **Queensland**, the first Monday in October in **New South Wales** and **South Australia**, and the second Monday in March in **Victoria**, Labour Day was marked by mass marches of labor union members in the cities and larger towns from the 1880s to the 1940s, but has faced rivalry from communist-dominated labor unions which favored May 1 for marches. Since the 1960s Labour Day has lost all of its original significance and is just another public holiday.

LAND SETTLEMENT As in the Americas, the lure of becoming a large landowner was a powerful attraction for immigrants to

Australia and, despite the dryness of much of the land, land hunger was a general aspiration in nineteenth-century Australia. Consequently, the process of land settlement in Australia was a central feature of its history in the nineteenth century and continued to be important in the first third of the twentieth century. Because of its isolation and sparse European population before 1830, **colonial governors** had the power to make grants of land to individuals as a reward for services to the colony, such as increasing its food supply or by aiding its economy. Before arriving in Australia, the leader of the **First Fleet** and the first colonial governor, Captain Arthur Phillip, was given the power to grant land to **emancipists** so they could support themselves since they had little likelihood of returning to **Britain**. In 1789 Phillip was given the power to make land grants to free settlers.

Once the hinterland had been opened up and large numbers of free settlers began arriving after 1820, this system began to break down. It was challenged by **squatting** (the illegal occupation of land) and by the need for the British government to recoup part of the large cost of running its Australian colonies. Under the Ripon regulations of 1831 the governors were told that henceforth all land was to be auctioned at five shillings (50 cents) an acre. This began a policy of reliance on land sales as a primary source of government revenue. In the law that set up the colony of **South Australia** in 1834 all land was to be sold at a minimum price of 12 shillings ($1.20) an acre to pay for the development and to raise money to assist further **immigration**. In 1840 the **New South Wales** governor, Sir George Gipps (1791-1847) fixed a minimum price of one pound ($2) per acre for land in the infant colony of **Victoria**.

The lure of the inland for pastoral use caused a land rush. By 1850 sheep and cattle ranchers had occupied the eastern half of the present state of New South Wales, virtually all of Victoria, most of the south-eastern parts of South Australia and **Queensland**. The 1850s and 1860s saw conflict between the squatters and the less-well off who wanted land. The newly created colonial governments tried to accommodate their wishes through what was called "closer settlement" legislation based on **free selection**.

There was a second great wave of land occupation between 1850 and 1890 based on **sheep** and **wheat** farming. By the end of this wave, the boundary of European occupation covered almost all of eastern Australia and about half of the area of **Western Australia**. The occupation of the land really only stopped when the deserts were reached in the interior or because the terrain was too rugged as in western **Tasmania**.

However well intentioned, land sale policy could not escape the dry reality of much Australian land. Attempts to settle more farmers on the land only worked in areas which were relatively well watered. Where the limits of settlement were overreached as they were by the early 1890s, severe **drought** brought devastation to thousands in **agriculture**. Nevertheless, governments refused to accept either the limitations imposed by Australia's low and variable rainfall or economic truths. Using the United States as a model, Australia was regarded as infinitely bounteous.

In the twentieth century, policies to encourage land settlement were directed at war veterans of **World War I**. Those veterans settled on the land between 1915 and 1929 often had a difficult time making a living, largely because of falling prices for agricultural products after the boom of 1918 to 1920. An investigation in 1929 of 37,561 soldier settlers found that 29 percent had left their farms.

The policy continued after **World War II**, although the demand was less. By 1954 a total of 21,428 applications had been made for cheap loans to assist veterans to become farmers and of these, 15,950 were approved. The largest endeavor to promote land settlement was based on the irrigation of the south-east interior made possible by the **Snowy Mountains Scheme**. The last important project used by governments to promote land settlement was the Ord River Scheme in northern **Western Australia** in the 1960s. Since then Australian governments, both federal and state, have grudgingly given greater attention to the economics of land settlement and environmental considerations in their preparation of land settlement policies.

LANG, JACK [JOHN THOMAS] (1876-1975)   Lang was twice **premier** of **New South Wales** and one of its most controversial politicians. Born in **Sydney**, he was elected to the New South Wales parliament in 1913 for the Sydney suburban electorate of Granville for the **Australian Labor Party** (ALP). He was a member of the New South Wales parliament until 1946. He was an anti-conscriptionist during **World War I** and in 1923 became leader of the ALP in New South Wales.

His first term as premier from May 30, 1925, to October 7, 1927, was notable for two pioneering initiatives in **social security**: child endowment and widows' pensions. His second term as premier from

October 25, 1930 to May 13, 1932, was dominated by the Depression.

Lang's populist economic policies, which included a reduction in the interest rate on Australia's large overseas borrowings, were opposed by the federal ALP government of **James Scullin** and even more so by its successor, the conservative **United Australia Party** government of **Joseph Lyons**. Lang's attempt to resist federal law over the collection of money claimed by it for interest charges led to his dismissal by the New South Wales governor, Philip Woolcott Game (1876-1961), but privately the two men remained friends for many years. Lang's government was defeated at the June 1932 New South Wales election. Lang lost his leadership of the New South Wales ALP to William McKell (1891-1985) in 1939 and in 1943 was expelled from the ALP for opposing the federal ALP government of **John Curtin** over **conscription**. He was readmitted to ALP membership in 1971, having outlived his enemies and become a legend in his own lifetime.

LAWLER, RAY [RAYMOND EVENOR] (1921-)   One of Australia's most notable playwrights, Ray Lawler was born in Footscray, **Melbourne**, **Victoria**. In 1955 he achieved international recognition for his play, *Summer of the Seventeenth Doll*. The play, which is set in Melbourne, is based on the relationships between two barmaids and two sugarcane cutters from **Queensland**. Written in Australian idiom, the *Doll* was one of the pivotal events in Australia's post-1945 cultural history. Although Lawler has written other plays, the *Doll* remains the work for which he is best known. (*See also* Literature)

LAWSON, HENRY (1867-1922)   Writer and poet, Lawson was born near Grenfell, **New South Wales**, and grew up in a poor rural environment. He moved to **Sydney** in 1884 and began writing for the ***Bulletin*** by 1887. His further ventures into the rural hinterland of Australia and **New Zealand** were the basis for his short stories, which made him one of the leading Australian writers of the 1890s and 1900s. After the success of *Joe Wilson and His Mates* (1901), Lawson gained a contract with the London publisher, Methuen. Thereafter he fought an increasingly losing battle with alcoholism. He died in poverty but was given a state funeral. (*See also* Literature)

LEGISLATIVE ASSEMBLY The title of most of the lower houses of parliaments in Australian **states** (or **colonies** before 1901) which were created by the granting of self-government to the Australian colonies from 1856. In **Tasmania** and **South Australia**, these legislatures are called the House of Assembly. Because these legislatures were elected directly, it became the convention that the **premier** and the ministers of a government were drawn from the legislative assembly, not the **legislative council**.

LEGISLATIVE COUNCIL The upper house of parliaments in Australian **states** (or **colonies** before 1901). Unlike the **legislative assembly**, the legislative council predated the granting of self-government. The first legislative council was created in 1823 in **New South Wales** and in **Tasmania** in 1828. Based on the idea of the British House of Lords, the membership of legislative councils was originally nominated by the **colonial governor**. In 1842 the legislative council of New South Wales was reformed: 12 of its members were to be nominated by the governor and the remaining 24 were to be elected based on a property qualification for the **franchise**.

With the granting of self-government, the legislative councils became "houses of review," that is, they could amend or reject legislation submitted to them by the legislative assembly. Although the legislative councils were also elected bodies, they required a property qualification in their franchise. This could, and did, create tensions between the two houses. Conflicts between them occurred in **Victoria** in 1867 and in Tasmania in 1924 and 1948. The **Australian Labor Party** sought to get rid of legislative councils on the grounds that they were undemocratic, but succeeded only in **Queensland** where the members of the legislative council voted to abolish themselves in 1922. The restrictions on the franchise for legislative councils were eliminated in Victoria in 1930, **Western Australia** in 1964, Tasmania in 1968, and **South Australia** in 1973. Between 1934 and 1978 the legislative council of New South Wales was entirely nominated, until an elective council was agreed on by a referendum.

LEICHHARDT, [FRIEDRICH WILHELM] LUDWIG (1813-1848) Born in Prussia, Ludwig Leichhardt earned his place in Australian history as a naturalist and explorer. Interested in botany and geology, Leichhardt explored the coastal regions of northern **New South Wales**. In 1844-45 he led a successful expedition from south-eastern **Queensland** to the north of the **Northern Territory** (near modern **Darwin**), an epic and difficult journey which took 14 and a half months and opened up much new land for **sheep** and/or cattle raising and **agriculture**. He made two attempts to cross Australia from east to west (from southeast Queensland to **Perth**, Western Australia) in 1846 and again in 1848. On the second attempt the entire expedition disappeared and its fate has never been established. After his death, Leichhardt's previously high reputation as a competent explorer and leader was tarnished by allegations of inefficiency and inflexibility. An inner **Sydney** suburb was named after him and the story of Leichhardt was used by the Nobel prize winner **Patrick White** for his best-selling novel *Voss* (1957).

LEND LEASE   Lend Lease was a system of mutual aid between the **United States** and its allies during **World War II**. It operated from March 11, 1941, to June 30, 1946. Part of the operation of Lend Lease consisted of several mutual aid agreements. Under Lend Lease the United States provided assistance to Australia of $1.15 billion, of which 39.6 percent was for war materials, 13.7 for transportation equipment, and 12.8 percent for petroleum products. The reciprocal aid provided by Australia was mainly foodstuffs and military clothing. (*See also* World War II)

LEWIS, ESSINGTON (1881-1961)   One of Australia's greatest industrialists, Lewis was born in Burra, **South Australia**. While studying mining engineering, he joined the **Broken Hill Proprietary Company Limited** (BHP) at Broken Hill in 1904 and began his progression up the managerial ladder overseeing **mining** and smelting operations and the construction phase of the **Newcastle** steelworks. He became general manager of the company in 1921, managing director in 1926, and chief general manager in 1938. Lewis's passions were hard work and efficiency, and he did much to improve the company's operations. After visiting **Japan** in 1934, he became alarmed at Australia's lack of military preparation and privately urged greater efforts in this direction to federal politicians. During **World War II**, Lewis played a critical and distinguished role in aircraft and munitions production. He returned to BHP after the war and was chairman of the board of directors from 1950 to 1952. He remained on the board until his death.

LIBERAL PARTY OF AUSTRALIA   The Liberal Party is Australia's most important conservative political party. It was formed by **Robert Gordon Menzies** and others in 1944 in **Victoria** from the former **United Australia Party** and other conservative groups. By 1948 the Party claimed 150,300 members, of whom two-thirds lived in the large cities. Menzies led the Liberals, in coalition with the **Country Party** (the present **National Party**), to a historic victory in the federal elections on December 10, 1949, and remained as **prime minister** until his retirement in 1966. Much of the electoral success of the Liberal Party from the mid-1950s to the early 1970s could be attributed to the favorable economic conditions of this period and to the split in the **Australian Labor Party** (ALP), which produced the breakaway **Democratic Labor Party**, which used the preferential voting system to direct its preferences to the Liberal Party.

The Liberal/Country Parties' success in federal elections from 1949 to 1983 was mirrored by their success in state elections. The Liberal/Country Party coalition governed **New South Wales** from 1965-76 and 1988-95; Victoria (Liberal Party only) from 1955-82 and 1992 to date; **Queensland** from 1957-89 (the Liberals were the junior party in government from 1983 to 1989) and 1996 to date; **South Australia** from 1944-67, 1968-70, 1979-82, and 1993 to date; **Western Australia** from 1959-71, 1974-83, and 1993 to date; and **Tasmania** from 1969-72, 1982-89, and 1992-98.

The unpopularity of the ALP federal government of **Gough Whitlam** in 1975 saw Liberal Party membership rise to 140,000, but with Liberal success in the elections of 1975, 1977, and 1980 membership declined to 103,000 by 1982 and by 1990 had fallen to 69,000. Victoria remained the heart of the Liberal Party with 20,000 members in 1990. In May 1995 the Liberal Party had 70,000 members.

The Liberal Party was defeated in the federal elections of March 5, 1983, and remained out of government largely because of internal disunity until March 2, 1996, when it was returned with a landslide majority under **John Howard** who had been elected leader of the party on January 30, 1995. In the 1996 elections, the Liberal Party gained 38.7 percent of the vote for the **house of representatives**; in the **senate**, it gained 40.7 percent of the vote in coalition with the **National Party**. In the national elections on October 3, 1998 the Liberal Party was re-elected, but with a reduced majority. Its vote for the house of representatives fell to 34.1 percent and to 35.8 percent in the senate (in alliance with the National Party). The Liberal Party is a member of the International Democrat Union and the Pacific Democrat Union. (*See also* Australia Party; Casey,

Richard Gardiner; Country/National Party of Australia; Lyons Forum)

LINDSAY, NORMAN [ALFRED WILLIAM] (1879-1969)   Artist and author, Lindsay was born at Creswick, **Victoria**. He moved to **Melbourne** in 1896 where he tried to make a living as a black and white illustrator. Despite his talent, he failed to succeed in the city's deeply depressed economy and moved to **Sydney** in 1901 where he worked for the *Bulletin*. He became notorious for his studies of nude sirens which offended religious sensibilities, but his fine work encompassed many other subjects including native fauna. Between 1910 and 1912 he furthered his artistic studies in London and Paris. He published his first novel, *A Curate in Bohemia*, in 1913 and went on to publish other works. His novel *Redheap* (1930) which portrayed the place of his birth, aroused the ire of the **censorship** authorities and was banned until 1959. Lindsay is best known today for the remarkable fineness and detail of illustrations and for his classic children's story, *The Magic Pudding*, which was published in 1918. His son Jack Lindsay (1900-1990) was a notable classics scholar and author in Britain.   (*See also* Literature)

LITERATURE   As with other aspects of Australian cultural life, the language and form of Australian literature was transplanted from **Britain**. Although accounts of early Australia were written in other languages, including French and Spanish, the bulk of these writings were in English. However, the utterly different landscape of Australia, and the peculiarities of its history and settlement, eventually gave rise to a different kind of literature. As the **convict** era passed—examined most notably in works like *His Natural Life* (1874) by Marcus Clarke (1846-1881)—the landscape assumed primacy as a subject along with its interaction with the people. Henry Kendall (1839-1882) wrote memorable poetry about the beauty of the natural landscape in the well-watered coastal areas of **New South Wales**.

With the publication of the *Bulletin* in 1880 and its promotion of Australian **nationalism**, Australian literature made a conscious effort to seek a national identity. This time it was found in the **land settlement** of Australia and the struggles of small farmers to make a living in a dry, often hostile, setting or "the bush." It was the landscape for the poetry and prose of **Henry Lawson** and writers like Steele Rudd (1868-1935), who wrote *On Our Selection* in 1899, and was the basis for successful (if inaccurate) film adaptations in the 1930s.

In 1908 the federal government set up the Commonwealth Literary Fund to assist writers, but it provided only limited assistance before 1939. The small size of Australia's population made the business of earning a living difficult for writers and the often provincial mode of thinking, reinforced by **censorship**, did not make for a congenial creative climate. Consequently, many of Australia's best writers have left Australia for varying periods, usually basing themselves in Britain. This **emigration** has been a persistent feature of Australian literature throughout most of the twentieth century.

The 1930s and 1940s saw renewed debate about the direction of Australian literature as seen by the creation of the *Jindyworobaks* and the **Angry Penguins** as well as the founding of literary journals, *Southerly* (1939) and *Meanjin* (1940). Nevertheless, Britain retained a powerful influence over Australian literature. In a much-quoted phrase coined in 1950, the writer and critic A. A. Phillips (1900-1986) referred to the "cultural cringe" of Australian authors towards British and European literature. Part of the reason for the "cultural cringe" was in the domination of the English departments in Australian **universities** by English-born staff. The first chair in Australian literature was not established until 1962 at the University of Sydney.

There are four main national literary awards in Australia: the Miles Franklin Award (1957), the National Book Council/Banjo Award (1974), the Patrick White Award for Literature (1974), and the Australian/Vogel Award (1980).

In 1973 **Patrick White** won the Nobel prize for Literature, the first Australian to do so, and by so doing, greatly enhanced the reputation of Australian literature both and within and outside Australia. White was not the first Australian writer to gain an international reputation, but since his success, other Australian writers, such as **Colleen McCulloch** and **Peter Carey**, seem to have found this path easier. (*See also* Angry Penguins; Archibald, Jules François; *Bulletin;* Carey, Peter; Dennis, Clarence Michael James; Franklin, Miles; Gibbs, Cecilia May; Herbert, Xavier; Ingamells, Rex; Jindyworobaks; Lawler, Ray; Lawson, Henry; Lindsay, Norman; Mackellar, Dorothea; Mcculloch, Colleen; Moorehead, Alan; Pritchard, Katherine Susannah; Richardson, Henry Handel; Slessor, Kenneth; Stead, Christina; Stewart, Douglas; Stow, Randolph; West, Morris; White, Patrick; Wright, Judith)

LONG SERVICE LEAVE   Long service leave is an employment benefit which is unique to Australia. Its origins date from provisions in Victorian and South Australian colonial legislation of 1862 for civil servants with 10 years employment to have up to 12 months paid leave. The Victorian legislation expected that the reason for the leave was to accommodate extended overseas travel such as to Europe. Access to such leave was not automatic but could be granted at the discretion of the governor. The principle of long service leave was adopted by the Commonwealth bureaucracy in 1902. Thereafter, long service provisions spread among public sector employees through the **award** system. In the private sector, long service leave was not granted without employer consent, and by the 1940s only in the brewing and liquor trades was this given.

In 1951 the government of **New South Wales** legislated to make long service leave generally available as a means of reducing labor turnover, rewarding long and faithful service and allowing employees time to recuperate from their work. The New South Wales example was followed by **Queensland** (1952), **Victoria** (1953), **Tasmania** (1956), **South Australia** (1957), **Western Australia** (1958) and the **Northern Territory** and the **Australian Capital Territory** (1961). Typical entitlements are three months of paid leave after 15 years in the private sector or 10 years of continuous service in government employment.

LYONS FORUM   The Lyons Forum is a conservative Christian pressure group in the **Liberal Party of Australia** which was formed secretly in the early 1980s. Named after Dame Enid Muriel Lyons (1897-1981), the wife of **Joseph Lyons**, mother of 12 children and conservative politician (she was the first woman elected to the federal **house of representatives** where she sat from 1943 to 1951), the Forum's policies include support for the traditional family structure, organized **religion**, and opposition to abortion and euthanasia. It has been claimed that the Forum had between 40 and 45 members or sympathizers in the first government of **John Howard** in September 1996, that is nearly a third of the total membership of the federal parliamentary **Liberal Party**. The Forum was credited with increasing government support in the federal budget of August 1996 for **women** with young children who wanted to stay at home rather than go to work.

LYONS, JOSEPH [ALOYSIUS] (1879-1939)   Australian **prime minister**, Lyons was born at Stanley, in north-western **Tasmania** of **Irish**-Catholic descent. He was a schoolteacher before entering Tasmanian politics by winning a seat for the **Australian Labor Party** (ALP) in 1909. He held various ministerial positions before becoming **premier** (1923-28). In the 1929 election he was elected to the **house of representatives** for the electorate of Wilmot and was made postmaster-general and minister for works and **railroads** in the **Scullin** government. He resigned from the government in March 1931 after the return of Edward G. Theodore (1884-1950) to the position of treasurer, following Theodore's clearing of fraud changes over a mining transaction in 1919. With some other members of parliamentary ALP and the **Nationalist Party** parliamentarians, Lyons formed the **United Australia Party** and became prime minister after the defeat of the Scullin government at the elections on December 19, 1931. He was prime minister from October 22, 1932, to April 7, 1939, governing in coalition with the **Country Party**. In office he cut public expenditure substantially and waited for the **economy** to improve. Because of his ALP past, Lyons had not been expected to remain in office long as a conservative leader, but he proved durable and was only removed from office by a fatal heart attack.

M

MABO JUDGMENT   The Mabo Judgment was a landmark decision of the **High Court of Australia** concerning native land title. Brought down on June 3, 1992, the Judgment was the conclusion of a case begun in 1982 by Eddie Mabo (pronounced "Marbo") (1936-1992) and four other indigenous Melanesian residents of Murray Island (or Mer), a tiny island on the eastern approach to Torres Strait, seeking confirmation of their traditional land rights. By a majority of six to one, the Court upheld the Islanders' claim. It recognized that although the British Crown had gained title to the land of Australia in 1788, this action did not wipe out existing native title. In reaching its decision, the Court followed the general approach of courts in the **United States**, **Britain**, Canada, and **New Zealand**. Although of political and symbolic significance, the practical impact of other land claims by Aboriginal and **Torres Strait Islanders** following the Mabo Judgment was expected to be limited because of the strict criteria laid down by the Court to establish such claims and because further test cases were needed to clarify the legal boundaries of native title.

In January 1994 the **Keating** government enacted the *Native Title Act* which was intended to clarify the legal uncertainties caused by the Mabo Judgment and to create a tribunal to hear land claims.

The limitations of the Mabo Judgment for land rights claims by indigenous Australians was made much less certain by the **Wik Decision** in December 1996. On December 11, 1997, the Supreme Court of Canada referred to the Mabo Judgment in a decision concerning a land and mineral right claim by indigenous Canadians.

MACKELLAR, [ISOBEL MARIAN] DOROTHEA (1885-1968)
Poetess and novelist, MacKellar was born in **Sydney** and completed her education at the University of Sydney. In 1908 she published her poem "Core of My Heart" in the London *Spectator*, which she revised and published as "My Country" in *The Closed Door* in 1911. This compelling hymn of praise to the Australian landscape was used widely in Australian secondary schools for decades and is probably the best-known Australian poem. Although she published three novels and four collections of poetry before 1926, they failed to have the impact of her earlier work.

MACQUARIE, LACHLAN (1762-1824) Macquarie was colonial governor of **New South Wales** from January 1, 1810, to November 30, 1821; his time in this office is generally considered one of the formative periods in Australian history. He was born on Ulva, an island in the Inner Hebrides, and arrived in New South Wales with his own regiment, the 73rd, after the **"Rum Rebellion."** Despite the large influx of **convicts** during his term in office, Macquarie tried to run New South Wales more as a colony than as simply an outdoor jail. He had virtually complete powers as governor and used them to govern as a benign autocrat. He used the convicts to build **roads** and public buildings and founded the towns of Liverpool, Bathurst, Penrith, and Cambelltown. He was sympathetic towards the **Aborigines** and tried to elevate the social standing of **Emancipists**, a policy which earned him the dislike of the wealthy free settlers and large landowners (the "Exclusives"). Macquarie was also concerned to elevate the public morals of the colony and to this end encouraged marriage, keeping the Sabbath, and **education**. During his term as governor, the barrier of the Blue Mountains west of **Sydney** was finally removed when they were successfully crossed in 1813, an event which opened the hinterland to **agriculture** and **sheep** and/or cattle raising. Towards the end of his office, his policies ran counter to the new private sector ideology developing in Britain. His activities were criticized in the **Bigge Reports**. Macquarie University, which was opened in northern Sydney in 1964, was named in his honor.

MANNIX, DANIEL (1864-1963) Catholic archbishop and a leader of the Catholic community in Australia, Mannix was born in Ireland and studied at St. Patrick's College, Maynooth. He came to **Melbourne** in 1913 as coadjutor archbishop in 1913 and became archbishop of Melbourne in May 1917, a position held until his death. He quickly assumed the role of leader of Australian **Catholicism**. He sought greater economic justice for Catholics, criticized freemasonry, marriages with non-Catholics, artificial birth control, and later, communism and Nazism. He became nationally prominent in his opposition to **conscription** (1916, 1917) during **World War I** and British policy in Ireland. In the 1940s and 1950s he encouraged the leader of the Catholic Studies Movement, Bartholemew A. Santamaria (1915-1998) to resist and defeat communist influence in the **labor unions**, a policy that led to a major split in the **Australian Labor Party** in 1955 and the creation of the **Democratic Labor Party**. Mannix was also a controversial figure within the Catholic Church. In 1957 the Vatican decided against his view that it was appropriate for Catholics to take separate political action against communism. (*See also* Catholicism)

MANUFACTURING Despite its growth after the 1870s, when it overtook **mining** as an employer, manufacturing still lagged behind **agriculture** as the largest single employer in the Australian economy. In 1911 manufacturing employed 20.6 percent of the labor force, but it was not until the late 1930s that its share of gross domestic product matched that of agriculture. Factories were often small-scale. In 1939, 68 percent of Australia's 26,941 factories employed 10 people or less. Most manufacturing was located in the larger urban centers.

　　World War II stimulated Australian manufacturing as did the postwar years. By 1954 there were 49,576 factories but manufacturing still retained its small-scale character because 71 percent of them employed 10 or fewer employees. Continued growth saw manufacturing contribute 29.9 percent of Australia's gross domestic product by 1961 and employ 28.2 percent of its **labor force**.

Since the mid-1970s manufacturing has declined as a large-scale employer; after 1978 more Australians have been employed in **wholesale and retail trade** than in manufacturing. In August 1991 manufacturing employed 14.4 percent of the employed labor force compared with 28 percent in the 1950s. Between 1982 and 1991, total employment in manufacturing was almost stationary, varying from only 1.1 to 1.2 million, but within manufacturing there have been significant changes in employment. Wood and paper products, publishing and fabricated metal products managed to increase their employment share, but there have been large job losses in the **iron and steel** industry. In August 1997 manufacturing employed 1.1 million people, of whom the largest single group, nearly a quarter, worked in machinery and equipment manufacturing.

Australian manufacturing is generally considered by economists to have suffered from being mainly designed for a small domestic market by policies of **protection** rather than being aimed at the international market. Since the fall in the value of the Australian dollar in 1985, manufacturing exports have increased. In 1997-98, manufacturing accounted for 13.2 percent of Australia's gross domestic product, and 12.9 percent of its employed labor force in August 1998. (*See also* Iron and Steel)

MARITIME STRIKE The Martime Strike was a milestone event in the history of organized labor in Australia. Despite its name, it was actually a series of large, interconnected **labor disputes** which occurred between August and November 1890. It was essentially a power struggle between a **labor union** movement grown confident by five years of unprecedented membership growth and well-organized employers determined to resist the unions' challenge to their authority. The unions' claim for the "closed shop" (that is, for workplaces where the employees were union members) was countered by the employers' principle of "freedom of contract" (that is, their freedom to employ whom they wanted).

The Maritime Strike had two immediate sources: a dispute in the wool shearing industry which began in late 1889 and a dispute between the Mercantile Marine Officers' Association of Australia and New Zealand (formed in 1889 with 187 members) and the shipowners who refused to negotiate with the association after it decided to affiliate with the Melbourne Trades Hall Council, the body representing labor unions in **Victoria**. After the dismissal of a member of the association, it declared a strike which attracted general support from organized labor on the waterfront, in mining and sheep shearing.

The strike soon enveloped **New South Wales**, Victoria, **South Australia**, **Queensland**, and **New Zealand**. British organized labor subscribed 4,000 pounds ($8,000) to support the strike, but the employers were too strong and had the backing of the governments, which used the police and military forces to defeat the strikers. By September 1890 about 50,000 men were estimated to have gone on strike in Australia and about 10,000 in New Zealand. The defeat of the Maritime Strike and other large strikes in wool shearing in 1891 and 1894, combined with the onset of a severe economic depression which was aggravated by **drought**, and greatly reduced union membership and power; between 1890 and 1901 the number of labor union members in Australia fell from 200,000 to 97,000. Within organized labor these defeats encouraged the unions to give greater prominence to politics as a means of achieving their goals and encouraged the formation of the **Australian Labor Party**.

MAY, ROBERT MCCREDIE (1936-) Ecologist, May was born in **Sydney** and studied science at the University of Sydney. He was Gordon Mackay lecturer in applied mathematics at Harvard University from 1959 to 1961. He returned to Australia where he held a succession of posts, culminating in a professorship in theoretical physics, at the University of Sydney, between 1962 and 1973. From 1973 to 1988 May was professor of biology at Princeton University. He made an important contribution to theoretical ecology by the use of models and showed the fragility of diverse environments, such as tropical rain forests to human intervention. (*See also* Environment)

MAYO, [GEORGE] ELTON (1880-1949) Generally regarded as the founder of the "human relations school" in management studies, Mayo was born in **Adelaide**, South Australia, and studied medicine at the universities of Adelaide, Edinburgh, and London. In London, his interest in medicine as a career waned and he became interested in adult education. He returned to Adelaide in 1905 and resumed his studies, this time in philosophy and psychology. In 1911 Mayo became foundation lecturer in mental and moral philosophy at the University of Queensland and held the chair of philosophy there from 1919 to 1923. In 1919 he published his first book, *Democracy and Freedom*. He also worked for the Workers' Educational Association. In 1922 he left Australia for the United States. He received a Rockefeller grant and worked at the Wharton School of the University of Pennsylvania.

Mayo became best known for the experiments he conducted at the Hawthorne plant of the Western Electric Company in Chicago between 1927 and 1932 while professor of industrial research at the Harvard Graduate School of Business. This research drew attention to the importance of informal organization and values among employees. Mayo published *The Social Problems of Industrial Civilization* in 1947. In the same year he retired and went to live in England.

MCCULLOCH, COLLEEN [MARGARETTA] (1937-) Best-selling novelist, McCulloch was born in Wellington, a country town in **New South Wales**, and studied science at the University of Sydney. After qualifying as a neurophysiologist, she worked in Britain for four years. She moved to the **United States** and lectured at the Yale School of Medicine for 10 years. McCulloch published her first novel, *Tim*, in 1974, which was made into a film in 1979 starring Mel Gibson, but the work which won her international renown was *The Thorn Birds*, which was published in 1977 and concerned several generations of an Irish-Australian family on a sheep ranch. This work sold 10 million copies and was made into a mini-series for television starring Rachel Ward and Richard Chamberlain. McCulloch's other novels are *An Indecent Obsession,* (1981) which was made into a film, *A Creed for the Third Millennium* (1985), and a novella, *The Ladies of Missalonghi* (1987). Since then she has moved into historical fiction, specifically the period of the late Roman Republic and the early Roman Empire. She has published a number of novels based on this period including *The First Man in Rome* (1990) and *Caesar* (1997). Since 1980 McCulloch has lived on **Norfolk Island**.

MCEWEN, JOHN (1900-1980) Country Party leader and **prime minister**, McEwen was born at Chiltern, Victoria. He enlisted in the **Australian Imperial Force** and was a farmer before being elected to the **house of representatives** in 1934 and secured his first ministerial portfolio in 1937 when he became minister for the interior, a post he held until 1939. Following the victory of the

Liberal-Country coalition in the elections of December 1949, McEwen became minister for commerce and agriculture, a post he held until 1956 when he became minister for trade, which was expanded to include industry in 1963. In 1958 he succeeded **Arthur Fadden** as leader of the Country Party, in which capacity he was deputy prime minister until his retirement in 1971.

After the presumed drowning of the prime minister, **Harold Holt**, he was caretaker prime minister from December 19, 1967, to January 10, 1968. McEwen maintained the independence of the Country Party within the coalition; for example, he excluded **William McMahon** from becoming prime minister. As a minister from 1958 to 1971, McEwen was responsible for raising **protection** to far higher levels than previously, a policy which has been much criticized later for hampering Australia's economic performance.

MCMAHON, WILLIAM (1908-1990) Australian **prime minister**, McMahon was born in **Sydney**. He was elected to the **house of representatives** for the **Liberal Party** in December 1949. He held various ministerial positions from 1951 onwards, of which the most important were labor and national service (1958-66) and treasurer (1966-69). Under his time as prime minister, from March 10, 1971, to December 5, 1972, a number of important reforms were made that were taken up and expanded by the succeeding **Whitlam** government. These included the setting up of the National Urban and Regional Development Authority, the establishment of an official inquiry into poverty, and the beginning of federal funding of child care. In the federal election of December 1972 McMahon's government was defeated.

MEDIA (*See* Keith Rupert Murdoch, Press, Television)

MELBA, NELLIE (1861-1931) Opera singer Nellie Melba was born Helen Porter Mitchell in Richmond, a suburb of **Melbourne**. Her father was a businessman and she was educated at Presbyterian Ladies' College in Melbourne. She made her debut as a singer in Melbourne in 1884 and moved to London in 1886, but met with no success. She moved to Paris and under the guidance of Mathilde Marchesi, she changed her name to a truncated form of Melbourne. Her performance as Gilda in *Rigoletto* in Brussels in October 1887 began her international career as an opera singer. She made her debut in Paris in 1889 to general acclaim and moved back to London where she was the leading opera singer until 1913. She also sang at the La Scala Opera House in Milan and at the Metropolitan Opera in New York.

In 1902 she made a triumphal tour of all Australian **states** and **New Zealand** and made a second tour in 1909. Melba returned to Australia in 1911 to be head of the Melba-Williamson Opera Company. She went back to London in 1914 and then returned to Australia after the outbreak of **World War I** in August 1914. She made three concert tours of North America to raise money for the Allies. She taught at Melbourne University and in the 1920s divided her time between Australia and **Britain**. She made gramophone recordings from 1904 and made pioneering direct radio broadcasts. In Australia Melba conducted herself in a regal manner. She was made a Dame Commander of the Order of the British Empire and a Dame Grand Dross of the Order of the British Empire in 1927. In her will she left a bequest for a singing scholarship with the Albert Street Conservatorium which she had founded in Melbourne.

MELBOURNE Melbourne is the capital of the state of **Victoria** and has been second largest city in Australia since 1901. Sited on the northern side of Port Phillip Bay, which was explored from the sea in 1802, Melbourne was not settled until 1835 when John Batman (1801-1839) and John Pascoe Fawkner (1792-1869) founded independent settlements on the banks of the Yarra River. Unique for the time, Batman made a treaty with the local **Aborigines** for ownership of 243,000 hectares of land in return for goods and annual tribute. The treaty was revoked by the governor of **New South Wales** Richard Bourke (1777-1855) on the grounds that the land belonged to the Crown. Bourke named the new settlement after the British prime minister, Lord Melbourne, in 1837 and arranged for the site to be surveyed on a regular grid layout. Melbourne was declared a city in 1847.

At first Melbourne's economy depended on the pastoral industry in the surrounding region. By 1851 Melbourne had a population of about 29,000. By 1854 the population had climbed to 76,560 but dropped to 52,500 by 1857 as residents flocked to the newly opened **gold** fields. By 1861 the population had recovered to 125,000, overtaking that of **Sydney** for the first time; Melbourne was Australia's largest city until 1891. By 1861, too, the beginnings of Melbourne's suburbs were evident as well as some of its most enduring institutions. Toorak, where the governor's residence was located from 1854 to 1876, became a socially exclusive area. Emerald Hill, Hotham, Saint Kilda, Essendon, Flemington, and Port Melbourne were all surveyed in the 1850s. The *Age* newspaper was founded in 1854. The University of Melbourne was opened in 1855. The first **Australian Rules** football game was played in 1858.

Until the 1890s, gold-based economic growth brought suburban expansion and investment in water, **roads**, streetcars, **railroads**, and communications. In 1880 the first telephone exchange in Australia was opened in Melbourne; it was privately operated with 44 subscribers. During the 1880s, Melbourne's population grew from 268,000 to 473,000, mainly in the suburbs. The 1880s saw the proportion of the population living in the City of Melbourne area fall from 25 to 15 percent. The prosperity enabled 41 percent of Melbourne's homes to be owner or buyer occupied by 1891. Melbourne was called "marvellous" and acquired the reputation as a brash, American-style city with businessmen alert for any opportunity. In contrast, Sydney was then seen as a slower, conservative place; Sydney's lower population was cited to support these views. Only in its failure to provide a sewerage system was Melbourne seen as inferior to Sydney. Melbourne's first sewerage connection was not made until 1897.

The speculative boom that had supported Melbourne's prosperity collapsed in 1893 with crashes by banks and building societies and a sharp rise in unemployment. Between 1891 and 1901 the population rose by only 6,000 to 478,100, indicating substantial population loss. Many Victorians in this period left to try their luck on the new gold fields of **Western Australia**. Melbourne retained something of its former importance when it was made the home of the new federal government and bureaucracy, which was moved to **Canberra** in 1927.

By the 1930s the reputation of Sydney and Melbourne had been reversed. Now it was Melbourne that was regarded as slow and conservative with Sydney being seen as the more go-ahead city. During **World War II** Melbourne was the Allied headquarters for the South Pacific. In the post-1945 period Melbourne became the home for many thousands of immigrants, particularly **Greeks** and **Italians**. In 1956 Melbourne hosted the **Olympic Games**, the first Australian city to do so. Melbourne became a center for large-scale **manufacturing**. In 1935 General Motors opened a car factory at Fishermen's Bend on the Yarra River, which became a producer of the Holden motor car after 1948. The Ford Motor Company built a large factory at Broadmeadows in 1959. A large petrochemical plant was built at Altona in western Melbourne in 1954-55.

In the 1960s two new universities were opened in Melbourne, Monash University (1961) and La Trobe University (1964). Although Melbourne remains an important center for older large companies, notably **Broken Hill Proprietary Company Limited** and the **Australian Council of Trade Unions**, it had been overtaken by Sydney as Australia's financial capital by 1986. In 1996 Melbourne had a population of 3.1 million.

MELBOURNE CUP   The Melbourne Cup is not only Australia's most important horse race, it is a national social institution. Begun in 1861, the Cup is held on the first Tuesday in November. It is a long race (3.2 kilometers). Many Australians bet on the Cup, but most participate in a "pool" at work or school. Among the horses that have won the Cup, the best remembered are *Phar Lap* (1930), *Rain Lover* (1968, 1969) and *Think Big* (1974, 1975). The Cup is an important occasion in women's fashion; the miniskirt was introduced into Australia at the Cup in 1965. (*See also* Sport)

MENZIES, ROBERT GORDON (1894-1978)   Australia's longest serving **prime minister**, Menzies was born at Jeparit, a country town in **Victoria**. His father and an uncle served as conservative politicians in **state** and federal politics. An outstanding student, Menzies graduated with a first-class honors degree from the University of Melbourne in 1916. He earned his reputation as a brilliant constitutional lawyer in the 1920s. In 1928 he won a seat in the **legislative council** of the Victorian parliament. In 1932 he became minister for railroads, attorney-general, and solicitor-general in the conservative government of Sir Stanley Argyle (1932-34). In 1934 he was elected to the **house of representatives** for the safe, conservative Melbourne electorate of Kooyong.

Following the death of **Joseph Lyons**, Menzies was elected leader of the **United Australia Party** and prime minister, a post he held from April 26, 1939, to August 29, 1941. Party in-fighting and dissatisfaction with his leadership made Menzies' first term as prime minister unstable, particularly after the elections on September 21, 1940, when his government had to depend upon the support of two Independents. While Menzies was absent in Britain, the Independents withdrew their support and the **Australian Labor Party** (ALP) formed a new government under **John Curtin**. During

1941 Menzies and Winston Churchill clashed behind the scenes. The motives of Menzies while in Britain have been the subject of controversy in recent years, but there seems little doubt that for some time at least he was attempting to rebuild his political fortunes there after his reverses in Australia. These maneuvers failed and he returned to Australia.

After 1943 when he again became leader of the United Australia Party, Menzies began to rebuild the conservative political parties. In 1944 he and others formed the **Liberal Party of Australia**, which was designed to represent, in Menzies' words, the "forgotten people," that is the middle class, particularly those who were self-employed. The conservatives made some gains at the federal elections in September 1946, but in the elections on December 10, 1949, they won by a landslide in an enlarged parliament with many new marginal seats.

From 1949 to his retirement on January 26, 1966, Menzies dominated Australian politics. His domination was made possible by the economic prosperity of the 1950s and 1960s and by the split in the ALP in 1955. Menzies was staunchly pro-British in sympathy, but was also a friend of the **United States** as the protector of Australian interests in the Asian region. His period in power was notable for the **Anzus Treaty** in 1951 and the **Petrov Affair** in 1954. Perhaps his greatest achievement was support for **universities** and for **education** generally.

METAL TRADES INDUSTRY ASSOCIATION (MTIA)   The MTIA was one of Australian main **employers' associations**. It was established in 1970, but its origins go back to the Iron Trades Employers' Union, which was formed in **New South Wales** in 1873. In 1990 the MTIA had 7,000 members, mainly in New South Wales and **Victoria**, who collectively employed about 450,000 people, and its annual budget was $10.5 million. In May 1998 the 6,990 members of the MTIA agreed to merge with the **Australian Chamber of Manufactures** to create the Australian Industry Group. (*See also* Amalgamated Metal Workers' Union)

METHODISM   The Methodist Church was established in Australia by meetings of lay followers in 1812. The first Methodist minister arrived in 1815. Wesleyan Methodism was the dominant form of Methodism in Australia. In 1855 the church became independent of British administration. Methodism grew with British **immigration**, particularly from mining areas such as Cornwall (tin), Wales, Durham and Northumberland (coal). The proportion of Methodists in the population rose from 5.6 percent to 13.4 percent between 1851 and 1901. A number of non-Wesleyan churches were formed in this period, notably the Bible Christians, the Methodist New Connexion, the Primitive Methodists, and the United Methodist Free Church, but by 1902 these groups had been united into one church. The Methodist church is traditionally associated with opposition to alcohol and gambling and support for keeping the Sabbath as well as social work through missions. At the 1976 Census there were 983,200 Methodists or 7.3 percent of the population. In 1977, 85 percent of Methodists voted to join with the Presbyterians and Congregationalists to form the **Uniting Church of Australia**. (*See also* Table 17 in Appendix 3)

MINERAL SANDS   Since the early 1970s Australia has been the world's largest producer and exporter of a relatively rare group of minerals extracted from coastal sands. These minerals are rutile, zircon, ilmenite, monazite, leucoxene, and xenotime. Sand mining began on the east coast in 1934 and on the coast of south-eastern **Western Australia** in 1956. Nearly all of the output is exported. Mineral sands have a variety of uses in pigments, ceramics, and other industrial processes. Although the final output from this form of mining is small—only a few thousand tonnes—it is very valuable. In 1994 Australia produced 56 percent of the world's output of zircon and in 1995-96 exports of mineral sands were worth $481 million.

MINING   Mining has been an important industry in Australia since 1850. Up to that time, the only significant mining was of **coal** at **Newcastle**, but only 41,384 tonnes had been extracted there by 1847 under a monopoly granted to the Australian Agricultural Company in 1824. In 1851 the first **gold** rush began and it became the dominant form of mining for the next 20 years, but its role was uneven and capricious. In contrast, coal production climbed steadily from 375,000 tonnes in 1860 to 1,029,000 tonnes in 1872 and continued to rise to meet the needs of a growing urban economy. Sustained copper mining began in 1844. Continuous tin mining began in 1872, zinc mining in 1889, tungsten mining in 1894, silver mining in 1900, and lead mining in 1902. Although some **iron ore** was mined between 1874 to 1877, sustained mining did not begin until 1903. The first bauxite was not mined until 1927, the first **mineral sands** mining did not begin until 1934. Uranium was first found in 1894, but no attempt was made to find significant reserves until 1944 following a request from both **Britain** and the **United States**. Australia is now known to have about 28 percent of the world's low-cost reserves of uranium. The mining of uranium, like that of mineral sands, has aroused opposition from groups concerned about the environment and the potential diversion of Australia's uranium by the receiving countries for nuclear weapons.

Mining was the economic basis for nearly all of the largest non-metropolitan towns in Australia: **Newcastle** and **Wollongong** (coal) and Broken Hill (silver, lead, and zinc) in **New South Wales**; Ballarat and Bendigo in **Victoria** (gold); Mount Isa (lead, zinc, and copper) in **Queensland**; Zeehan (lead and silver) in **Tasmania**; and Kalgoorie and Coolgardie (gold) in **Western Australia**.

Although some of the output from these various mining endeavors was destined for domestic use, exports were always an important aspect of the Australian mining industry even though the share of the output exported has varied considerably. For example, Australia was a major supplier of coal to the Pacific region between 1860 and 1924, but this market fell away and exports did not again become a significant part of the industry until 1953.

Since the 1960s Australia has once more become a major exporter of mining products with much of these exports going to Japan and, from the 1980s, to other parts of the Asia-Pacific region. In 1996-97 mining products accounted for 27 percent of Australia's total exports. Coal made up 10 percent of total exports in 1996-97 and its largest markets were **Japan** (47 percent), the Republic of **Korea** (12 percent), India (8 percent), and Taiwan (7 percent). Gold made up 6 percent of total exports in 1996-97 and its largest market was the Republic of Korea which accounted for 53 percent of gold exports. Iron ore made up 4 percent of total exports in 1996-97 and its three largest markets were Japan (45 percent), the People's Republic of China (21 percent), and the Republic of Korea (13 percent).

The contribution of mining to Australia's gross domestic product has varied. It reached its highest level in 1861 (17.8 percent) and was 11.5 percent in 1901. By 1961 it had fallen to 1.8 percent, but since that time it has recovered strongly. There was a mining boom in the late 1960s based on the discovery of large deposits of iron ore and **nickel**. The mining of mineral sands was given a new lease of life. The boom fueled a surge in the stock market, which had collapsed in the early 1970s. Mining accounted for 8.4 percent of Australia's gross domestic product in 1990-91, although by 1997-98 it had fallen to 3.7 percent, largely in response to changes in global demand and price fluctuations.

As an employer, mining accounted for a peak of 19.4 percent of the employed **labor force** in 1861, a proportion that had fallen to 7.3 percent in 1901. In 1921 mining employed 2.7 percent of the labor force in Australia. Even in 1998 mining employed 1 percent of the Australian labor force. (*See also* Aluminum; Diamonds; Petroleum; Tables 23, 27, 30, 33, and 35 in Appendix 3)

MITCHELL, THOMAS LIVINGSTONE (1792-1855) Born in Craigend, Stirlingshire, Scotland, Mitchell arrived in **New South Wales** as deputy surveyor-general in 1827 and became surveyor-general in 1828. He is mainly remembered for his extensive explorations of the river systems of northern and central New South Wales (1831-32 and 1835-36), **Victoria** (1836) and **Queensland** (1846). A controversial figure because of his insubordination, bad temper, and cruelty towards **Aborigines**, Mitchell was nevertheless a good writer and his published accounts of his travels built his reputation as an important explorer. He was knighted in 1839.

MONASH, JOHN (1865-1931) Generally regarded as Australia's greatest military leader, Monash was born in **Melbourne** to Jewish-Prussian parents from western Poland. He studied arts, engineering, and law at Melbourne University. He became interested in military matters in 1884 and by 1913 was a colonel. He commanded the 4th Infantry Brigade at **Gallipoli** and was made a major-general in 1916. In May 1918 the Australian forces under his command played a major role in the German defeat at the battle of Hamel, using coordinated artillery, tank, and infantry attacks, which helped the Allies break through the Hindenburg Line (September 1918), techniques that anticipated the Germans' use of blitzkrieg during **World War II**. After the war, Monash was made chairman of the State Electricity Commission of Victoria, where he began using brown coal to generate electricity. He was a committed Zionist. Monash University in Melbourne, which was opened in 1961, is named after him.

MOOREHEAD, ALAN [MCCRAE] (1910-1983)   Journalist and author, Moorehead was born in **Melbourne** where he worked for the Melbourne *Herald* newspaper. In 1936 he went to London and during **World War II** was the correspondent for the *Daily Express* which was the basis for his *African Trilogy* (1944). A popular historian he wrote biographies of Winston Churchill and Field Marshall Montgomery, and accounts of the **Gallipoli** campaign, the explorations to find the source of the Nile in the nineteenth century, and the effects of the European intrusion into the Pacific.

MORMONISM   The Mormons, or Church of the Latter Day Saints, first visited Australia in 1840 and some missionaries arrived in **Sydney** in 1851, but the faith made little headway. The **census** shows that there were only 405 Mormons in 1891. Between 1911 and 1947 their numbers rose from 1,088 to 3,499. Thereafter they were not separately identified in the national census until 1981 although a non-census source claims that there were 7,488 adherents by 1961. In 1976 the president of the Mormon Church, Spencer W. Kimball, and other leaders from the **United States** visited Australia for the first time. Since 1981 the number of Mormons in Australia has increased from 32,400 to 38,400 in 1991, and to 45,100 in 1996. Although only 0.3 percent of Australians are Mormons, they are important because of their wealth and because they are one of the few Christian denominations which actively and systematically proselytize for new members. (*See also* Religion)

MURDOCH, [KEITH] RUPERT (1931-)   International media magnate, Murdoch was born in **Melbourne** and educated at Geelong Grammar School and Worcester College, Oxford. His father, Keith Arthur Murdoch (1886-1952) was a correspondent during **World War I**, editor of the Melbourne *Herald*, and, from 1922, owner of the *News*, an afternoon newspaper in **Adelaide**. On the death of his father, he inherited the *News* and was soon embroiled in a war with the other Adelaide press owners. He beat his rivals and bought the *Sunday Times* in **Perth**. In 1960 he bought the *Daily Mirror* in **Sydney** and in 1964 set up the *Australian*, Australia's first daily national newspaper; unlike his other newspapers, it was a money loser for his group for many years.

   In 1969 Murdoch bought the British tabloid newspaper, the *News of the World* and the ailing British *Sun* newspaper and set up News Group Newspapers Limited. He revamped the *Sun* and boosted its circulation to make it into a major earner for his group. In 1972 he bought the Sydney *Daily Telegraph*. In 1973 he bought his first U.S. newspapers in Texas, began a national weekly, the *Star*, and bought the *New York Post* in 1976. In 1981 he bought the London *Times*, Britain's most prestigious newspaper, but then in financial trouble.

From the 1950s Murdoch showed an accurate understanding of what the general mass of the public wanted in a newspaper—often in defiance of what their managements wanted to give them—and the importance of good political connections. He also made sure that his newspapers reflected his generally conservative view of the world. Naturally these attitudes made him a controversial figure in Australia, in **Britain**, and the **United States**. At the same time he has also consistently been a maverick in his business dealings and prided himself on not being an establishment figure. He was made a Companion of the Order of Australia in 1984 for his services to newspaper publishing.

In the 1980s he shifted the focus of his News group towards **television** and film. Murdoch had previously acquired television stations in Sydney and Melbourne and went on to buy six U.S. stations in 1985. These he combined with his purchase of 20th Century Fox Corporation to create a new group. He also became a pioneer of satellite broadcasting. The scale and diversity of Murdoch's holdings have led to massive legal and financial tangles (particularly in 1991), over which he has largely triumphed. In 1985 he was forced to become a U.S. citizen to comply with American media laws. In the 1990s Murdoch has turned to sport as a means of providing product for his broadcasting outlets. Between 1995 and 1997 he fought an expensive battle in the Australian rugby league to establish his own teams. In 1997 he bought the Los Angeles Dodgers baseball team and in 1998 he bought the famous English soccer club, Manchester United. On November 11, 1998 Murdoch successfully floated part of his Fox Entertainment Group Inc. on the U.S. stock market. (*See also* Press)

MYALL CREEK MASSACRE On June 9, 1838, 20 **Aborigines**, accused of stealing cattle, were massacred by seven convicts working for settlers in north-eastern **New South Wales**. The convicts were tried and hanged, but they were given much support by other settlers who regarded the Aborigines as pests. After 1838 the murder of Aborigines by settlers was carefully concealed.

N

NATIONAL ANTHEM   From 1788 to 1974, the national anthem of Australia was the British anthem "God Save the Queen (King)." In April 1974 the **Australian Labor Party** government of **Gough Whitlam** replaced this song with "Advance Australia Fair" as the national anthem. In 1976 the **Liberal-Country** coalition **Fraser** government made "God Save the Queen" the national anthem for regal and vice-regal occasions. In 1984 the **Hawke** government declared that "Advance Australia Fair" was Australia's national anthem for all occasions except during visits by members of the British royal family when "God Save the Queen" was to be played as the *Royal* Anthem.

In 1974 a poll by the Australian Bureau of Statistics on the relative popularity of choices for the national anthem found that 43 percent favored "Advance Australia Fair"; 28 percent favored "Waltzing Matilda"; 19 percent favored "God Save the Queen"; and 10 percent supported "Song of Australia."

"Advance Australia Fair" was composed by a Scottish immigrant, Peter Dodds McCormick (c.1834-1916) and first sung in 1878. During **World War II** it was used with news broadcasts. "Waltzing Matilda" was composed by "Banjo" [Andrew Barton] Paterson (1864-1941) and first sung in 1895. It remains one of Australia's best known songs and deals with the social conflict between sheep shearers and large rural land owners (or "squatters") who occupied their land by **squatting**.

NATIONAL FARMERS' FEDERATION (NFF)   The NFF was established in 1979 to provide a single, national voice for Australian **agriculture**. It is a federal body and by 1997 represented about 120,000 farmers through 30 affiliated organizations. The objectives of the NFF are to promote the development of Australia's agricultural, pastoral, fishing, and forestry resources; to be a single, national policy forum for agriculture; to act for the improvement of Australian agriculture; and to collect and disseminate information concerning rural industries. Although the NFF is not a political organization as such, its policies and activities favor the conservative side of politics. For example, it is critical of the power of **labor unions** and its president between 1984 and 1988, Ian McLachlan (1936-), a prominent member of the **Liberal Party**, was minister of defense from 1996 to 1998. During the first half of 1998 the NFF was an active participant in a long-running dispute to break the power of the Maritime Union of Australia over the supply of labor on the waterfront.

NATIONAL PARTY (*See* Country/National Party of Australia)

NATIONALISM   Compared to many other countries, nationalism in Australia has always been subdued. Australia lacked many of the prerequisites for overt national feeling. The European settlement of the country took place over a large area, separated by considerable differences. Colonial and then **state** loyalties have been paramount for much of Australian history, despite the **federation** of the **colonies** in 1901. British **immigration** fed a pride in being part of the British Empire. Although a majority of Australians were Australian-born by 1871, the British-born dominated the older age groups until the 1900s. Neither was there any shared sense of struggle to establish democracy in Australia, which was freely granted by British governments. The **Gallipoli** landing was used as an opportunity by Australian governments to try to forge national feeling.

There was also an attitude of dependence among Australian foreign policymakers for much of the twentieth century. They saw Australia as a vulnerable European outpost liable to be overwhelmed by its Asian neighbors and therefore dependent upon outside support, whether British or American for its **defense**.

The Australian press too reflected the strength of state loyalties and concerns. Newspapers like the *Sydney Morning Herald* and the *Age* viewed Australia from the prism of their capital cities or states. There was no national daily newspaper (the *Australian*) until 1964 although the *Australian Financial Review*, a national newspaper catering to business and economic news had been published from 1951.

In political terms, Australian nationalism was more a feature of the **Australian Labor Party** than its conservative opponents. This became much more evident under the **Whitlam** government between 1972 and 1975 by its promotion of Australian nationalism (seen, for example, in its creation of the **Australian honors system**) and by its questioning of the level of foreign investment and American military bases. Despite symbols such as the **Australian flag** and the **national anthem,** Australia is still in the process of defining itself as a nation. Both the flag and the national anthem have aroused much debate. In recent years there has also been debate about **republicanism**, but it too has been inconclusive and devoid of enthusiastic support. (*See also* Citizenship and Naturalization)

NATIONALIST PARTY   The Nationalist Party was the main conservative party in Australia between 1917 and 1932. It was formed in February 1917 when the pro-conscription members of the federal **Australian Labor Party** (ALP) parliament led by **William Morris Hughes** merged with the opposition **"Fusion" Liberal Party**. The Nationalists continued to be the federal government until December 1922 when it was forced into coalition with the new **Country Party**, which refused to accept Hughes as **prime minister**. Hughes was replaced by **Stanley Melbourne Bruce** who remained prime minister until he was defeated in the 1929 election. In May 1932 the Nationalist parliamentarians joined with a breakaway ALP group from the federal **Scullin** government to form the **United Australia Party**. At the **state** level, the Nationalist Party formed governments in **New South Wales** in 1916-20, 1922-25, and 1927-30 (in coalition with the Country Party); in **Victoria** in 1917-23, 1923-24 (in coalition with the Country Party), 1924, 1928-29; in **Queensland** in 1929-32 (with the Country Party); in **South Australia** in 1917-20; and in **Western Australia** in 1917-24 and 1930-33.

NATURALIZATION (*See* Citizenship and Naturalization)

"NEW AUSTRALIANS"   New Australians was a term applied to immigrants to Australia after 1945 from non-English speaking countries. The term was one of a number suggested by the minister for immigration, Arthur Augustus Calwell (1896-1973), in 1949 to help immigrants assimilate more easily into Australian society and to discourage offensive alternatives. (*See also* Immigration)

NEWCASTLE   Located on the coast north of **Sydney**, Newcastle has been the second largest city in **New South Wales** since 1861 and was the sixth largest city in Australia until 1981. It has been a heavy industry city since 1915. In the nineteenth century it was the center of Australia's black **coal** mining industry. Newcastle is also the port for the Hunter River valley, a major region whose economy was, and is, based on **agriculture**, **wine** growing, and coal mining. After the discovery of the entrance to the Hunter River in 1797, a **convict**

settlement was established to mine its coal (1801-1802). A larger settlement was made in 1804 and Newcastle remained a convict center until 1823.

The beginning of large-scale coal mining in the district from the late 1850s to meet domestic demand, particularly the growth in **urbanization**, and later a vigorous export trade, caused Newcastle's population to grow rapidly from 7,810 in 1861 to 49,900 in 1891. The decline of local coal mining hurt the economy in the 1900s, and its stagnation was reversed by the establishment of Australia's **iron and steel** industry at Newcastle by the **Broken Hill Proprietary Company Ltd**. (BHP) in April 1915. Newcastle was Australia's sole iron and steel producer until 1929, when it was joined by a plant at **Wollongong**. By 1933 Newcastle had a population of 104,500. In 1938 the city's 11 local governments were amalgamated to form a single greater city government.

Since 1947 the bulk of Newcastle's suburban expansion has been southward. A university college was founded in 1951 and it became a full university in 1965. On December 28, 1989, Newcastle became the first Australian city to be extensively damaged by an earthquake. Measuring 5.6 on the Richter Scale, the earthquake killed 12 people, injured 120 others, and caused an estimated $1.2 billion in damage, mainly in the inner city.

In 1982 a large part of the iron and steel **labor force** was retrenched and Newcastle was effectively put on notice that the industry may not survive in the city. The same process occurred in steel-making centers in Western Europe and the north-eastern **United States**. By 1996 the industry employed only 3,000 in Newcastle compared to 13,000 in the early 1980s. On April 29, 1997, BHP announced that the Newcastle steelworks would close in 1999 as a part of program to rationalize production and reduce costs. In 1996 urban Newcastle had a population of 270,300 and was the center of a region with a total population of 449,800.

NEW GUARD   The New Guard was a right-wing organization that operated in **New South Wales** from 1931 to 1935. It was formed by Eric Campbell (1893-1970), a lawyer and former military officer with fascist sympathies. The New Guard spent much of its time disrupting **Communist Party** meetings and fed off the misery and alarm for the social order caused by the Depression. A member of the New Guard disrupted the official opening of the **Sydney Harbor**

Bridge in March 1932. At its height in 1933, the New Guard had about 50,000 members.

NEW RIGHT The term "New Right" was invented in the late 1970s to describe neo-conservatives in the **United States** and **Britain**. It has been used in Australia in the 1980s to describe a small, loose but influential group of conservative politicians, businessmen, lawyers, academics, press commentators, and officials from private think tanks who want to reduce the role of government in the economy generally and the power of **labor unions** in particular. They support the selling of government businesses to private enterprise and the economic policies of former President Ronald Reagan and former British Prime Minister Margaret Thatcher. Their leading thinker and guide has been the U.S. economist Milton Friedman. Unlike the "old" Right, the "New Right" tends to have little interest in questions of private morality. Although the "New Right" has been credited with having much influence over the **Liberal Party** since the late 1970s, its influence has also been evident in the economic policies of the **Australian Labor Party** governments of **Bob Hawke** and **Paul Keating**.

NEW SOUTH WALES New South Wales (NSW) is Australia's oldest and most populous **state**. Named in 1770 by Captain **James Cook** New South Wales originally covered half the Australian mainland east of 136 degrees of longitude. With the British annexation of all of Australia in 1829, the boundary was pushed even farther westward to 129 degrees east. After 1834 this area was reduced substantially, beginning with the separation of **South Australia** as a separate colony in 1836, **Victoria** in 1851, and **Queensland** in 1859. These separations defined the present boundaries of New South Wales until the setting up of the **Australian Capital Territory** in the south-east as the seat of the federal government in 1911. Since that time New South Wales has had an area of 801,600 square kilometers or about 10 percent of Australia's area.

New South Wales operated as a **convict** colony from 1788 to 1840. Its early years were hard as the colonial administration tried to organize a regular food supply. Up to 1813, when a crossing was found across the heavily forested Blue Mountains, most settlement had been confined to the **Sydney** region. The colony's population had reached only 8,300 by 1813, but with the opening up on the plains west of the Blue Mountains, the pastoral economy became the engine of economic growth; by 1833 the population had risen to 60,000. In 1855 New South Wales was granted self-government by Britain. Although **gold** was discovered in New South Wales in 1851, it was the greater gold discoveries of Victoria that enabled it to overtake New South Wales in population until the 1890s. However, New South Wales had natural advantages that enabled it to regain the lead in population from Victoria, namely Sydney's excellent natural harbor and, most importantly, its possession of the bulk of Australia's black **coal** deposits, which underlay Sydney in an inverted arc and surfaced north at **Newcastle** and the Hunter valley region and south in the **Wollongong** district, the basis of important provincial cities. After 1915 New South Wales was the center of Australia's **iron and steel** industry. As the **railroads** grew out of Sydney from 1855, they formed a network that feeds trade back to the city.

By 1861 New South Wales had a population of 350,900; it had 1.1 million by 1891, 2.1 million by 1921, and 4.2 million by 1966. In 1996 the population of New South Wales was 6 million, of whom 70 percent lived in the coastal cities of Sydney, Newcastle, and Wollongong. The growth of the cities, particularly Sydney, has been fed not just by **immigration** but also by migration from country areas since the 1890s. New South Wales has also benefited from the growth of the federal capital, **Canberra**, in the southern part of the state since the 1960s.

The most striking fact of the history of New South Wales in the twentieth century has been the dominance of Sydney. Between 1901 and 1996, Sydney increased its share of total New South Wales population from 36 to 62 percent. Sydney is not just the political and economic capital of New South Wales, it has been the financial capital of Australia since the mid-1980s.

New South Wales has a long history of **Australian Labor Party** (ALP) governments. The ALP was founded in New South Wales in 1891 and first won government in 1910. **Jack Lang** was the state's most controversial **premier**, having two terms in office, in 1925-27 and 1930-32. But it was the ALP's victory under William McKell (1891-1985) in 1941 that saw the start of Labor's longest spell in office (1941-65). Unlike the ALP in **Victoria**, the ALP in New South Wales did not split in the 1950s. This was a period of important reforms: the 40-hour working week (1947) and 10 p.m. closing of hotel bars (1955), and a new system of secondary education, which came into force in 1962. **Liberal-Country** Party coalition governments ran New South Wales from 1965 to 1976, when Neville Wran (1926-) regained government for the ALP. In March 1988 the Liberal-National coalition again won government and instituted widespread reforms in **education** and government administration. On March 25, 1995, the ALP was again returned to power, if narrowly, under Bob Carr (1947-).

New South Wales is the main destination for international tourists to Australia; it received 64 percent of these tourists in 1994-95 and accounts for a third of the domestic tourist market. Much of its tourist appeal comes from the development of Sydney as a truly global city, the attractiveness of its harbor setting, its beaches, and the natural beauty of its hinterland.

NEW ZEALAND Since its establishment as a British colony in 1840, there have been continuous relations between New Zealand and Australia. When the Australian colonies federated in 1901, the preamble of the **Australian Constitution** made provision for New Zealand to become an Australian **state**.

The two countries have been allies in both world wars, in **Korea**, and **Vietnam**, and they share the **Anzac** tradition. The two countries do not always agree on military and foreign relations; for example, the Australian government did not support New Zealand's opposition in 1985 to the visit of American military ships carrying nuclear weapons under the **Anzus Treaty**. Nevertheless, military and **defense** cooperation between Australia and New Zealand remains close.

There has also always been much population movement between the two countries. Since the 1970s Australia has attracted far more New Zealanders than New Zealand has Australians because of the decline of opportunity in the New Zealand economy following **Britain's** joining the European Economic Community. In 1996 the number of New Zealanders living in Australia had risen to 291,381 or the equivalent of nearly 9 percent of the resident population of New Zealand.

Despite their similarities, there are many important historical differences between Australia and New Zealand. New Zealand has been a unitary state since 1876 whereas Australia has been a federation since 1901 and shows no sign of becoming a unitary state. Although the two countries each received large numbers of British immigrants, proportionally far fewer **Irish** emigrated to New Zealand. Since World War II, Australia has received far higher proportions of immigrants from non-English speaking countries than Australia with the result that New Zealand society lacks the multicultural aspect evident in Australia. Because of its restricted manufacturing base, **labor unions** have been also less powerful in New Zealand than in Australia.

In 1983 Australia and New Zealand signed the Closer Economic Relations Trade Agreement to free up trade. The agreement has worked well, though it has been claimed that it favors New Zealand manufacturing exporters unduly. Between 1982-83 and 1997-98, Australia's exports to New Zealand rose from 5.3 to 6.4 percent. Over the same period, the Australian share of imports from New Zealand rose from 3.2 to 4.1 percent.

Since the mid-1980s New Zealand government has deregulated much of the economy and severely cut government services and outlays with the object of improving economic performance. One outcome of these changes and the abolition of the **awards** system in 1991 and its replacement by a system of employment contracts was a reduction in the power and membership of labor unions. Between 1985 and 1996 the proportion of New Zealand employees who were union members fell from 43.5 to 19.9 percent. These changes have hurt the New Zealand Labor Party, which has not been in government since 1990. These policies have been much admired by conservative governments in Australia as worthy of emulation.

NICKEL Australia is a major producer of nickel, which is used in the production of stainless steel and construction steel. Nickel was produced on a small-scale in **Tasmania** from 1913 to 1938, but until the 1960s known reserves were tiny. Between 1966 and 1970 large reserves of nickel were discovered in the interior of south-eastern and northern **Western Australia** and **Queensland**. Production of nickel concentrates rose from 2,610 tonnes in 1967, to 34,900 in 1971, and to 66,000 by 1990. By 1988 Australia was the world's largest producer of nickel. In 1997-98 Australia produced 134,000 tonnes of nickel and nickel accounted for 0.8 percent of total Australian merchandise exports. (*See also* Mining)

NOLAN, SIDNEY [ROBERT] (1917-) Born in **Melbourne**, Nolan is one of Australia's best painters. In 1938 he helped found the Contemporary Art Society. In 1947-48 he painted the memorable *Kelly* series in which he used the fact and myth of the bushranger **Ned Kelly** as a motif for persecution and alienation. He is also known for his interpretations of the Australian landscape. He was knighted in 1981.

NORFOLK ISLAND Norfolk Island is a small island (3,455 hectares) in the South West Pacific Ocean, 1,676 kilometers from **Sydney**. Discovered by **James Cook** in 1774, it was a **convict** settlement from 1788 to 1814 and again from 1825 to 1856. It had no indigenous people. While a part of the convict system, it was used as a place of punishment for those convicts convicted of crimes in Australia; as such, it was one of the most brutal outposts of the convict system. Between 1840 and 1844 the governor, Alexander Maconachie (1787-1860), tried to introduce more humane programs for the convicts, but he was given neither the opportunity nor the resources to prove his methods.

In 1856, 194 descendants of the *Bounty* mutiny of 1789 were transferred from Pitcairn Island to Norfolk Island. Norfolk Island has a permanent population of about 1,500, of whom about a third are descendants of the *Bounty* mutineers. Norfolk Island has been a **territory** of the Australian government since 1913 and has had self-government since 1979. Tourism is the major industry. The Island's best-known resident is the novelist **Colleen McCulloch**.

NORTHERN TERRITORY (NT) The NT occupies the northern central part of the Australian mainland. It covers 1,346,200 square kilometers, or 17.5 percent of the total area of Australia. Despite its large area, it is not a **state**, but a territory. Its largest towns are **Darwin** and Alice Springs. The coast of the NT was probably explored by the Portuguese in the sixteenth century, but was definitely known by the Dutch, who explored it in detail from 1623 to 1642. Between 1675 and 1700, fishermen from modern **Indonesia** began visiting the coast for trepang or sea slugs to supply to China. To discourage the French or the Dutch, the British maintained three military bases on the coast at various times between 1824 and 1849, but they failed to develop as permanent settlements. From 1858 to 1862 the explorer **John McDouall Stuart** explored much of the NT from south to north. His discoveries were the basis for **South Australia** making a claim to administer the NT, which was reluctantly granted by the British government in 1863.

In 1911, after 47 years of neglect, the administration of the NT passed to the federal government. Its European population numbered just 3,310 and its public debt was four million pounds (or about $332 million at 1997 prices). The NT economy depended then, and largely still does, on **sheep** and/or cattle raising, and **mining**. In the 1960s large-scale mining of **iron ore**, bauxite, and manganese began and to these have been added uranium, and offshore reserves of oil and gas in the 1970s. By 1966 the population had reached 37,400 and in 1996 had grown to 195,100.

The NT has two major tourist attractions, both entered on the World Heritage List: **Ayers' Rock** in the south-west corner and Kakadu National Park in the north. **Aborigines** are an important part of the NT population and since 1976 have been granted about a third of the area of the NT in the form of reserves. In 1996, 23.7 percent of the population were Aborigines. In 1978 the NT was granted full self-government, but it remains very dependent upon the federal government for much of its funding. In 1997 Shane Stone (1950-) became **chief minister** of the NT leading a **Liberal-National** Party coalition government. On August 11, 1998 the federal government announced that it would support a **referendum** on statehood for the NT from January 1, 2001, an idea first suggested by **Malcolm Fraser** in 1975. The referendum was held in conjunction with the national elections on October 3, 1998 and rejected by 52 to 48 percent.

NOSSAL, GUSTAV [JOSEPH VICTOR] (1931-) Immunologist, Nossal was born in Bad Ischl, Salzburg, Austria. He came to Australia in 1939 with his parents who were fleeing Nazi persecution. He studied science at the Universities of Sydney and Melbourne. Between 1959 and 1961 he was an assistant professor at the department of genetics in the School of Medicine at Stanford University. Since 1965 he has been professor of medical biology at the University of Melbourne and has been director of the Walter and Eliza Hall Institute of Melbourne, a post formerly held by **Macfarlane Burnet**. His concept of "one cell, one antibody" is fundamental to immunology. As well as contributing to scientific research, he has promoted science as a federal government priority and encouraged the commercial development of the research done by the Walter and Eliza Hall Institute.

O

OLIPHANT, MARK [MARCUS LAURENCE ELWIN] (1901-)
Physicist, Oliphant was born in **Adelaide**, where he worked in a jeweler's shop and in a public library to support himself while he studied physics at the University of Adelaide. He was inspired by a visit to Australia by Ernest Rutherford and later joined him at Trinity College at Cambridge University in 1927 where he pursued his studies in nuclear research and gained his doctorate in 1929. During **World War II** he made notable contributions to the development of microwave radar and the atomic bomb. After World War II, he supported nuclear power, but opposed nuclear weapons. He returned to Australia in 1950 where he was director of the Research School of Physical Sciences at the Australian National University until 1963. He is best known for his work in the development of atomic accelerators. In 1971 he was made governor of **South Australia** and held the position until 1976.

OLYMPIC GAMES   Australia has competed in every summer Olympic games since they began in Athens in 1896 and at only four of these games—1904 (St. Louis), 1920 (Antwerp), 1936 (Berlin), and 1976 (Montreal)—have its competitors failed to win any gold medals. The relatively poor showing of Australians at the Montreal games provoked widespread public criticism which led the federal government to establish the Australian Institute of Sport which was opened in **Canberra** in 1981 by the **Fraser** government. This, along with other initiatives, has boosted Australia's success at subsequent Olympic games. At the Atlanta games in August 1996, Australians won nine gold medals, nine silver medals, and 23 bronze medals. Because of its climate, Australia has not been a particularly successful competitor in the winter Olympic games, although in 1994 an Australian relay team won a bronze medal, the first time Australia won a medal since these games began in 1926.

Melbourne was the host city of the summer Olympics in 1956 and on September 24, 1993, it was announced that **Sydney** will be the host city of the games in 2000. (*See also* Sport)

ONE NATION PARTY   The One Nation Party is the right-wing, populist party which was formed in Ipswich, a suburb of **Brisbane**, on April 11, 1997, by an independent member of the **house of representatives**, Pauline Hanson (1954-). Hanson was originally endorsed for the federal electorate of Oxley by the **Liberal Party**, but her endorsement was withdrawn because of her extremist views just before the national elections on March 2, 1996. Hanson won the seat as an independent and began to campaign against assistance programs for **Aborigines**, land rights for Aborigines in the aftermath of the **Wik Case**, and **immigration**, particularly from Asia. Her views gained her notoriety and widespread coverage in the Australian and international media. Support for the party in public opinion polls declined from 9 percent nationally at its formation to 3 percent by April 1998, but rebounded to 9 percent in June 1998. At the **Queensland** state elections on June 13, 1998, the party won 22.6 percent of primary vote, mainly from the ruling **National Party**. Polls show that the bulk of the party's support comes from Queensland and that it has most appeal for poorly educated, low-paid, blue-collar workers, rural dwellers, the unemployed, retirees, and homemakers. Support for the One Nation Party also reflected wider discontent with the economic policies of the Liberal and National Parties, particularly cuts to government services and jobs in rural areas. In July 1998 the party had about 10,000 members. At the national elections on October 3, 1998 the party attracted 8.4 percent of the vote for the **house of representatives** and 9 percent for the **senate**. Although Pauline Hanson failed to win a seat in the house of representatives, one member of the party was elected to the senate in Queensland. (*See also* Political Parties)

OVERLANDERS   Overlanders were cattle and sheep owners who drove their herds great distances across inland Australia to find better grazing lands. The word "overlander" was used by 1841 to describe those who drove stock mainly from **New South Wales** to **South Australia**. The great age of the Overlanders was from 1837 to 1885. One of the best- known Overlanders was the Durack family, who moved cattle from south-western **Queensland** to northern **Western Australia** from 1883 to 1885. (*See also* Sheep and Wool)

OVERLAND TELEGRAPH   The Overland Telegraph was the first direct electric telecommunication link between Australia and the world. It was opened in 1872 and ran across Australia from **Darwin** in the north to Port Augusta, **South Australia**, a distance of 3,175 kilometers. The route of the Telegraph followed that first explored by **John McDouall Stuart**.

P

PAGE, EARLE [CHRISTMAS GRAFTON] (1880-1961) Country Party leader and **prime minister,** Page was born in Grafton, a country town in north-eastern **New South Wales**, and received his education at the Sydney High School and then the University of Sydney, where he qualified as a surgeon. After service with the **Australian Imperial Force** in **World War I** in the medical corps, he returned to Grafton to practice medicine and engage in rural politics. In 1919 he was elected to the federal parliament as the member for Cowper. In 1920 he became leader of the Country Party, a post he held until 1939. Page was a particularly effective advocate for rural development; he supported hydro-electricity and the creation of new **states** within the federal system. He was a vigorous party leader who molded the Country Party into a formidable political force. He acted as prime minister in 1926-27, 1935, and 1937 and occupied the post temporarily between April 7 to April 26, 1939. He was knighted in 1938.

PAINTING Painting has been practiced in Australia for at least 4,000 years. Analysis of beeswax overlaying rock paintings by **Aborigines** in Arnhem Land in the **Northern Territory** have been dated from 2,000 B.C. to the nineteenth century. The main themes of Aboriginal rock paintings were animals and tribal myths and motifs. With the coming of European settlement in 1788, this art form was, like its creators, swept aside.

The earliest European artists were concerned with documenting the landscape and its exotic flora and fauna and charting the progress of settlement. Paintings tended to celebrate the European conquest of the landscape and its transformation from wilderness to property. The style of many early Australian paintings was British which conveyed little of the sunlit nature of Australia. Aboriginal art was regarded as primitive and had no influence on the evolution of Australian painting which followed Western European conventions. The best-known of the early Australian painters were Joseph Lycett (1775-1828), John Glover (1767-1849), and Conrad Martens (1801-1878).

The **gold** rushes boosted Australia's population and attracted several important artists such as S. T. Gill (1818-1880) and Eugen von Guérard (1811-1901). Gill produced some marvelous work inspired by gold digging, bushfires, and **bushrangers**. Von Guérard depicted the Australian landscape through the prism of German Romanticism. In the 1880s Australian painting came of age in a remarkable outburst of creativity led by artists such Frederick McCubbin (1855-1917), Arthur Streeton (1867-1943), and **Tom Roberts**. In their works, which were influenced by French Impressionism, the sunshine of Australia shone brightly and their influence dominated Australian painting into the 1920s. However, the economic climate for artists in Australia remained poor and many left to study and work in Europe in the 1890s and 1900s.

The isolation of Australia and the dominance of an English-oriented establishment among the trustees of the art galleries of the state capitals meant that it was not until 1939 that Australia was exposed to the art of pathfinders such as Picasso, Braque, and Cézanne when the Melbourne *Herald* sponsored an exhibition of their works. The isolation of Australia also gave rise to the "Melbourne School" or "Antipodean Group" in the 1940s and 1950s led by artists such as John Brack (1920-).

Since the 1960s there has been a higher level of interest and support for Australian painting by Australians, a consequence of rising **education** levels and higher incomes. In 1968 the federal government began to seriously collect Australian art. In 1974 its acquisition of *Blue Poles* by the American artist Jackson Pollock for $1.2 million aroused controversy, but the decision was eventually accepted as wise. In October 1982 the Australian National Gallery was opened in **Canberra** as a home for the national art collection and has provided an important national focus for Australian and overseas art.

Although international trends have made their presence felt in Australian painting, it retains its distinctiveness, particularly in its reaction to the power of the landscape to challenge and inspire. William Drysdale (1912-1981) and Fred Williams (1927-1982) are just two Australian artists especially famous for their portrayal of the Australian interior.

From the 1970s there has also been a resurgence in Aboriginal art by artists in the central and western desert regions who use acrylic paint to depict traditional motifs. Their work has won critical acclaim both in Australia and internationally. (*See also* Lindsay, Norman Alfred William; Nolan, Sidney; Roberts, Tom)

PALMER, [EDWARD VIVIAN] VANCE (1885-1959) Born in Bundaberg, **Queensland**, into a literary household, Palmer worked as a journalist in **Brisbane** and London before military service in **World War I**. He returned to Australia with his wife, Nettie [Janet Gertrude] Palmer (1885-1964), whom he married in 1914 and with whom he had a lifelong literary partnership. Palmer set about developing a specifically Australian national **literature**, most notably through his foundation of the Pioneer Players in 1922, which was dedicated to Australian drama. His play *The Black Horse* (1924) was written for this purpose. He went on to write a total of 12 novels including *The Passage* (1930), the trilogy *Golconda* (1948), and *The Big Fellow* (1960), a study of power politics in Queensland. He also wrote an important non-fiction work, *The Legend of the Nineties* (1954). Palmer was an important and constructive literary critic and served on the board of the Commonwealth Literary Fund from 1942 to 1953. (*See also* Literature)

PAPUA NEW GUINEA Papua New Guinea is the name of the eastern half of the island of New Guinea. The western half was taken over by the Dutch in 1828 (who had proved it to be an island by 1597), but the eastern half remained unclaimed until 1883 when the government of **Queensland** tried to annex it to avoid it being taken over by anyone else; this was vetoed by the British government. In 1884 Germany took over the north-eastern part of New Guinea, and in 1888 **Britain** took over the remaining south-east part (Papua). By 1906 Australia had been given power over Papua, and after capturing German New Guinea in 1914, was given a mandate over the captured territory by the League of Nations. Papua New Guinea was invaded by the Japanese in 1942 and was the scene of protracted jungle fighting with Australian and American forces.

     After **World War II** Australia made a greater effort to develop the economy and society of Papua New Guinea. In 1975 Papua New Guinea was granted its independence, but it remains the main recipient of Australia's foreign aid ($319.5 million in 1996-97 or 22 percent of Australia's total foreign aid program). (*See also* Indonesia)

PARKES, HENRY (1815-1896) Colonial politician, Parkes was born in Stoneleigh, Warwickshire, England. After a business failure, he emigrated to **New South Wales** in 1839, where he established a newspaper, the *Empire*, in 1850. He was elected to the **legislative council** in 1854 and became one of Australia's leading politicians in the pre-1890 period. He became colonial secretary in 1866 and served as **premier** of New South Wales five times (1872-75, 1877, 1878-83, 1887-89, and 1889-91). Parkes instituted or supported many reforms in land sale policy, hospitals, prisons, and mental institutions and, most importantly, was instrumental in establishing the public **education** system in New South Wales (1866, 1880). In economic management, he was a free trader and opposed tariffs and duties. In 1889-90 he played a significant role in mobilizing political support for the **federation** of the Australian colonies. In the period of factional politics in New South Wales (1860-90) Parkes was very successful, but his authoritarian approach failed as **factions** were replaced by mass political parties. Always a controversial figure, Parkes was an able and honest administrator.

PERFORMING ARTS (*See* Percy Aldridge Grainger; Robert Murray Helpman; Joan Sutherland)

PERTH   Perth is the capital city of the state of **Western Australia**. Located on the south-eastern coast on the Swan River, Perth was named after Perthshire, Scotland, the birthplace and parliamentary seat of the then British secretary of state for war and the colonies. It was founded in 1829 by Captain James Stirling (1791-1865) as Australia's first colony of free settlers. Growth was slow. By 1848 Perth had 1,148 people, and its port, Fremantle, had 426. **Convicts** were brought in from 1850 to 1868 to ease the shortage of servants. Nevertheless, Perth's growth remained slow and even by 1881 its population had reached only 8,500. During the 1880s, Perth's population doubled and continued to rise as a result of the 1890s **gold** rushes to 61,000 by 1901 and reached 106,000 by 1911. Between 1861 and 1901, about a third of Western Australia's population lived in Perth. Until the 1960s, Perth grew comparatively slowly; by 1966 it had a population of 500,000, but with the mineral boom—particularly of **iron ore**—from the late 1960s to the early 1970s, it grew much faster. By 1996 Perth's population was 1.2 million.

The movement for amalgamating local governments had some success in Perth: four municipalities were amalgamated between 1906 and 1912. In 1928 the Western Australian government passed Australia's first town planning act which was to be applied to Perth. Plans for metropolitan Perth were prepared in 1955 and again in 1970. Perth was, and is, the most isolated of Australia's major cities. Transport links to the eastern states came late. There was no rail link with Adelaide until 1917 and although a rough road link (the Eyre Highway) was made during **World War II**, it was not fully bitumen sealed until 1976. Fremantle, the port of Perth, was an important U.S. submarine base during World War II, and it has been estimated that its submarines accounted for half of all Japanese tankers sunk in the war.

The *Western Australian*, Western Australia's main newspaper, began production in Perth in 1885. The University of Western Australia was opened in Perth in 1913. A second university, Murdoch, was opened in 1975. Two more universities have been created since then: the Curtin University of Technology (1987) and the Edith Cowan University (1991).

PETROLEUM   Although forms of petroleum (which includes oil and natural gas) were known to exist in Australia as early as 1839 (when crude bitumen was found in the **Northern Territory**), it was not until 1964 that the first commercial oil field began production at Moonie, near Roma, **Queensland**. Other discoveries of petroleum followed offshore from northern **Western Australia** and eastern **Victoria**. Most oil produced in Australia is "light" and "heavy" crude still needs to be imported, mainly from the Middle East. In 1971 a large natural gas field was discovered off the coast of northern Western Australia known as the North West Shelf. By 1985 Australia was producing 96 percent of its crude oil needs. In 1997-98 Australia produced 33,947 mega liters of crude oil and 30,619 giga liters of natural gas. In 1997-98 petroleum and petroleum products accounted for 4.4 percent of Australia's total merchandise exports. (*See also* Mining)

PETROV AFFAIR   The Petrov Affair was a pivotal event in post-1945 Australian politics. In April 1954 Vladimir Mikhailovich Petrov (1907-1991), third secretary of the Soviet embassy in **Canberra**, defected and was granted asylum by the federal government. The Soviet government tried to fly Petrov's wife, Evdokia (1914-), back to Moscow, but the aircraft was stopped at **Darwin** and she too was granted political asylum. The Petrovs provided details of their spying in Australia and implicated two members of the staff of **Herbert Vere Evatt**, the leader of the federal parliamentary **Australian Labor Party** (ALP), then in opposition. Unwisely Evatt personally appeared before the royal commission of inquiry (1954-

55) to defend his staff, but the commission refused to clear them and Evatt's reputation suffered.

The Petrov Affair helped to split the ALP in 1955, which led to the formation of the **Democratic Labor Party**. As a result, the **Menzies** government was able to stay in power with comparative ease and the ALP remained in opposition federally until 1972. As a spy case, the Petrov Affair was significant for the defection of the highly trained Mrs. Petrov who was an expert in codes. In 1956 the Petrovs published an account of their story called *Empire of Fear*. (*See also* Australian Security Intelligence Organisation)

PHAR LAP *Phar Lap* was Australia's most famous racehorse in the 1920s and 1930s. He won 37 of his 51 races largely because his heart was twice normal size. Raised in **New Zealand**, he won the **Melbourne Cup** in 1930. *Phar Lap* was taken to the **United States**, but died in San Francisco after a few weeks (1932). Although it was suggested that he was killed by gangsters because he was too fast, he probably died from poisoning caused by eating fermentable green pasture. The name *Phar Lap* came from the Thai word for "lightning." *Phar Lap's* heart was preserved at the Institute of Anatomy in **Canberra** and his stuffed hide was put on display in the Melbourne Museum. (*See also* Melbourne Cup; Sport)

PLAYFORD, THOMAS (1896-1981) Playford was the longest serving **premier** in Australia's history and the most important premier of **South Australia**. Born in Norton Summit, South Australia, he became a fruit grower before enlisting in the **Australian Imperial Force** where he saw service both at **Gallipoli** and on the Western Front in **France**. One of his grandfathers, also called Thomas Playford (1837-1915), had been premier of South Australia from 1887-89 and 1890-92.

Playford was elected to the house of assembly (**legislative assembly**) in 1933 for the Liberal and Country League and in March 1938 was made Crown lands commissioner and minister of repatriation and irrigation. On November 11, 1938, he became premier, a post he retained until March 10, 1965. During his record-breaking term of 27 years in office, Playford actively sought to change the basis of the **economy** of South Australia from **agriculture** to **manufacturing**. The Depression had hit the state's economy very hard and Playford was determined to create employment. During his period in power, total employment in manufacturing increased from 41,000 to 114,200. The industrial towns of Whyalla and Elizabeth were developed under these policies.

Knighted in 1957, Playford maintained his rule by a gerrymander (dubbed the "Playmander") which was biased in favor of rural voters. In March 1965 his administration was defeated by the **Australian Labor Party**, but he hung on as leader of the opposition until July 5, 1966.

POLITICAL PARTIES   Modern political parties begin in Australia with the formation of the **Australian Labor Party** (ALP) in 1891. The ALP was the first modern Australian political party because of its use of a policy platform and by use of disciplined voting by its parliamentary members. From the 1850s Australian politics had been characterized by **factions** or "interests" based on strong personalities, such as **Henry Parkes**, with loosely organized parliamentary supporters, rather than political parties as such with the result that there was a high turnover of administrations; for example, there were 26 governments in **New South Wales** between 1856 and 1889. The main axis of difference in politics from 1860 to 1890 was between those who favored **free trade** (mainly New South Wales) and those who favored **protection** (mainly **Victoria**). Parties with names such as Free Trade and Protectionist were used by the late 1880s in New South Wales and Victoria, but other political labels included Conservative, Liberal, and National. The tenor of politics was generally conservative—although British liberalism, represented by politicians like **Alfred Deakin**, was also important— because until members of parliament were given a salary in 1889, it was difficult for other than wealthy individuals to become politicians.

The success of the ALP in winning concessions from the conservative groups in the 1890s and 1900s and in forming national governments in 1904 and 1909-10, forced these groups to adopted the disciplined voting tactics of the ALP. In 1909 the conservative and liberal groups combined to create the first united conservative party, the **"Fusion" Liberal Party**. In late 1916 the ALP split over **conscription**, some of its parliamentary members joined the "Fusion" Liberal Party and later formed the **Nationalist Party** in February 1917.

Australian politics was run by two parties until January 1920 when the **Country Party** was formed. Unlike similar parties in

North America, the Country Party, although also based on rural populism, has always been a conservative political party with no radical associations. In 1922 the Country Party showed its power when it refused to accept **William Morris Hughes** as prime minister. It has been the partner of conservative governments ever since 1920 while retaining its independence and right to disagree over policy. In 1982 the Country Party renamed itself the National Party of Australia.

The next important change in the makeup of Australian political parties occurred in May 1931 when the ALP government again split with some of its parliamentary members joining the Nationalist Party to create the **United Australia Party**. This was Australia's leading conservative party until 1944 when **Robert Gordon Menzies** and others reorganized it and other conservative groups to form the modern **Liberal Party of Australia**.

In 1956 there was a third split in the ALP which produced the **Democratic Labor Party** in 1957. This party, although not a formal member of the governing conservative coalition of the Liberal and Country Parties, was instrumental in maintaining it in federal government between 1957 and 1972 through directing the preferences of its voters away from the ALP.

Splits in the conservative parties have also occurred and like those in the ALP have given rise to new parties. In July 1969 the **Australia Party** was formed, largely from Liberal Party members who opposed the war in **Vietnam**. Preferences from this party helped to bring about the election of the **Whitlam** government in December 1972, thereby ending 23 years of continuous conservative federal governments. In 1977 a disillusioned Liberal, Don Chipp, formed the **Australian Democrats**, a party which has since been very important in holding the balance of power in the **senate**.

In 1984 a system of federal funding was introduced for political parties. To be eligible, parties must be registered and receive at least 4 percent of the formal first preference vote in elections for the senate. In 1996 there were 26 separate political parties registered under this legislation.

Because of the dominance of Australian politics since 1910 essentially two political parties, the ALP and conservative coalitions, minor parties have often been devoted to single issues and short-lived. Some have achieved limited success based mainly on disenchantment with the major political parties. For example, the Nuclear Disarmament Party was formed in June 1984, attracted tens of thousands of supporters, and succeeded in having one of its candidates elected to the senate, but had largely petered out after two years.

Australia's most recent minor party, the **One Nation Party**, was formed on April 11, 1997, by Pauline Hanson (1954-), who was elected for the federal seat of Oxley in Queensland in March 1996. Originally nominated by the Liberal Party, Hanson lost her endorsement before the election because of her strident anti-Asian views. The **One Nation Party** opposes **immigration**, particularly from Asia, and special consideration of the needs of **Aborigines**. (*See also* Franchise)

POPULATION   The population history of Australia falls into four main periods: 1788 to 1861; 1861 to 1891; 1891 to 1945; and 1945 to the present.

The first period from 1788 through to 1860 was when permanent British settlements were made along the coast and inland in the south-eastern corner of the mainland. During this time the European population grew from about 1,000 to 1.1 million. The number of **Aborigines** fell from somewhere between 315,000 (and possibly as many as 750,000) to about 180,000 by 1861, and continued to fall to 74,000 by 1933. **Immigration** stimulated by the gold rush, **convicts**, and the distance from **Britain** made Australia's European population heavily masculine. In the early 1840s males outnumbered females by more than two to one. By 1861 there were 138 males for every 100 females. Of the total population growth, 80 percent came from immigration.

From 1861 to 1891 Australia's population almost trebled from 1.1 million to 3.2 million which reflected and boosted its high level of economic growth. Immigration, particularly the government-assisted immigration programs from the late 1870s to 1890, did much to boost population growth, particularly in the capital cities and large towns. Immigration contributed 37 percent of total population growth. The proportion of males per 100 females fell from 138 to 116. Although the birth and death rates remained high by later Australian levels, both were slowly declining over the period. The population was very youthful. In 1871 half the population of 1.6 million was under 20 years of age. Because of high infant mortality, life expectancy at birth hardly changed. Between 1881 and 1890, life expectancy at birth was 47 years for males and 51 years for females.

The period from 1891 to 1945 marked the transition from a society with high birth and death rates to one where both rates continued to fall (generally known as "demographic transition"). Acute economic depression in the 1890s and the increased use of contraceptives by married couples resulted in a sharp fall in the birthrate, which continued into the 1900s and became the subject of a royal commission in **New South Wales** (1903-04).

Between 1890-92 and 1910-12, average births per 1,000 women aged 15 to 44 fell from 159 to 117. Even with improved economic conditions, the birthrate never recovered to its pre-1890 levels and collapsed to its lowest point in the early 1930s (71 births per 1,000 women aged 15 to 44 for 1932-34). The death rate fell too, mainly as a result of the continued fall in infant mortality (from 110 per 1,000 births in 1890-92 to 28 in 1946-48). Immigration made a variable contribution to population growth. It was important from 1910 to 1914 and from 1920 to 1929, but not for the rest of the period because of the Depression and **World War II**. In this period Australia's population rose from 3.2 to 7.4 million, but only 14 percent of the total population gain of 4.3 million came from immigration.

Between 1945 and the late 1990s Australia's population again underwent much growth and change. In all the resident population increased two and a half times from 7.4 to 18.5 million of which 39 percent came from immigration. For the first time in the nation's history, immigration from non-English speaking countries made a significant contribution to population growth, although the British Isles remained the main source of immigrants. The bulk of immigration from continental Europe, which was dominated by **Italians** and **Greeks**, occurred between 1950 and 1970.

The birthrate slowly recovered in the 1940s, and rose in the 1950s, and into the first half of the 1960s but since the early 1970s fell steadily. The death rate fell, too, but the fall in the infant death rate was much more impressive from an average of 28 per thousand in 1946-48 to 6 in 1995-97. By the 1980s only the Aborigines had high levels of infant deaths. In 1980-82 the average Aboriginal infant mortality rate was 31 per 1,000 births, or three times the national rate. Government concern about population, its pattern of growth and prospects for the future led to Australia's first national population inquiry, which released its report in 1975.

The period from 1946 to the late 1990s was also notable for the growth in the number of females in the population who have outnumbered males slightly since the early 1980s. Because immigration policies favored younger people, the median age of the Australian population fell from 31 in 1946 to 28 by 1966. It was again 31 by 1986 and in 1996 was 34. Immigration also fed the long-established trend towards **urbanization**. Between 1947 and 1996 the proportion of Australians who were urban dwellers (using the U.S. definition) rose from 70.2 to 82.3. Since 1975 public debate about population has been chiefly concerned with the impact of population growth on the **environment** and the rise in Asian immigration. (*See also* Emigration; Immigration; Tables 11 to 20 in Appendix 3)

PREMIER The elected leader of the government of an Australian **state**, or before 1901, an Australian colony. The term was in use by 1858. With the rise of modern **political parties** after 1910, premiers are the leaders of majority party in the lower house, usually called the **legislative assembly**. Since the federal government gained control of income tax, in 1942 the power of premiers has waned, although collectively they can exercise much influence on the federal government. (*See also* Deakin, Alfred; Lang, Jack; Playford, Thomas; Reid, George Houston; Territories)

PRESBYTERIANISM Up to the 1930s Presbyterianism vied with **Methodism** as the third largest religion in Australia. The first Presbyterian congregation began in 1803 and it erected Australia's oldest surviving church building in 1809. The number of Presbyterians grew with Scottish immigration which was actively promoted by the first Presbyterian minister, John Dunmore Lang (1799-1878). Before 1870, there was considerable disunity within Presbyterianism in Australia, but these differences were largely resolved and a federal body, the Presbyterian Church of Australia, was set up in 1901, at which date 11.9 percent of Australians claimed to be Presbyterians. The church has been notable for its interest in and promotion of **education** and has always had strong support from the better-off members of society. Since 1933 Presbyterianism in Australia has declined in parallel with Methodism. By 1971 only 8.1 percent of Australians were Presbyterians compared to 8.6 percent for Methodists. In 1977 the two denominations joined with the Congregationalist church to form the **Uniting Church of Australia**. However, not all Presbyterians supported the amalgamation. The 1996 population **census** showed that although there were no Congregationalists or Methodists,

675,500 Australians—3.8 percent of the total population—claimed the Presbyterian and Reformed Church as their denomination. (*See also* Religion; Table 17 in Appendix 3)

PRESS The first newspaper to be produced in Australia was the *Sydney Gazette and New South Wales Advertiser* which was first printed on March 5, 1803, and continued until 1842. It was a weekly organ of the governor and his administrations. A second similar newspaper was begun in **Tasmania** in 1810. The first privately owned newspaper, the *Australian*, was begun in **Sydney** by William Charles Wentworth (c.1792-1872) and Robert Wardell (1794-1834) in 1824. Printed without a government license, it championed self-government. Australia's oldest continuously printed newspaper, the *Sydney Morning Herald*, first appeared in April 1831. The oldest continuously printed newspaper in Victoria, the *Age*, began in October 1854. Overseas news was derived from Britain and its dissemination became much faster after the setting up of a direct cable link with Reuter's London office in July 1872 through the **Overland Telegraph**.

The general prosperity of the period from 1860 to 1890 gave rise to a profusion of newspapers and periodicals catering to humor, literature, and politics, of which the most influential was the *Bulletin* which was first published in 1880.

Weekly photographic newspapers were common in the 1900s. Before the 1920s the layout of most of the larger Australian newspapers was reversed to what it is today. Advertising usually occupied the first few pages and the news section the middle pages. Reflecting the move of the federal government from **Melbourne** to **Canberra**, the *Canberra Times* began publication in 1926.

The first telegraphic transmission of pictures took place in 1929 and a commercial telephone service with Britain began in 1930, developments which improved the timeliness of the delivery of news. The hugely successful *Australian Women's Weekly* was begun by Frank Packer (1906-1974), the father of media magnate Kerry Packer (1937-) in 1933.

In 1951 the *Australian Financial Review* was first published by the Fairfax group (the then owners of the *Sydney Morning Herald*). Originally, a biweekly until 1963 when it was published daily, it became an important source of political as well as economic news.

After the death of his father, Keith Murdoch (1886-1952), **Rupert Murdoch** became head of News Ltd. in **Adelaide** and used it as a base for building a media conglomerate in Australia before creating his global media empire. On July 15, 1964, he began Australia's first national daily newspaper, the *Australian*. Although not at first a particularly financially successful newspaper, it came to occupy an important place in the Australian press by the early 1970s.

Over the last 20 years there has been a greater concentration of media ownership in fewer hands. This was a reflection not just of a harder economic climate but also of the demise of the John Fairfax group which went into receivership after a family member, Warwick Fairfax (1960-), tried to buy back the group in 1987 to become sole owner; the debts he incurred in this operation led to the carving up of the group. The group was finally acquired by the Canadian media magnate, Conrad Black in 1991. Technology has also continued to offer new challenges and opportunities to the press. There was a general changeover to electronic production in the 1970s and since 1996 greater use has been made of the Internet for advertising and news. (*See also* Television)

PRIME MINISTER   The elected leader of an Australian federal government, in contrast to **premier** in the **states**. By convention the prime minister must be a member of the **house of representatives**. The office of prime minister is not recognized in the **Australian Constitution**. (*See* Appendix 2)

PRITCHARD, KATHERINE SUSANNAH (1883-1969)   Novelist, Pritchard was born in Fiji, but spent her early years in **Melbourne** and **Tasmania**. Her father was a journalist and she worked as a journalist in Melbourne before going to London in 1908 where she worked as a feelance writer and wrote her first novel, *The Pioneers* (1915). She also worked as a journalist in the **United States**. Pritchard returned to Australia and was a foundation member of the **Communist Party of Australia** and remained a member throughout her life. She traveled throughout Australia to gather material for her books before settling in **Western Australia**. Her best-known works are *Working Bullocks* (1926) and *Coonardoo* (1929). (*See also* Literature)

PROTECTION   Along with **free trade**, protection was an important part of the political language of Australia from 1856 to 1900. The debate was over whether tariffs should be mainly for raising revenue or whether they should be designed to "protect" local industry from external competition. The debate about which approach gave the greatest benefits was strongest in **Victoria** (whose governments favored protection) and **New South Wales** (where governments favored free trade). To counteract the sharp decline in government revenue from **gold** exports, Victoria introduced a mildly protective tariff in 1866 to assist local industry. Higher levels of protection were introduced in 1877 and 1892. New South Wales was able to follow "free trade" policies because it could raise more revenue from land sales and duties on **mining**. Until the **federation** of the Australian colonies in 1901, all the colonies levied different duties on one another's products.

After federation protection became a fundamental part of national economic policy. Lower tariffs were granted for British goods. The system of protection developed by successive federal governments had many aims. In 1907 the **Harvester Judgment** began the principle of protection for manufacturers who paid "fair and reasonable" wages to their employees. Further protection measures were introduced during **World War I**, which were incorporated and extended into a comprehensive tariff by the minister for trade and customs, Walter Massy-Greene (1874-1952), in 1921. During the 1920s assistance and export subsidies were given to rural producers. In 1929 the Bridgen Inquiry reported favorably on the protection system, claiming that it maintained a higher standard of living.

From the early 1950s a system of import licensing was introduced, which covered most imported goods. Protection had the active support of **John McEwen**. In 1965 the Vernon Inquiry into the economy argued that protection should be set at levels that would encourage Australian producers to be competitive with imports. Its report was ignored by the **Menzies** government. The **Whitlam** government made the first large-scale reforms of the protection system. In 1973 tariffs were cut by 25 percent but the effect on particular goods was variable. The average effective rate of protection fell for some goods but remained high for others, namely cars, textiles, clothing, and footwear. In May 1988 the **Hawke** government abolished import quotas and cut tariffs in manufacturing by 20 percent. In a report to the Hawke government, Professor Ross Garnaut (1946-) recommended that all protection be dismantled by the year 2000.

Although well received protection policy remained a highly controversial economic and political issue largely because of the likely fall in employment in towns and regions with narrowly based economies. Since the late 1980s Australian governments have consistently supported greater liberalization of international trade barriers. (*See also* Asia Pacific Economic Cooperation, Cairns Group of Fair Traders in Agriculture; Economy; Free Trade; Labor Force; Manufacturing)

Q

QANTAS Qantas has been Australia's national airline since 1947 when it was bought by the federal **Chifley** government. It is one of the oldest airlines in the world. It began in 1922 as the Queensland and Northern Territory Aerial Services Limited and was Australia's first commercial air service. In 1934 it made the first international passenger flight by an Australian airline from **Brisbane** to Singapore, linking up the service with Britain's Imperial Airways to form a connection with **Britain**. In 1967 it became Qantas Airways Ltd. It introduced the world's first business class in 1979. In 1989 a Qantas Boeing 747-400 plane established a distance record for a commercial jet aircraft for a flight from London to **Sydney**. On June 1, 1992, the federal government announced that Qantas was to be merged with the government-owned domestic airline, Australian Airlines (formed in 1946) and then sold. Despite difficult trading conditions for international aircraft companies since then, Qantas has prospered. In 1998 Qantas had services to 29 countries. On September 29, 1998, its management announced that Qantas had entered into an alliance with British Airways, American Airlines, Canadian Airlines and Cathay Pacific Airways to form a strategic alliance called One World, which was planned to come into effect in February 1999. (*See also* Charles Kingsford Smith)

QUEENSLAND Queensland is the third largest of Australia's **states** in area (1,727,200 square kilometers) and population. It occupies the north-eastern part of Australia and was named in honor of Queen Victoria, who suggested the name. It accounts for 22.5 percent of the total area of Australia. Its capital city is **Brisbane**. The first permanent European settlement was a **convict** settlement at Moreton Bay (modern Brisbane) in 1824. The settlement, which was later moved up the Brisbane River, was a place of punishment for convicts who had committed offenses in **New South Wales**. In 1833 Queensland held 1,200 convicts, but by 1841 this had been reduced to 200. Land explorations by Allan Cunningham (1791-1839) in 1827 and **Thomas Mitchell** in 1846 proved the potential of Queensland for **agriculture** and **sheep** and cattle raising, which became the mainstay of the economy. From 1840 the land was opened to development by free settlers.

In 1859 Queensland was made a separate colony from New South Wales; at its first census in 1861 as a separate colony, Queensland had a population of 30,100. The European occupation was resisted by the **Aborigines**, particularly in the north, from the 1850s through to the 1890s. It is estimated that the fighting cost between 10,000 and 20,000 Aboriginal and 1,000 European lives. In 1863 sugarcane was added to wool as a major cash crop. An attempt to establish cotton growing to exploit the shortage caused by the American Civil War in the 1860s failed. Sugar production was then believed to need "colored" labor and from 1863 to 1904 **Kanakas** (Melanesians) were brought in as contract laborers. Their presence caused racial tensions with European workers as did the presence of **Chinese**, who had come to Queensland during the gold rush of the early 1870s.

By 1891 Queensland had overtaken **South Australia** as Australia's third most populous colony with a population of 393,700. Some industrial development occurred, but generally the economy remained dependent on agriculture and **mining**.

Queensland was unusual among Australia's colonies in its population distribution. Brisbane, the capital, had only 26 percent of the colony's population of 391,500 in 1891; 41 percent lived in other towns and 33 percent were rural dwellers. Even by 1961 when the population had reached 1.5 million, only 41 percent lived in Brisbane, 35 percent in other towns, and 25 percent in rural areas. As a result, the provincial and rural vote in Queensland has always been a strong force in state politics, regardless of which political party was in government. Both the **Australian Labor Party** (ALP) (1932-57) and the **Country/National** and **Liberal** coalition parties (1957-89) have used gerrymanders to retain power.

In the early 1920s Queensland enjoyed a brief reputation for political radicalism and reform. In 1922 it became the first (and only state) to abolish its **legislative council** and the only one to experiment with unemployment insurance. But since the 1920s Queensland politics has been remarkable for its conservatism. Under National Party **premier**, Jo Bjelke-Petersen (1911-), Queensland gained the reputation for being the most conservative state in Australia between 1968 and 1989. It was generally hostile to environmental concerns and pursued an aggressive policy of encouraging **tourism** and coastal real estate development. In December 1989 the ALP under Wayne Goss (1951-) won government for the first time since 1957, but lost support and was barely returned in the elections on July 15, 1995. An unsuccessful by-election saw the fall of the government in February 1996 and the installation of a coalition National/Liberal Party government under Rob Borbidge (1954-) as premier. At the state elections on June 13, 1998 the **One Nation Party** gained 22.6 percent of the vote, split the conservative vote as a whole, and enabled the ALP under Peter Beattie (1952-) to form a minority government with the support of an independent.

Although Queensland attracted Chinese and **German** immigrants before 1900 and **Italians** in the inter-war years, non-English-speaking **immigration** has not been the important feature of its post-1945 history the way it has in New South Wales and **Victoria**. In 1991, for example, only 8.4 percent of Australia's foreign-born from non-English speaking countries lived in Queensland compared to 39.1 percent for New South Wales and 34 percent for Victoria. What is especially significant about the demography of Queensland since the 1960s has been the attractiveness of its south-eastern corner for Australian-born as a place to live and retire, especially for older, better-off, residents of Victoria and New South Wales.

Another feature of Queensland has been its significantly lower than average income per head among all states except Tasmania since 1948-49. This is despite the development of mining and tourism since the 1960s. In 1996 Queensland residents had a median personal weekly income of $286 compared to $298 for residents of New South Wales, and $290 for residents of Victoria. At the 1996 census Queensland had a resident population of 3,369,000 compared to 2,977,800 in 1991. Its main tourist attractions are the **Gold Coast** and the **Great Barrier Reef**. (*See also* Cairns; Townsville)

R

RADCLIFFE-BROWN, ALFRED REGINALD (1881-1955) Anthropologist, Radcliffe-Brown was born in Birmingham, England, and completed his education at Cambridge University. Between 1921 and 1937 he held foundation chairs in social anthropology at the universities of Cape Town, **Sydney**, and Oxford which he held until 1946. While in Australia, he carried out studies of kinship among **Aborigines**, which he published as *The Social Organization of Australian Tribes* in 1931. He used surveys and interviews as well as previous studies, and his work has enduring status as a contribution to ethnography. (*See also* Aborigines)

RAILROADS   The first government-owned railroad in Australia was opened in 1854 in **Melbourne**, Victoria. In **New South Wales** the failure of a private company to build a railroad from **Sydney** to Goulburn caused it to be taken over by the government in 1855. In the other colonies, government railroads began in **South Australia** in 1856, in **Queensland** in 1863, in **Tasmania** in 1871, and in **Western Australia** in 1879. Between 1871 and 1901 the length of government-operated railroad (private railways in Australia have largely been confined to mining sites) grew from 1,561 to 20,240 kilometers. In October 1917, the Trans-Australia railroad was completed between South Australia and Western Australia, providing an east-west rail link across Australia, but no north-south rail link across the center of Australia was ever built.

By 1942 the railroad system had reached its greatest extent— 43,831 kilometers—but this achievement was spoilt by the **colonies** having built their railroads using different-sized rail gauges. New South Wales and South Australia used a standard track width of 1.60 meters, Victoria used 1.44 meters, and Queensland and Western Australia used 1.07 meters. Thus although the railroads of New South Wales and Victoria were linked at Albury in 1883, passengers had to change trains until 1962 because of different-sized railroad gauges.

Passenger use of the railroads peaked in 1945 at 535 million passenger journeys and declined to 447 million journeys by 1996. However, the railroads continue to be important for moving bulk commodities such as **coal**, **iron ore**, and **wheat**. Between 1945 and 1996 the amount of freight moved by the railroads increased from 41 to 216 million tonnes.

REFERENDUM   The **Australian Constitution** (section 128) can only be changed by referendum which must be approved by a majority of voters and a majority of **states**. Between 1906 and 1988, 42 referendums have been submitted to the voters, of which only eight were carried: senate elections (1906), state debts (1910, 1928), social services (1946), **Aborigines** (1967), **senate** casual vacancies, referendums, and retirement of judges (1977). Referendums are also required for certain sorts of constitutional changes in **New South Wales**, **Queensland**, and **South Australia**. (*See also* Australian Constitution)

REID, GEORGE HOUSTON   (1845-1918)   Colorful conservative colonial **premier** and **prime minister**, Reid was born in Johnstone, near Paisley in Scotland. He emigrated with his family to **Victoria** in 1852, but moved to **New South Wales** in 1856. In 1879 he qualified as a lawyer and, despite being little known, was elected to the lower house of the New South Wales parliament in 1880, campaigning on a platform of **free trade**. After being minister of public instruction (1883-84) and leader of the opposition (1891-94), he became premier in 1894 and held the post until 1899 when he showed his skill as an administrator when the colony was badly hit by economic depression and **drought**. He played an active, if controversial, role in **federation**.

Reid was elected to the **house of representatives** in 1901 where he was the first leader of the opposition (1901-04) and prime minister from August 18, 1904 to July 5, 1905, as head of a coalition made up of the Free Trade Party and some members of the Protectionist Party. Reid was knighted in 1909 and in 1910, he became Australia's first high commissioner in London, a position he held until 1916. Just before his term in this office ended, he was offered a seat in the British House of Commons which he accepted. A rotund figure in middle age, and an entertaining speaker, Reid was a gift for caricaturists in the 1890s and 1900s.

RELIGION   Apart from the traditional religions practiced by the **Aborigines**, religion in Australia has largely been a by-product of European **immigration**. With the growth of **Irish** immigration, there was much official concern from the 1820s onwards about the growth of **Catholicism** which might challenge the dominance of the **Church of England**. Hence, unlike either **Britain** or the **United States**, the changes in the numerical balance of religions was carefully monitored through the population **census** from 1828 onward. The 1881 census in **Tasmania** was the only Australian census to omit a question on religion. Divisions between Protestants and Catholics were a significant feature of Australian society until the 1960s. The census did not fully enumerate the smaller religions between 1954 and 1981, but has done so since then.

Presbyterianism was associated with Scottish immigration and **Methodism** with immigration from provincial England. Similarly, Judaism has been brought to Australia from immigration by **Jews**. Sensitivities over religious divisions led the framers of the **Australian Constitution** to forbid the federal government under section 116 from legislating to make any religion the established religion (that is, like the Church of England in the United Kingdom), imposing any religious observance, prohibiting the free exercise of any religion, imposing any religious test for any office or public trust under the control of the federal government.

Judaism was the largest single non-Christian denomination until 1981 when it was overtaken by Islam which claimed 200,900 followers or 1.1 percent of Australians. **Mormonism** is the only religion which has been imported to Australia from the **United States** and not dependent upon immigration.

As in other countries, the incidence of churchgoing on a Sunday has declined steadily in Australia. In 1947 35 percent of Australians were regular churchgoers and 32 percent were in 1958, but by 1978 this figure had fallen to 19 percent and in 1998 it was estimated that only 8 percent were regular churchgoers.

There is also a substantial minority of Australians who do not profess any religion. From the 1933 census onward, it has not been compulsory to answer the question on religious belief. Up to 1961 about 11 percent of Australians did not answer the question on religion and the proportion has been rising steadily ever since. At the 1996 census 25.1 percent of Australians did not respond to the religion question. (*See also* Table 17 in Appendix 3)

REPUBLICANISM Although there was some support for Australia becoming a republic in the nineteenth century, notably from the *Bulletin* in the 1890s, interest largely died for the next hundred years. Support for the monarchy, fed by British **immigration**, remained very high. A poll in 1953 found that 77 percent of Australians favored continuing as a constitutional monarchy and only 15 percent supported Australia becoming a republic. Since that time support for the monarchy has slowly fallen. By 1998 only 37 percent supported the monarchy and 52 percent supported a republic, but, other polling showed that half of respondents said that they did not feel strongly either in favor of the monarchy or a republic.

The Australian Republican Movement was formed in 1991 and claimed 7,000 members; its formation prompted the creation of Australians for Constitutional Monarchy in 1992. In 1993 the **Keating** government set up a committee to advise the government on how Australia might become a republic while keeping constitutional change to a minimum. Voting for a constitutional convention to discuss Australian becoming a republic was held between November and December 1997. Conducted on a voluntary basis (**compulsory voting** is the norm in Australia), 46.6 percent of the electorate voted with voting favoring supporters of a republic both in total and by state (these are necessary conditions if the **Australian Constitution** is to be changed). The constitutional convention met between February 2-13, 1998. Consisting of 152 delegates, 89 backed the idea of a republic in principle, but because of a split among republicans, only 73 supported a proposal to appoint the president by a two-thirds majority of both the **senate** and the **house of representatives**. However, it did agree that this option should be put to the electorate at a **referendum**. The **Howard** government accepted this recommendation and the referendum was scheduled for November 1999. If the referendum is successful, it is intended to introduce the change on January 1, 2001 to coincide with the centenary of **federation**.

RETURNED SERVICES LEAGUE (RSL)   The RSL has been Australia's largest single organization of war veterans since its formation in 1916 when it was called the Returned Sailors' and Soldiers' Imperial League of Australia. The present title was adopted in 1965. The aim of the RSL was to ensure that returned soldiers, sailors, and air crew as well as their wives and children received their fair share of benefits in postwar society. Organizations like the RSL succeeded in gaining improved pensions for veterans and war widows and also in gaining employment preference for veterans in the bureaucracies of the federal government and the **states**. Membership of the RSL was 2,000 by 1930, but by 1946 had reached its peak of 374,000; since that time it has averaged about 250,000 members and was 230,000 in 1997. Until the 1980s the RSL exerted considerable influence on governments, but as the number of veterans from **World War II** has declined, so has its influence. (*See also* Australian Imperial Force)

RICHARDSON, HENRY HANDEL (1870-1946) This was the pseudonym of novelist Ethel Florence Lindesay Robertson, who was born in **Melbourne**. Her writings were much influenced by the madness and death in poverty of her father. She was educated at Melbourne Presbyterian Ladies' College and left for Europe in 1887. She married John George Robertson in 1895 and only came back to Australia once, in 1912, during her lifetime. Originally planning to be a concert pianist, she abandoned this career for writing. Her first novel *Maurice Guest* (1908) was set in Germany. She followed this by a far more successful novel based on her adolescence, *The Getting of Wisdom* in 1910. Between 1917 and 1929 she published her trilogy, *The Fortunes of Richard Mahony*, which was based on her father's life. Richardson was one of the first Australian novelists to gain an international reputation. (*See also* Literature)

ROADS Because of its large land area and relatively small and scattered population, Australia's road system was extensive, but of poor quality outside of the cities before **World War II**. The **railroads** and ships were the main movers of people and goods within and outside Australia before 1945. In 1940 Australia had 724,800 kilometers of roads—compared to 43,800 kilometers of railroads—but only about 4 percent of this extensive network was either concrete or bitumen sealed. There were also many gaps in the road system. There was no road bridge over the Hawkesbury River linking **Sydney** with the northern part of New South Wales until 1945 even though a railroad bridge had been built in 1889. Most interstate and intercity transportation was by railroad. The administration of roads was also undeveloped and left in the hands of local government. There were no state road boards before 1913 when the first was formed in **Victoria**; the purpose of the board was to centralize road construction and maintenance. The other **states** followed suit between 1920 and 1939.

World War II demonstrated the need for a better road system, but the real stimulus to road construction did not come until the advent of large-scale car ownership from the 1950s. By 1954 the road system had grown to 831,200 kilometers of which only 7.3 percent was concrete or bitumen sealed. An east-west road link was made between **Adelaide** and **Perth** during World War II, but the whole road was not bitumen sealed until 1976. Neither was there a fully sealed north-south road link between **Darwin** and Adelaide until

1979. Since the mid-1960s the quality of Australia's road network has improved greatly although accurate measurement of its progress is hindered by the reliance on statistics provided by about 800 local governments. By 1997 Australia had 803,100 kilometers of roads, but there had been an unquestioned improvement in the quality of roads. Between 1965 and 1997 the proportion of concrete or bitumen sealed roads had increased from 15 to 39 percent.

ROBERTS, TOM [THOMAS WILLIAM] (1856-1931) One of Australia's greatest artists, Roberts was born in Dorchester, England and immigrated to **Melbourne** in 1869. After study in Australia, he continued as an artist in **France** and Spain. He returned to Australia in 1885 and was a founder of the Australian Artists' Association. With other notable artists like Frederick McCubbin (1855-1917) and Arthur Streeton (1867-1943), Roberts introduced "impressionist" painting to Australia. He is best known for his paintings, often heroic, of rural life such as *Shearing the Rams* and a robbery by **bushrangers** (*Bailed Up*, 1895), but he also did many portraits and was commissioned to paint the opening of the new federal parliament in 1901. Since his death his reputation has grown enormously. (*See also* Painting)

ROYAL AUSTRALIAN AIR FORCE (RAAF) Based on the British Royal Air Force, the Royal Australian Air Force was formed in 1921 out of resources from the wartime Australian Flying Corps. It was poorly equipped and, until 1932, was under threat of being broken up and divided between the army and the **Royal Australian Navy**. But with the threat of war in the late 1930s, it was expanded and upgraded. During **World War II**, the RAAF was part of the Australian forces in all conflicts. A total of 189,700 men and 27,200 women served in the RAAF, of whom 6,447 were killed (5,116 in Europe and 1,331 in the south-east Pacific and Asia). After the war, the RAAF was engaged in the wars of **Korea**, Malaya, and **Vietnam**. In 1996 the air force component of the Australian Defence Force had 17,212 personnel.

ROYAL AUSTRALIAN NAVY (RAN) The Royal Australian Navy is the national navy of Australia. It was formed in 1911 from the naval forces of the formerly separate Australian **colonies**. During **World War I** the RAN had a major success in sinking the German raider the *Emden* (1914) in the Indian Ocean. Ships of the RAN also fought in the Atlantic and Pacific oceans and in the Mediterranean. By 1918 the RAN had 5,050 personnel. Greatly reduced in size and power in the interwar years, the RAN was expanded for the needs of **World War II**. During the war the RAN suffered 2,742 casualties, of whom 1,740 died. At the war's end in 1945, the RAN had 39,900 men and 2,700 women. The RAN was reorganized around its two aircraft carriers, but its fleet air arm was disbanded. The RAN took part in the wars in **Korea** and **Vietnam**. In 1996 the naval component of the Australian Defence Force had 14,404 personnel.

ROYAL FLYING DOCTOR SERVICE The Royal Flying Doctor Service was established in 1928 by the Rev. John Flynn (1880-1951) of the Presbyterian Church to provide medical care to people living in remote areas. The service, a product of aircraft and reliable radio communication, began in **Queensland** and spread to other states. It was the inspiration for the popular **television** soap opera of the late 1980s, *The Flying Doctors*.

"RUM REBELLION" The "Rum Rebellion" was the name given to a coup on January 26, 1808, which deposed William Bligh (1754-1817), the former captain of the *Bounty*, as governor of **New South Wales**. It was led by John Macarthur (1766-1834), a leading citizen and former army officer, and Major George Johnston (1774-1823). The cause of the coup was Bligh's attempt to stop the use of rum or spirits as a form of **currency**, a practice that reduced the wealth of the officers of the soldiers who had been sent to the colony to guard the **convicts**. Bligh returned to Britain; Johnston was court-martialed and cashiered; and Macarthur, who had gone to England in 1809 to argue for constitutional changes, was not allowed to return to Australia until 1817.

S

SCHOOL OF THE AIR The School of the Air is a two-way radio service begun in 1951 in **South Australia** to provide an **education** to children living in isolated rural areas who were unable to attend school. The idea was to supplement correspondence teaching and bring the teacher's voice to the children. In 1985 the Aussat satellite was launched, partly to improve the reception of School of the Air broadcasts. In the late 1980s the School had made use of fax machines and experimental use of two-way television as teaching aids. In 1990 the School was examined by a visiting Russian delegation as a possible model for teaching children in remote areas. (*See also* Education)

SCIENCE (*See* Bragg, William Henry and Bragg, William Lawrence; Commonwealth Scientific Industrial Research Organisation; Burnet, Frank Macfarlane; Doherty, Peter Charles; Fleay, David Howells; Florey, Howard Walter; Gregg, Norman McCalister; May, Robert McCredie; Nossal, Gustav Joseph Victor; Oliphant, Mark Laurence Elwin)

SCULLIN, JAMES [HENRY] (1876-1953) Australian **prime minister** Scullin, was born at Trawalla, **Victoria**. Largely self-educated, he joined the **Australian Labor Party** (ALP) in 1903 and was a member of the **house of representatives** from 1910 to 1913. He was a leading opponent of **conscription** during **World War I**. He was re-elected to the house of representatives in 1922, became leader of the parliamentary ALP in 1928, and became prime minister after the ALP won the national elections on October 12, 1929.

Scullin was prime minister from October 22, 1929, to January 6, 1932. His term in office was dominated by the Depression and by the fact that although the ALP had won a majority in the house of representatives, it had failed to win a majority in the **senate** whose members frustrated his government's efforts to ease the very high unemployment caused by the Depression. Scullin's government also faced opposition from the ALP in **New South Wales** led by its **premier**, the forceful **Jack Lang**, and from the board of the **Commonwealth Bank**. His own cabinet was also divided about the best policies to adopt towards the Depression. His government was defeated in the elections on December 19, 1931, by the newly formed **United Australia Party**. Scullin remained leader of the ALP in the federal parliament until 1935 and a member of parliament until 1949. The experience of the Scullin government with the banks convinced his minister for defense, **Ben Chifley**, to try to nationalize the banks when he was prime minister in the late 1940s. (*See also* Joseph Aloysius Lyons)

SECRET BALLOT Voting by ballot (as opposed to open voting by hand at meetings) for parliamentary elections had been a goal of radical political reformers in England since the 1780s. In Australia, the ballot was first advocated in **New South Wales** in the 1840s, but it was the Victorian *Electoral Act* of 1856 that introduced the secret ballot to the world and made it an integral part of the **franchise**. The secret ballot was adopted by New South Wales, **South Australia**, and **Tasmania** in 1858, **Queensland** in 1859, and **Western Australia** in 1879. The principle of the "Australian" ballot was adopted by **New Zealand** in 1870, **Britain** in 1872, and Canada in 1874. The first American state to adopt the ballot was Massachusetts in 1888, with all the other states following its lead by 1903. (*See also* Compulsory Voting; Franchise)

SENATE The upper chamber of the Australian federal parliament, the senate was created by the **Australian Constitution** in 1901. Modeled on the U.S. Senate, it is elected on a state basis. It was intended to be the guardian of the rights of the **states** within the federal government as opposed to the **house of representatives** which is elected by a majority of voters only. The role of the senate is mainly to review legislation submitted to it by the house of representatives. The original role of the senate has been changed by the rise of **political parties**, which drew more on ideology than state loyalty, and by the emergence of minor parties since the 1950s, such as the **Democratic Labor Party** and the **Australian Democrats**, which have been able to use their senate representation to hold the balance of power.

SHEEP AND WOOL Sheep and wool have been major products of **agriculture** in Australia since the 1830s and an integral part of the hinterland landscape as well as the **economy**. The first sheep were brought to Australia in 1794 by John Macarthur (1766-1834). During his absences from Australia (1801-05 and 1809-1817, his wife Elizabeth Macarthur (1766-1850) did much to improve the quality of his sheep. By 1850 there were about 17 million sheep in Australia. This figure had grown to 50 million by 1875, 100 million by 1890, and 180 million by 1970, the highest number ever recorded.

By the 1840s wool was a leading Australian export. In 1840 Australia supplied 20 percent of Britain's wool imports; by 1850, it supplied over half. Up until the 1950s most wool went to **Britain**, but since then **Japan** has been the largest single customer. About 75 percent of the wool Australia exports is unprocessed. Between 1990-91 and 1997-98 wool production in Australia fell from 1 million to 641,794 tonnes. In 1996-97 live sheep and wool accounted for 3.9

percent of the total value of Australia's exports; 5.2 million live sheep were exported in 1996-97. In 1997-98 wool accounted for 3.5 percent of Australia's merchandise exports. (*See also* Agriculture; Overlanders, Squatting)

SHEFFIELD SHIELD The Sheffield Shield is a silver trophy that has been the prize of inter-colonial/state **cricket** matches since 1893. The Shield arose out of an English cricket tour of Australia led by W. G. Grace, paid for by the Earl of Sheffield, in 1891-92. He also donated 150 pounds (or about $13,000 in 1997 prices) for the development of cricket in Australia. (*See also* Sport)

SHENANDOAH **INCIDENT** The *Shenandoah* was one of 18 cruisers used by the South against the merchant shipping of the North during the American Civil War. Between January 25 and February 18, 1865, the *Shenandoah* was docked in **Melbourne** harbor where captain J. J. Wadell was not only allowed to make repairs and take on provisions, but also to recruit new crew. The failure of the Victorian government to prevent his recruiting was regarded as a violation of British neutrality by the U.S. Consul in Melbourne and was part of the U.S. claims against Britain before the Tribunal of Arbitration in Geneva (1871-72). Britain was forced to pay U.S. $15.5 million for damage caused by the *Shenandoah* and other raiders.

SLESSOR, KENNETH [ADOLPH] (1901-1971) Poet, journalist, and war correspondent, Slessor was born in the inland country town of Orange, **New South Wales**, and educated in **Sydney**. He worked for the Sydney *Sun* newspaper in the early 1920s and with **Norman Lindsay** on the magazine *Vision* (1923-24). As a poet he is best known for *Five Bells* (1939) and *One Hundred Poems* (1944). He was the Australian army's Official War Correspondent during **World War II**. In 1944 he became literary editor of the *Sun* newspaper. (*See also* Literature)

SMITH, BERNARD [WILLIAM] (1916-) Art historian, Smith was born in **Sydney**. He was educated at the University of Sydney, the Warburg Institute in London, and the Australian National University. He was a high school teacher between 1935 and 1944 and was a member of the staff of the Art Gallery of New South Wales from 1944 to 1952. Smith held three posts at the University of Melbourne between 1955 and 1963 and was art critic for the *Age* newspaper from 1963 to 1966. He was professor of contemporary art and director of the Power Institute of Fine Arts at the University of Sydney from 1967 to 1977. His publications include *European Vision and the South Pacific* (1960), *Australian Painting* (1962), and *The Boy Adeodatus* (1984), his autobiography. (*See also* Painting)

SNOWY MOUNTAINS SCHEME The Snowy Mountains Scheme was the largest construction project in Australian history. It diverted the Snowy River inland through the Great Dividing Range in south-eastern Australia and into the Murrumbidgee river in southern **New South Wales** to generate hydro-electricity and to provide extra water for irrigation. First suggested in 1881, the work was carried out between 1949 and 1972. Many European immigrants worked on the project, which consisted of 16 storage dams, seven power stations, and a total of 225 kilometers of aqueducts and tunnels. Construction of the Snowy Mountains Scheme cost 121 lives. In recent years the diversion of all but one percent of the water from the Snowy river to hydro-electricity has been criticized for destroying the ecosystem of the river. On October 23, 1998 a government report recommended that 15 percent of the water be returned to the Snowy river.

SOCIAL SECURITY Australia's social security system began nationally in 1909 when the federal government began to pay old age and invalid pensions. The old age pension was available for men at 65 and women at 60. It replaced state age pensions, which had been introduced in **New South Wales** and **Victoria** in 1900 and in **Queensland** in 1908, and an invalid pension, which had begun in New South Wales in 1908. In 1912 the federal government began paying a maternity lump sum to mothers on the birth of a child. Until **World War II**, there was no extension to the federal social security system, apart from providing benefits for **World War I** veterans and their dependants. In the **states** there were some important initiatives. In 1923 Queensland introduced an unemployment insurance scheme. In New South Wales the government of **Jack Lang** introduced a widows' pension in 1926 and child endowment in 1927.

During the 1940s the federal Australian Labor Party governments of **John Curtin** and **Ben Chifley** completed the basis of the current national social security system. The main additions to the system in this period were the child endowment scheme (1941), the widows' pension (1942), and unemployment and sickness benefits (1945). The federal government was able to undertake these initiatives as it gained control of the states' powers over income tax in 1942. Its powers were also strengthened by the passing of a **referendum** in 1946 extending its power to make legislation for social security and **health and medical services** under the **Australian Constitution**.

Since the 1940s the main new social security programs have been the pharmaceutical benefits scheme (1948), the age pensioner medical service (1951), a supporting mother's benefit for unmarried mothers not entitled to the widow's pension (1973), an extended version of child allowances, the Family Allowance Scheme (1976), and the Family Income Supplement (1983), an allowance paid to low-income families with children who were not receiving any other form of social security payment. By the mid-1990s social security and welfare payments represent about 35 percent of expenditure by the federal government. (*See also* Commonwealth-State Relations, Women)

SOUTH AFRICA   Before the opening of the Suez Canal in 1869, Australia's links with South Africa were unavoidable because it was a critical part of the sea lanes between Australia and Britain. Even after the opening of the canal, South Africa remained an important part of these sea lanes. It was shipments from South Africa that saved the **convict** settlement at **Sydney** from starvation in the early 1790s. With the regularity of sea travel between the two countries, there was some interchange of population usually based on employment in **mining**. During the Boer war (1899-1902) 16,175 Australians fought on the British side and about 5,000 opted to remain there.

In 1901 there were 6,500 Australians in South Africa and 1,500 South Africans in Australia. By 1951 there were about 5,000 of each nationality living in the other's country, but with the introduction of apartheid in South Africa and increasingly domestic unrest after 1960, the number of South Africans of European descent migrating to Australia rose while the number of Australians in South Africa fell. During and after his term as Australian prime minister (1975-83), **Malcolm Fraser**, made a notable contribution to international efforts to abolish the apartheid system and encourage a democratic, multicultural society in South Africa. At the 1996 census there were 55,717 South Africans living in Australia compared to 15,565 in

1976. Because of the similarities in the economies of Australia and South Africa, **trade** between them is limited.

SOUTH AUSTRALIA South Australia was founded as a British colony in 1836 according to the idea of "systematic colonization" developed by Edward Gibbon Wakefield (1796-1862). The **population** was to be built up by **immigration** using profits from land sales. There were to be neither **convicts** nor an established church. After a difficult start the colony began to pay its way from 1844. Copper **mining**, which began in 1842, augmented the agricultural economy. **Adelaide**, the capital of the colony, was planned by William Light (1786-1839), making it the only nineteenth-century Australian city to be systematically planned. The present boundaries of South Australia date from 1861 and cover 984,000 square kilometers or 12.8 percent of the area of Australia.

From its beginning, South Australia was a center of religious toleration and attracted German immigrants after the 1840s seeking religious freedom. It also became a center for political freedom. In 1856 it was granted its own constitution which provided for a house of assembly (**legislative assembly**) elected by secret ballot with manhood suffrage and no property qualification to vote. South Australia was the source of several significant reforms. It was the first Australian colony to legalize **labor unions** (1878) and to give **women** the vote (1894).

From a starting population of 14,600 in 1841, South Australia had 276,400 people by 1881 making it the third largest of Australia's **colonies**. Thereafter its population growth rate was relatively slow. During the 1880s it was overtaken by Queensland. By 1933 its population had reached 580,900.

Apart from the south-east corner, most of South Australia is desert or semi-desert, which limited its potential for **agriculture** and population growth. In an effort to broaden the economic base of the state, the conservative government of **Thomas Playford**, who was **premier** from 1938 to 1965, actively promoted and assisted industrial development. Steel making (1938) and shipbuilding (1940) were established at Whyalla. A new satellite township, Elizabeth (1954), was founded north of Adelaide based on car building and metal fabrication. The empty space of the interior was also used. Woomera, a federal government township built after 1947, was a center for missile and nuclear weapons testing. In 1976 one of the world's largest deposits of uranium and copper was discovered at Roxby Downs in southern-central South Australia. South Australia has been a particularly popular destination for British immigrants in the post-1945 period. Between 1947 and 1966 the population of South Australia rose from 646,100 to 1,091,900. Despite the broadening of the economic base, South Australia has continued to experience a relatively low level of population growth. In 1986 it was overtaken by **Western Australia** as Australia's fourth most populous state.

Since 1933 South Australia has been ruled mainly by conservative governments with the **Australian Labor Party** (ALP) holding government only from 1967 to 1968, 1970 to 1979, and 1982 to 1993. Its leading figure in this period was Don Dunstan (1926-) who was premier in the two administrations between 1967 and 1979 and who introduced important reforms in consumer law, labor relations, and the protection of the environment. In contrast, the ALP administration of John Bannon (1943-) between November 6, 1982, and September 1, 1991, ended disastrously with huge financial losses by the government-owned State Bank amounting to $2.2 billion. The **Liberal Party** enjoyed a landslide victory in the elections on December 11, 1993, but suffered an unexpected collapse in its vote on October 11, 1997, although retaining government. Since November 1997, John Olsen (1945-) has led the Liberal government as premier.

SOUTH PACIFIC FORUM The South Pacific Forum was formed in September 1972 at Suva, Fiji, with the objective of promoting greater regional cooperation and trade. It has 15 members: Australia, **New Zealand**, Kiribati, Fiji, Marshall Islands, the Federated States of Micronesia, Nauru, Niue, Palau, **Papua New Guinea**, Solomon Islands, Tonga, Tuvalu, Vanuatu, and Western Samoa. The dominant economic powers of the Forum are Australia and New Zealand. Representatives of the Forum met in **Cairns** for the first time in 1997.

SPENCE, WILLIAM GUTHRIE (1846-1926) One of Australia's leading labor leaders in the late nineteenth century, Spence was born on one of the Orkney Islands of Scotland and emigrated with his family to Geelong, **Victoria**, in 1852. He had no formal education and worked as a butcher's boy, miner, and shepherd. He assisted with the recruiting drive which led to the formation of the Amalgamated Miners' Association (AMA) at the gold mining town of Bendigo in 1874. In 1878 he became secretary of the Creswick Miners' Union. Spence was an early supporter of industrial unionism and wanted the AMA to cover all miners in Australia and **New Zealand**. A number of mining unions did affiliate with the AMA, but the idea of a single union for the whole **mining** industry did not survive beyond the nineteenth century.

At the 1884 Intercolonial Trade Union Congress Spence tried unsuccessfully to persuade the unions to amalgamate along trade or industry lines and to set up a Federal Council to "deal with matters affecting the well-being of the working classes generally," a move which foreshadowed the formation of the **Australian Council of Trade Unions** in 1927. Although he supported conciliation as a means of settling disputes with employers, he was quite willing to use strikes as well. An excellent organizer and negotiator, he was appointed the first president of the Amalgamated Shearers' Union of Australasia in 1886 and in 1894 combined this union with several others to form the **Australian Workers' Union** in 1894; Spence served as its secretary from 1894 to 1898 and as its president from 1898 to 1917. He also wrote a history of the union in 1911.

From the mid-1880s Spence was a supporter of the need for organized labor to have political representation. He was a member of the legislative assembly of the New South Wales parliament for the **Australian Labor Party** (ALP) from 1898 to 1901 and of the **house of representatives** from 1901 to 1917. In 1917 he was permitted to resign from the ALP rather than be expelled for his support of **conscription**.

SPORT Australia's generally benign climate has been a powerful inducement to the popularity of sport of all kinds. Australians not only watch sport on television, they play it too. By 1984 the top 10 sports—**cricket**, **Australian Rules**, soccer, lawn bowls, golf, netball, tennis, basketball, field hockey, and Rugby League—claimed a total of 3.1 million participants. British **immigration** in the nineteenth century provided the foundation for the popularity of cricket and Rugby League. Australian Rules football, was an exception being an Australian invention although based on Gaelic football. The popularity of soccer has grown greatly since 1945 because of support from European immigrants. Horse racing is also strongly supported with the **Melbourne Cup** being a national institution. The premier yachting event is the **Sydney** to **Hobart** race, which began in 1945 and which attracts competitors from many countries. In 1983 Australia scored a yachting coup by being the first country other than the **United States** to win the America's Cup.

Australians have been participants in most major international sporting competitions. They participated in every **Olympic Games** since 1896, and in 1956 Australia hosted the Games in **Melbourne**, Victoria. As well, Australians have been participants in the Festival of Empire Games (1911-30) and the Commonwealth Games, which began as the Empire Games in Hamilton, Canada, in 1930. Australia hosted these Games in 1938, 1962, and 1982. In September 2000, Australia will host the Olympic Games in **Sydney**.

In 1997 an official survey found that 30 percent of Australians over 15 participated in organized sport, 33.3 percent of males and 27 percent of women. (*See also* Melbourne Cup; Sheffield Shield)

SQUATTING   Squatting was the illegal occupation of Crown (that is, government-owned) land before 1846. The word first appeared in print in Australia in 1828 and came from the late eighteenth-century American word "squatter" meaning a settler on uncultivated land without legal title. Drawn by the opportunities of **sheep** and cattle raising, many settlers moved beyond the limits of settlement set by governments to occupy or "squat" on lands they saw as unused. Their activities conflicted with colonial governments which wanted to use the sale of this land to generate revenue. (*See also* Free Selection; Land Settlement)

STATES   Under the **Australian Constitution**, the former **colonies** of Australia—**New South Wales**, **Victoria**, **Queensland**, **South Australia**, **Western Australia**, and **Tasmania**—became new legal entities, that is states within the new federal constitution.

STATUTE OF WESTMINSTER   The Statute of Westminster was a piece of British legislation which came into effect on December 11, 1931, and which officially renamed the British Empire as the British Commonwealth of Nations and effectively gave the dominions, such as Australia, sovereignty. The statute aroused little interest in Australia, which did not formally endorse it until October 9, 1942, and it was held to have taken effect from September 3, 1939.

STEAD, CHRISTINA [ELLEN] (1902-1983)   Expatriate novelist, Christina Stead was born in **Sydney** and educated at the University of Sydney. She worked as a teacher and in other jobs until she left Australia for **Britain** in 1928. Thereafter, she lived mainly in the **United States** and Europe. A cosmopolitan rather than a national author, Stead published her first work, *The Salzburg Tales*, in 1934. In 1935 she published *Seven Poor Men of Sydney,* her only novel to be set wholly in Australia. In 1937 she went to live in the United States. In 1940 she published *The Man Who Loved Children* in New York, a work often considered to be her best. Despite her success, Stead was largely ignored in Australia. In 1946 one of her novels, *Letty Fox: Her Luck*, was banned in Australia on the grounds that its heroine was immoral. After the death of her husband, she returned to Australia in 1968 and in 1974 became the first person to receive a literary award established by **Patrick White**. (*See also* Literature)

STEWART, DOUGLAS [ALEXANDER] (1913-1985)   Poet, playwright and critic, Stewart was born in Eltham, **New Zealand**, and educated at Victoria University College. After working as a journalist, he moved to Australia in 1938 where he joined the staff of the *Bulletin*. He became interested in Australian bush ballads and was joint editor of an anthology of them in 1955. He wrote a play about **Ned Kelly** in 1943, but is best remembered for his radio play, *The Fire on the Snow* (1944) which deals with Scott's expedition in **Antarctica** in 1912. (*See also* Literature)

STOW, [JULIAN] RANDOLPH (1935-)   Poet and novelist, Stow was born in the country town of Geraldton, **Western Australia**, and was educated at the University of Western Australia. He worked as a missionary with **Aborigines,** as an English teacher, and as an assistant anthropologist in **Papua New Guinea**. He lectured in English at the University of Leeds and returned to Australia in 1966. He is best known for *To the Islands* (1958), *Visitants* (1979), and *The Suburbs of Hell* (1984). In 1979 he won the **Patrick White** Literary Award. (*See also* Literature)

STRIKES   (*See* Labor Disputes)

STUART, JOHN MCDOUALL (1815-1866)   One of Australia's greatest land explorers, Stuart was born in Fife, Scotland. He joined the army and emigrated to **South Australia** in 1839 where he used his military experience to work as a surveyor. In 1844-45 he was a member of the expedition led by **Charles Sturt** into central

Australia where he learned the skills to survive in a harsh, arid land. His own remarkable expedition of 1861-62 succeeded in crossing the Australian mainland from south to north. The route he opened up was used for the **Overland Telegraph** (1872), which provided Australia's first direct communications link with the world. Stuart was poorly rewarded for his achievements and left Australia in 1864 with his health broken by the hardship of his expeditions. The government of South Australia used his expedition to lay claim to the control of the **Northern Territory**. (*See also* Exploration)

STURT, CHARLES (1795-1869) Born in Bengal, India, to an English judge, Sturt is famous in Australian history for his **exploration** of the inland river systems of south-eastern Australia in 1829-30. He followed the Murrumbidgee River to where it met the Murray River and then the Murray River until it met the sea. His expedition disproved the common belief that these rivers flowed into an inland sea. In 1844-46 Sturt led an expedition into the Simpson desert which proved conclusively that there was no inland sea in the interior. (*See also* Exploration)

SUTHERLAND, JOAN (1926-) Opera singer, Sutherland was born in Point Piper, an eastern suburb of **Sydney**. Her musical talent was fostered by her mother and she made her singing debut in August 1947 in Sydney. Winning competitions in 1949 and 1950 enabled her to study in London. She became a soprano with Covent Garden in 1952. In 1954 she married one of her teachers, Richard Alan Bonynge (1930-), an Australian pianist with whom she formed a remarkably productive musical partnership. Sutherland became an international opera star after her performance in Donizetti's *Lucia di Lammermoor* in 1959. She and Bonynge returned to Australia in 1965 for a one season and in 1974 they came back again. Sutherland was a regular guest singer with Australian Opera and Bonynge became its musical director from 1975 to 1986. Sutherland was named a Companion of the Order of Australia in 1975 for her services to opera and was made a Dame Commander of the British Empire in 1979. She announced her retirement in September 1990.

SUBURBIA (*See* Urbanization)

SYDNEY Sydney is Australia's oldest and, for most of its history, largest city. It is the capital of its most populous state, **New South**

Wales. Based on an outstanding natural harbor, Sydney was a natural center for trade and economic development, as well as being a political capital.

Founded in 1788 with about 1,000 Europeans, its population grew slowly until the 1830s and even by 1851 had only reached 54,000. Thereafter Sydney grew rapidly in parallel with the Australian **economy** and as a city in its own right. Between 1861 and 1891 it lagged behind **Melbourne** in population size. By 1881 the population had reached 225,000, of whom 55 percent lived in the suburbs rather than the inner city. In 1901 Sydney contained 496,000 people and had regained from Melbourne its position as the largest Australian city. The two cities were often compared. In the 1880s, Melbourne was frequently described as the progressive, American-style city and Sydney as the slower, conservative city.

Since 1901 Sydney's population has grown nearly seven and a half times from 496,000 to 3.7 million by 1996. Buttressed by the industrial center of **Newcastle** and the commuter and resort center of the **Central Coast** to the north and the industrial center of **Wollongong** to the south, Sydney is at the center of the largest urban system in Australia. By the 1930s the reputations of Sydney and Melbourne had been reversed. Melbourne was now called the staid, conservative city whereas Sydney was seen as the go-ahead city of Australia.

Not only does Sydney easily dominate New South Wales, it is home to a significant part of the total Australian population. Between 1901 and 1996, the proportion of the population of New South Wales living in Sydney rose from 37 to 62 percent. Over the same period, the proportion of all Australians living in Sydney has increased from 13 to 21 percent. This growth has been based on its port, its commerce and manufacturing, and its role as a political capital. Mascot airport was established in 1919.

The University of Sydney was established in 1852. A major event in the growth of Sydney was the opening of the **Sydney Harbor Bridge** in 1932, which enabled large-scale settlement of the city's north, largely for the better-off residents. In 1942 Japanese submarines carried out a daring raid on shipping in Sydney harbor.

The **Sydney Opera House** was opened in 1973 and soon gained an international reputation for its revolutionary architecture. Since the mid-1970s there has been much redevelopment of the inner harbor area of Sydney. In 1979 the eastern suburbs were linked to the inner city by an underground electric railway, a project which had been planned in the 1880s.

In January 1988 Sydney was the focal point of Australia's bicentennial celebrations. In 1990 the National Maritime Museum was opened at Darling Harbour. In 1991 the Museum of Contemporary Art was opened at Circular Quay. In 1995 Sydney's first legal casino was opened at Darling Harbour. In 1996, 1.6 million people, 42 percent of Sydney's population, lived in the city's west, an area largely opened up for settlement in the post-1945 period.

In the last half of the 1980s Sydney overtook Melbourne as Australia's financial capital. By 1989, 60 of Australia's largest 100 companies had their head offices in Sydney. In the process it has become Australia's truly global city although at the price of also becoming Australia's most socially divided city with its most expensive real estate.

Sydney is a major tourist destination. In 1994-95, 64 percent of international visitors to Australia came to Sydney and the most popular attractions were its shopping, the Sydney Opera House, Darling Harbour, the Rocks, the Sydney Tower, and the beaches, particularly Bondi. On September 23, 1993, Sydney was named as the venue for the summer **Olympic Games** in September 2000. (*See also* Urbanization)

SYDNEY HARBOR BRIDGE   One of Australia's best-known landmarks and icons, the **Sydney** Harbor Bridge is the widest and heaviest arc bridge in the world. Construction began in 1923 and the bridge was opened in 1932. The official opening of the bridge on March 19, 1932, by **Jack Lang**, was disrupted by a member of the **New Guard**. The bridge is 503 meters long and 134 meters above average sea level. It has eight traffic lanes and two railroad lines. By the 1980s the bridge carried 40 million rail and bus passengers a year and over 80 million by private vehicles. In August 1992 the Sydney Harbor Tunnel was opened to relieve traffic pressure on the bridge.

SYDNEY MORNING HERALD   Australia's oldest continuous newspaper, the *Herald* was first produced in 1831 as the *Sydney Herald*. It was renamed the *Sydney Morning Herald* in 1842 by its new owners John Fairfax and Charles Kemp. Throughout its history it has been a conservative newspaper, but since the 1960s it has become more critical about social issues. In 1996 the *Herald* 's circulation was 235,000 from Monday through Friday and 400,300 on Saturdays.

SYDNEY OPERA HOUSE Opened on October 20, 1973, the Sydney Opera House is Australia's best known modern building. Located on Bennelong Point on the south side of **Sydney** harbor, it was designed by the Danish architect Jørn Utzon (1918-) and was built between 1959 and 1973 at a cost of $100 million which was raised from special lottery ticket sales. Notable for its pioneering design and use of concrete, sail-like structures, the Opera House covers 2.2 hectares and can accommodate about 7,000 people at any one time. The Opera House is a major attraction for both domestic and international tourists.

T

TARIFFS (*See* Protection)

TASMANIA Tasmania is Australia's only island **state**. It has an area of 68,800 square kilometers and lies south of the south-east coast of the Australian mainland. Around 22,000 years ago there was a drop in the sea level which created a land bridge between the mainland and Tasmania enabling its peopling by mainland **Aborigines**. A rise in the sea level around 10,000 years ago cut the land bridge and again isolated Tasmania. It was discovered in 1642 by the Dutch navigator Abel Janszoon Tasman (c.1603-1659), who named it Van Diemen's Land after the **governor-general** of the Dutch East Indies. To preempt suspected French designs, the British used **convicts** from **Sydney** to establish a presence in Tasmania in 1803. **Hobart**, the capital of Van Diemen's Land, as Tasmania was officially known until January 1, 1856, was founded in 1804. The colony was administratively under **New South Wales** until 1825. Van Diemen's Land was a major convict colony until 1853. Between 1803 and 1850, 62,300 convicts were sent there, 43 percent of all the convicts transported to Australia. Even as late as 1848, 38 percent of the colony's population of 28,460 were convicts.

Despite several decades of resistance, the Aborigines were defeated and deprived of their lands by the late 1820s. The remainder spent their last days in European captivity. The last surviving tribal Tasmanian Aborigine, Truganini, died in 1876.

After the end of the transportation of convicts in 1853, Tasmania made slow economic progress. Mineral discoveries, notably of **gold**, tin, silver-lead, and copper, at the end of the nineteenth century boosted the economy, but generally Tasmania's rate of economic growth has been poor and the state has suffered from sustained population loss to the mainland since 1900. Most who left were the young. More than any other state, Tasmania has become particularly dependent upon grants from the federal government. Since 1948-49, household income per head in Tasmania has been the lowest of any Australian state or **territory**, a fact that had encouraged out-migration. Successive state governments, especially since the 1920s, sought to stimulate the economy by large-scale, hydro-electric schemes and by encouraging industrialization. Tasmania has its own **franchise** system: the Hare-Clark system, a unique system of proportional representation based on multi-member constituencies.

After the creation of Lake Pedder to generate hydro-electricity in 1972, the pro-development government and bureaucratic policies clashed with the growing Tasmanian environmental movement. The formation of the United Tasmania Group in March 1972 was the first "green" political party in the world, anticipating the German Greens by six years. The Group, which became the Tasmanian Wilderness Society in 1979, won a notable victory in its campaign to stop the state government from flooding the Franklin River in 1983.

At the state elections on May 13, 1989, the environmental party, the Greens, won 18 percent of the vote and agreed to allow the **Australian Labor Party** (ALP) led by Michael Field (1948-) to form a government based on a written accord, which by late 1990 had broken down. At the state elections on February 1, 1992, the ALP government was heavily defeated by the **Liberal Party** led by Ray Groom (1945-), although the government lost support at the elections on February 24, 1996. Tony Rundle (1939-) replaced Groom as **premier**. On April 28, 1996, Tasmania gained international notoriety when a deranged gunman killed 35 people and wounded 21 others at Port Arthur, a former convict settlement and important tourist attraction. His action led to tighter gun laws throughout Australia.

Tasmanian policies have always been renowned for their conservatism. Homosexual behavior was only legalized in 1994 and then only because of pressure from the federal government after the United Nations Human Rights Commission found that Tasmania's harsh homosexual laws violated the human rights charter. Only one

Tasmanian premier had ever been **prime minister** of Australia, **Joseph Aloysius Lyons**. At the 1996 census Tasmania had a resident population of 459,700 compared to 452,800 in 1991.

Following the state elections on August 29, 1998 the Liberal government of Tony Rundle was defeated by the ALP led by Jim Bacon (1950-). As a result of a change in the state constitution which reduced the number of parliamentarians from 35 to 25, the number of Green representatives fell from five to one, thereby eliminating them as power brokers in Tasmanian politics.

TAYLOR, [THOMAS] GRIFFITH (1880-1963) Australia's first significant geographer, Taylor was born in Walthamstow, Essex, England and emigrated to **New South Wales** with his family in 1893. He was educated at the Universities of Sydney and Cambridge. In 1910 he went with Robert Falcon Scott in his expedition to **Antarctica** as meteorologist where he carried out pioneering research into its climate and topography. In 1920 he became associate professor of geography at Sydney University, a position he held until 1928. In books and articles about the climate and geography of Australia, Taylor argued that Australia did not have unlimited potential for a large **population** because of its mainly arid climate.

These views were highly unpopular in official circles in the 1920s (though some other geographers and economists agreed with Taylor). The official view at the time was that Australia had virtually unlimited potential for economic and population growth. His estimate that Australia's population would be about 19 or 20 million by the end of the twentieth century based on environmental constraints proved remarkably accurate. The education authorities in **Western Australia** banned his books from its schools after he described the state as mostly desert. Taylor left Australia in 1928 after failing to be made a full professor and became professor of geography at the Universities of Chicago (1928-35) and Toronto (1935-51). In 1940 he became the first non-American to be elected president of the Association of American Geographers. He returned to Australia in 1951. During his career he wrote over 40 books.

TELECOMMUNICATIONS Because of the great distances within Australia and its isolation from **Britain**, advances in telecommunications have been quickly adopted in Australia. The telegraph was first operated in **Melbourne**, Victoria, in 1854, 10 years after its invention in the **United States**. **Sydney**, Melbourne and **Adelaide** were linked by telegraph in 1858. The **Overland Telegraph** connected Australia with the outside world in 1872.

The telephone was first used in Australia in 1878, two years after its invention. By 1887 all the capital cities had telephone exchanges operated by the colonial governments. The first public telephone was installed in 1893. Under section 51(v) of the **Australian Constitution**, telecommunications were made a responsibility of the federal government. Administration of these powers was passed to the postmaster general's department. In 1930 the first overseas telephone call was made between the prime ministers of Australia and Britain. The number of telephone subscribers reached half a million in 1929, fell during the Depression and did not reach half a million again until 1939. By 1952 there were a million subscribers; there were 2 million by 1965 and 5 million by 1981. Overseas telecommunications were made the responsibility of the Overseas Telecommunications Commission in 1946, services previously provided by private companies.

In 1975 the Australian Telecommunications Commission (Telecom) was created to run the telephone network. Telecom became the largest single public sector employer in Australia. In 1975 it employed 86,000 and in 1991, 72,200. Since the 1970s there have been strong pressures on Telecom to operate more like a private company and to share its operations with the private sector. In late 1997 a third of Telecom was privatized with 1.7 million Australians buying shares. Meanwhile, employment has fallen as technology had advanced.

Australia's satellite communications are managed by AUSSAT Proprietary Limited, a company set up by the federal government in November 1981. The first two Australian satellites were launched by the Space Shuttle in 1985 and the third by the Ariane rocket in 1987. (*See also* School of the Air; Television)

TELEVISION Under section 51(v) of the **Australian Constitution**, the power to make laws with respect to broadcasting rests entirely with the federal government. In 1954 the Royal Commission into Television recommended its gradual introduction based on government licenses for private owners, that is, using similar arrangements to those under which radio stations had operated since 1923. In 1956 a dual television service began. The first commercial broadcast began on September 16, 1956, and the first broadcast by the government-owned **Australian Broadcasting Commission** (ABC) began on November 5, 1956. Television sets were expensive at first and relied heavily on British and American programs.

Notable events in the 1960s included the beginning of *Four Corners*, a current affairs program by the ABC in 1961 and the first Australian satirical program, the *Mavis Bramston Show* in 1964. In 1974 the system of individual licenses for television and radio was abolished. In 1976 cigarette and tobacco advertising were banned on television and radio. Color television broadcasting began in March 1975.

On October 24, 1980, broadcasts began by the Special Broadcasting Service, a government-owned agency designed to cater to the information and entertainment needs of Australia's non-English speaking peoples. The service has been highly successful and provides a global emphasis on world affairs not generally given in most other areas of Australian television.

The politics of Australian television have mainly revolved around the question of ownership, particularly cross-ownership with the **press**, the level of Australian content in broadcasting, and the implications of technological advances. Television ownership is almost universal and a major leisure activity. In 1992 a survey found that Australians watch on average 179 minutes of television a day.

TERRITORIES The territories of Australia are those administrative areas which are not defined as states in the **Australian Constitution**. The internal territories are the **Northern Territory** and the **Australian Capital Territory** which includes Jervis Bay on the south coast of **New South Wales**.

There are seven external territories off the Australian mainland: the Coral Sea Islands Territory (Willis Group and Cato Island); **Norfolk Island**; the Australian Antarctic Territory which is comprised of two slices of **Antarctica**; the Territory of Heard and MacDonald Islands off the coast of Antarctica; and three territories which lie due south of **Indonesia**, that is the Cocos (or Keeling) Islands, Christmas Island, and Ashmore and Cartier Islands. With the exception of the Northern Territory and the Australian Capital Territory, these territories have either no permanent populations (the Coral Islands and Antarctica) or very small populations. At the 1996 **census** the total population of Australia's external territories was only 3,323 compared to 2,697 in 1991. (*See also* Australian Capital Territory; Northern Territory)

TORRES STRAIT ISLANDERS   Torres Strait Islanders are the smaller group of Australian indigenous people, the larger group being by far **Aborigines**. They are mainly a Melanesian people with some mix from Asian, Polynesian, and Europeans. They inhabit an archipelago of 17 islands in Torres Strait between the north-eastern Australian mainland at Cape York and **Papua New Guinea**. The islands were the scene of missionary activity and pearl fishing from 1871. In 1879 the islands became part of **Queensland** whose governments included them under the administration of Aborigines and treated them in a paternal manner. Some limited autonomy was restored to them in 1939, but this did not satisfy the Torres Strait Islanders.

During the 1870s the Islanders became much more politically active following the decline of pearl fishing in the 1950s and the movement of more Islanders to the Australian mainland. In 1978 the Islanders attempted unsuccessfully to overturn the takeover by Queensland of their islands through the **High Court of Australia**. Isolation and concern over their possible handover to Papua New Guinea gave the Islanders a heightened sense of separateness and cohesion and concern for their rights to their land. This gave rise to what became known as the **Mabo Judgment** in 1992 which, in effect, gave the Islanders what they wanted, that is, legal confirmation of their ownership of the land. But in the process, it was a legal decision with enormous implications for land ownership in Australia and the land rights claims of indigenous Australians.

Torres Strait Islanders have only been separately identified in the national **census** of population and housing since 1971. Since that time, their recorded numbers have grown greatly as Australia's indigenous people have shown a greater willingness to identify themselves as either Aborigines or Torres Strait Islanders. The number of Torres Strait Islanders has risen from 9,663 in 1971 to 15,232 in 1981, to 26,883 in 1991, and to 38,850 in 1996. In 1996, only 14.8 percent of those Australians who identified themselves as Torres Strait Islanders lived on islands in the Torres Strait. Most of the remainder, 39.6 percent, lived in Queensland. Like the Aborigines, their level of **urbanization** is less than for Australians generally.

TOURISM   Domestic tourism in Australia developed in the wake of the **railroads** from the 1880s. State government tourist bureaus grew out of the railroad booking offices. The first government tourist bureau was established in **New South Wales** in 1906 followed by **Victoria** and **South Australia** in 1908, **Tasmania** in 1915, **Western Australia** in 1921, and **Queensland** in 1926. The railroads enabled the residents of the large cities to visit mountain and beach resorts. **Sydney**, the Blue Mountains to its west, and Gosford to its north, were established tourist areas by the 1920s. In the mid-1930s an international tourist trade began in the form of cruises to **New Zealand** and the introduction of tourist class berths on liners to **Britain**. Before 1945 though, mass domestic tourism was constrained by the slow rise in living standards, low levels of car ownership, and lack of paid annual holidays.

In 1924 the federal government began to collect statistics on short-term population movements between Australia and other countries. The figures show that before 1940 only about 20,000 people a year visited Australia and a similar number of Australians visited other countries. Most visitors came from New Zealand and Britain. Less than a thousand a year came from the **United States**. The pattern of movements by Australian residents was similar, with most going to New Zealand or Britain and only a few hundred to the United States.

After 1950, there was a slow but steady growth in mass domestic tourism based on rising incomes, rising car ownership, and more paid leisure time. Beginning in New South Wales in 1951, **long service leave** began to be extended to most employees. In 1958 the annual leave given to New South Wales employees was extended to three weeks; the other states and territories followed by 1963. The entry of jet aircraft into domestic travel in the 1960s gave further impetus to domestic tourism as exemplified by the growth of the **Gold Coast** in Queensland from the late-1950s.

These same forces gave rise to greater international tourism. In 1950, 31,400 Australians visited other countries, a figure which by 1960 had only risen to 77,700. But after the introduction of jumbo jets in the early 1970s, the number of Australians going overseas soared from 352,200 in 1970 to 911,700 in 1975 and to 1.2 million by 1980. In 1995-96, 2.7 million Australians traveled overseas on trips of less than 12 months. Of these travelers, 37.4 percent went to Asia, 15.2 percent to New Zealand, 12.1 percent to the United States, and 11.3 percent to Britain and Ireland.

In contrast to the growth of domestic tourism, Australia's development as an international tourist destination was much slower. In 1929 the federal government established the Australian National

Travel Association to promote Australia as a tourist destination. In 1930 the Association established offices in London and San Francisco; Australia thus became the first foreign country to establish a tourist promotion center on the west coast of the United States. Despite the Association's efforts, the number of international tourists was small. In 1950, there were 43,600 overseas visitors to Australia; 84,600 came in 1960, and 516,000 in 1975, a poor result given that 911,800 Australians visited other countries in that year. Since 1975 the number of overseas visitors to Australia has increased sharply; 904,600 came in 1980 and 4.2 million came in 1995-96.

In 1995-96 the largest groups of visitors came from Asia (50.2 percent), New Zealand (16.1 percent), Britain and Ireland (9.3 percent), and the United States (7.6 percent). Part of this growth could be attributed to the promotional work of the Australian Tourist Commission, a statutory body established by the federal government in 1967, made up of representatives of government and the tourist industry to promote domestic and international tourism. The Bureau of Tourism Research estimated that in 1993-94 international tourism contributed 6.6 percent of Australia's gross domestic product directly and supported 6.9 percent of the employed **labor force**.

In 1995-96 international tourism was responsible for 12.8 percent of Australia's total export earnings. Despite the growth in international tourism over the past decade, Australia still receives only about 0.5 percent of the world's tourist arrivals. The fall in the value of Asian currencies reduced tourist numbers during 1997-98, but the consequent fall in the value of the Australian dollar has made Australia a more attractive destination for British and American tourists.

The most popular attractions for tourists are Sydney and its surroundings, the **Gold Coast** and the **Great Barrier Reef** in **Queensland**, and **Ayer's Rock** and Kakadu National Park in the **Northern Territory**, and the federal capital of **Canberra**.

TOWNSVILLE Townsville is the third largest town in the state of **Queensland**. It was named after Robert Towns (1794-1873), a Sydney merchant and pioneer cotton grower. Although the district around Townsville was explored by Captain **James Cook** in 1770, it was not settled until 1865. Its economy was based on agriculture (particularly meat processing), serving as an export port for cane sugar and as a mineral processing center. During **World War II**

Townsville was an important base for Australian and American forces. Townsville was bombed by the Japanese in July 1943.

By 1933 the population of Townsville had reached 25,900. In 1943 the presence of the military swelled the population to about 90,000. By 1966 Townsville had a population of 56,800 and continued to grow thereafter, partly in response to the growth of tourism. In 1996 the urban center of Townsville-Thuringowa had a population of 104,900. On January 11, 1998, Townsville received half its average annual rainfall in 24 hours causing severe flooding and $50 million in damage.

TRADE With its relatively small **population**, the Australian **economy** has always been more dependent upon trade than nations with larger economies. In 1921 the trade dependence—that is the value of imports as a percentage of gross domestic product—of Australia was 25.5 percent. The development of the **manufacturing** from the 1930s onward reduced the trade dependence of the Australian economy to 14 percent by 1990-91.

Similarly, exports have always amounted to a higher percentage of gross domestic product in Australia for the same reason. In 1921 exports were equivalent to 19.4 percent of the gross domestic product of Australia. In 1990-91 exports as a proportion of gross domestic product had fallen to 13.1 percent.

For much of its history as a country of European settlement, Australia was heavily reliant on the British economy, not just as a source of investment and labor through **immigration**, but also as a market for its exports, particularly **wool** and **gold**. Between 1861 and 1891 about two-thirds of all Australian exports went to **Britain**. Although the figures are not available nationally before 1887, it would seem that Britain was also the source for a comparable proportion of Australia's imports before 1901. Essentially, Australia was a raw or unfinished commodities (minerals and agricultural products) exporter and an importer of finished or value-added goods. Elements of this trade pattern persist into the 1990s with the Australian dollar being regarded by money markets as a **currency** which reflects the price of commodities and minerals.

In spite of its small population, Australia has still made a disproportionately large contribution to world trade. In 1901 Australia accounted for 0.2 percent of the world's population, but 2 percent of world trade. Between 1913 and 1938 Australia's share of world trade was between 1.8 and 1.9 percent. In 1950 its share had risen to 2.8 according to the International Monetary Fund, as a result of the abnormal trading conditions prevailing after **World War II**. By 1970 this figure had fallen to 1.7 percent and to 1.2 percent by 1990. In 1996 Australia's share of world trade was down to 1 percent, but still a significant result for a country which had only 0.3 percent of the world's population. Such a decline was also to be expected given the recovery of the Western European economies and the rise of the Japanese economy in this period.

The fundamental features of the trade component of Australia's economy shifted considerably after World War II. Between 1951 and 1961 the share of Australian exports taken by Britain fell from 32.6 to 21.5 percent and continued to decline, especially so after Britain joined the European Economy Community in 1973. Between 1970-71 and 19997-98 Australia's exports to Britain fell from 9.8 to 3.5 percent and its imports from 21.4 to 6.2 percent.

Much of the decline in the trading relationship between Britain and Australia after 1955 was because of the rise of **Japan** as an importer of Australian products, especially **iron ore**. Between 1954-55 and 1970-71 Japan's share of Australian exports rose from 7.6 to 23.7 percent. In 1997-98 Japan took 20 percent of Australia's exports.

Trade between Australia and the **United States** fluctuated before 1940 although there was a consistent pattern of Australia importing more from the United States than it exported. In 1920-21 the United States accounted for 22 percent of Australia's imports, but only took 5.4 percent of its exports. Since World War II Australia's trade with the United States was also influenced by the Cold War with Australia buying much military hardware from the United States. In 1997-98 the United States accounted for 8.8 percent of Australia's exports, but 21.9 percent of its imports.

Yet despite the growth of Australian trade with Asia and the United States since 1945, Australia's trading links with the European Union are still very important, despite the decline in trade with Britain on a country-to-country basis. In 1995-96, the European Union overtook Japan as Australia's largest partner in merchandise trade. In 1997-98 the European Union accounted for 11.7 percent of Australia's exports and 24.1 percent of its imports.

In terms of two-way trade (that is the combination of exports and imports), Australia's largest trading partners in 1997-98 were the European Union (18 percent), Japan (17 percent), the United States

(15.5 percent), and the Association of South-East Asian Nations (12.3 percent). (*See also* Agriculture; Economy; Mining)

TRADE UNIONS (*See* Labor Unions)

TRANSPORTATION (*See* Railroads, Roads)

U

UNITED AUSTRALIA PARTY (UAP) The UAP was Australia's largest conservative political party between 1931 and 1944. It was formed in May 1931 when a number of conservative federal **Australian Labor Party** (ALP) parliamentarians joined **the Nationalist Party** led by **William Morris Hughes** because they opposed the economic policies of the government of **James Scullin** in coping with the Depression. The UAP elected a former ALP member, **Joseph Aloysius Lyons**, leader and won the national elections on December 19, 1931. The UAP was able to govern alone from 1931 to 1934 when it was forced into coalition with the **Country Party**. The UAP suffered continually from disunity. After Lyons's death in 1939, **Robert Gordon Menzies** was elected leader and **prime minister** but because of internal attacks on his leadership he resigned in August 1941.

   In state politics, the UAP ruled in coalition with the Country Party in **New South Wales** (1932-41) and in **Victoria** (1932-35 and 1943-45, but as the junior party). At the federal elections in September 21, 1940, the UAP coalition and the ALP each won 36 seats in the **house of representatives** with two independents holding the balance of power. The independents withdrew their support from the UAP government in October 1941, and the ALP formed a government under **John Joseph Curtin**. As a political party, the UAP was unduly prone to in-fighting and excessively reliant on certain sections of the business community. After being heavily defeated in the federal elections on August 21, 1943, Menzies regained the leadership of the UAP and with others used it as the basis for creating a new conservative party, the **Liberal Party of Australia**, which was formed between December 14-16, 1944.

UNITED KINGDOM (*See* Britain)

UNITED STATES OF AMERICA Australia's contacts with the United States date from 1792 when American ships came to **Sydney** for trade. The first person naturalized in Australia was a Bostonian, Timothy Gordon Pitman (1791-1832) in 1825. The first American consul office was opened in Sydney in 1839. The California gold rush of 1849 was linked directly to the Australian gold rushes of the 1850s because it was the experience that Edward Hargraves (1816-1891) gained on those fields that enabled him to train assistants to discover payable **gold**. The stage coach company of **Cobb and Co** was founded by Americans. Later in the century, the U.S. Constitution was used as a model for the **Australian Constitution** in its use of bodies such as the **senate** and the **house of representatives**. For most Australians their images of the United States came at first from the American films which dominated their cinemas from the 1920s.

World War II and the presence of over a million American servicemen provided Australians with their first mass contact with Americans. The contact made Australians aware that their standard of living was inferior to that of the Americans. The Battle of the **Coral Sea** (February to May 1942), at which the American navy inflicted a strategic reverse on the Japanese navy, was interpreted as having saved Australia from invasion. The battle is commemorated each year and the American navy is invited to participate. After the war about 12,000 Australian women went to the United States as war brides. Australian military forces have fought with the Americans in **Korea** and **Vietnam**, and the Gulf war. During the Vietnam war, a total of 276,885 U.S. troops took rest and recreation leave in Australia between October 1967 and January 1972.

The military connection between the two countries remains important as indicated by Australia's commitment to the **Anzus Treaty**. Since 1963 there have been a number of American bases in Australia. Pine Gap in the **Northern Territory** is run by the Central Intelligence Agency to monitor foreign military communications. These bases have long been considered to be vital to the defense of the United States.

Population interchanges between Australia and the United States have been limited and of a similar size since 1870. In 1901 there were 7,500 American-born living in Australia compared to 7,000 Australians living in the United States. In 1991 there were 43,800 Americans living in Australia compared to 52,500 Australians living in the United States. Since 1860 the most popular U.S. state for the Australian-born has been California.

Recent American immigrants to Australia tend to be young and of high socioeconomic status. For example, at the 1991 **census**, 26.6 percent of the United States-born were in the highest income category compared to 11.1 percent of Australian-born. The census data also indicate that many of the United States-born in Australia do not intend to stay permanently in Australia. In 1996 there were 49,500 United States-born in Australia, of whom only 42.7 percent had become Australian citizens.

American economic and cultural influences on Australia began to grow significantly from about 1920 and has accelerated since World War II. In the 1920s Hollywood films swamped the infant Australian **film** industry. With the start of **television** in Australia in 1956, many American programs were shown, particularly on the commercial channels, and this has heightened American influence and the adoption of American words into **Australian English**. Since the 1950s the United States, not **Britain**, has been the most important general external influence on Australia.

The United States has also become a major investor in Australia, particularly since 1960. American firms such as General Motors (which produced the first mass-produced Australian car, the "Holden," in 1948), Coca-Cola, Mobil, Kodak, General Electric, Otis, K Mart, and Microsoft are well-known names in Australia. By 1986 the United States had emerged as the largest single investor nation in Australia, a position it maintained in 1996-97 when it accounted for 25 percent of all foreign investment.

Throughout the twentieth century, Australia has had an unfavorable balance of **trade** with the United States. Since 1960 the United States has accounted for roughly 20 percent of Australia's imports by value, but only for about 10 percent of its exports. In 1997-98 the United States accounted for 21.9 percent of Australia's imports, but only 8.5 percent of its exports. (*See also* Great White Fleet, Lend Lease, *Shenandoah* Incident; Tables 6 to 10 in Appendix 3)

UNITING CHURCH OF AUSTRALIA   The Uniting Church of Australia was created on June 22, 1977, when the **Methodists** voted to amalgamate with the **Presbyterians** and Congregationalists. At the 1976 **census** these three faiths had a combined following of 1.9 million (53,400 Congregationalists, 983,200 Methodists, and

900,000 Presbyterians), but by the 1981 census, only 712,600 Australians claimed to be members of the Uniting Church, although this figure had risen to 1.2 million by the time of the 1986 census. In 1996 the Uniting Church had 1.3 million members—that is 7.5 percent of the population—making it Australia's third largest **religion**. (*See also* Religion)

UNIVERSITIES   The first Australian university was founded in **Sydney** in 1852. It was followed by the establishment of universities in **Melbourne** (1853), **Adelaide** (1874), **Tasmania** (1890), **Queensland** (1909), and **Western Australia** (1911). The number of university students was small: there were only 1,900 in 1902 and their numbers grew very slowly, reaching 7,800 by 1922 and 9,900 by 1932. Even by 1938 there were only 157 professors, 814 other staff, and 12,126 students in all of Australia's universities.

Until the 1940s most universities were dedicated to teaching, not research. Until the late 1950s students wishing to carry out post-graduate research usually had to go to **Britain** or to the **United States** often with the assistance of scholarships granted by the Carnegie Corporation. Australian universities lacked the prestige of their British counterparts. The first Australian students were admitted to Oxford University in 1880 and Rhodes scholarships first became available to Australian students in 1904.

As institutions, the universities were undeveloped, hampered by a lack of funds and lack of appreciation of their importance. Between 1903 and 1923 no Australian **prime minister** held even a bachelor's degree. It was not until 1925 that the University of Sydney became the first Australian university to have a full-time administrative head (called a vice chancellor). There was no university press until 1923 and no course in Australian history until 1927; both of these were achievements of the University of Melbourne. Of the total revenue received by universities in 1938 (846,414 pounds or $1.7 million), 40 percent came from government grants, 32 percent from fees, and 19 percent from private foundations. The main extension classes of the universities were conducted through the Workers' Educational Association, which was set up in all **states** in 1913.

In 1946 the federal government established the Australian National University to provide a center for post-graduate research, but building did not begin until the 1950s. Recognition of the need for university research began in the 1930s and was raised by the demands of **World War II**. Nevertheless, acceptance of the value of university graduates was slow. It was not until 1963 that a system was introduced to regularly recruit graduates into the federal bureaucracy.

In 1964 the Martin Report recommended that there should be a general expansion of university education in Australia. The Report was accepted and was the basis for a growth in tertiary education, particularly colleges of advanced education, which lasted until 1974. Between 1963 and 1975 the number of universities increased from 10 to 18. In 1981, 8 percent of the Australian **labor force** had a university degree compared with 19 percent in the United States. Despite the growth of higher education, its output still lagged behind the United States and Western Europe. In 1986 Australian universities and colleges of advanced education produced 77,800 graduates or 490 per 100,000 population compared with 545 per 100,000 population for bachelor's and advanced degree four-year institutions in the United States.

By 1987 there were 19 universities, 46 colleges of advanced education, 16 colleges of technical and further education, and eight other institutions providing higher education. In December 1987 the federal government announced major changes to higher education, which brought about a "unified national system" of higher education with fewer and larger institutions. The number of non-university educational institutions was reduced by amalgamation and upgraded to universities. In 1991 there were 30 universities, three university colleges, and 16 institutions providing higher education. In 1997 there were 43 universities. In 1996 a total of 634,100 students were enrolled in some form of university study compared to 534,538 in 1991. Between May 1994 and May 1996, the proportion of Australians aged 15 to 64 with university qualifications rose from 11.5 to 12.8 percent. In recent years Australian universities have had their budgets and staffs greatly reduced by cuts in federal government funding which has forced them to rely more on fees and an additional tax on graduates, which now account for 24 percent of the income of universities. (*See also* Education)

URBANIZATION A high level of urbanization has always been an outstanding feature of European settlement in Australia. Towns were established first, rural life developed later as free settlers opened up the interior from the 1820s. The British convicts brought to Australia were, more often than not, urban rather than rural dwellers. By 1851, 38.1 percent of the 403,000 European residents lived in towns with more than 2,500 people (using the widely used U.S. definition of urbanization) compared to 54.0 percent in England and Wales and 11 percent in the **United States**. By 1851 too, all of Australia's present major coastal cities had been founded: **Sydney** (1788), **Hobart** (1804), **Brisbane** (1824), **Perth** (1829), **Melbourne** (1836), and **Adelaide** (1840) along with the important regional centers of **Newcastle** (1894), **Wollongong** (1826) and **Geelong** (1837).

The gold rushes slowed urban growth, but it resumed from the 1870s. The last half of the nineteenth century saw the emergence of the foundations of the modern pattern of urbanization. The six main cities grew and maintained their dominance of their respective colonial economies because they were the principal ports as well as being their capital cities. Sydney and Melbourne were easily Australia's largest cities. Sydney grew from 54,000 in 1851 to 496,000 in 1901; over the same period, Melbourne grew from 29,000 to 478,000 and was Australia's largest city between 1861 and 1891. Together, Australia's capital cities accounted for 29 percent of the whole population in 1851 and 35 percent in 1901. Outside of the capital cities, mining was often the basis for the larger urban centers such as Newcastle (coal), Ballarat and Bendigo (gold) and Broken Hill (silver and lead). Other centers founded in this period were **Townsville** (1865), **Darwin** (1869), and **Cairns** (1873).

Better transportation, particularly **railroads** and street cars, enabled the growth of suburbs in the main cities from the 1870s and led to a spreading out of the population from the inner areas. Smaller cities like Hobart, unless they acquired manufacturing centers like Newcastle, tended to fall behind. Sydney was the first Australian city to reach the one million population mark (1924), followed by Melbourne (1934), Brisbane (1976), and Adelaide (1986). An important change in Australia's cities occurred in 1911 when the federal capital, **Canberra**, was created, but its population was small until the 1950s. Like Adelaide, Canberra was only the second notable Australian city to be systematically planned.

The pace of urbanization in Australia has quickened since 1911 when 50.6 percent of the population were classified as urban (using the U.S. definition of a minimum population 2,500). By 1933 urbanization had reached 63.5 percent and had risen to 80.9 percent by 1966. The capital cities have easily retained their dominant position among the urban centers of their respective states. Between them, these cities were home to 47 percent of all Australians in

1933, 58 percent in 1966, and 62 percent in 1996. The ranking of Sydney and Melbourne as Australia's two leading cities has continued and their share of total population has increased. In 1901 these two cities accounted for 26 percent of all Australians, 38 percent by 1996.

The degree of domination by the coastal capital cities of their respective states varies considerably. The highest proportions of populations living in their capital cities since 1901 have been in **Victoria** and **South Australia**, closely followed by **Western Australia** and **New South Wales**. **Queensland** and **Tasmania** have the smallest proportions of their populations living in their capital cities. At the 1996 census, 70 percent of the residents of Victoria, South Australia, and Western Australia lived in their respective capital cities; in New South Wales the figure was 62 percent, 44 percent in Queensland, and 41 percent in Tasmania.

Urbanization in Australia has been remarkable not just for its high level, but for the concentration of its urban population in cities with more than one million. In 1970 cities of this size contained 51 percent of Australians. Australia's capital cities have also been the main settlement areas of immigrants as well as their main centers of cultural, economic, and political life. Since the late 1960s there has been a revival in the formerly declining inner suburbs of the main cities as better-off residents have renovated older housing in a process known as "gentrification." For example, in Sydney, 35 percent of the population lived in the original inner core of suburbs in 1911; this proportion had fallen to only 5 percent by 1976, but in 1996 these suburbs accounted for 8 percent of the population, a noteworthy reversal of the general outward spread of Sydney's population over this period. The other noteworthy trend in the pattern of Australian urbanization has been the growth of large coastal urban centers based on commuting, tourism, and retirees, most notably on the **Gold Coast** in Queensland and the **Central Coast** in New South Wales. (*See also* Population; Tables 18 to 20 in Appendix 3)

V

VICTORIA The **state** of Victoria occupies the south-eastern end of the Australian mainland. Its area is 227,600 square kilometers or 3 percent of the total area of Australia. Most of the state has a temperate, moist climate. Its main centers of population are

Melbourne (the capital), **Geelong**, Ballarat, and Bendigo. **George Bass** made the first detailed examination of the Victorian coast in 1798, but found it unpromising.

It was not until the 1830s that the agricultural potential of the land was recognized by **squatters**, who became its first permanent European residents. John Batman (1801-1839) and John Pascoe Fawkner (1792-1869), both sons of **convicts**, established rival camps on the opposite sides of the Yarra River, the site of the future capital city of Melbourne. The Melbourne area was officially opened for settlement in 1836 by the **New South Wales** government. In the same year **Thomas Mitchell** explored much of the interior and publicized its value for farming. In the ensuing land rush, migrants came from New South Wales and directly from **Britain** to raise the population from 11,700 in 1841 to 77,300 by 1851. The influx was disastrous for the **Aborigines**, whose numbers are believed to have fallen by about two-thirds over the same period.

On July 1, 1851, Victoria was proclaimed a separate colony from New South Wales. Over the next few days **gold** discoveries in the interior set off a gold rush that transformed Victoria. The main finds were at Ballarat and Bendigo. Between 1851 and 1861 Victoria produced 594.2 tonnes of gold and the **population** soared from 77,300 to 538,600. Gold enabled Victoria to have the highest population and greatest affluence of any Australian colony from the late 1850s to the 1890s when New South Wales again took the lead.

In 1855 Victoria was granted self-government by the British government and given its own constitution. Gold accelerated the desire for greater democracy. In December 1854 gold miners fought troops at the **Eureka Stockade** over the system of licensing. At the elections of 1856 the government was elected by **secret ballot** and the next year the **legislative assembly** abolished the property qualification for voting. However, the **legislative council**, the upper house, remained elected by the wealthy, and the two houses were in conflict until the 1880s. Eventually a coalition of liberals and conservatives governed Victoria. The comparative strength of liberalism in Victoria compared with its weakness in New South Wales inhibited the growth of the **Australian Labor Party** (ALP).

Primed by the gold rush, the Victorian economy diversified into wheat growing, dairy farming, and **manufacturing** between 1865 and 1890. Unlike other colonies, the closer settlement laws of 1865-69 designed to settle more people on the land and break up large land holdings worked better in Victoria because of its more abundant rainfall. The 1880s were a boom period in Victoria, marked by much speculation in land and borrowing from Britain to pay for building the cities and the transportation system. This gave way to severe depression in the early 1890s and a slow recovery thereafter. Victoria gained a new reputation for conservatism as shown by its being the last Australian state to give women the vote in 1908.

The greatest single development of the interwar period was the development of the brown **coal** deposits of the Latrobe Valley in eastern Victoria in the 1920s, which provided the state with an independent source of coal for electricity generation, freeing it from the uncertainties of supplies from the New South Wales black coal industry. In 1928-29 the value of manufacturing in Victoria exceeded that of **agriculture**.

Victoria nevertheless remained important. It was the seat of the federal government from 1901 to 1927 before it was transferred to **Canberra** and the source of many federal **prime ministers** and politicians. The success of conservatives in Victorian politics since 1950 owed much to the weakness of the ALP. The split of the ALP in 1955 and the creation of the **Democratic Labor Party** were largely Victorian events.

Since 1891 Victoria has been a highly urbanized society with more people living in the cities and towns than in rural areas. In 1891, 51.9 percent of Victorians were urban dwellers (using the U.S. definition of urbanization of a minimum population of 2,500). Melbourne has always been the largest single center of population. Between 1901 and 1996 the proportion of the population of Victoria living in Melbourne has risen from 39.8 to 71.8 percent.

From 1949 to 1967 Victoria has had the highest income per head of any Australian state, reflecting its position as Australia's financial capital until the mid-1980s. At the 1996 census Victoria had a resident population of 4,373,500 and a median weekly income of $290 (compared to $298 in New South Wales).

In 1982 the ALP under John Cain (1931-), whose father, John Cain (1882-1957) had been Labor **premier** from 1952-55, was elected to government. On August 7, 1990, Cain resigned after revelations about the size of Victoria's public debt and financial mismanagement, specifically the $1 billion loss incurred by the merchant bank arm of the State Bank of Victoria. He was replaced on August 9, 1990, by Joan Kirner (1938-), Victoria's first woman premier. In the state elections on October 3, 1992, the **Liberal**

Party convincingly defeated the ALP and its leader, Jeff Kennett (1948-), became premier. (*See also*, Eureka Stockade; Mannix, Daniel; Monash, John)

VIETNAM   Australia's relations with Vietnam began in 1962 when 32 military "advisers" were sent to help the South Vietnamese government in its war with North Vietnam. In May 1965 the government began to commit Australian troops to the war. This decision was in order to demonstrate Australia's reliability to the **United States** as an ally and predated a formal request for assistance by the government of South Vietnam. The government introduced selective **conscription** based on a ballot when young men turned 20; if their birthday was selected, they were called up for military service. Despite growing opposition to Australia's participation in the war after 1967, Australian troops were not withdrawn until 1972 by the newly elected **Whitlam** government. In all, 40,207 Australian soldiers fought in Vietnam, of whom 423 were killed and 2,398 were wounded; 43 percent of the casualties were conscripts.

After the Communist victory in 1975, many Vietnamese fled the country by boat; of these **"boat people,"** 2,011 arrived in Australia between 1977 and 1981. In 1996 there were 151,085 Vietnamese in Australia (compared to 83,044 in 1986), most of whom lived in **Melbourne** and **Sydney**. (*See also* Australia Party; Chinese)

W

WATSON, JOHN CHRISTIAN (1867-1941)   Watson was the first leader of the **Australian Labor Party** (ALP) to become **prime minister**. He was born in Valparaiso, Chile, during his parents' emigration from Scotland to **New Zealand** and he became a printer in that country. He arrived in **New South Wales** in 1886 and became president of the Sydney Trades and Labour Council (the federation of the city's **labor unions**) in 1893 and of the Australian Labour Federation, which was the first attempt to form a national labor union body; it advocated the direct representation of labor in parliament. Watson joined the ALP and presided over the labor union conference in New South Wales in 1894 at which ALP candidates for parliament had to sign a pledge that bound them to follow the majority decisions of the parliamentary party (caucus). In 1894 he was also elected to the **legislative assembly** of New South Wales.

In 1901 Watson was elected to the **house of representatives** and was made leader of the parliamentary ALP. Because of the pledge, the ALP members were disciplined in their voting and therefore able to exert disproportionate influence on their relatively less organized opponents. The ALP increased its representation in the federal parliament after the elections on November 23, 1903, and Watson was able to form the first ALP government on April 27, 1904, with himself as prime minister and treasurer; he held office until August 17, 1904. It was the first time that a political party based on labor unions had formed a national government anywhere in the world.

During his brief period in office, Watson tried, unsuccessfully, to bring in a labor arbitration law that would have included giving employment preference to members of labor unions. Watson resigned as ALP leader in October 1907 because of ill health and was succeeded by **Andrew Fisher**. In 1916 Watson, like many other founding members of the ALP, supported **conscription** and was expelled from the party. Watson went on to have a business career and was one of the founders of the National Roads and Motorists' Association in New South Wales.

WEALTH AND INCOME The first national estimates of the wealth of Australia were made by **Timothy Augustine Coghlan** in the late 1880s with the objective of showing the remarkable economic progress of Australia during the nineteenth century and comparing it to other countries. The economic depression of the 1890s and earlier 1900s killed off official interest in the measurement of wealth and the distribution of income, but interest revived in the late 1900s with rising inflation. A question on incomes was proposed for inclusion in the first national **census** in 1911, but was rejected by the **senate** as too intrusive. However, the distribution of wealth in Australia was first investigated by the War Census in 1915. After 1920 official interest in the subject again lapsed and it was not until the third national census in 1933 that an income question was included.

The first national surveys of income distribution were made using payroll tax data in 1960 and the first national household expenditure survey was undertaken in 1974-75. The next official investigation of the topic took place in 1968-69. An income question has been included in every census since 1976.

Since that time a number of studies have found that there are large disparities in the distribution of wealth in Australia and that there is evidence that these disparities have increased since the

1970s. One study found that between 1993 and 1998 the wealthiest 10 percent of the population increased its ownership of Australia's wealth from 44 to 48 percent, particularly as a result of the growth of superannuation since 1990 and the rise of home prices in **Sydney**. About 60 percent of household wealth in Australia is held in the form of **home ownership**.

WEST, MORRIS [LANGLO] (1916-) A novelist, West was born in **Melbourne** and completed his education there and in **Hobart**. He joined the Christian Brothers, a Catholic teaching order, and taught in **New South Wales**. He later left the order, served in the **Australian Imperial Force** during **World War II**, and moved to Europe in the 1950s which he used as the setting for his many best-selling works that often have themes concerning **Catholicism**. He is the best-known Australian author of the post-1945 period and his success, like that of **Patrick White**, has made it easier for Australian authors to achieve international success. Among his many works are *Children of the Sun* (1957), *The Devil's Advocate* (1959), and *The Shoes of the Fisherman* (1963). (*See also* Literature)

WESTERN AUSTRALIA Western Australia is Australia's largest state in area. It covers a third of the mainland: 2,525,500 square kilometers. Much of the state is arid. Only in the south-west is there sufficient rainfall to support **agriculture**. The main urban center is the state capital, **Perth**, located on the Swan River in the south-eastern corner. The Portuguese almost certainly explored its northern coast in the first half of the sixteenth century, and the Dutch and English are known to have explored its western and northern coasts in the seventeenth century. Because much of the country was arid and forbidding, these voyages did not result in settlement and interest died. It was revived by the French in the early 1800s, and their explorations led to British fears that they might found a settlement. In 1826 a British military settlement was made at modern Albany on the south-western coast. In 1829 the British government annexed the whole of Western Australia and founded Perth. In 1840-41 **Edward John Eyre** explored the south-western coastal strip on the edge of a large desert called the Nullabor Plain after 1860 because it was devoid of trees.

The **Aborigines** on the coast were crushed after some five years of fighting, but the struggle continued as European settlement moved inland. With the end of the transportation of **convicts** to eastern

Australia, Western Australia became the new destination and some 10,000 were sent there from 1850 to 1868 to provide cheap labor for landowners. Nevertheless, the dryness of most of the colony restrained agriculture, and it was not until a series of gold rushes between 1888 and 1893 that the economy became buoyant. The finds at Coolgardie and Kalgoorlie were especially important. Between 1891 and 1901 the population of Western Australia increased from 49,800 to 184,120, largely because of the gold boom.

Western Australia suffered from isolation from the more economically advanced eastern Australian states. The telegraph did not link Perth with **Adelaide** until 1877 and there was no **railroad** link until 1917 when the Trans-Australian Railway was opened. The first regular air service with Adelaide did not begin until 1929, and although there was a road link made to Adelaide during **World War II**, it was not fully sealed until 1976.

Although 70 percent of Western Australian voters had supported **federation** of the colonies in 1900, federation was believed to have harmed local manufacturing. Western Australia has been the only Australian state where secession from the Commonwealth has been a political issue. In 1906 the state government passed a resolution of secession and in 1933 two-thirds of voters agreed to leave the Commonwealth at a state **referendum**. The state government sent a delegation to the British Parliament which rejected its arguments for secession.

Western Australia's economy after 1910 was based on agriculture (mainly **wheat** and dairy farming) and **gold** mining. In the 1960s, however, the state's relatively sluggish economy was transformed by a mineral boom. Huge deposits of **iron ore** were discovered in the north of the state, and oil and natural gas were found off-shore. **Diamonds** have also become an important part of the mining industry. The boom increased the state's population from 836,700 in 1966 to 1,459,000 in 1986. At the 1996 census Western Australia had a resident population of 1,726,100, compared to 1,586,825 in 1991.

Because of the aridity of the state outside of the south-western corner, Perth and the surrounding towns have always been the dominant urban centers. Between 1901 and 1996 Perth increased its share of state's population from 33.1 to 72.1 percent.

The **Australian Labor Party** (ALP) gained office in 1983 under Brian Burke (1947-) but the government became the object of increasing controversy in the late 1980s over the closeness of its financial dealings with large corporations. On October 12, 1990, Carmen Lawrence (1948-) became **premier**. She was first woman premier of any Australian state and held the position until the defeat of her government at the elections on February 6, 1993, by the **Liberal Party** led by Richard Court (1947-), the son of the former Liberal Party premier, Charles Court (1911-).

WHALING AND SEALING   Whaling and sealing were Australia's first significant export industries. The first recorded British whaling in **New South Wales** waters was in 1791, but it was not until 1805 that a local industry began to emerge. Fur sealing began on the islands in Bass Strait between the Australian mainland and **Tasmania** after 1797 and attracted whalers and sealers from New England as well as **Britain**. By 1833 whaling had become Australia's most valuable export industry, after which time it was overtaken by **sheep and wool**. Between 1832 and 1841 whale exports were worth a total of about 1.4 million pounds ($2.8 million) in export earnings to New South Wales. The sealing industry was largely destroyed by the 1830s by the sealers killing too many seals and not allowing their numbers to be maintained. With the replacement of whale oil by kerosene after 1853, whaling entered a long decline, with the last whaling taking place in **Western Australia** in 1978 when 624 whales were caught. The decision to end whaling was taken to protect the marine **environment**. Australia has since opposed any further whaling in the world.

WHEAT   Wheat has been Australia's most important crop for more than a century. It was first grown in **New South Wales** in 1788, but it was not until the 1860s that it was grown on a large scale with the opening up of the inland plains. The dryness of the land limited the bulk of wheat production to New South Wales, **Victoria**, **South Australia**, and **Western Australia**. Drought and wheat diseases limited production, but by 1900, thanks largely to the work of William James Farrer (1845-1906) in the 1890s, disease resistant varieties of wheat had been developed.

By the 1920s wheat had become a significant export commodity with about 40 percent of exports going to **Britain**. The Depression hit the industry hard, and its problems were the subject of a royal commission of inquiry in 1934-36. In 1939 the **Lyons** government created the Australian Wheat Board to buy and sell all domestically produced wheat.

Wheat production rose from 1 to 3.5 million tonnes between 1901-2 and 1921-22 and to 5.3 million tonnes by 1952-53. The highest production was 18.1 million tonnes in 1979. In 1995-96 wheat production was 17.2 million tonnes and accounted for 4.1 percent of Australia's merchandise exports in 1997-98.

WHITE, PATRICK [VICTOR MARTINDALE] (1912-1990) Winner of Australia's first Nobel prize for Literature in 1973, White was born in London during a visit there by his Australian parents. He grew up on his parents' ranch near Muswellbrook, a country town in the upper Hunter valley of **New South Wales**, but also spent much time in **Sydney** and in inland areas because of his severe asthma. He graduated from Cambridge University in 1935, and published his first novel, *Happy Valley*, which was set in rural Australia, in 1939; it was published in the United States in 1940. In 1941 he published *The Living and Dead* in the United States, but it was not published in Britain and Australia until 1962. Both *The Aunt's Story* (1948) and the *Tree of Man* (1955) were also published in the United States before they were published in Britain. After war service in North Africa, White returned to Australia in 1947.

White was generally poorly received in Australia until the late 1950s when his *Voss* (1957), based on the life of the explorer **Ludwig Leichhardt**, became a best-seller. Along with novels, such as *The Vivisector* (1970) and *The Twyborn Affair* (1979), White also wrote short stories, poems, and plays, notably *Big Toys* (1978) and *Signal Driver* (1983). He used the prize money from his Nobel prize to establish the Patrick White Literary Award for Australian writers. He died in Sydney on September 29, 1990.

WHITE AUSTRALIA POLICY "White Australia" was the term generally used to describe the objectives of Australia's **immigration** policy from 1901 to the late 1960s. When the federal government assumed responsibilities for immigration from the **colonies** in 1901 under section 51(xxvii) of the **Australian Constitution**, it was able to build on existing anti-**Chinese** laws and practices. The principle behind the policy was that only "white," preferably British, immigrants should be admitted to Australia and that all others should be excluded. In 1902 a **Dictation Test** was applied to nonwhite (mainly Asian) immigrants. In 1906 the last of the laborers from Melanesia (**Kanakas**) were deported.

The White Australia Policy was based on a number of premises: the superiority of the white races; the expectation that the **Aborigines** would eventually die out; and the need to protect Australian workers' living standards from low-cost Asian workers. It was also hoped to create a society free from racial divisions. The White Australia Policy had the support of all the major political parties until the 1960s.

The first real weakening of the White Australia Policy came after 1951 when the first of 12,000 Asian students came to Australia under the Colombo Plan. The good example set by these students helped to undermine long-held racial prejudices. The political independence and economic growth of Asia from the 1950s made the policy seem increasingly offensive and earned Australia criticism from countries like Singapore and the Philippines. From the late 1960s federal governments gradually dismantled the White Australia Policy and replaced race with other criteria for immigration. In January 1973 the policy was officially abandoned.

WHITLAM, [EDWARD] GOUGH (1916-)   Australian **prime minister**, Whitlam was born in **Melbourne** and graduated in arts and law from Sydney University. He was elected to the **house of representatives** in 1952 as **Australian Labor Party** (ALP) member for Werriwa, an electorate in south-western **Sydney**. Narrowly elected deputy leader of the parliamentary ALP in 1960, he was resented by the leader Arthur Augustus Calwell (1896-1973), who tried to have Whitlam expelled from the ALP. In 1967 Whitlam was elected leader after the ALP's massive defeat in the elections of November 26, 1966. He set about reforming the ALP organization and advocated policies designed to attract support from the younger voters and the middle class in the outer suburbs of the large cities. Whitlam gained a remarkable swing of 7 percent to the ALP in the elections of October 25, 1969. Whitlam led the ALP to victory in the elections of December 2, 1972. However, Labor did not win a majority in the **senate** where the non-Labor parties were able to frustrate the government's programs of reform.

Whitlam was prime minister from December 5, 1972, to November 11, 1975. Building on a number of initiatives of the last months of the previous **McMahon** government, he undertook a wide-ranging series of reforms. In foreign relations the government ended Australia's participation in the war in **Vietnam**, recognized the People's Republic of China, made arrangements to grant independence to **Papua New Guinea**, and generally displayed a level of independence that surprised and sometimes alarmed interested parties like the **United States**, whose government regarded his administration as too radical. The government upgraded **social security**, introduced universal health insurance, revised the **divorce** law, and devised programs to improve life in the cities, assist **Aborigines**, and improve the status of **women**.

The Whitlam government faced two great problems: the inflation and recession caused by the 1973 oil crisis, and the hostility of the **Liberal-Country** coalition, which used its majority in the senate to force the government to hold elections on May 18, 1974. Despite the re-election of Whitlam's government, the senate refused to pass the budget (October 1975). Unexpectedly, the **governor-general**, Sir John Kerr (1914-1991), a Whitlam appointee, intervened; he dismissed Whitlam and installed the leader of the opposition, **Malcolm Fraser**, as prime minister of a caretaker government on November 11, 1975. At the elections on December 13, 1975, Whitlam and the ALP were defeated. Whitlam remained as leader until 1977, when he resigned after a second electoral defeat on December 10, 1977. In May 1983 the ALP government of **Bob Hawke** (1929-) appointed Whitlam to be Australia's ambassador to UNESCO.

WHOLESALE AND RETAIL TRADE   Large-scale retailing developed in Australia after the 1850s with the growth of **urbanization**. Wholesaling developed, too, but did not become a powerful force in its own right until the 1890s. The early twentieth century saw the foundation of many of Australia's largest current retailers: Myer (Melbourne, 1900); G. J. **Coles** (Melbourne, 1914); David Jones (Sydney, 1906), and Woolworths (Sydney, 1924). (This Woolworths had no connection with the U.S. chainstores of Woolworths.) The next major change was the appearance of "cash and carry" stores, the first supermarkets, in the 1920s.

The first Australian census of retailing was taken in 1947-48. Apart from **Newcastle** consumer cooperatives never became a significant feature of Australian retailing. By 1983 the 10 largest retailers accounted for a third of total retail sales. In 1978 wholesale and retail trade overtook **manufacturing** to become the largest single employer of any industry group. In August 1998 wholesale and retail trade employed 20.6 percent of the labor force.

WIK CASE The Wik are a group of about 1,500 **Aborigines** who live on the central western coast of Cape York peninsula in **Queensland**. They are made up of small clans of about 20 people. About 12 languages are spoken by the Wik peoples. Because of their isolation, they have managed to maintain their traditional way of life and intimate connection with the land to a far greater extent than the great majority of Aborigines.

On December 23, 1996, the Wik peoples came to national attention when the **High Court of Australia** handed down its judgment in a case they had initiated against the state of Queensland. The Wik peoples claimed native title rights over land subject to pastoral leases; such leases are peculiar to Australia and are a product of the process of **land settlement** and the historic importance of pastoral activities in Australian **agriculture**. It had been assumed before the Wik Decision that pastoral leases precluded land claims by indigenous Australians, following the **Mabo Judgment**. The court found that indigenous rights could coexist with the rights of a holder of a pastoral lease. The Wik Decision is complicated and presented an array of political problems which were often at the forefront of debates in the federal parliament in late 1997 and early 1998 because it seemed to widen the scope for land rights claims by indigenous Australians. After lengthy negotiations, the legal procedure for land claims raised by the Wik Case was clarified by amendments to the *Native Title Act* in July 1998.

WILLIAMSON, DAVID [KEITH] (1942-) Australia's leading contemporary playwright, Williamson was born in **Melbourne** and became a mechanical engineer. He lectured in mechanical engineering and psychology, an experience he used for his plays. His first major play was *The Removalists* (1972), which he followed by *Don's Party* (1973), *Traveling North* (1980), and *Emerald City* (1987); all these plays have been made into **films**. Not all his works have received critical acclaim; *Celluloid Heroes*, for example, deals with the world of the Australian **film** industry and was not popular with those who were prominent in the industry. Williamson's plays are typically about the affluent middle class—for instance, *Top Silk* is about the legal profession—or conflict in organizations (such as

The Club, which deals with **Australian Rules** football), but all are characterized by an accurate understanding of the contemporary Australian scene. Along with writing plays, Williamson has also written screen scripts for the movies *Gallipoli* (1981) and *The Year of Living Dangerously* (1983).

WINE The first attempt to plant vine cuttings in Australia was made in 1788 by the government, which saw wine as a healthier alternative to rum, the main alcoholic drink of the 1790s and 1800s. These attempts failed because of disease and lack of expertise. The first commercial vineyard was planted by John Macarthur (1766-1834) and three of his sons in 1817 using French techniques. James Busby (1801-1871), a Scottish immigrant, is credited as the founding father of the Australian wine industry. He arrived in 1824 and was granted land in the Hunter Valley in **New South Wales** to plant vineyards. The 1830s saw the establishment of commercial wine growing in **Victoria**. Wine growing began in **South Australia** in the Barossa Valley in 1847. Its pioneers, particularly Christopher Dawson Penfold (1811-1870) and Joseph Ernest Seppelt (1813-1868), founded firms that continue to this day. The South Australian industry gained much from the destruction of many vineyards in Victoria and New South Wales in the 1890s by the disease phylloxera. In the 1880s, wine growing was established in **Western Australia**.

By the 1980s about 60 percent of Australia's wines came from South Australia. Apart from diseases, the main problem for Australian wine growers was the historic Australian preference for **beer**. In 1971-72 Australians over 15 years consumed on average an estimated 6.7 liters of unfortified wine per head compared with 174.3 liters of beer. Since the mid-1970s domestic consumption of wine has risen from 10.6 liters a head in 1974-75 to 18.2 liters in 1994-95 (compared to 95.4 liters of beer). This change in consumption was a reflection on the improved quality of Australian wine—to the point where Australian wine has gained an international reputation—the influence of Southern European immigrants, and more discrimination by Australians in their choice of alcoholic drinks. An official survey conducted in May 1998 found that 37.3 percent of Australians over had drunk some form of wine in the previous week. (*See also* Beer; "Rum Rebellion")

WOLLONGONG　Wollongong was the third largest city in **New South Wales** from 1921 to 1991 and is located south of **Sydney**. Its coast was explored by **George Bass** and **Matthew Flinders** in 1796, and outcrop **coal** was discovered the next year. The name Wollongong is of Aboriginal origin and means "sound of the sea." The first settlement was made in 1826. **Agriculture** and timber were the region's first industries, and these were joined by coal mining in 1849. Over the next 40 years a string of coal mining towns grew up north of Wollongong. By 1901 the population of the Wollongong area was 17,400. Between 1921 and 1933 the population grew from 32,370 to 42,850 based on the 1947 definition of the urban area.

Apart from a copper smelting plant (1907), **manufacturing** was slow to develop at Wollongong. In 1928 an **iron and steel** works was established at Port Kembla, and this provided the economic foundation of Wollongong. In 1938-39 Wollongong was the scene of protests about the shipment of Australian pig iron to **Japan**.

Growth continued during **World War II** and into the postwar period. In 1947 the local governments of the area were combined to form the City of Greater Wollongong. Its industries attracted much **immigration**, particularly from non-English speaking countries, in the 1950s and 1960s. By 1971, 30.1 percent of the total population of 192,300 was foreign-born, of whom half had come from **Britain** and the other half from other parts of Europe. In 1996 Wollongong, as an urban center, had a population of 219,760 having been overtaken by the **Central Coast** as the third largest urban center in New South Wales. (*See also* Newcastle)

WOMEN　Until the 1830s most of Australia's European women were either **convicts** or former convicts. The first six free women settlers arrived in **New South Wales** in 1793, but only 576 in all had arrived by 1831. Because 85 percent of the convicts were men and most free immigrants were also males, the population was heavily male dominated. In 1828 only a quarter of the European population of 54,700 were females, and even by 1841 only a third of the population of 206,700 were females. After 1832 assisted **immigration** schemes improved the balance between the sexes. Between 1832 and 1851, 68,863 adults were assisted to immigrate to New South Wales, of whom 54 percent were women, but of the 25,288 unassisted adults who arrived in New South Wales in this period, only a third were women. The shortage of women continued and raised their level of marriage. In 1851, 77 percent of women in

New South Wales over 20 years old were married compared with 57 percent in Britain.

The **gold** rushes of the 1850s in New South Wales and **Victoria** attracted thousands of immigrants, but again, most were men. By 1861, 42 percent of the population of 1.1 million were females, and with the passing of the frontier society, the sexes became better balanced. By 1901, the number of males per 100 females was 110 compared to 138 in 1861.

Following the British law of 1870, all the Australian colonies passed laws that recognized a married woman's right to own property separately from her husband: Victoria (1870), New South Wales (1879), **Tasmania** (1883), **South Australia** (1884), **Queensland** (1890), and **Western Australia** (1892).

Women began to play a more prominent role in public affairs, such as in the temperance movement in 1880s. They gained the right to vote first in South Australia in 1894, in 1902 in New South Wales, and in federal elections also in 1902. Victoria was the last state to give women the right to vote in 1908. Because they tended to vote the same way as their husbands or their families, the women's vote made little difference to the political scene, although the defeat of the two **referendums** on **conscription** in 1916 and 1917 was attributed by many to the "women's vote." In the 1950s and 1960s more women than men tended to vote for the conservative parties.

Opportunities for women to work in paid employment in the **labor force** were limited until the 1880s, when factory and office work increased. By 1911, 17 percent of women aged 15 or over were in paid employment. Of those who worked, most worked in either the services sector or in **manufacturing**.

The introduction of **social security** programs was of immediate benefit to women. A national means tested age pension was available to women aged 60 or more in 1908, and a maternity allowance was introduced in 1912. A widows' pension was begun in New South Wales in 1926 and nationally in 1942.

As in other Western countries, an increasing proportion of women entered the labor force and higher **education** after 1960. Their presence led to pressure for changes to work and pay discrimination against women. In 1966 married women were allowed to become permanent appointees in federal government employment. In February 1972 the Women's Electoral Lobby was formed to raise awareness of women's issues in political processes.

In 1973 the **Whitlam** government appointed the first adviser on women's affairs.

A persistent aspiration among Australian women since 1900 has been to gain pay equality with men. In the 1920s and 1930s, **industrial tribunals** set women's pay rates at 55 percent that of men's. This was raised to 75 percent of men's pay in 1950. In 1958 New South Wales introduced the first "equal pay for equal work" legislation, which was followed by the other **states** by 1968. In 1969 and 1972 the federal industrial tribunal handed down equal pay for equal work for employees covered by federal **awards**. Nevertheless, despite these decisions, women's pay in the private sector still lags behind men's.

Behind these events has been the sustained rise in the proportion of women in the labor force. In August 1966, 36.6 percent of women over 15 were in the labor force; by August 1997, it was 52.7. Much of this increase has come about because of married women. In August 1966, 29.1 percent of married women were in the labor force; by August 1997, this proportion had risen to 54.3 percent. The federal **Hawke** government brought in two national laws to assist women: the *Sex Discrimination Act 1984*, which provided legal redress against discrimination on the grounds of sex, marital status, and pregnancy, and the *Affirmative Action (Equal Employment Opportunity for Women) Act 1986*, which was aimed at removing discrimination against women in employment and required companies with over 100 employees to prepare statements on how they were complying with this law. (*See also* Chisholm, Caroline; Country Women's Association; Divorce; Fertility; Gibbs, Cecilia May; Immigration; Population)

WOOL (*See* Sheep and Wool)

WORLD WAR I (1914-18) For a country with only 4.9 million people in 1914, Australia made a significant contribution to the Allied effort in World War I. The war was a watershed in Australia's twentieth-century history. Early victories in 1914 were Australia's occupation of German New Guinea and the destruction of the German raider *Emden* off the Cocos islands in the Indian Ocean. A total of 416,809 enlisted in the armed services, of whom 330,714 left Australia in the **Australian Imperial Force** (AIF). Australian forces played a notable part in the assault on the **Gallipoli** peninsula in north-western Turkey (April 25 to December 20, 1915), a campaign that gave rise to Anzac Day. The Australian Light Horse continued the war against Turkey in the south (1916-18). But for most Australian troops the bulk of the fighting was conducted on the Western Front in **France**. During 1916 deaths among the AIF in France reached 12,823 and 20,628 in 1917.

The federal government attempted to introduce **conscription** by **referendum** in two bitterly fought campaigns, but each time the vote was negative (October 1916, December 1917). By doubling living costs, the war caused much hardship among the working class and this, together with the huge loss of life, fed anti-war feeling. There was a massive **labor dispute** in **New South Wales**, which spread to **Victoria** (August-October 1917). The **Australian Labor Party** split over conscription in November 1916. The war stimulated ship building and the new steel industry, which had began at **Newcastle** in April 1915.

During 1918 the AIF helped to stabilize the Western Front against the German offensive. Of particular importance was the innovative attack led by General **John Monash** near Hamel (June 10, 1918). Because Australians were frequently used to lead attacks, they suffered a high casualty rate. A total of 53,884 were killed or died of wounds, 155,133 were wounded, and 4,084 were captured. The prime minister, **William Morris Hughes**, used Australia's high casualty rate to gain a separate place for Australia at the Versailles peace conference to press its national interests and territorial claims over German New Guinea. (*See also* Anzac; Papua New Guinea; Royal Australian Navy)

WORLD WAR II (1939-45) As in **World War I**, Australia made a substantial contribution to the Allied war effort in World War II. Australia joined with **Britain** in declaring war on Germany on September 3, 1939, and against Italy on June 11, 1940. The first contribution to Britain's war effort was participation in the Empire Air Training Scheme; the first Australian trainees reached Canada in September 1940. In all, 5,036 Australians died in the air war against Germany. Australian troops (Sixth Division) were sent to Egypt where they captured Bardia, Tobruk, and Benghazi from the Italians (January-February 1941), but a counterattack by the German Afrika Corps saw many of these gains lost except for Tobruk. Australian forces were then committed to Greece, where they were quickly routed by overwhelming German forces. They withdrew to Crete until evacuated or forced to surrender (June 1, 1941). The Greece-Crete campaign cost 1,595 Australian casualties and 5,174 captured.

Concern over the intentions of **Japan** in south-east Asia led the Australian government to send the Eighth Division to reinforce the British forces at Singapore (February-August 1941). After the Japanese attack on American territories in the Pacific, Australia declared war (December 9, 1941). In the next three months the Japanese conquered most of south-east Asia. Singapore fell on February 15, 1942. Among the 133,814 Allied troops captured were 15,384 Australians. By this time, the Japanese had landed on New Britain and Bougainville off the north-eastern coast of New Guinea, islands that were then part of Australian territory. The Japanese launched a series of raids on the Australian mainland; they bombed **Darwin** and Broome, and Wyndham in northern **Western Australia** and **Townsville**. Japanese submarines made attacks on **Newcastle** and **Sydney** (June 8, 1942), the most southerly point of their war effort, as well as sinking 17 ships off the Australian coast.

Australia feared invasion and the federal government looked to the **United States** for protection and help. On February 23, 1942, the government overruled Winston Churchill and brought the Seventh Division back to Australia instead of sending it to Burma. The battle between the Japanese and American naval forces in the **Coral Sea** was interpreted as having saved Australia from invasion (May 4-8, 1942). In March the government agreed to the appointment of General Douglas MacArthur as supreme commander of Allied forces in the south-west Pacific. The first American troops arrived in Australia on April 6, 1942. Australia also served as the base for U.S. submarine operations against Japan, most notably at **Brisbane** and Fremantle, the port of **Perth**. American submarines based at Fremantle sank about half of the Japanese tankers sunk during the war. Australia was a recipient of **Lend Lease** assistance during the war.

Between August 25 and September 6, 1942, Australian forces inflicted the first land defeat of Japanese forces in their drive into south-east Asia at Milne Bay, New Guinea. Thereafter the fighting centered upon driving the Japanese out of New Guinea across the Kakoda Trail (January 1943). In North Africa, the Australian Ninth Division played a leading role in the battle of El Alamein (October 23-November 5, 1942). On September 19, 1943, **conscription** was introduced for the war in the Pacific.

From November 1942 to October 1943 about 10,000 Australians, along with 51,000 prisoners of war and about 100,000 conscripted Asian laborers, worked as slave laborers under horrific conditions building a railway from Thailand to Burma; more than 12,000 prisoners died, 2,800 of them Australians. Australian forces defeated the Japanese in eastern-central **Papua New Guinea** (September 1943-April 1944), thereby enabling American forces to press on up the northern coast of New Guinea to the Philippines. In October 1944, Australian forces launched a series of campaigns against groups of Japanese bypassed by the American advance, campaigns that have been criticized as lacking military justification.

World War II ended in the Pacific on September 15, 1945. A total of 396,661 men and women served in the Australian armed services of whom 33,826 were killed, 180,864 were wounded, and 23,059 were captured at some time.

The total direct cost of the war was 2 billion pounds ($4 billion) or over twice Australia's gross domestic product in 1939. The war changed Australia in many ways. It stimulated **manufacturing** and by early 1942 led to full employment, which lasted until 1973. The exposure to thousands of American soldiers dented Australian assumptions about their high standard of living. The war showed the vulnerability of Australia to attack from Asia. It led to the new commitment by the federal government to mass **immigration** in order to build up the **population**. On May 26, 1944, the acting prime minister, **Frank Forde**, announced that this policy would start after the war. The inability of Britain to fulfill the role of Australia's protector had been demonstrated by the war and led Australian governments to supplement Britain with the United States as the new protector. (*See also* Anzus Treaty; Australian Imperial Force; Japan; Royal Australian Air Force; Royal Australian Navy)

WRIGHT, JUDITH [ARUNDELL] (1915-) A poetess, Wright was born in Armidale, **New South Wales**, and was raised on her parent's sheep ranch. She was educated at the University of Sydney and spent a year traveling in Europe. Her first collection of poems was published in 1946 as *The Moving Image*. Wright's poems are remarkable for her affinity with the Australian landscape and its antiquity as well as the passage of time, metaphysics, and feminine experience. She has also published children's books and short stories and a work about her pioneering family, *The Generations of Men* (1959). She played a leading part in a campaign to ban mining of the **Great Barrier Reef** and has been nominated for a Nobel prize. (*See also* Literature)

BIBLIOGRAPHY

Structure of the Bibliography

The Bibliography is set out as follows:

1. Bibliographies and Guides to Sources: General
2. Bibliographies and Guides to Sources: Specific Topics
3. Computer Databases
4. Collections of Primary Sources
5. Statistical Sources
6. General Reference Works
7. Atlases and Map Collections
8. Biographical Collections
9. Journals
10. National Histories and Survey Works
11. Travel Accounts
12. Environmental Works
13. Aborigines: Prehistory and Ethnography
14. Aborigines and Europeans
15. Discovery of Australia
16. First European Settlements and Convicts
17. Early Colonial Governors
18. Land Explorers
19. Land Settlement
20. States, Regions, Cities, and Towns
21. Politics: General
22. Parliamentary Biographical Registers
23. Political Parties and Movements
24. Political Autobiographies and Biographies
25. Australia and the British Empire
26. Australia and the United States
27. Foreign Relations, Antarctica, and Australian Territories
28. Economic History: General
29. Industry and Business Histories
30. Employment and Labor Relations
31. Social Investigation and Analysis
32. Social Welfare
33. Education
34. Sport and Gambling
35. Population and Immigration
36. Religion

Introduction
Australia's past as a European country is richly documented and nearly all of it in English. There is a wide selection of published material on all aspects of its history and numerous bibliographical guides to manuscript and published sources. In contrast, Australia's ancient Aboriginal past is still being explored as are relations between Aborigines and Europeans over the past 200 years. Knowledge and understanding of these areas have grown greatly in the past 20 years and much more can be expected in the future.

For reasons of space, the bibliography lists mainly books or monographs published since 1970 and omits journal articles. Most of the better-known books published before 1970 are listed in the first edition of this dictionary which was published in 1992. The main exceptions to this policy are bibliographies, collections of sources, books which have become sources in their own right, and works on dictionary entries where no more recent authoritative work has been published. Most of the books listed are based on original research and give detailed bibliographies, which provide signposts to particular journal articles. Major journal articles can be found in the *Social Sciences Citation Index*. The principal journals dealing with Australian history are listed in section 9. The inclusion of a work in the bibliography does not necessarily imply any recommendation; it is simply to note its importance and possible interest to the reader. If a book is available for an entry, it is included.

Although the more recent works have been favored over older ones, this is not to say that the older works are either inferior or no longer worth reading. Indeed, in some instances, they may be superior to later works, but the aim has been to reflect the current scholarly view of the topic and to capture the older works in their bibliographies. Along with being designed to be used independently as a starting point for studying Australian history, the bibliography is also intended to be a guide to further reading for entries in the dictionary.

It is important to realize that works like these can only reflect the scholarly consensus about a subject. The scale and range of topics makes it impossible for any single author to be an expert on everything and lack of time makes it impossible to check all primary sources. At times, there may not be a scholarly consensus about an important topic.

Beginning Australian history

Before anyone plunges directly into Australian history, it is recommended that they first spend some time acquiring a general appreciation of the British Empire of which Australia was so long a part. Angus Calder, *Revolutionary Empire* (New York: E. P. Dutton, 1981) is a valuable general account of the rise of the British Empire within the British Isles, in North America and Asia up to the 1780s. In the same vein, Bernard Bailyn's, remarkable *Voyagers to the West: Emigration from Britain to America on the Eve of the Revolution* (London: I. B. Tauris, 1986) contains much that is also relevant to early Australian history particularly on emigrants' attitudes to land and the process of settlement.

There are two excellent general survey works on the subject, namely Lawrence James, *The Rise and Fall of the British Empire* (London: Little, Brown and Company, 1994) and P. J. Marshall, (ed.). *The Cambridge Illustrated History of the British Empire* (Cambridge: Cambridge University Press, 1996). Despite these newcomers, Colin Cross, *The Fall of the British Empire, 1918-1968* (London: Hodder and Stoughton, 1968) retains its value as an excellent, accurate introductory survey; it is particularly useful to students coming fresh to the subject. After that, readers can explore the works listed in sections 15 and 16 of the Bibliography, particularly the works listed for Oskar Spate and Alan Frost.

Victorian England exerted a major influence on shaping Australian society. Two useful works providing general background to the period are Geoffrey Best, *Mid-Victorian Britain, 1871-75* (London: World University, 1971) and Asa Briggs, *Victorian Cities* (Ringwood: Penguin, 1963). Briggs's study is unusual in including a chapter on Melbourne in his studies of large English cities. For more advanced students, the stimulating work of Martin J. Weiner, *English Culture and the Decline of the Industrial Spirit, 1850-1980* (New York: Cambridge University Press, 1981) is recommended; it deals with the interesting question of British attitudes and ideas, many of which they passed on to their colonies.

For most readers, the best introduction to Australia's history is by reading some of the general works. The books on Australia by the

American author C. Hartley Grattan are still important. His book *The Southwest Pacific: A Modern History* (2 vols. Ann Arbor: University of Michigan Press, 1963) retains much value as an introduction to the history of Australia as well as New Zealand, the islands of the southwest Pacific, and Antarctica. Both volumes contain annotated bibliographies. There is an important study of Hartley Grattan's connection with Australia by Laurie Hergenham, *No Casual Traveller: Hartley Grattan and Australia* (St. Lucia, Queensland: Queensland University Press, 1995).

Given the increasingly narrow nationalist approach of most Australian history writing since Grattan, this wider perspective retains its importance. For a recent general history of the Pacific, see the history trilogy of Oskar Spate, *The Pacific Since Magellan* (Canberra: Australian National University Press, 1979, 1983, 1988).

There are many good single-volume works about Australia. C. Hartley Grattan's *Introducing Australia* (New York: John Day, 1942) was based on the author's experiences in Australia in 1927 and as a Carnegie Fellow in 1937-38. A recent general history is John Maloney, *The Penguin History of Australia* (Ringwood: Penguin, 1988), which includes an annotated bibliography. Stephen R. Graubard (ed.), *Australia: the Daedalus Symposium* (Sydney: Angus and Robertson, 1985) is also interesting as an introduction, particularly the contribution by Geoffrey Blainey. Douglas Pike, *Australia: The Quiet Continent* (2nd ed. Cambridge: Cambridge University Press, 1970) was unusual among works of this period in giving an urban stress to Australia's history. Manning Clark, *A Short History of Australia* (revised ed., Melbourne: Macmillan, 1986) provides an introduction to the views of this influential and controversial historian, which are elaborated in his six-volume history.

Peter Luck's *This Fabulous Century* (Melbourne: Milgrom and Schwartz, 1979) is a readable and accurate popular account of Australian history since 1900. It is extremely good in conveying the flavor of Australian life and covers topics such as heroes, humor, sport, fads and fashions, and events, which are usually outside the interests of academic historians. The same author's *A Time to Remember* (Melbourne: Mandarin Australia, 1991) is also recommended.

Research guides

For those wanting to undertake research into Australian history, sections 1 and 2 set out a comprehensive list of bibliographies and research aids. Despite its title, the book by Gillian M. Hibbins and others *Local*

History: A Handbook for Enthusiasts (Sydney: George Allen and Unwin, 1985) provides an excellent general introduction to the main sources and their uses. It is not just about local history. Similarly, Henry Mayer and Liz Kirby's *ARGAP: A Research Guide to Australian Politics and Cognate Subjects* (Melbourne: Cheshire, 1976) and its companion *ARGAP 2* (Melbourne: Longman Cheshire, 1984) give a broad introduction to many aspects of Australia, not just politics.

More specialized researchers are directed to the computer databases for Australia listed in section 3. Since the late 1970s these databases have become an essential means for research. The Royal Melbourne Institute of Technology (G.P.O. Box 2476V, Melbourne, Victoria, 3001) offers a set of social science and education databases on CD-ROM covering a number of the databases mentioned in the Bibliography.

Dietrich H. Borchardt (ed.) *Australians: An Historical Library Vol. VII: A Guide to Sources* (Sydney: Fairfax, Syme and Weldon, 1987) is indispensable as a guide as it contains not only a detailed bibliography of 3,000 references but also essays on the development of the study of Australian history, archives, libraries, museums, and galleries. It is indexed by name and subject. It can be usefully complemented by John J. Mills, *Information Resources and Services in Australia* (2nd ed., Wagga Wagga, New South Wales: Centre for Information Studies, Charles Sturt University, 1992). For significant books published on Australia since Borchardt's work see the *Guide to New Australian Books* published by the National Centre for Australian Studies since October 1990.

John Thawley (ed.), *Australasia and South Pacific Islands Bibliography* (Lanham, Maryland, and London: Scarecrow Press, 1997) is a landmark work which contains 5,933 items published up to 1996; of these items, 2,870 relate directly to Australia. Thawley's is the latest and easily the best work of its kind. Unlike the bibliography in this work, it includes secondary works published before 1970. The bibliography in this dictionary adds just over 100 items to those listed in Thawley's work which have been published since 1996.

Another starting point for research into Australian history is through the official yearbooks published by federal and state governments (Section 5). Unlike the British *Annual Abstract of Statistics* or the *Statistical Abstract of the United States*, these works contain commentaries, chronologies, and bibliographies as well as statistics. Some series, like the annual *Year Book Australia* published by the

Australian Bureau of Statistics, contain expert special articles that can save much time and labor.

Reference works

The most lasting gain from Australia's bicentennial in 1988 was a number of new reference works. The three most important were *Australians: An Historical Library*, a 10-volume work of which five (Volumes VI to X) are reference books; James Jupp (ed.), *The Australian People: An Encyclopedia of the Nation, Its People and Their Origins* (Sydney: Angus and Robertson, 1988); and William S. Ramson (ed.), *The Australian National Dictionary: A Dictionary of Australianisms on Historical Principles* (Melbourne: Oxford University Press, 1988). These works represented a major advance in Australian history and no library claiming an interest in the field can afford to be without them.

The same applies to the on-going *Australian Dictionary of Biography* (Melbourne: Melbourne University Press) which began publication in 1966; 14 volumes had been produced by 1996 plus an index volume covering the period 1788 to 1939. The volumes covering up to 1939 are also available as CD-ROM. In addition, information on individuals not listed in the *Australian Dictionary of Biography* may be available in a supplementary listing by H. J Gibbney and Ann G. Smith, *A Biographical Register, 1788-1939: Notes from the Australian Dictionary of Biography* (2 vols. Canberra: Printing Service, Australian National University, 1987).

Specific topics

Australia's environment and how it has been changed by human settlement is the subject of section 12 of the Bibliography. The best modern work is *Australia: A Geography* edited by Denis Jeans (2 vols. Sydney: University of Sydney, 1986, 1987). The first volume is devoted entirely to the natural environment and the second to man's impact upon it.

The study of Australia's first occupiers, the Aborigines, has expanded enormously since the 1960s. Long treated as a footnote in the earlier general histories of Australia, their prehistory and conquest by the Europeans has at last received detailed attention. For an excellent general introduction see Geoffrey Blainey, *Triumph of the Nomads* (Melbourne: Macmillan, 1982). The most recent large-scale treatment of their history is in D. J. Mulvaney and J. Peter White (eds.), *Australians to 1788* (Sydney: Fairfax, Weldon and Syme, 1987). About a quarter of the authoritative encyclopedia edited by James Jupp, *The Australian People* (Sydney: Angus and Robertson, 1988) is also devoted to Aborigines. The reader should be aware that new discoveries about the history and prehistory of Aborigines will mean continual revisions of their place in Australian history. David Horton (ed.), *Encyclopaedia of Aboriginal Australia: Aboriginal and Torres Strait Islander History, Society and Culture* (2 vols. Canberra: Aboriginal Studies Press, 1994) is also available as a CD-ROM.

There are some excellent thought-provoking single-volume books about Australia. Kenneth G. McIntyre, *The Secret Discovery of Australia* (revised ed., Sydney: Pan, 1982) argues that Australia's eastern coastline was known to the Portuguese 250 years before the voyage of Captain Cook in 1770. Geoffrey Blainey, *The Tyranny of Distance* (revised ed., Melbourne: Macmillan, 1982) first appeared in 1966 and encouraged consideration of distance and isolation as factors in Australian history.

Since its European colonization, Australia has attracted many travelers who have written about their experiences and observations. Section 11 of the Bibliography lists a small selection of these works, which have a special claim to significance or interest. An obvious starting point from an American point of view is Mark Twain's *Follow the Equator* (1897), the Australian and New Zealand parts of which Penguin Books published as *Mark Twain in Australia and New Zealand* (Harmondsworth: Penguin, 1974).

Overseas interest in Australia was at its height from 1901 to 1914, when it was regarded as a center of social and government experiments. One of the seminal works of this period was W. Pember Reeves, *State Experiments in Australia and New Zealand* (2 vols. London: Grant Richards, 1902). Republished by George Allen and Unwin in 1923, it was reissued by Macmillan in 1969. Convicts rightly figure prominently in writings about Australian history for the pre-1850 period. The work of the well-known art critic Robert Hughes on the convict system, *The Fatal Shore* (London: Collins Harvill, 1987), is now the best-known account, but readers are warned that the pervasive impression of gloom presented by Hughes does not command scholarly support which sees the convict experience in a far more optimistic light. In particular, readers should consult Alan Frost, *Botany Bay Mirages: Illusions of Australia's Convict Beginnings* (Melbourne: Melbourne University Press, 1994), Stephen Nicholas (ed.), *Convict Workers: Interpreting Australia's Past* (Sydney: Cambridge University Press, 1988), and Portia Robinson, *The Women of Botany Bay: A Reinterpretation of the*

Role of Women in the Origins of Australian Society (Sydney: Macquarie Library, 1988). They might also consult A. Roger Ekirch, *Bound for America: The Transportation of British Convicts to the Colonies, 1718-1775* (New York: Oxford University Press, 1987) for the American background to the British convict system.

Books abound on Australian politics. William G. McMinn, *A Constitutional History of Australian History* (Melbourne: Melbourne University Press, 1972) is a reliable introduction to the evolution of the political framework (sections 21 to 24). D. Jaensch, *The Australian Party System* (Sydney: Allen and Unwin, 1983) provides a general account of the political parties from 1945 to 1982.

Ross McMullin, *The Light on the Hill: The Australian Labor Party, 1891-1991* (Melbourne: Oxford University Press, 1991) is a comprehensive account of Australia's oldest continuous political party. It can be supplemented by works such as Andrew Scott, *Fading Loyalties: The Australian Labor Party and the Working Class* (Sydney: Pluto Press, 1991) and Graham Freudenberg, *Cause for Power: The Official History of the New South Wales Branch of the Australian Labor Party* (Sydney: Pluto Press and the New South Wales Branch of the Australian Labor Party, 1991), but a fully satisfying history remains to be written. P. L. Reynolds, *The Democratic Labor Party* (Brisbane: Jacaranda Press, 1974) is an excellent analysis of its subject as well as providing valuable data on the social aspects of the Australian Labor Party. For the Liberal Party see Gerald Henderson, *Menzies' Child: The Liberal Party of Australia, 1944-1994* (Sydney: Allen and Unwin, 1994). Clement Mcintyre, *Political Australia: A Handbook of Facts* (Melbourne: Oxford University Press, 1991) contains a useful compilation of political and other related data.

On foreign relations (sections 25 to 27), the quality of scholarship has risen greatly as greater access has been permitted to official documents. David Day, *Menzies and Churchill at War* (Sydney: Angus and Robertson, 1986) argues that Menzies entertained political ambitions in Britain in the early 1940s, a view challenged by A. W. Martin in *Robert Menzies: A Life, Volume 1, 1894-1943* (Melbourne: Melbourne University Press, 1993).

The economy has been of perennial interest in Australia and it has been the subject of some remarkable books (sections 28 and 29). Timothy A. Coghlan, *Labour and Industry in Australia* (4 vols.), first published by Oxford University Press in 1918 and reprinted by Macmillan in 1968, remains a marvelously well-informed panorama of Australia's economy, politics, and society up to 1901. Coghlan knew most of the principal colonial personalities in the late nineteenth century, and this gives his work for the period added insight.

The works of Australia's leading economic historian, Noel G. Butlin are magisterial, but difficult for non-economic readers; for a "user-friendly" introduction see R. V. Jackson's *Australian Economic Development in the Nineteenth Century* (Canberra: Australian National University Press, 1977). For a general account of the economy in the twentieth century, see E. A. Boehm, *Twentieth Century Economic Development in Australia* (Melbourne, 2nd ed., 1979). The five-volume *Pelican History of World Economy in Twentieth Century* (general editor Wolfram Fischer published between 1977 and 1986) is helpful in placing the Australian economy in its international setting.

Labor relations (section 30) is an important chapter in Australian history. For an introduction to the current scene, the reader can consult the *Australian* number of the U.S. Department of Labor, Bureau of International Affairs' series *Foreign Labor Trends* (Washington, D.C.: Government Printing Office), which has been issued annually since 1987. It is based on information compiled by the U.S. Embassy in Canberra and contains commentary and statistics.

There is now a great range of books on aspects of Australian social history; a selection of them is set out in sections 30 to 35. For immigration (section 35), the great work is James Jupp (ed.), *The Australian People: An Encyclopedia of the Nation, Its People and Their Origins* (Sydney: Angus and Robertson, 1988), an extraordinarily rich book covering all aspects of immigration and immigrant groups in Australia. As mentioned, about a quarter of this work is devoted to Aborigines. For a short recent introduction see James Jupp, *Immigration* (Sydney: Sydney University Press, 1991), the first of the *Australian Retrospective Series*.

As with other immigrant societies, there are many religions in Australia, but scholarly treatment of them is comparatively recent (section 36). Hans Mol conducted the first household survey of religion in 1966; the results were published in his *Religion in Australia: A Sociological Investigation* (Melbourne: Nelson, 1971). For an all too rare Australian and New Zealand study see Hugh R. Jackson, *Churches and People in Australia and New Zealand, 1860-1930* (Auckland, New Zealand: Allen and Unwin, 1987). Readers are also referred to Michael Hogan, *The Sectarian Strand: Religion in Australian History* (Ringwood: Penguin, 1987). More generally, there is a first-rate recent series of monographs under the general editorship of Philip J. Hughes which were published by the Australian Government Printing Services in 1995 and 1996 which give a current profile of the religious faith concerned, census statistics, and a bibliography. These works are listed in section 36 under their particular author.

War has given rise to one of the largest topics for writing in Australian history (section 40). There are official histories of Australia's part in both world wars, in Korea and Vietnam; those for the world wars also include separate medical volumes.

William S. Ramson (ed.), *The Australian National Dictionary: A Dictionary of Australianisms on Historical Principles* (Melbourne: Oxford University Press, 1988) gives meanings and documents the derivations of Australian words.

For the arts, there are a number of reliable reference works. Bruce Bennett and Jennifer Strauss (eds.) *The Oxford Literary History of Australia* (Melbourne: Oxford University Press, 1998) provides a detailed up-to-date account of Australian literature. Alan McCulloch, and Susan McCulloch (eds.), *Encyclopedia of Australian Art* (3rd ed. Sydney: Allen and Unwin, 1994) performs the same function for Australian art. For interpretative works, one starting point is A. G. Serle, *From the Deserts the Prophets Come: The Creative Spirit in Australia, 1788-1972* (Melbourne: Heinemann, 1973). David Marr, *Patrick White: A Life* (Sydney: Random House Australia, 1991) is a biography truly worthy of Australia's first Nobel prize winner for Literature. It has much to say about Australia's literary, theatrical, and artistic worlds since the late 1940s. In its own way, it is also an introduction to many themes in Australian history such as artists' relations with Britain. John F. Williams, *The Quarantined Culture: Australian Reactions to Modernism, 1913-1939* (Melbourne: Cambridge University Press, 1995) provides a long overdue account of the effect of censorship on Australia's culture.

Finally, mention should be made of the Australian Consortium for Social and Political Research Inc. at the Australian National University in Canberra. Founded in 1976, it is a national organization designed to encourage the use of computer-based social science data including a growing number of public opinion polls. It is a repository of Australian and overseas survey data which are assuming greater historical importance over time.

1. BIBLIOGRAPHIES AND GUIDES TO SOURCES: GENERAL

Albinski, Nan B. (ed.). *Australian Literary Manuscripts in North American Libraries: A Guide*. Canberra: Australian Scholarly Editions Centre, University College, Australian Defence Force Academy and National Library of Australia, 1998. Provides details for about 850 Australian and Australian-related authors, publishers, artists and organizations.

———— (ed.). *Directory of Resources for Australian Studies in North America*. Melbourne: National Centre for Australian Studies and the Australia-New Zealand Studies Center, Pennsylvania State University, 1992.

Argus Newspaper. *Argus Index*. Melbourne: Argus Newspaper, 1910-49.

Arnold, John, and Peter Browne (eds.). *Australia: A Reader's Guide*. Melbourne: National Centre for Australian Studies, 1996. A guide to about 1,350 works.

Australian Bureau of Statistics. *Catalogue of Australian Statistical Publications, 1804 to 1901*. Canberra: Australian Bureau of Statistics, 1989 (ABS Catalogue No. 1115.0).

————. *Catalogue of Official Statistical Publications, 1901-1984*. Canberra: Australian Bureau of Statistics, 1987 (ABS Catalogue No. 1112.0).

Australian Institute of Urban Studies. *Bibliography of Urban Studies in Australia*. Canberra: National Library of Australia, 1966-81.

Australian Periodicals in Print. Melbourne: D. W. Thorpe, 1972 to date. A convenient checklist.

Beed, Terence W. and others (compilers). *Australian Opinion Polls, 1941-1990: An Index*. Melbourne: D. W. Thorpe and National Centre for Australian Studies, 1993.

———— (compilers). *Australian Opinion Polls, 1941-1977*. Sydney: Hale and Iremonger and University of Sydney Sample Survey Centre, 1978.

Borchardt, Dietrich H. *Australian Bibliography: A Guide to Printed Sources of Information.* 3rd ed. Sydney: Pergamon, 1976.

———— (ed.). *Australians: An Historical Library*, Vol. VII: *A Guide to Sources*. Sydney: Fairfax, Syme and Weldon, 1987. The outstanding single-volume work of its kind. Edited by Australia's foremost bibliographer and incorporating the contributions of 60 scholars, it remains the first resort for serious students of Australian history and contains references to more than 3,000 works published before 1983.

———— (ed.). *Australian Official Publications*. Melbourne: Longman Cheshire, 1979.

Brady, Barbara (ed.). *Australian Sourcebooks: Social Sciences.* Melbourne: D. W. Thorpe with Australian Library and Information Association, 1992. Annotated bibibliography of about 700 books, periodicals, and databases.

Burnstein, Susan and others (eds.). *Directory of Archives in Australia.* O'Connor, A.C.T.: Australian Society of Archivists Inc., 1992.

Choate, Ray. *A Guide to Sources of Information on the Arts in Australia.* Sydney: Pergamon Press, 1983.

Cook, John, Nancy Lane, and Michael Piggott. *A Guide to Commonwealth Government Sources.* Sydney: Pergamon Press, 1988.

Crittenden, Victor. *Index to Journal Articles on Australian History, 1983.* North Balwyn, Victoria: Australian Reference Publications, 1990.

Crittenden, Victor, and Dietrich Borchard. *Index to Journal Articles on Australian History, 1984-1988.* North Balwyn, Victoria: Australian Reference Publications, 1994.

Crittenden, Victor, and John Thawley. *Index to Journal Articles on Australian History, 1974-1978.* Kensington, New South Wales: Australia 1788-1988, A Bicentennial History, 1981.

————. *Index to Journal Articles on Australian History for 1979.* Kensington, New South Wales: Australia 1788-1988, A Bicentennial History, 1981.

————. *Index to Journal Articles on Australian History for 1980.* Kensington, New South Wales: Australia 1788-1988, A Bicentennial History, 1982.

Crittenden, Victor, Barry Tie, and Des Rowney. *Index to Journal Articles on Australian History for 1981.* Kensington, New South Wales: Reference Section of History Project Incorporated, University of New South Wales, 1983.

————. *Index to Journal Articles on Australian History for 1982.* North Balwyn, Victoria: Australian Reference Publications, 1987.

Ferguson, John Alexander (ed). *Bibliography of Australia.* 7 vols. Sydney: Angus and Robertson, 1941-69. A facsimile edition was published by the National Library of Australia, Canberra, between 1975 and 1977.

———— (ed.). *Bibliography of Australia: Addenda, 1784-1850* (Volumes I to IV). Canberra: Australian National Library, 1986.

Fetherstone, Guy (ed.). *A Bibliography of Victorian History, 1850-1900.* rev. ed. Ascot Vale, Victoria: Red Rooster Press, 1986.

Hagger, A. J. (ed.). *A Guide to Australian Economic and Social Statistics.* Sydney: Pergamon Press, 1983.

Hall, Nick V. (ed.). *Parish Registers in Australia: A List of All Known Originals, Transcripts, Microforms and Indexes of Australian Parish Registers.* Melbourne: The Author, 1989.

————. *Tracing Your Family History in Australia: A Guide to Sources.* 2nd ed. Melbourne: Scriptorium Family Australia Centre, 1994.

Harrington, Michael. *The Guide to Government Publications in Australia.* Canberra: Australian Government Publishing Service, 1990.

Hibbins, Gillian M., Charles Fahey, and Mark R. Askew. *Local History: A Handbook for Enthusiasts*. Sydney: George Allen and Unwin, 1985. Contains much more than its title suggests.

Hogan, Terry, A. T. Yarwood, and Russell Ward (compilers). *Index to Journal Article on Australian History.* Armidale: University of New England, 1976.

Index to British Parliamentary Papers on Australia and New Zealand, 1800-1899. 2 vols. Dublin: Irish University Press, 1974.

Jurgensen, Manfred. *Eagle and Emu: German-Australian Writing, 1930-1990.* Brisbane: Queensland University Press, 1992.

Kepars, Indulis (ed.). *Australia.* 2nd ed. Oxford, Eng., Santa Barbara, Calif., Denver, Colo.: Clio Press, 1994. One of the World Bibliographical Series, this excellent work contains an annotated bibiography with over 1,000 entries. Because of the omission of important earlier works, the first edition, published in 1984, also needs to be consulted.

Mander-Jones, Phylllis (ed.). *Manuscripts in the British Isles Relating to Australia, New Zealand and the Pacific.* Canberra: Australian National University Press, 1972. The principal work on the subject.

Marshall, Julie, G. (ed.). *Literature on Royal Commissions, Select Committees of Parliament and Boards of Inquiry Held in Australia.* Melbourne: La Trobe University Library, 1990.

Mayer, Henry, and Liz Kirby (eds.). *ARGAP: A Research Guide to Australian Politics and Cognate Subjects.* Melbourne: Cheshire, 1976; a supplementary work, *ARGAP 2*, was published by Longman Cheshire, Melbourne, in 1984. Despite its title, these works covers many topics other than politics.

McNaught, Jean (ed.). *Index to Certificates to Depasturing Licences: Licence to Depasture Crown Lands beyond the Limit of Location, 1837-1860.* Lismore: Richmond-Tweed Regional Library, 1997.

Mills, C. M. (ed.). *A Bibliography of the Northern Territory: Monographs.* 5 vols. Canberra: Canberra College of Advanced Education Library, 1977-83.

Mills, John J. (ed.) *Information Resources and Services in Australia.* 2nd ed. Wagga Wagga, New South Wales: Centre for Information Studies, Charles Sturt University, 1992. A first-rate guide.

Mitchell Library, Sydney. *Dictionary Catalog of Printed Books.* 38 vols. Boston, Mass.: G. K. Hall, 1968. Supplements have been issued since 1968.

Monie, Joanna (compiler). *Index to English Language Journal Articles on Australia Published Overseas to 1900.* Sydney: History Project Incorporated, 1983.

Muir, Marcie, and Kerry White (compilers). *Australian Children's Books: A Bibliography, 1774-1988.* 2 vols. Melbourne: Melbourne University Press, 1992.

National Centre for Australian Studies. *Guide to New Australian Books.* Melbourne: D. W. Thorpe. A comprehensive bimonthly journal containing brief reviews, October 1990 to date.

———. *International Directory of Australian Studies.* Melbourne: National Centre for Australian Studies and the International Development Program of Australian Universities and Colleges, 1992.

National Library of Australia. *APAIS: Australian Public Affairs Information Service.* Canberra: 1945 to date. The major guide to periodical literature.

———. *Australian Books: A Select List of Recent Publications and Standard Works in Print 1990.* Canberra: National Library of Australia, 1991.

———. *Australian Joint Copying Project Handbook.* Canberra: National Library of Australia and the State Library of New South Wales, 1972 to date.

———. *Australian National Bibliography, 1901-1950.* 2 vols. Canberra: National Library of Australia, 1988.

———. *Australian National Bibliography.* Canberra: National Library of Australia, 1961-1996. As from 1996 the Library ceased publication of this work because of competition from on-line bibliographies.

————. *Guide to Collections of Manuscripts Relating to Australia.* Canberra: National Library of Australia, 1965 to date.

————. *Newspapers in Australian Libraries: A Union List.* 4th ed. Canberra: National Library of Australia, 1984-5. This work consists of two parts: part 1 covers holdings of foreign newspapers and part 2 covers holdings of Australian newspapers.

————. *Principal Manuscript Collections in the National Library of Australia.* Canberra: National Library of Australia, 1992.

Newcastle Morning Herald and Miners' Advocate Index. Newcastle: Newcastle Public Library, 1861 to date. This is the only newspaper index in Australia covering the period from 1861 to the present.

Nicholson, Ian. *Log of Logs: A Catalogue of Logs, Journals, Shipboard Diaries, Letters, and All Forms of Voyage Narratives, 1788 to 1988, for Australia and New Zealand and Surrounding Oceans.* Yaroomba, Queensland: The Author and Australian Association for Maritime History, 1990.

Nunn, G. Raymond (ed.). *Asia and Oceania: A Guide to Archival and Manuscript Sources in the United States.* 5 vols. London and New York: Mansell Publishing Limited, 1985. Lists some Australian materials.

Peake, Andrew G. (ed.). *Sources for South Australian History.* Dulwich, South Australia: Tudor Australia Press, 1987.

Philips, Margaret E. (ed.). *Australian Joint Copying Project: Handbook* Part 7: *Public Record Office Admiralty Records.* Canberra: National Library of Australia, 1993.

Pong, Alfred (ed.). *Checklist of Nineteenth Century Australian Periodicals.* Bandoora, Victoria: Latrobe University, 1985.

Price, Charles A. (ed.). *Australian Immigration: A Bibliography and Digest.* 4 vols. Canberra: Department of Demography, Australian National University, 1966-81.

Richards, Ronald (ed.). *A Guide to the Sources for the History of South Western Australia.* Nedlands, Western Australia: University of Western Australia Press, 1993.

Robert, W. C. H. (ed.). *Contributions to a Bibliography of Australia and the South Sea Islands.* 4 vols. Amsterdam: Philo Press, 1968-75.

Sharp. N. D., and M. A. Smith. *Late Pleistocene Archaeological Sites in Australia, New Guinea and Island Melanesia.* Australian Heritage Commission Bibliography Series No. 6, Canberra: Australian Government Publishing Service, 1991.

Sheehan, Joy. *A Guide to Sources of Information on Australian Business.* Sydney: Pergamon Press, 1983.

Stone, Beth. (ed.). *Guide to Microform Research Collections in the National Library of Australia.* Canberra: National Library of Australia, 1992.

Stuart, Lurline (ed.). *Nineteenth Century Australian Periodicals: An Annotated Bibliography.* Sydney: Hale and Iremonger, 1979.

Sydney Morning Herald Index. Sydney: Sydney Morning Herald, 1927-61. After 1961 the Index was kept in index card form, and since 1987 its business, politics, economics, and finance sections have been available as a computer database.

Symons, Jane. *Photographic Resources of Australia, 1990.* Sydney: Watermark Press, 1989. A comprehensive guide to the photographic holdings of governments, institutions and societies.

Thawley, John (ed.). *Australasia and South Pacific Islands Bibliography.* Lanham, Md., and London: Scarecrow Press, 1997. Contains 5,933 references and is the most comprehensive and up-to-date work of its kind.

Thorpe, D. W. *Australian Periodicals in Print.* Melbourne: D. W. Thorpe, 1981 to date. Annual.

———. *Subject Guide to Australian Books in Print.* Port Melbourne: D. W. Thorpe, 1990 to date. Annual.

Walsh, Kay, and Joy Hooton (eds.). *Australian Autobiographical Narrative.* 2 vols. Canberra: Australian Scholarly Editions Centre, University College, Australian Defence Force Academy and National Library of Australia, 1993, 1998. Covers the period up to 1900.

York, Barry (ed.). *Our Multicultural Heritage, 1788-1945: Annotated Guide to the Collections of the National Library of Australia.* Canberra: National Library of Australia, 1995.

2. BIBLIOGRAPHIES AND GUIDES TO SOURCES: SPECIFIC TOPICS

Adelaide, Debra (ed.). *Australian Women Writers: A Bibliographic Guide.* Sydney: Pandora Press, 1988.

———— (ed.). *Bibliography of Australian Women's Literature, 1795-1990.* Melbourne: D. W. Thorpe and National Centre for Australian Studies, 1991.

Australian Bureau of Statistics. *A Guide to Labour Statistics.* Canberra: Australian Bureau of Statistics, 1986 (ABS Catalogue No. 6102.0).

Australian Institute of Aboriginal Studies. *Current Bibliography.* Canberra: The Institute, 1961-75. Continued as *Annual Bibliography.* Canberra: The Institute, 1975 to date.

Bartlett, Ann M. (ed.). *Local and Family History Sources in Tasmania.* Launceston: Genealogical Society of Tasmania Inc., 1991.

Beedie, N. K. (ed.). *Bibliography of Captain James Cook, R. N., F. R. S., Circumnavigator.* 2nd ed. Sydney: Council of the Library of New South Wales, 1970.

Bennett, Bruce, and others. (eds.). *Western Australian Writing: A Bibliography.* Fremantle, Western Australia: Fremantle Arts Centre, 1990.

Bettison, M., and Ann Summers (eds.). *Her Story: Australian Women in Print, 1788-1975.* Sydney: Hale and Iremonger, 1980.

Bourke, Margaret M. (ed.). *Bibliography of Australian Finance, 1900-1968.* Sydney: Reserve Bank of Australia, Occasional Paper No. 5, 1971.

Brockwell, C. J. (ed). *Aborigines and the Law: A Bibliography.* Canberra: Law Department, Research School of Social Sciences, Australian National University, 1979.

Burkhardt, Geoffrey (ed.). *Australian School Centenary and Jubilee Histories: A Select Bibliography.* Angaston, South Australia: Magpie Books, 1995.

Chambers, Margaret (ed.).   *Finding Families: The Guide to the National Archives of Australia for Genealogists.* Canberra/Sydney: National Archives of Australia in association with Hale and Iremonger, 1998.

Commonwealth Department of Community Services and Health, *Bibliography of Australian Medicine and Health Services to 1950.* 4 vols. Canberra: Australian Government Publishing Service, 1988.

Craig, John. *Australian Politics: A Source Book.* 2nd edition Sydney: Harcourt Brace and Co., 1993. A guide to recent sources on politics for students with a chronology and glossary.

Department of Immigration and Ethnic Affairs. *Asia-Pacific and Trans-Tasman Migration*: An *Annotated Bibliography.* Canberra: Department of Immigration and Ethnic Affairs, 1998.
———. *Immigration Policies, 1945-1991: An Annotated Bibliography.* Canberra: Australian Government Publishing Service, 1991.

———. *Migrants and Religion: An Annotated Bibliography.* Canberra: Australian Government Publishing Service, 1996.

———. *Racism in Australia, 1990-1996.* Canberra: Australian Government Printing Service, 1997.

———. *Second Generation Australians: An Annotated Bibliography.* Canberra: Department of Immigration and Ethnic Affairs, 1998.

————. *The Social and Cultural Impact of Immigration on Australia: An Annotated Bibliography.* Canberra: Department of Immigration and Ethnic Affairs, 1998.

Dillon, J. L., and G. C. McFarlane (eds.). *An Australian Bibliography of Agricultural Economics, 1788-1960.* Sydney: New South Wales Government Printer, 1967.

Duwell, Martin, and others (eds.). *The ALS Guide to Australian Writers: A Bibliography, 1963-1995.* 2nd ed.   St. Lucia, Brisbane: Queensland University Press, 1997.

Evans, Heather (ed.).   *The Aboriginal People of Victoria: Select Bibliography of Pre-1960 Printed Sources in the Collections of the State Library of Victoria.* Melbourne: State Library of Victoria, 1993. This is also an excellent annotated bibliography.

Fielding, J., and Robert O'Neill (eds.).   *A Select Bibliography of Australian Military History, 1891-1939.* Canberra: Australian National University, Australian Dictionary of Biography, 1978.

Fitzpatrick, Georgina (comp.).   *Religion in Australian Life: A Bibliography of Social Research.* Bedford Park, South Australia: Australian Association for the Study of Religions and National Catholic Research Council, 1982.

Flesch, Juliet (ed.). *Love Brought to Book: A Bio-Bibliography of 20th Century Australian Romance Novels.* Melbourne: National Centre for Australian Studies, 1995.

Foster, S. G., Susan Marsden, and Roslyn Russell (eds.).   *Federation: The Guide to Records.* Canberra: Australian Archives, 1998.   An authoritative guide to the manuscript records of the federation of the Australian colonies in 1901.

Gandevia, B., and others (eds.).   *An Annotated Bibliography of the History of Medicine and Health in Australia.* Sydney: Royal Australasian College of Physicians, 1984.

Gunew, Sneja, and others (eds.).   *A Bibliography of Australian Multicultural Writers.* Geelong: Centre for Studies in Literary Education, Deakin University, 1992.

Hall, Sandra (ed.). *Australian Film Index: A Guide to Australian Films Since 1900.* Melbourne: D. W. Thorpe, 1992.

Hurley, Michael (ed.). *A Guide to Gay and Lesbian Writing in Australia.* Sydney: Allen and Unwin, 1996.

Jones, Gregory P. *A Guide to Sources of Information on Australian Industrial Relations.* Sydney: Pergamon Press, 1988.

Knight, Russell W. (ed.). *Australian Antarctic Bibliography.* Hobart: University of Tasmania, 1987.

Kyle, Noeline. *Tracing Family History in Australia.* Sydney: Methuen Australia, 1985.

Magery, Susan, and Lyndall Ryan (eds.). *A Bibliography of Australian Women's History.* Parkville, Victoria: Australian Historical Association, 1990.

Mason, M., and G. Fitzpatrick (eds.). *Religion in Australian Life: A Bibliography of Social Research.* Australian Association for the Study of Religions and National Catholic Research Council, 1982.

McIntosh, Lawrence D. (ed.). *Religion and Theology: A Guide to Current Reference Resources.* Wagga Wagga, New South Wales: Centre for Information Studies, 1977.

Mills, Carol, and June Dietrich (eds.). *Melbourne Review Index, 1876-1885.* Wagga Wagga, New South Wales: Centre for Information Studies, Charles Sturt University, 1992.

Murray, Sue, John Arnold, and others (eds.). *Bibliography of Australian Poetry, 1935-1955.* Melbourne: D. W. Thorpe, 1991.

Plomley, N. J. B. (ed.). *An Annotated Bibliography of the Tasmanian Aborigines.* London: Royal Anthropological Institute of Great Britain and Ireland, 1969. This work was continued by C. Sagona (see below).

Royal Australian Air Force Historical Section. *Units of the Royal Australian Air Force: Chiefs of the Air Staff, Aircraft, Bibliography.* Canberra: Australian Government Printing Service, 1995.

Sagona, C. (ed.). *An Annotated Bibliography of the Tasmanian Aborigines, 1970-1987.* Caufield, Victoria: Art School Press, 1989. This is a continuation of a work begun by N. J. B. Plomley listed separately in this bibliography.

Schaeffer, Irene (ed.). *Land Musters, Stock Returns, and Lists: Van Diemen's Land, 1803-1822.* Hobart: St. David's Park, 1992.

Smith, Hugh, and Sue Moss (eds.). *A Bibliography of Armed Forces and Society in Australia.* Canberra: Australian Defence Force Academy, 1987.

Swain, Tony (ed.). *Aboriginal Religion in Australia: A Bibliographical Survey.* New York: Greenwood Press, 1991.

Symons, Beverley, and others (eds.). *Communism in Australia: A Resource Bibliography.* Canberra: National Library of Australia, 1994.

Thomson, Neil, and Patricia Merrifield (eds.). *Aboriginal Health: An Annotated Bibliography.* Canberra: Australian Institute of Aboriginal Studies, 1988.

Wescombe, Christabel and Geoffrey Sherington (eds.). *Education in New South Wales: A Guide to State and Commonwealth Sources.* Sydney: Hale and Iremonger, 1993.

3. COMPUTER DATABASES

Note: For details of databases relating to Australia see the latest issue of *Directory of Online Databases* (New York: Cuadra/Elsevier) and Jenny Williams and Sherrey Quinn (eds.), *Directory of Australian Databases on CD ROM.* Hawthorn, Victoria: Australian Database Development Association, 1993. Those most relevant to Australian history are:

Australian Books in Print. Issued in book form since 1956.

Australian Business Index, 1981 to date.

Australian Database Association. *Directory of Australian and New Zealand Databases.* 3rd ed. Melbourne: Australian Database Association, 1988.

Australian Family and Society Abstracts, 1980 to date.

Australian Financial Review, 1982 to date.

Australian Industrial Relations Index, 1983 to date.

Australian Municipal Information System, 1968/69 to date.

Australian National Bibliography, 1980 to date.

Australian Public Affairs Information Service, 1978 to date.

National Library of Australia. *AHRR* (*Australian Historic Records Register*). National Library of Australia: Canberra, 1988. This register covers 3,500 records and is also available on microfiche.

4. COLLECTIONS OF PRIMARY SOURCES

Alomes, Stephen, and Catherine Jones (eds.). *Australian Nationalism: A Documentary History.* Sydney: Angus and Robertson, 1991.

Bertrand, Ina (ed.). *Cinema in Australia: A Documentary History.* Sydney: University of New South Wales Press, 1989.

Bessant, B. (ed.). *Readings in Australian History: The Occupation of a Continent.* Melbourne: Eureka Publishing Co., 1979.

Cannon, Michael (ed.). *Historical Records of Victoria.* 6 vols. Melbourne: Victorian Government Printing Office, 1981 to date. Concentrates on Aborigines, and land settlement up to 1840.

Clark, C. M. H. (ed.). *Select Documents in Australian History, 1788-1850.* Sydney: Angus and Robertson, 1955. Often reprinted since 1955.

———— (ed.). *Select Documents in Australian History, 1851-1900.* Sydney: Angus and Robertson, 1962.

———— (ed.). *Sources of Australian History.* London: Oxford University Press, 1957.

Clark, Patricia, and Dale Spender (eds.). *Life Lines: Australian Women's Letters and Diaries, 1788-1840.* Sydney: Allen and Unwin, 1996.

Crawford, John G., and others (eds.). *Australian Trade Policy, 1941-1966: A Documentary History.* Canberra: Australian National University Press, 1968. See also Snape in this section.

Crowley, Frank K. (ed.). *A Documentary History of Australia.* 6 vols. Melbourne: Nelson, 1980-85.

Dorling, Philip (ed.). *Diplomasi: Australia and Indonesia's Independence: Documents, 1947.* Canberra: Australian Government Publishing Service, 1994.

Ebbels, R. Noel (ed.). *The Australian Labor Movement: Extracts from Contemporary Documents.* Melbourne: Cheshire-Lansdowne, 1960.

Evans, Raymond, and others (eds.). *1901: Our Future's Past—Documenting Australia's Federation.* Melbourne: Macmillan, 1997.

Flannery, Tim (ed.). *The Explorers.* Melbourne: Text Publishing, 1998.

Gordon, Harry (ed.). *An Eyewitness History of Australia.* 3rd. ed. Melbourne: Lloyd O'Neill, 1986.

Hassam, Andrew (ed.). *No Privacy for Writing: Shipboard Diaries, 1852-1879.* Melbourne: Melbourne University Press, 1995. Contains eight diaries written by working-class men and women.

Hudson, W. J. (ed.). *Documents on Australian Foreign Policy, 1937-49.* Canberra: Australian Government Publishing Service, 1975 to date. By 1997, 11 volumes had been published for the period 1937-48.

Johnston, R. (ed.). *Documentary History of Queensland.* St. Lucia, Queensland: Queensland University Press, 1982.

Kelly, Max. *A Certain Sydney, 1900: A Photographic Introduction to a Hidden Sydney.* Sydney: Doak Press, 1977.

———. *Faces of the Street: William Street, Sydney, 1916.* Sydney: Doak Press, 1982. A photographic collection.

Kingston, Beverley (ed.). *The World Moves Slowly: A Documentary History of Australian Women.* Camperdown, New South Wales: Cassell, 1979.

Lack, John, and Jacqueline Templeton (eds.). *Sources of Australian Immigration History, 1901-1945.* Melbourne: Melbourne University Press, 1988.

Lee, David (ed.). *Australia and Indonesia's Independence: The Transfer of Sovereignty - Documents, 1949.* Canberra: Department of Foreign Affairs and Trade, 1998.

Lloyd, Clem, and Richard Hall (eds.). *Backroom Briefings: John Curtin's War.* Canberra: National Library of Australia, 1997. Confidential briefings given to senior journalists between 1941 and 1945.

Louis, L. J., and Ian Turner (eds.). *The Depression of the 1930s.* Melbourne: Cassell Australia, 1968.

Martin, A. W., and Patsy Hardy (eds.). *Dark and Hurrying Days: Menzies' 1941 Diary.* Canberra: National Library of Australia, 1993.

McAllister, Ian, and Rhonda Moore (eds.). *Party Strategy and Change: Australian Electoral Speeches since 1946.* Melbourne: Longman Cheshire, 1991.

McKinlay, Brian (ed.). *Australian Labor History in Documents.* 3 vols. Burwood, Victoria: Collins Dove, 1990. A revised version of a work originally published in 1979.

Meany, Neville. *Australia and the World: A Documentary History from the 1870s to the 1970s.* Melbourne: Longman Cheshire, 1985.

Moore, D., and R. Hall. *Australia: Image of a Nation, 1850-1950.* Sydney: Collins, 1983.

Reece, R. H .W., and R. Pascoe. *A Place of Consequence: A Pictorial History of Fremantle.* Fremantle, Western Australia: Freemantle Arts Centre, 1983.

Robson, L. L. (ed.). *Australian Commentaries: Select Articles from the "Round Table," 1911-1942.* Melbourne: Melbourne University Press, 1975.

Shaw, A. G. L. (ed.). *Gipps-La Trobe Correspondence, 1839-1846.* Melbourne: Melbourne University Press, 1989.

Snape, Richard H. and others (eds.). *Australian Trade Policy, 1965-1997: A Documentary History.* Sydney: Allen and Unwin, 1998. A collection of over 400 documents. See also Crawford in this section.

Starr, Grahame (ed.). *The Liberal Party of Australia: A Documentary History.* Melbourne: Drummond/Heinemann, 1980.

Stone, D. I. (ed.). *Gold Diggers and Diggings: A Photographic Study of Gold in Australia, 1854-1920.* Melbourne: Lansdowne, 1974.

Tampke Jürgen (ed.). *Wunderbar Country: Germans Look at Australia, 1850-1914.* Sydney: Hale and Iremonger, 1982.

Ward, Russel (ed.). *Such Was Life: Selected Documents in Australian Social History, 1788-1850.* Milton, Queensland: Jacaranda Press, 1972.

Ward, Russel, and John Robertson (eds.). *Such Was Life: Selected Documents in Australian Social History.* 2 vols. Sydney: Alternative Publishing Co-operative, 1980, 1986. Covers the period from 1851 to 1983.

Wilson, John, and others (eds.). *The Australian Welfare State: Key Documents and Themes.* Melbourne: Macmillan, 1996.

5. STATISTICAL SOURCES

Australian Bureau of Statistics. *Australian Economic Indicators.* Canberra: Australian Bureau of Statistics, ABS Catalogue No. 1350.0, February 1991 to date. A monthly publication which contains a wide range of economic, demographic, and labor statistics.

————. *Australian Women's Year Book.* Canberra: Australian Bureau of Statistics, ABS Catalogue No. 4124.0, 1994 to date.

————. *Population Survey Monitor.* Canberra: Australian Bureau of Statistics, ABS Catalogue No. 4103.0, August 1993 to date.

————. *Year Book Australia.* Canberra: Commonwealth Government Printer, 1977-78 to date. This important publication is much more than a compilation of statistics. It contains a chronology and valuable special articles. Earlier issues were published from 1908 by the Commonwealth Bureau of Census and Statistics as the *Official Year Book of the Commonwealth of Australia.*

Commonwealth Bureau of Census and Statistics [Australian Bureau of Statistics after 1975] New South Wales Office. *Official Year Book of New South Wales.* Sydney: Government Printer, 1904 to date.

———— Queensland Office. *Official Year Book of Queensland.* Brisbane: Government Printer, 1901, 1937 to date.

———— South Australian Office. *Official Year Book of South Australia.* Adelaide: Government Printer, 1912-13, 1966 to date.

———— Tasmanian Office. *Official Year Book of Tasmania.* Hobart: Government Printer, 1967 to date.

———— Victorian Office. *Official Year Book of Victoria.* Melbourne: Government Printer, 1873 to date.

———— Western Australian Office. *Official Year Book of Western Australia.* Perth: Government Printer, 1886-1905, 1957 to date.

Coppell, W. G. (ed.). *Australia in Facts and Figures.* rev. ed. Melbourne: Penguin, 1994. First published in 1974.

Docherty, James C. (ed.). *Selected Social Statistics of New South Wales, 1861-1976.* Historical Statistics Monograph No. 1. Sydney: History Project Incorporated, 1982.

Ethnic Affairs Commission of New South Wales. *The People of New South Wales: Statistics from the 1996 Census.* Sydney: Ethnic Affairs Commission of New South Wales, 1998. Mainly concerned with birthplace, language, and religion at the local government area level.

Keating, Michael. *The Australian Workforce, 1910-11 to 1960-61.* Canberra: Department of Economic History, Research School of Social Sciences, Australian National University, 1973.

Liesner, Thelma (ed.). *One Hundred Years of Economic Statistics: United Kingdom, United States of America, Australia, Canada, France, Germany, Italy, Japan, Sweden.* London: The Economist Publications Ltd., 1989.

Parker, Philip M. (ed.). *National Cultures of the World: A Statistical Reference.* Westport, Conn.: Greenwood Press, 1997.

Reserve Bank of Australia. *Australian Economic Statistics, 1949-50 to 1984-85.* 2 vols. Sydney: Reserve Bank of Australia, 1985.

Schmitz, C. J. *World Non-Ferrous Mineral Production and Prices, 1770-1976.* London: Frank Cass, 1979. Contains some statistics for Australia.

Vaus, David de, and Ilene Wolcott. *Australian Family Profiles: Social and Demographic Patterns.* Melbourne: Australian Institute of Family Studies, 1997. Draws together a wealth of data mainly from between 1980 and 1995 and includes commentary and extensive references.

6. GENERAL REFERENCE WORKS

Adams, J. D. (ed.). *AUSCHRON: Chronology of Australian History and Current Events.* Melbourne: RMIT (Royal Melbourne Institute) Internet [CD-ROM], 1997.

Australian Dictionary of Biography. 14 vols. Melbourne: Melbourne University Press, 1966 to date. A CD-ROM version of this work was issued in 1996 covering the volumes for period from 1788 to 1939.

Australian Geographic. *Australian Encyclopaedia.* 5th ed. 12 vols. Sydney: Australian Geographic, 1988.

Australians: An Historical Library. 10 vols. Sydney: Fairfax, Syme and Weldon, 1987. Five of these volumes are reference volumes: VI. *A Historical Atlas.* VII. *A guide to Sources.* VIII. *Events and Places.* IX. *A Historical Dictionary.* X. *Historical Statistics*

Bambrick, Susan (ed.). *The Cambridge Encyclopedia of Australia.* Melbourne: Cambridge University Press, 1994.

Bassett, Jan. *The Concise Oxford Illustrated Dictionary of Australian History.* Melbourne: Oxford University Press, 1996.

Bishop, Bernie, and Deborah McNamara (eds.). *The Asia-Australia Survey, 1997-98.* Melbourne: Macmillan Education, 1997.

The Book of Australian Facts. Sydney: Reader's Digest: 1992.

Corcoran, Robert (ed.). *Collins Australian Dictionary of Political Terms.* North Blackburn, Victoria Collins Dove, 1994.

Davison, Graeme, John Hirst, and Stuart Macintyre (eds.). *The Oxford Companion to Australian History.* Melbourne: Oxford University Press, 1998.

Dawson, Sarah (ed.). *The Penguin Australian Encyclopedia.* Ringwood: Viking O'Neill, 1990.

Fraser, Bryce, and Ann Atkinson (eds.). *The Macquarie Encyclopedia of Australian Events.* Sydney: Macquarie Library Ltd., 1997. A revised version of a work first published in 1983. It includes a reading guide at the end of each chapter.

Jaensch, Dean, and Max Teichman (eds.). *The Macmillan Dictionary of Australian Politics.* 4th ed. Melbourne: Macmillan, 1992.

Jupp, James (ed.). *The Australian People: An Encyclopedia of the Nation, Its People and Their Origins.* Sydney: Angus and Robertson, 1988. The major reference work on Australian immigration.

Murphy, Brian P. (ed.). *Dictionary of Australian History.* Sydney: McGraw-Hill Book Company, 1982.

Murray-Smith, Stephen (ed.). *The Dictionary of Australian Quotations.* Melbourne: Heinemann, 1987.

Palmer, Alan (ed.). *Dictionary of the British Empire and Commonwealth.* London: J. Murray, 1996. Contains many entries on Australia.

Pierce, Peter. *The Oxford Literary Guide to Australia.* Melbourne: Oxford University Press, 1987.

Shaw, John. (ed.). *Collins Australian Encyclopaedia.* Sydney: Collins in association with David Bateman Ltd., 1984.

Trood, Russell, and Deborah McNamara (eds.). *The Asia-Australia Survey, 1994.* South Melbourne: Pan Macmillan, 1994 to date.

Who Owns Whom: Australasia and Far East. London: Dun and Bradstreet, 1971 to date.

7. ATLASES AND MAP COLLECTIONS

Australian Electoral Commission and Australian Survey and Land Information Group. *Commonwealth of Australia, 1901-1988: Electoral Distributions.* Canberra: Commonwealth Department of Administrative Services, 1989.

Australian Surveying and Land Information Group and New Zealand Department of Survey and Land Information. *Macquarie Illustrated World Atlas.* rev. ed. Sydney: Macquarie Library in association with the Division of National Mapping, Canberra, and the Department of Lands and Survey, Wellington, 1994. A CD-ROM version was released in 1997.

Camm, Jack, C. R., and John McQuilton (eds.). *An Historical Atlas.* Vol. VI of *Australians: An Historical Library.* Sydney: Fairfax, Syme and Weldon, 1987. The best historical atlas of Australia.

Clancy, Robert. *The Mapping of Terra Australis: A Guide to Early Printed Maps of Australia, Antarctica, and the South Pacific.* Macquarie Park, New South Wales: Universal Press, 1995.

Green, Colin, and Tony Milne (eds.). *The Australian Atlas: Resource Units of Australia and the World.* 2nd ed. Melbourne: Rigby/Philip, 1978.

Griffin, T. L. C., and M. McCaskill (eds.). *Atlas of South Australia.* Adelaide: South Australian Government Printer, 1986.

Hugo, Graeme, and Chris Maher. *Atlas of the Australian People-1991 Census: National Overview.* Canberra: Australian Government Publishing Service, 1995.

Jeans, D. N. *An Historical Geography of New South Wales to 1901.* Sydney: Reed Education, 1972.

Johnson, Ken. *Ausmap Atlas of Australia.* Cambridge: Cambridge University Press, 1992.

Kelly, Max, and Ruth Crocker. *Sydney Takes Shape: A Collection of Contemporary Maps from Foundation to Federation.* Sydney: Macleay Museum, University of Sydney, 1977. Only 1,000 copies of this valuable work were printed.

Kunz, Egon, and Elsie Kunz. *A Continent Takes Shape.* Sydney: Collins, 1971.

Lines, John D. *Australia on Paper: The Story of Australian Mapping.* Box Hill, Victoria: Fortune Publications, 1992.

Nile, Richard, and Christian Clerk (eds.). *Cultural Atlas of Australia, New Zealand and the South Pacific.* Sydney: Hodder Headline/RD Press, 1996. This well-illustrated work mainly deals with indigenous peoples.

Perry, Thomas M. *The Discovery of Australia: The Charts and Maps of the Navigators and Explorers.* Melbourne: Nelson, 1982.

Poulsen, Michael, and Peter Spearritt. *Sydney: A Social and Political Atlas.* Sydney: George Allen and Unwin, 1981.

Rauchle, N. M. (ed.). *Map Collections in Australia: A Directory.* 3rd. ed. Canberra: National Library of Australia, 1980.

Taylor, Peter. *The Atlas of Australian History*. Sydney: Child and Associates, 1990.

Whitehouse, Eric B. *The Northern Approaches: Australia in Old Maps, 1770-1820.* Brisbane: Boolarong Press, 1994.

Wilson, Lee. *Mystery Continent: Historical Atlas of European Exploration in Australia*. Sydney: CCH Australia, 1984.

8. BIOGRAPHICAL COLLECTIONS

Atkinson, Ann (ed.). *The Dictionary of Famous Australians.* 2nd ed. Sydney: Allen and Unwin, 1995.

Australian Dictionary of Biography. 14 vols. Melbourne: Melbourne University Press, 1966 to date. A CD-ROM version of this work was issued in 1996 covering the volumes for period from 1788 to 1939.

Carment, David, Robyn Maynard, and Alan Powell (eds.). *Northern Territory Dictionary of Biography.* 2 vols. Casuarina, Northern Territory: Northern Territory University Press, 1990, 1992.

Dahlitz, Raymond A. (ed.). *Secular Who's Who: A Biographical Dictionary of Freethinkers and Secularists.* Melbourne: Ray Dahilitz, 1994.

Dicky, Brian (ed.). *The Australian Dictionary of Evangelical Biography.* Sydney: Evangelical History Association, 1994.

Erickson, Rica (ed.). *The Bicentennial Dictionary of Western Australians, Pre-1829-1888.* 4 vols. Nedlands, Western Australia: University of Western Australia Press, 1987-88.

Forth, G. J. (ed.). *A Biographical Register and Annotated Bibliography of Anglo-Irish Colonists in Australia.* Geelong, Victoria: Deakin University Press, 1992.

Game, Cathryn (ed.). *Monash Biographical Dictionary of 20th Century Australia.* Melbourne: Reed Reference Publishing, 1994. Contains 2,220 entries.

Gibbney, H. J., and Ann G. Smith (eds.). *A Biographical Register, 1788-1939: Notes from the Australian Dictionary of Biography.* 2 vols. Canberra: Australian National University, 1987.

Gillen, Mollie (ed.). *The Founders of Australia: A Biographical Dictionary of the First Fleet.* Sydney: Library of Australian History, 1988.

Green, Neville (ed.). *Aborigines of the Albany Region, 1821-1898.* (Vol. VI of *The Bicentennial Dictionary of Western Australians, Pre-1829-1888*). Nedlands, Western Australia: University of Western Australia Press, 1990.

Hallam, Sylvia, and Lois Tilbrook (eds.). *Aborigines of the Southwest Region, 1829-1840.* (Vol. VIII of *The Bicentennial Dictionary of Western Australians, Pre-1829-1888*). Nedlands, Western Australia: University of Western Australia Press, 1990.

Kirkland, Frederick (ed.). *Order of Australia, 1975-1995: The First Twenty Years.* Sydney: Plaza Historical Services, 1995. Provides a listing of those who have received Australian honors.

Moore, Andrew, and John Shields, (eds.). *A Biographical Register of the Australian Labour Movement, 1788-1975.* Sydney: University of New South Wales Press. In preparation.

National Centre for Australian Studies. *List of Australian Writers: 1788-1992.* 2 vols. Melbourne: National Centre for Australian Studies: Bibliography of Australian Literature Project, 1995. Contains biographical and bibliographical information on 9,500 Australian authors.

Reed Reference Australia. *Contemporary Australians, 1995-96.* Melbourne: Reed Reference Australia, 1995. A "Who's Who" type publication.

Robb, Gwenda, and others (eds.). *Concise Dictionary of Australian Artists.* Melbourne: Melbourne University Press, 1993.

Salsbury, Stephen, and Kay Sweeney (eds.). *Sydney Stockbrockers: Biographies of Members of the Sydney Stock Exchange.* Sydney: Hale and Iremonger, 1992.

Stratham, Pamela, and Rica Erickson (eds.). *Dictionary of Western Australians*. 3 vols. Nedlands, Western Australia: University of Western Australia Press, 1979. Covers the period up to 1868.

9. JOURNALS

Aboriginal History (Canberra), 1977 to date.

Archives and Manuscripts (Canberra), 1955 to date.

Australian Aboriginal Studies (Canberra), 1983 to date.

Australian and New Zealand Journal of Criminology (Sydney), 1967 to date.

Australian and New Zealand Journal of Sociology (Melbourne), 1965 to date.

Australian Archaeology (Canberra), 1974 to date.

Australian Book Review (Melbourne), 1961-73, 1978 to date.

Australian Economic History Review (Melbourne), 1956 to date.

Australian Feminist Studies (Adelaide), 1986 to date.

Australian Folklore (Perth), 1987 to date.

Australian Foreign Affairs Record (Canberra), 1929 to date. An important source of official information.

Australian Geographical Studies (Canberra), 1963 to date.

Australian Jewish Historical Society Journal (Sydney), 1939 to date.

Australian Journal of Chinese Affairs (Canberra), 1977 to date.

Australian Journal of International Affairs (Melbourne), 1947 to date. Published as *Australian Outlook* from 1947 to 1989.

Australian Journal of Politics and History (Brisbane), 1955 to date.

Australian Society (Melbourne), 1982 to date.

Australian Studies, London, 1988 to date. Formerly *BASA Magazine* (London), 1983-87, the journal of the British-Australian Studies Association.

Bulletin (Bibliographical Society of Australian and New Zealand), (Canberra), 1970 to date.

Current Affairs Bulletin (Sydney), 1947-98.

Flinders Journal of Politics and History (Adelaide), 1969 to date.

Historical Records of Australian Science (Canberra), 1980 to date.

Historical Studies (Melbourne), 1949 to date.

Italian Historical Society Journal (Melbourne), 1992 to date.

Journal of Australian Political Economy (Sydney), 1977 to date.

Journal of Australian Studies (Melbourne), 1977 to date.

Journal of Industrial Relations (Sydney), 1959 to date.

Journal of Northern Territory History (Darwin), 1990 to date.

Journal of the Australian Catholic Historical Society (Sydney), 1960 to date.

Journal of the Australian Population Association (Canberra), 1973 to date.

Journal of the Australian War Memorial (Canberra), 1982 to date.

Journal of the Historical Society of South Australia (Adelaide), 1975 to date.

Journal of the Royal Australian Historical Society (Sydney), 1906 to date.

Journal of the Royal Historical Society of Queensland (Brisbane), 1914 to date.

Labour and Industry (Brisbane/Geelong), 1987 to date.

Labour History (Canberra, Sydney), 1962 to date.

Melbourne Journal of Politics (Melbourne), 1968 to date.

Oral History Association of Australia Journal (Perth), 1978 to date.

Papers and Proceedings (Tasmanian Historical Research Association), 1878 to date.

People and Place (Melbourne), 1992 to date. A journal devoted to population and urban research.

Studies in Western Australian History (Perth), 1977 to date.

Victorian Historical Journal (Melbourne), 1911 to date.

10. NATIONAL HISTORIES AND SURVEY WORKS

Alomes, Stephen. *A Nation At Last?   The Changing Character of Australian Nationalism, 1889-1988.* Sydney: Angus and Robertson, 1988.

Atkinson, Alan. *The Europeans in Australia: A History. Volume One: The Beginning.* Melbourne: Oxford University Press, 1997.

Australians: An Historical Library. I. *Australians to 1788.* II. *Australians 1838.* III. *Australians 1888.* IV. *Australians 1938.* V. *Australians from 1939.* Sydney: Fairfax, Syme and Weldon, 1987.

Boeze, Frank. *Island Nation: A History of Australians and the Sea.* Sydney: Allen and Unwin, 1998.

Bolton, Geoffrey. *The Middle Way, 1942-1988.*   Vol. 5 of *Oxford History of Australia.* Melbourne: Oxford University Press, 1990.

Clark, C. M. H. *A History of Australia.* 6 vols. Melbourne: Melbourne University Press, 1962-88. This work covers the history of Australia up to 1935.

——. *A Short History of Australia.* rev. ed. Melbourne: Macmillan, 1986.

——. *Manning Clark's History of Australia.* Melbourne: Melbourne University Press, 1993. Abridged edition of Clark's six-volume history published between 1962 and 1988.

Clarke, F. G. *Australia: A Concise Political and Social History.* 2nd ed. Sydney: Harcourt Brace Jovanovich, 1992.

Grattan, C. Hartley. *The Southwest Pacific: A Modern History.* 2 vols. Ann Arbor: University of Michigan Press, 1963.

Graubard, Stephen R. (ed.). *Australia: The Daedalus Symposium.* Sydney: Angus and Robertson, 1985.

Grimshaw, Patricia, and others. *Creating a Nation, 1788-1990.* Melbourne: Penguin Books/McPhee Gribble, 1994. This work emphasizes the role of women in Australian history.

Hudson, Wayne, and Geoff Bolton (eds.). *Creating Australia: Changing Australian History.* Sydney: Allen and Unwin, 1997.

Kingston, Beverley. *Glad, Confident Morning, 1860-1900.* Vol. 3 of the *Oxford History of Australia.* Melbourne: Oxford University Press, 1988.

Kociumbas, Jan. *Possessions, 1770-1860.* Vol. 2 of the *Oxford History of Australia.* Melbourne: Oxford University Press, 1992.

MacIntyre, Stuart. *The Succeeding Age, 1901-1942.* Vol. 4 of the *Oxford History of Australia.* Melbourne: Oxford University Press, 1986.

Molony, John. *The Penguin History of Australia: The Story of 200 Years.* Ringwood: Penguin, 1988. First published by Viking in 1987.

Rickard, John. *Australia: A Cultural History*. New York: Longman Inc., 1988. An introductory text which covers more than its title indicates.

Ward, R. B. *Australia Since the Coming of Man*. Sydney: Lansdowne, 1982.

Younger, R. M. *Australia and the Australians: A New Concise History*. Melbourne: Hutchinson, 1982.

11. TRAVEL ACCOUNTS

Ackermann, Jessie. *Australia From a Woman's Point of View*. London: Cassell and Co., 1913. Reprinted in facsimile in 1981.

Adams, Francis W. L. *The Australians: A Social Sketch*. London: T. Fisher and Unwin, 1893.

Breton, William H. *Excursions in New South Wales, Western Australia and Van Dieman's Land During the Years 1830, 1831, 1832 and 1833*. 2nd ed. London: Richard Bentley, 1835.

Buley, E. C. *Australian Life in Town and Country*. London: Newnes; and New York: G. P Putnam's Sons, 1905.

Fullerton, Mary E. *The Australian Bush*. London and Toronto: J. M. Dent and Sons, n.d. c.1927.

Hügel, Baron Charles von. *New Holland Journal: November 1833- October 1834*. Trans. Dymphna Clark. Melbourne: Melbourne University Press, 1994.

Inglis, James. *Our Australian Cousins*. London: Macmillan and Co., 1880.

Lawrence, D. H. *Kangaroo: The Corrected Edition*. Melbourne: HarperCollins Publishers/Imprint Classics, 1992. First published in 1923. A novel based on a visit to Australia.

McGuire, Paul. *Australian Journey*. London and Toronto: William Heinemann Ltd., 1939.

Métin, Albert. *Socialism without Doctrine.* Sydney: Alternative Publishing Co-operative, 1977. Originally published as *Le Socialisme sans Doctrines* in Paris in 1901.

Pesman, Ros. *Duty Free: Australian Women Abroad.* Melbourne: Oxford University Press, 1996.

Reeves, W. Pember. *State Experiments in Australia and New Zealand.* 2 vols. London: Grant Richards, 1902. Republished by George Allen and Unwin in 1923, it was reissued by Macmillan, Melbourne, in 1969.

Rowland, Percy F. *The New Nation: A Sketch of the Social, Political and Economic Conditions and Prospects of the Australian Commonwealth.* London: Smith, Elder and Co., 1903.

Trollope, Anthony. *Australia.* 2 vols. New York: Hippocrene Books, 1987. Originally published in 1873.

Twain, Mark. *Mark Twain in Australia and New Zealand.* Harmondsworth: Penguin, 1974. A facsimile reprint of part of Mark Twain's *Follow the Equator*, originally published in 1897.

Twopeny, R. E. N. *Town Life in Australia.* London: Eliot Stock, 1883. Reissued in facsimile by Penguin, 1973.

Ussher, Kathleen. *The Cities of Australia.* London and Toronto: J. M. Dent and Sons, 1928.

12. ENVIRONMENTAL WORKS

Australian Bureau of Statistics. *Australia's Environment—Issues and Facts.* Canberra: Australian Bureau of Statistics, 1992 (ABS Catalogue No. 4140.0).

Bennett, Isobel. *The Great Barrier Reef.* Sydney: Collins/Australian Museum, 1987.

Bergmann, Meredith, and Verity Bergmann. *Green Bans, Red Union: Environmental Activism and the New South Wales Builders Labourers' Federation.* Sydney: University of New South Wales Press, 1998.

Bureau of Mineral Research Palaeogeographic Group. *Australia—The Evolution of a Continent.* Canberra: Australian Government Publishing Service, 1990.

Cawte, Alice. *Atomic Australia: 1944-1990.* Sydney: University of New South Wales Press, 1992.

Clayton, M. N., and R. J King. (eds.). *Marine Botany: An Australian Perspective.* Melbourne: Longman Cheshire, 1981.

Collis, Brad. *Snowy: The Making of Modern Australia.* rev. ed. Canberra: Tabletop Press, 1998. An illustrated history of the Snowy Mountains Scheme.

Dawson, Terence J., Anne Musser, and Jillian Hallam. *Kangaroos: Biology of the Largest Marsupials.* Sydney: University of New South Wales Press, 1995.

Department of Enviroment, Sport and Territories. *State of the Environment, 1996.* Melbourne: CSIRO Publishing, 1996. The most comprehensive and up-to-date work in one volume.

Eckersley, Richard (ed.). *Measuring Progress: Is Life Getting Better?* Melbourne: CSIRO Publishing, 1998. Explores the possible use of a broadly-based genuine progress indicator (GPI) to monitor economic, social, and environmental change as a substitute for the traditional gross domestic product.

Encyclopedia of Australian Wildlife. Sydney: Reader's Digest, 1997. Well illustrated and comprehensive.

Gilpin, Alan. *An Australian Dictionary of Environment and Planning.* Melbourne: Oxford University Press, 1990.

Hall, Colin M. *Wasteland to World Heritage: Preserving Australia's Wilderness.* Melbourne: Melbourne University Press, 1992.

Hill, R. S. (ed.). *The History of the Australian Vegetation: Cretaceous to Recent.* Cambridge: Cambridge University Press, 1994.

Jeans, D. N. (ed.). *Australia: A Geography.* Vol. 1: *The Natural Environment;* Vol. 2: *Space and Society.* Sydney: Sydney University Press. 1986, 1987. Originally published in one volume in 1977.

Jeans, D. N., and Peter Spearritt. *The Open-Air Museum: the Cultural Landscape of New South Wales.* Sydney: Allen and Unwin, 1981.

Lines, William J. *Taming the Great South Land: A History of the Conquest of Australia.* Sydney: Allen and Unwin, 1991.

O'Conner, Mark. *This Tired Brown Land.* Sydney: Duffy and Snellgrove, 1998.

Oosterzee, Penny Van. *The Centre: The Natural History of Australia's Desert Regions.* Sydney: Reed Books, 1994.

Papadakis, Elim. *Politics and the Environment: The Australian Experience.* Sydney: Allen and Unwin, 1993.

Powell, John M. *An Historical Geography of Modern Australia: The Restive Fringe.* Melbourne: Cambridge University Press, 1988.

Price, A. Grenfell. *Island Continent: Aspects of the Historical Geography of Australia and its Territories.* Sydney: Angus and Robertson, 1972.

Pybus, Cassandra and Richard Flanagan. *The Rest of the World Is Watching.* Sydney: Pan Macmillan, 1990. A series of essays dealing with environmental politics in Tasmania.

Pyne, Stephen J. *Burning Bush: A Fire History of Australia.* New York: Henry Holt and Company, 1991.

Rolls, Eric C. *They All Ran Wild: the Story of Pests on the Land in Australia.* Sydney: Angus and Robertson, 1984.

Strahan, R. (ed.). *The Australian Museum Complete Book of Australian Mammals.* Sydney: Angus and Robertson, 1983.

Tapper, N. and L. Hurry. *Australia's Weather Patterns: An Introductory Guide.* Mt. Waverly, Victoria: Dellasta, 1993.

The Heritage of Australia: the Illustrated Register of the National Estate. Melbourne: Macmillan in association with the Australian Heritage Commission, 1981.

Warner, R. F. (ed.). *Fluvial Geomorphology of Australia.* Sydney: Academic Press, 1988.

Young, Ann. *Environmental Change in Australia since 1788.* Melbourne: Oxford University Press, 1996.

13. ABORIGINES: PREHISTORY AND ETHNOGRAPHY

Blainey, Geoffrey N. *Triumph of the Nomads: A History of Ancient Australia.* rev. ed. Melbourne: Macmillan, 1982.

Butlin, Noel G. *Economics and the Dreamtime: A Hypothetical History.* Melbourne: Cambridge University Press, 1993. The last work by Australia's leading economic historian of the post-1945 period.

————. *Our Original Aggression: Aboriginal Populations of Southeastern Australia, 1788-1850.* Sydney: Allen and Unwin, 1983. A pioneering work in the field.

Horton, David. *Recovering the Tracks: The History of Australian Archaeology.* Canberra: Aboriginal Studies Press, 1991.

Horton, David, and others (eds.). *Encyclopaedia of Aboriginal Australia: Aboriginal and Torres Strait Islander History, Society and Culture.* 2 vols. Canberra: Aboriginal Studies Press, 1994. Also available on CD-ROM.

Jones, Philip. *Boomerang: Behind an Australian Icon.* Adelaide: Wakefield Press, 1996.

Keast, A. (ed.). *Ecological Biogeography of Australia.* 3 vols. The Hague: W. Junk Publishers, 1981.

Layton, Robert. *Australian Rock Art: A New Synthesis.* Sydney/ Melbourne: Cambridge University Press, 1992.

Mulvaney, D. J., and J. Peter White (eds.). *Australians to 1788.* Sydney: Fairfax, Weldon and Syme, 1987.

Murray, Tim. *Archaeology of Aboriginal Australia.* Sydney: Allen and Unwin, 1998.

Reynolds, Henry. *Fate of a Free People: A Radical Re-Examination of the Tasmanian Wars.* Melbourne: Penguin Books, 1995.

Spencer, W. B., and F. J. Gillen. *The Native Tribes of Central Australia.* London: Macmillan, 1899. A facsimile edition was published by Dover, New York, in 1968.

Webb, Stephen. *Palaeopathology: Health and Disease Across a Hunter-Gatherer Continent.* Melbourne: Cambridge University Press, 1995.

White, J. P., and J. F. O'Connell. *A Prehistory of Australia, New Guinea and Sahul.* Sydney: Academic Press, 1982.

14. ABORIGINES AND EUROPEANS

Bartlett, Richard H. *The Mabo Decision.* Sydney: Butterworths, 1993.

Beckett, Jeremy. *Torres Strait Islanders: Custom and Colonialism.* Cambridge: Cambridge University Press, 1987.

Brennan, Frank. *One Land, One Nation: Mabo-Towards 2000.* St. Lucia: Queensland University Press, 1995. Includes a chronology as well as references.

Butt, Peter and Robert Eagleson. *Mabo, Wik, and Native Title.* Sydney: Federation Press, 1998.

Chesterman, John and Brian Galligan. *Citizens without Rights: Aborigines and Australian Citizenship.* Melbourne: Cambridge University Press, 1997.

Commonwealth Department of Aboriginal Affairs. *Aboriginal Social Indicators, 1984.* Canberra: Australian Government Publishing Service, 1984. A useful compendium of statistics.

Critchett, Jan. *A Distant Field of Murder: Western District Frontiers, 1834-1848.* Melbourne: Melbourne University Press, 1990.

French, Maurice. *Conflict on the Condamine: Aborigines and the European Invasion.* Toowoomba: Darling Downs Institute Press, 1989.

Gardner, P. D. *Gippsland Massacres: The Destruction of the Kurnai Tribe, 1800-1860.* West Gippsland and Latrobe Valley Education Centre, 1983.

Goodall, Heather. *Invasion to Embassy: Land in Aboriginal Politics in New South Wales.* Sydney: Allen and Unwin, 1996.

Graham, Hiley. *The Wik Case: Issues and Implications.* Sydney: Butterworths, 1997.

Griffiths, Max. *Aboriginal Affairs: A Brief History, 1788-1995.* Sydney: Kangaroo Press, 1995.

Hall, R. A. *The Black Diggers: Aborigines and Torres Strait Islanders in the Second World War.* Sydney: Allen and Unwin, 1989.

Harris, John. *One Blood: 200 Years of Aboriginal Encounter with Christianity.* Sydney: Albatross, 1990.

Henson, Barbara. *A Straight Out Man: F. W. Albrecht and Central Australian Aborigines.* Melbourne: Melbourne University Press, 1992.

Hunter, Ernest. *Aboriginal Health and History: Power and Prejudice in Remote Australia.* Melbourne: Cambridge University Press, 1993.

Kolig, E. *The Silent Revolution: The Effect of Modernization on Australian Aboriginal Religion.* Philadelphia: Institute for the Study of Human Issues, 1981.

Lippmann, L. *Generations of Resistance: The Aboriginal Struggle for Justice.* Melbourne: Longman Cheshire, 1981.

Maddock, K. *Your Land Is Our Land: Aboriginal Land Rights.* Ringwood: Penguin, 1983.

Milliss, Roger. *Waterloo Creek: The Australia Day Massacre of 1838, George Gipps and the British Conquest of New South Wales.* Melbourne: Penguin/McPhee Gribble, 1992.

Morphy, Howard. *Ancestral Connections: Art and an Aboriginal System of Knowledge.* Chicago: University of Chicago Press, 1991.

Pepper, Phillip, and Tess De Araugo. *What Did Happen to the Aborigines of Victoria?* Volume 1: *The Kurnai of Gippsland.* Melbourne: Hyland House, 1985.

Peterson, Nicolas and Will Sanders. *Citizenship and Indigenous Australians: Changing Conceptions and Possibilities.* Melbourne: Cambridge University Press, 1998.

Plomley, N. J. B. *Weep in Silence: A History of the Flinders Island Aboriginal Settlement.* Hobart: Blubber Head Press, 1987.

Rae-Ellis, Vivienne. *Black Robinson: Protector of Aborigines.* Melbourne: Melbourne University Press, 1988.

Read, Peter, and Jay Read. *Long Time, Olden Time: Aboriginal Accounts of Northern Territory History.* Alice Springs: Institute for Aboriginal Development Publishing, 1992.

Reece, R. H. W. *Aborigines and Colonists: Aborigines and Colonial Society in New South Wales in the 1830's and 1840's.* Sydney: Sydney University Press, 1974.

Reece, R. H. W. and C. T. Stannage (eds.). *European-Aboriginal Relations in Western Australian History.* Perth: University of Western Australia Press, 1984.

Reynolds, Henry. *Aboriginal Sovereignty: Reflections on Race, State and Nation.* Sydney: Alllen and Unwin, 1996.

———. *Frontier: Aborigines, Settlers, and Land.* Sydney: Alllen and Unwin, 1987.

———. *The Other Side of the Frontier: Aboriginal Resistance to the European Invasion of Australia.* Ringwood, Victoria: Penguin, 1982.

Ryan, Lyndall. *The Aboriginal Tasmanians.* Brisbane: University of Queensland Press, 1981.

Stephenson, Margaret A. *Mabo: The Native Title Legislation.* St. Lucia: Queensland University Press, 1995.

Stevens, Christine. *White Man's Dreaming: Killalpaninna Mission, 1866-1915.* Sydney: Oxford University Press, 1994.

Watson, Pamela. *Frontier Lands and Pioneer Legends: How Pastoralists Gained Karuwali Land.* Sydney: Allen and Unwin, 1998.

Willey, K. *When the Sky Fell Down: the Destruction of the Tribes of the Sydney Region, 1788-1850.* Sydney: Collins, 1979.

Yarwood, A. T., and M. J. Knowling. *Race Relations in Australia: A History.* Sydney: Methuen, 1982.

15. DISCOVERY OF AUSTRALIA

Dampier, William. *A New Voyage Round the World.* London: J. Knapton, 1697. A reprint of the 1729 edition was issued in 1968 by Dover Publications, New York.

Duyker, Edward (ed.). *The Discovery of Tasmania: Journal Extracts from the Expeditions of Abel Janszoon Tasman and Marc-Joseph Marion Dufresne, 1642 and 1772.* Hobart: St. David's Park, 1992.

Eisler, William, and Bernard Smith. *Terra Australis: The Furthest Shore.* Sydney: International Cultural Corporation of Australia for the Art Gallery of New South Wales, 1988.

Estensen, Miriam. *Discovery: The Quest for the Great South Land.* Sydney: Allen and Unwin, 1998.

Frost, Alan. *The Voyage of the Endeavour: Captain Cook and the Discovery of the Pacific.* Sydney: Allen and Unwin, 1998.

Horner, Frank. *Looking for La Pérouse: D'Entrecasteaux in Australia and the South Pacific, 1792-1793.* Melbourne: Melbourne University Press, 1995.

Hough, Richard. *Captain James Cook: A Biography*. London: Hodder and Stoughton, 1994.

Ingleton, Geoffrey. *Matthew Flinders: Navigator and Chartmaker*. Melbourne: Hedley Australia, 1986.

Marchant, L. *France Australe: A Study of French Explorations and Attempts to Found a Penal Colony and Strategic Base in South Western Australia, 1503-1826*. Perth: Artlook Books, 1982.

McIntyre, Kenneth G. *The Secret Discovery of Australia: Portuguese Ventures 250 Years before Captain Cook*. rev. ed. Sydney: Pan, 1982.

Robert, W. C. H. *The Dutch Explorations, 1605-1756, on the North and Northwest Coast of Australia: Extracts from Journals, Log Books, and Other Documents Relating to These Voyages*. Amsterdam: Philo Press, 1973.

Robertson, Jillian. *The Captain Cook Myth*. Sydney: Angus and Robertson, 1981.

Shilder, G. *Australia Unveiled: The Share of the Dutch Navigators in the Discovery of Australia*. Amsterdam: Theatrum Orbis Terrarum, 1976.

Smith, Bernard. *European Vision and the South Pacific, 1768-1850: A Study in the History of Art and Ideas*. 2nd ed. New York: Harper and Row, 1985. First published in 1960.

Spate, Oskar H. K. *The Pacific Since Magellan*. Vol. I: *The Spanish Lake*. Vol. II: *Monopolists and Freebooters*. Vol. III: *Paradise Lost and Found*. Canberra: Australian National University Press, 1979, 1983, 1988.

Williams, Glyndwr, and Alan Frost (eds.). *Terra Australis to Australia*. Melbourne: Oxford University Press, 1988.

16. FIRST EUROPEAN SETTLEMENTS AND CONVICTS

Andrews, Alan E. J. *Major Mitchell's Map 1834: The Saga of the Survey of the Nineteen Counties*. Hobart: Blubber Head Press, 1992.

Blainey, Geoffrey, N. *The Tyranny of Distance: How Distance Shaped Australia's History.* rev. ed. Melbourne: Macmillan, 1982.

Damousi, Joy. *Female Convicts, Sexuality, and Gender in Colonial Australia.* Melbourne: Cambridge University Press, 1997.

Daniels, Kay. *Convict Women.* Sydney: Allen and Unwin, 1998.

Forster, Colin. *France and Botany Bay: The Lure of a Penal Colony.* Melbourne: Melbourne University Press, 1996.

Frost, Alan. *Botany Bay Mirages: Illusions of Australia's Convict Beginnings.* Melbourne: Melbourne University Press, 1994.

―――. *Convicts and Empire: A Naval Question.* Oxford: Oxford University Press, 1980.

Fry, Ken. *Beyond the Barrier: Class Formation in a Pastoral Society, Bathurst, 1818-1848.* Bathurst, New South Wales: Crawford House Press, 1994.

Hirst, J. B. *Convict Society and Its Enemies: A History of Early New South Wales.* Sydney: Allen and Unwin, 1983.

Hughes, Robert. *The Fatal Shore: A History of the Transportation of Convicts to Australia, 1787-1868.* London: Collins Harvill, 1987.

King, Robert J. *The Secret History of the Convict Colony: Alexandro Malaspina's Report on the British Settlement of New South Wales.* Sydney: Allen and Unwin, 1990. A translation of the first Spanish account of Sydney.

Lyte, Charles. *Sir Joseph Banks: Eighteenth Century Explorer, Botanist, and Entrepreneur.* Sydney: Reed, 1980.

Martin, Ged (ed.). *The Founding of Australia: The Argument about Australia's Origins.* Sydney: Hale and Iremonger, 1978.

Mawer, Granville A. *Most Perfectly Safe: The Convict Shipwreck Disasters of 1833-42.* Sydney: Allen and Unwin, 1997.

Nicholas, Stephen (ed.). *Convict Workers: Interpreting Australia's Past.* Sydney: Cambridge University Press, 1988.

Oxley, Deborah. *Convict Maids: The Forced Migration of Women to Australia.* Melbourne: Melbourne University Press, 1996.

Robinson, Portia. *The Women of Botany Bay: A Reinterpretation of the Role of Women in the Origins of Australian Society.* Sydney: Macquarie Library, 1988.

Robson, Lloyd L. *A History of Tasmania.* Vol. I: *Van Diemen's Land From the Earliest Times to 1855.* Oxford: Oxford University Press, 1983.

Steven, M. *Trade, Tactics and Territory: Britain in the Pacific, 1783-1823.* Melbourne: Melbourne University Press, 1983.

Weidenhofter, Maggie. *Port Arthur: Place of Misery.* Port Arthur, Tasmania: Port Arthur Historic Site Management Authority, 1990. First published by Oxford University Press in 1981.

17. EARLY COLONIAL GOVERNORS

Fletcher, Brian H. *Ralph Darling: A Governor Maligned.* Melbourne: Oxford University Press, 1984.

Frost, Alan. *Arthur Phillip: His Voyaging, 1738-1814.* Melbourne: Oxford University Press, 1987.

King, Alice H. *Richard Bourke.* Melbourne: Oxford University Press, 1971.

King, J., and J. King. *Philip Gidley King: A Biography of the Third Governor of New South Wales.* Sydney: Methuen, Australia, 1981.

Ritchie, John. *Lachlan Macquarie: A Biography.* Melbourne: Melbourne University Press, 1986

18. LAND EXPLORERS

Beale, E. *Sturt: The Chipped Idol. A Study of Charles Sturt, Explorer.* Sydney: Sydney University Press, 1979.

Crowley, Frank K. *Forrest, 1847 to 1918.* Vol. I: *Apprenticeship to Premiership, 1847-91.* St. Lucia: University of Queensland Press, 1971.

Cunningham, Chris. *Blue Mountains Rediscovered: Beyond the Myths of Early Australian Exploration.* Sydney: Kangaroo Press, 1996.

Dutton, Geoffrey, P. H. *The Hero As Murderer: The Life of Edward John Eyre, Australian Explorer and Governor of Jamaica, 1815-1901.* Ringwood: Penguin, 1977.

McMinn, W. G. *Allan Cunningham: Botanist and Explorer.* Melbourne: Melbourne University Press, 1970.

Moorhead, Alan. *Cooper's Creek.* Melbourne: Macmillan, 1977. Illustrated edition of a work first published in 1963.

Webster, E. M. *Whirlwinds in the Plain: Ludwig Leichhardt-Friends, Foes and History.* Melbourne: Melbourne University Press, 1980.

19. LAND SETTLEMENT

Abbott, G. J. *The Pastoral Age: A Re-Examination.* Melbourne: Macmillan, 1971.

Bolton, Geoffrey C. *A Fine Country to Starve In.* Perth: University of Western Australia Press, 1972.

Campbell, K.O. *Australian Agriculture: Reconciling Change and Tradition.* Melbourne: Longman Cheshire, 1980.

Dutton, Geoffrey. *The Squatters: An Illustrated History of Australia's Pastoral Pioneers.* Melbourne: Viking O'Neil, 1989.

Fletcher, Brian H. *Landed Enterprise and Penal Society: A History of Farming and Grazing in New South Wales before 1821.* Sydney: Sydney University Press, 1976.

Glynn, S. *Government Policy and Agricultural Development: A Study of the Role of Government in the Development of the Western Australian Wheat Belt, 1900-1930.* Perth: University of Western Australia Press, 1975

Williams, M. *The Making of the South Australian Landscape: A Study in the Historical Geography of Australia.* London: Academic Press, 1974.

20. STATES, REGIONS, CITIES, AND TOWNS

Ashton, Paul. *The Accidental City: Planning Sydney since 1788.* Sydney: Hale and Iremonger, 1993.

Bate, Weston A. *Lucky City: the First Generation of Ballarat, 1851-1901.* Melbourne: Melbourne University Press, 1978.

————. *Life after Gold: Twentieth-century Ballarat.* Melbourne: Melbourne University Press/Miegunyah Press, 1993.

Blainey, Geoffrey. *Our Side of the Country: The Story of Victoria.* Sydney: Methuen Haynes, 1984.

Bowman, M. (ed.). *Beyond the City: Case Studies in Community Structure and Development.* Melbourne: Longman Cheshire, 1981.

Boyd, Robin. *Australia's Home: Its Origins, Builders and Occupiers.* Ringwood: Penguin, 1978.

Broome, Richard, Tony Dingle, and Susan Priestly. *The Victorians.* 3 vols. Sydney: Fairfax, Syme and Weldon Associates, 1984. An official history of Victoria.

Cannon, Michael. *Life in the Cities.* Melbourne: Currey O'Neil, 1983.

Cashman, Richard, and Chrys Meader. *Marrickville: Rural Outpost to Inner City.* Sydney: Hale and Iremonger, 1991.

Cole, J. R. *Shaping a City: Greater Brisbane, 1925-1985.* Brisbane: Brooks, 1984.

Davidson, Jim (ed.). *The Sydney—Melbourne Book.* Sydney: Allen and Unwin, 1986.

Davison, Graeme J. *The Rise and Fall of Marvellous Melbourne.* Melbourne: Melbourne University Press, 1978.

Docherty, James C. *Newcastle: The Making of an Australian City.* Sydney: Hale and Iremonger, 1983.

Fitzgerald, Ross. *A History of Queensland.* Vol. I: *From the Dreaming to 1915.* Vol. II: *From 1915 to the 1980s.* St. Lucia, Brisbane: Queensland University Press, 1982, 1984. An important account with an emphasis on the twentieth century.

Freestone, Robert. *Model Communities: The Garden City Movement in Australia.* Melbourne: Nelson, 1989.

Garden, Donald S. *Victoria: A History.* Melbourne: Nelson, 1984.

Gibbney, Jim. *Canberra, 1913-1953.* Canberra: Australian Government Publishing Service, 1988.

Hagan, Jim and Andrew Wells. *A History of Wollongong.* Wollongong: University of Wollongong Press, 1998.

Karskens, Grace. *Holroyd: A Social History of Western Sydney.* Sydney: University of New South Wales Press, 1991.

Kelly, Max. *Paddock Full of Houses: Paddington, 1840-1890.* Sydney: Doak Press, 1978.

Kennedy, Brian E. *Silver, Sin and Sixpenny Ale: A Social History of Broken Hill, 1883-1921.* Melbourne: Melbourne University Press, 1978.

Lawson, Ronald. *Brisbane in the 1890s: A Study of an Australian Urban Society.* St. Lucia: Queensland University Press, 1973.

Linge, Godfrey J. R. *Industrial Awakening: A Geography of Australian Manufacturing, 1788 to 1890.* Canberra: Australian National University Press, 1979.

Lloyd, Clem, and others. *For the Public Health: The Hunter District Water Board, 1892-1992.* Melbourne: Longman Cheshire, 1992.

Logan, T. *Urban and Regional Planning in Victoria.* Melbourne: Shillington House, 1981.

McCalman, Janet. *Struggletown: Public and Private Life in Richmond, 1900-1965.* Melbourne: Melbourne University Press, 1984.

McCarty, John W., and C. B. Schedvin. *Australian Capital Cities: Historical Essays.* Sydney: Sydney University Press, 1978.

Neutze, Max. *Urban Development in Australia: A Descriptive Analysis.* rev. ed. Sydney: Allen and Unwin, 1981.

Peachment, Alan (ed.). *The Business of Government: Western Australia, 1983-90.* Perth: Federation Press, 1991.

Peel, Victoria, and others. *A History of Hawthorn.* Melbourne: Melbourne University Press, 1993.

Powell, Alan. *Far Country: A Short History of the Northern Territory.* 3rd ed. Melbourne: Melbourne University Press, 1996.

Priestley, Susan. *South Melbourne: A History.* Melbourne: Melbourne University Press, 1995.

Reynolds, Peter, and Max Solling. *On the Margins of the City— Leichhardt: A Social History of Leichhardt and the Former Municipalities of Annandale, Balmain, and Glebe.* Sydney: Allen and Unwin, 1997.

Richards, Eric S. (ed.). *The Flinders History of South Australia: Social History.* 3 vols. Adelaide: Wakefield Press, 1986-87.

Robson, Lloyd. *A History of Tasmania.* 2 vols. Melbourne: Oxford University Press, 1983, 1990.

Sandercock, Leonie. *Property, Politics, and Urban Planning: A History of Australian City Planning.* New Brunswick, New Jersey: Transaction Books, 1990.

Sparke, Eric. *Canberra, 1954-1980.* Canberra: Australian Government Publishing Service, 1988.

Spearritt, Peter. *Sydney Since the Twenties.* Sydney: Hale and Iremonger, 1978.

Stannage, C. T. *The People of Perth: A Social History of Western Australia's Capital City.* Perth: Carroll's for Perth City Council, 1979.

Stratham, Pamela (ed.). *The Origins of Australia's Capital Cities.* Sydney: Cambridge University Press, 1989.

Thorpe, Bill. *Colonial Queensland: Perspectives on a Frontier Society, 1840-1900.* St. Lucia, Queensland: University of Queensland Press, 1996.

Townsley, W. A. *Tasmania: From Colony to Statehood, 1803-1945.* Hobart Tasmanian Government Printing Office, 1991.

Whitelock, Derek. *Adelaide, 1836-1976.* Brisbane: Queensland University Press, 1979.

Withycombe, Susan M. *Town in Transition: Queanbeyan, 1945-1985.* Canberra: Canberra Publishing and Printing Company, 1986.

21. POLITICS: GENERAL

Aitkin, Don. *Stability and Change in Australian Politics.* 2nd ed. Canberra: Australian National University Press, 1972.

Campbell, Andrew A. *The Australian League of Rights: A Study in Political Extremism and Subversion.* Melbourne: Outback Press, 1978.

Clune, David. *The New South Wales State Election: 1953.* Sydney: New South Wales Parliamentary Library and Department of Government, University of Sydney, 1996.

Considine, Mark, and Brian Costar (eds.). *Trials in Power: Cain, Kirner and Victoria, 1982-1992.* Melbourne: Melbourne University Press, 1992.

Crisp, L. F. *Australian National Government.* 4th ed. Melbourne: Longman Cheshire, 1978.

Cuneen, Christopher. *Kings' Men.* Sydney: Allen and Unwin, 1984. Deals with the office of governor-general from 1901 to 1936.

Davidson, Alastair. *The Invisible State: The Formation of the Australian State, 1788-1901.* Sydney: Cambridge University Press, 1991.

Eddy, John J., and John Nethercote (eds.). *Towards National Administration: Studies in Australian Administration History.* Sydney: Hale and Iremonger, 1994.

Foley, Carol A. *The Australian Flag: Colonial Relic or Contemporary Icon.* Sydney: The Federation Press, 1996.

Galligan, Brian. *Politics of the High Court: A Study of the Judicial Branch of the Government of Australia.* Brisbane: University of Queensland Press, 1987.

Hawker, Geoffrey N. *The Parliament of New South Wales, 1856-1965.* Sydney: Government Printer, 1971.

Hughes, Colin A. (ed.). *A Handbook of Australian Government and Politics, 1965-1974.* Canberra: Australian National University Press, 1977.

———— (ed.). *A Handbook of Australian Government and Politics, 1975-1984.* Sydney: Pergamon Press and Australian National University Press, 1986.

Hughes, Colin A., and B. D. Graham (ed.). *A Handbook of Australian Government and Politics, 1890-1964.* Canberra: Australian National University Press, 1968.

Irving, Helen. *To Constitute A Nation: A Cultural History of Australia's Constitution.* Cambridge: Cambridge University Press, 1997.

Jaensch, Dean. *The Australian Politics Guide.* Melbourne: Macmillan Education, 1996.

Jaensch, Dean, and Max Teichmann,. *The Macmillan Dictionary of Australian Politics.* 4th ed. Melbourne: Macmillan Education, 1992.

Kelly, Paul. *The End of Certainty: The Story of the 1980s.* rev. ed. Sydney: Allen and Unwin, 1994.

Lance, Armstrong. *Good God, He's Green: A History of Tasmanian Politics, 1989 to 1996.* Taroona, Tasmania: Pacific Law Press, 1997.

La Nauze, John A. *The Making of the Australian Constitution.* Melbourne: Melbourne University Press, 1972.

Lovell, David and others. *The Australian Political System.* Melbourne: Addison Wesley Longman Australia, 1998. Introductory text.

MacIntyre, Clement. *Political Australia: A Handbook of Facts.* Melbourne: Oxford University Press, 1991.

Manne, Robert. *The Petrov Affair: Politics and Espionage.* Sydney: Pergamon Press, 1987.

McKnight, David. *Australia's Spies and Their Secrets.* Sydney: Allen and Unwin, 1994. Deals with the Australian Security Intelligence Organisation.

McMinn, Winston G. *A Constitutional History of Australia.* Melbourne: Oxford University Press, 1979.

————. *Nationalism and Federalism in Australia.* Melbourne: Oxford University Press, 1994.

Mills, Stephen. *The Hawke Years: The Story from the Inside.* Melbourne: Penguin Books/Viking, 1993.

Moore, Andrew. *The Right Road? A History of Right Wing Politics in Australia.* Melbourne: Oxford University Press, 1995.

Norris, R. *The Emergent Commonwealth: Australian Federation, Expectations and Fulfillment, 1889-1910.* Melbourne: Melbourne University Press, 1975.

Power, John, and others. *Local Government Systems of Australia.* Canberra: Australian Government Publishing Service, 1981.

Rickard, John D. *Class and Politics: New South Wales, Victoria and the Early Commonwealth, 1890-1910.* Canberra: Australian National University Press, 1975.

Russell, Roslyn, and Philip Chubb. *One Destiny! The Federation Story: How Australia Became a Nation.* Melbourne: Penguin Books, 1998.

Rydon, Joan, and others. *New South Wales Politics, 1901-1917: An Electoral and Political Chronicle.* Sydney: New South Wales Parliamentary Library and Department of Government, University of Sydney, 1996.

Simms, Marion (ed.). *The Paradox of Parties: Australian Political Parties in the 1990s.* Sydney: Allen and Unwin, 1996.

Souter, Gavin. *Acts of Parliament: A Narrative History of Australia's Federal Legislature.* Melbourne: Melbourne University Press, 1988.

Wicks, Bertram. *Understanding the Australian Constitution: The Plain Words.* Hobart: Libra Books, 1997.

Wright, Raymond. *A People's Counsel: A History of the Parliament of Victoria 1856-1990.* Melbourne: Oxford University Press, 1992.

22. PARLIAMENTARY BIOGRAPHICAL REGISTERS

Bennett, S. C., and G. Bennett (eds.). *Biographical Register of the Tasmanian Parliament, 1851-1960.* Canberra: Australian National University Press, 1960.

Bolton, Geoffrey C., and Anne Mozley (eds.). *The Western Australian Legislature, 1870-1930.* Canberra: Australian National University Press, 1961.

Browne, G. (ed.). *Biographical Register of the Victorian Parliament, 1900-84.* Melbourne: Library Committee, Parliament of Victoria, 1985.

Connolly, Christopher N. (eds.). *Biographical Register of the New South Wales Parliament, 1856-1901.* Canberra: Australian National University Press, 1983.

Coxon, H., and others (eds.). *Biographical Register of the South Australian Parliament, 1857-1957.* Adelaide: Wakefield Press, 1985.

Radi, Heather, and others (eds.). *Biographical Register of the New South Wales Parliament, 1901-1970.* Canberra: Australian National University Press, 1979.

Rydon, Joan (ed.). *A Biographical Register of the Commonwealth Parliament, 1901-1972.* Canberra: Australian National University Press, 1975.

Thomson, K., and G. Serle (eds.). *A Biographical Register of the Victorian Parliament, 1851-1900.* Canberra: Australian National University Press, 1972.

Waterson, D. B. (ed.). *A Biographical Register of the Queensland Parliament, 1860-1929.* Canberra: Australian National University Press, 1972.

Waterson, D. B., and John Arnold (eds.). *Biographical Register of the Queensland Parliament, 1930-1980, with an Outline Atlas of Queensland Electorates, 1859-1980.* Canberra: Australian National University Press, 1982.

23. POLITICAL PARTIES AND MOVEMENTS

Aitkin, Donald. *The Country Party in New South Wales: A Study in Organisation and Survival.* Canberra: Australian National University Press, 1972.

Alexander, Malcolm and Brian Galligan (eds.). *Comparative Political Studies: Australia and Canada.* Melbourne: Longman Cheshire, 1992.

Beilharz, Peter. *Transforming Labor: Labor Tradition and the Labor Decade in Australia.* Melbourne: Cambridge University Press, 1994.

Bongiorno, Frank. *The People's Party: Victorian Labor and the Radical Tradition, 1875-1914.* Melbourne: Melbourne University Press, 1996.

Coghill, Ken (ed.). *The New Right's Australian Fantasy.* Sydney: McPhee Gribble/ Penguin, 1987.

Connell, R. W. and T. H. Irving. *Class Structure in Australian History: Documents, Narrative and Argument.* Melbourne: Cheshire, 1980.

Farrell, Frank. *International Socialism and Australian Labour: The Left in Australia, 1919-1939.* Sydney: Hale and Iremonger, 1981.

Freudenberg, Graham. *Cause for Power: The Official History of the New South Wales Branch of the Australian Labor Party.* Sydney: Pluto Press and the New South Wales Branch of the Australian Labor Party, 1991.

Hagan, James and Ken Turner. *A History of the Labor Party in New South Wales 1891-1991.* Melbourne: Longman Cheshire, 1991.

Henderson, Gerald. *Menzies' Child: The Liberal Party of Australia, 1944-1994.* Sydney: Allen and Unwin, 1994.

Jaensch, Dean. *The Australian Party System, 1945-1982.* Sydney: Allen and Unwin, 1983.

Kelly, Paul. *November 1975: The Inside Story of Australia's Greatest Political Crisis.* Sydney: Allen and Unwin, 1995. Concerns the dismissal of the federal government by the governor-general in 1975.

Loveday, Peter, and others (eds.). *The Emergence of the Australian Party System.* Sydney: Hale and Iremonger, 1977.

Macintyre, Stuart. *The Reds: The Communist Party of Australia from Origins to Illegality.* Sydney: Allen and Unwin, 1998.

Markey, Ray. *The Making of the Labor Party in New South Wales, 1880-1910.* Sydney: Sydney University Press, 1988.

Matthews, Race. *Australia's First Fabians: Middle-Class Radicals, Labor Activists and the Early Labour Movement.* Melbourne: Cambridge University Press, 1993.

McMullin, Ross. *The Light on the Hill: The Australian Labor Party, 1891-1991.* Melbourne: Oxford University Press, 1991.

Moore, Andrew. *The Secret Army and the Premier: Conservative Paramilitary Organisations in New South Wales, 1930-32.* Sydney: University of New South Wales Press, 1989.

Murray, Robert. *The Split: Australian Labor in the Fifties.* Melbourne: Cheshire, 1970. Reprinted by Hale and Iremonger, Sydney, in 1984.

O'Brien, Patrick. *The Liberals—Factions, Feuds, and Fancies.* Ringwood: Penguin, 1986.

Reynolds, Margaret. *The Last Bastion: Labor Women Working Towards Equality in the Parliaments of Australia.* Chatswood, New South Wales: Business and Professional Publishing, 1995.

Reynolds, P. L. *The Democratic Labor Party.* Brisbane: Jacaranda, 1974.

Saunders, Malcolm, and Ralph Summy. *The Australian Peace Movement: A Short History.* Canberra: Peace Research Centre, Australian National University, 1986.

Scott, Andrew. *Fading Loyalties: The Australian Labor Party and the Working Class.* Sydney: Pluto Press, 1991.

Simms, Marion. *A Liberal Nation: The Liberal Party and Australian Politics.* Sydney: Hale and Iremonger, 1982.

Singleton, Gwynnoth. *The Accord and the Australian Labour Movement.* Melbourne: Melbourne University Press, 1990.

Tsokhas, Kosmas. *Class Apart: Businessmen and Australian Politics, 1960-1980.* Melbourne: Oxford University Press, 1984.

Warhurst, John. *Keeping the Bastards Honest: The Australian Democrats First Twenty Years.* Sydney: Allen and Unwin, 1997.

24. POLITICAL AUTOBIOGRAPHIES AND BIOGRAPHIES

Abjorensen, Norman. *John Hewson: A Biography.* Port Melbourne: Lothian Books, 1993.

Ayers, Philip J. *Malcolm Fraser: A Biography.* Melbourne: William Heinemann Australia, 1987.

Barnett, David, and Pru Goward. *John Howard: Prime Minister.* Melbourne, Viking, 1997.

Barwick, Garfield. *A Radical Tory: Garfield Barwick's Recollections and Reflections.* Sydney: Federation Press, 1996.

Bebbington, G. *Pit Boy to Prime Minister: The Story of the Rt. Hon. Sir Joseph Cook.* Keele, England: University of Keele, 1988.

Blazey, Peter B. *Bolte: A Political Biography.* Brisbane: Jacaranda, 1972.

Buckley, Ken. *Doc Evatt.* Melbourne: Longman Cheshire, 1994.

Cain, John. *John Cain's Years: Power, Parties and Politics.* Melbourne: Melbourne University Press, 1995. The author was premier of Victoria in the 1980s.

Carew, Edna. *Paul Keating: Prime Minister.* Sydney: Allen and Unwin, 1992.

Cockburn, Stewart. *Playford: Benevolent Despot.* Kent Town, South Australia: Axiom Publishers and Distributors, 1991.

Crockett, Peter. *Evatt: A Life.* Sydney: Oxford University Press, 1993.

Cumpston, Ina M. *Lord Bruce of Melbourne.* Melbourne: Longman Cheshire, 1989.

Dodd, Helen J. *Pauline: The Hanson Phenomenon.* Brisbane: Boolarong Press, n.d. [1998]. An account of the central figure in recent political debates about Asian immigration.

Edwards, John. *Keating: The Inside Story.* Melbourne: Penguin/Viking, 1996.

Fitzgerald, Ross. *Red Ted Theodore.* St. Lucia, Queensland: Queensland University Press, 1994.

Fitzhardinge, L. F. *William Morris Hughes: A Political Biography.* 2 vols. Sydney: Angus and Robertson, 1964, 1979.

FitzSimons, Peter. *Beazley: A Biography.* Melbourne: HarperCollins, 1998.

Glass, Margaret. *Charles Cameron Kingston: Federation Father.* Melbourne: Melbourne University Press, 1997.

―――. *Tommy Bent: "Bent by Name, Bent by Nature."* Melbourne: Melbourne University Press, 1993.

Golding, Peter. *Black Jack McEwen: Political Gladiator.* Melbourne: Melbourne University Press, 1996. An overdue biography of one of the leading figures in Australian federal politics in the 1950s and 1960s.

Gunnar, Peter. *Good Iron Mac: The Life of Australian Federation Father Sir William McMillan, KCMG.* Sydney: The Federation Press, 1995.

Hawke, Bob. *The Hawke Memoirs.* Melbourne: Reed Books/Mandarin, 1996.

Hewat, Tim, and David Wilson. *Don Chipp.* Melbourne: Vista Books, 1978. A life of the founder of the Australian Democrats.

Hocking, Jenny. *Lionel Murphy: A Political Biography.* Melbourne: Cambridge University Press, 1997. A life of an important Australian Labor Party politician and High Court judge.

Hudson, W. J. *Casey.* Melbourne: Oxford University Press, 1986.

Hughes, Colin, A. *Mr. Prime Minister: Australian Prime Ministers, 1901-1972.* Melbourne: Oxford University Press, 1975.

Lunn, Hugh. *Johannes Bjeke-Peterson: A Political Biography.* St. Lucia: University of Queensland Press, 1984.

Marr, David. *Barwick: The Classic Biography of a Man of Power.* rev. ed. Sydney: Allen and Unwin, 1992.

Martin, Alan W. *Henry Parkes: A Biography.* Melbourne: Melbourne University Press, 1980.

———. *Robert Menzies: A Life, Volume 1, 1894-1943.* Melbourne: Melbourne University Press, 1993.

McMinn, Winston G. *George Reid.* Melbourne: Melbourne University Press, 1989.

Nairn, Bede. *The "Big Fella": Jack Lang and the Australian Labor Party, 1891-1949.* Melbourne: Melbourne University Press, 1986.

O'Reilly, David. *Cheryl Kernot: The Woman Most Likely.* Sydney: Random House Australia, 1998.

Pasquarelli, John. *The Pauline Hanson Story by the Man Who Knows.* Sydney: New Holland, 1998. An account of the founder of the controversial One Nation Party by her former senior political adviser.

Rickard, John. *H. B. Higgins: The Rebel as Judge.* Sydney: Allen and Unwin, 1985.

Robertson, John. *J. H. Scullin: A Political Biography.* Perth: University of Western Australia Press, 1974.

Ross, Lloyd. *John Curtin: A Biography.* Melbourne: Sun Books, 1983. First published in 1977.

Snedden, Billie M., and M. Bernie Schedvin. *Billie Snedden: An Unlikely Liberal.* Melbourne: Macmillan Australia, 1990.

Spaull, Andrew. *John Dedman: A Most Unexpected Labor Man.* Melbourne: Hyland Press, 1998.

Uren, Tom. *Straight Left.* Sydney: Random House, 1994.

Wilkinson, Marian. *The Fixer: The Untold Story of Graham Richardson.* Port Melbourne: Reed Books/William Heinemann, 1996. A study of a prominent figure in the federal Labor government from 1983 to 1992.

25. AUSTRALIA AND THE BRITISH EMPIRE

Black, Jeremy. *British Foreign Policy in an Age of Revolutions, 1783-1793.* Cambridge: Cambridge University Press, 1994.

Constantine, Stephen (ed.). *Emigrants and Empire: British Settlement in the Dominions between the Wars.* Manchester and New York: Manchester University Press/St. Martin's Press, 1990.

Drummond, I. A. *Imperial Economic Policy, 1917-1939.* London: Allen and Unwin, 1974.

Dunn, Michael. *Australia and the Empire.* Sydney: Collins/Fontana, 1981.

Edelstein, M. *Overseas Investment in the Age of High Imperialism: The United Kingdom, 1850-1914.* New York: Columbia University Press, 1982.

Fedorowich, Kent. *Unfit for Heroes: Reconstruction and Soldier Settlement in the Empire between the Wars.* Manchester and New York: Manchester University Press, 1995.

James, Lawrence. *The Rise and Fall of the British Empire.* London: Little, Brown and Company, 1994. A detailed general account.

Marshall, P. J. (ed.). *The Cambridge Illustrated History of the British Empire.* Cambridge: Cambridge University Press, 1996.

Somerville, Christopher. *Our War: How the British Commonwealth Fought the Second World War.* London: Weidenfeld and Nicholson, 1998

26. AUSTRALIA AND THE UNITED STATES

Adam, Hugh G. *An Australian Looks at America: Are Wages Really Higher?* Sydney: Cornstalk Publishing Company, 1927. Also published by Allen and Unwin, London, 1928.

Aitchison, Ray. *The Americans in Australia.* Blackburn, Victoria: Australasian Educa Press, 1986.

Ashbolt, Allan. *An American Experience.* London: Gollancz. An Australian's view of the United States in the late 1950s and early 1960s.

Ball, Desmond. *A Suitable Piece of Real Estate: American Installations in Australia.* Sydney: Hale and Iremonger, 1980.

Bell, Coral. *Dependent Ally: A Study in Australian Foreign Policy.* Sydney: Allen and Unwin, 1993.

Bell, Phillip, and Roger Bell (eds.). *Americanization and Australia.* Sydney: University of New South Wales Press, 1998.

Bell, Roger J. *Unequal Allies: Australian-American Relations and the Pacific War.* Melbourne: Melbourne University Press, 1977.

Brash, Donald T. *American Investment in Australian Industry.* Canberra: Australian National University Press, 1966. Pioneer study of 208 companies with some historical data.

Bureau of Immigration, Multicultural and Population Research. *Community Profiles: 1991 Census: United States of America Born.*

Canberra: Australian Government Publishing Service, 1995. This publication, which is one of a series, not only provides a comprehensive view of the United States-born in Australia in 1991 based on census tabulations otherwise expensive to obtain, but also a historical introduction and a bibliography.

Churchward, Lloyd. *Australia and America, 1788-1972: An Alternative History.* Sydney: Alternative Publishing Cooperative Limited, 1979.

Cuddy, Dennis L. *The Yanks are Coming: American Immigration to Australia.* San Francisco: R. and E. Associates, 1977. Primarily a survey of 200 American immigrants to Australia, but with much important background information. Particularly interesting for its report on attitudes both favorable and unfavorable toward Australia.

Daniel, E. and Annette Potts (eds.). *A Yankee Merchant in Goldrush Australia: The Letters of George Francis Train, 1853-55.* Melbourne: Heinemann, 1970.

Dashefsky, A., and others. *Americans Abroad: A Comparative Study of Emigrants from the United States.* New York: Plenum Press, 1992.

Frame, Tom. *Pacific Partners: A History of Australian-American Naval Relations.* London: Hodder and Stoughton, 1992.

Gunther, John and William H. Forbis. *Inside Australia.* New York: Harper and Row, 1972.

Harper, Norman (ed.). *Australia and the United States: Documents and Readings in Australian History.* Melbourne: Nelson, 1971.

————. *A Great and Powerful Friend: A Study of Australian American Relations between 1900 and 1975.* St. Lucia: Queensland University Press, 1987.

Hergenham, Laurie. *No Casual Traveller: Hartley Grattan and Australia.* St. Lucia, Queensland: Queensland University Press, 1995.

Joint Standing Committee on Foreign Affairs, Defence and Trade. *ANZUS After 45 Years: Seminar Proceedings, 11-12 August 1997*. Canberra: Parliament of the Commonwealth of Australia, 1997.

Moore, John H. (ed.). *Australians in America, 1876-1976*. St. Lucia: Queensland University Press, 1977.   A selection of Australian travelers' impressions of the United States.

Mosler, David and Bob Catley. *America and Americans in Australia*. Westport, Conn.: Praeger, 1998.

Phillips, Dennis. *Ambivalent Allies: Myth and Realities in the Australian-American Relationship*. Melbourne: Penguin, 1988.

Potts, E., and A. Potts. *Yanks Down Under, 1941-45: The American Impact on Australia*. Melbourne: Oxford University Press, 1985.

Potts, A., and L. Strauss. *For the Love of a Soldier: Australian War-Brides and their GIs*.   Crow's Nest, New South Wales: ABC Enterprises, 1987.

Tow, William (ed.). *Australian-American Relations: Looking Toward the Next Century*. Melbourne: Macmillan Education, 1998.

Withers, Glenn (ed.). *Commonality and Difference: Australia and the United States*. Sydney: Allen and Unwin, 1991.

27.   FOREIGN   RELATIONS,   ANTARCTICA,   AND AUSTRALIAN TERRITORIES

Andrews, Eric M. *The Anzac Illusion: Anglo-Australian Relations during World War I*.   Melbourne: Cambridge University Press, 1993.

————. *Australia and China: The Ambiguous Relationship*. Melbourne: Melbourne University Press, 1985.

————. *A History of Australian Foreign Policy: From Dependence to Independence*. Melbourne: Longman Cheshire, 1979.

————. *A History of Australian Foreign Policy: From Dependence to Independence.* Melbourne: Longman Cheshire, 1979.

Ball Desmond, and David Horner. *Breaking the Codes: Australia's KGB Network.* Sydney: Allen and Unwin, 1998.

Ball Desmond, and Helen Wilson (eds.). *Strange Neighbours: The Australia-Indonesia Relationship.* Sydney: Allen and Unwin, 1991.

Bowden, Tim. *The Silence Calling: The Australians in Antarctica, 1947-97.* Sydney: Allen and Unwin, 1997.

Brawley, Sean. *The White Peril: Foreign Relations and Asian Immigration to Australasia and North America, 1919-78.* Sydney: CCH Australia Ltd., 1995.

Day, David. *The Great Betrayal: Britain, Australia and the Onset of the Pacific War, 1939-42.* Sydney: Angus and Robertson, 1988.

————. *Menzies and Churchill at War.* Sydney: Angus and Robertson, 1986.

————. *Reluctant Nation: Australia and the Allied Defeat of Japan, 1942-45.* Melbourne: Melbourne University Press, 1992.

————. *Brave New World: Dr. H. V. Evatt and Australian Foreign Policy, 1941-1949.* St. Lucia, Queensland: Queensland University Press, 1996.

Edwards, Peter. G. *Prime Ministers and Diplomats: The Making of Australian Foreign Policy, 1901-1949.* Melbourne: Oxford University Press in association with the Australian Institute of International Affairs, 1983.

Edwards, Peter. G., and Gregory Pemberton. *Crisis and Commitments: The Politics and Diplomacy of Australia's Involvement in Southeast Asian Conflicts, 1948-1965.* Sydney: Allen and Unwin and Australian War Memorial, 1992.

Frei, Henry P. *Japan's Southward Advance and Australia: From the Sixteenth Century to World War II.* Melbourne: Melbourne University Press, 1991.

George, Margaret. *Australia and the Indonesian Revolution.* Carlton, Victoria: Melbourne University Press and Australian Institute of International Affairs, 1980.

Gurry, Meg. *India: Australia's Neglected Neighbour?: 1947-1996.* Griffith University, Queensland: Centre for the Study of Australia-Asia Relations, 1996.

Hasluck, P. M. C. *A Time for Building: Australian Administration in Papua and New Guinea, 1951-1963.* Melbourne: Melbourne University Press, 1976.

Hoare, M. *Norfolk Island: An Outline of Its History, 1774-1977.* 2nd ed. St. Lucia: Queensland University Press, 1978.

Hosel, J. *Antarctic Australia.* Melbourne: Currey O'Neil, 1981.

Hudson, W. J. *Blind Loyalty: Australia and the Suez Crisis, 1956.* Melbourne: Melbourne University Press, 1989.

Jackson, Keith and Alan McRobie. *Historical Dictionary of New Zealand.* Lanham, Md.: Scarecrow Press, 1996.

Millar, T. B. *Australia in Peace and War: External Relations since 1788.* 2nd ed. Melbourne: Maxwell Macmillan/Australian National University Press, 1992.

Osmond, Warren. *Frederic Eggleston: An Intellectual in Australian Politics.* Sydney: Allen and Unwin, 1985.

Ralston, Kathleen. *A Man for Antarctica: The Early Life of Phillip Law.* Melbourne: Hyland Publishing, 1993.

Rolls, Eric. *Flowers and the Wide Sea: The Epic Story of China's Century-Old Relationship with Australia.* 2 vols. St. Lucia, Queensland: Queensland University Press, 1993, 1996.

Smith, Gary, and others. *Australia in the World: An Introduction to Australian Foreign Policy.* Melbourne: Oxford Unversity Press, 1997.

Strahan, Lachlan. *Australia's China: Changing Perceptions from the 1930s to the 1990s.* Melbourne: Cambridge University Press, 1996.

Thompson, R. C. *Australian Imperialism in the Pacific: the Expansionist Era, 1820-1920.* Melbourne: Melbourne University Press, 1980.

Trainor, Luke. *British Imperialism and Australian Nationalism: Manipulation, Conflict and Compromise in the Late Nineteenth Century.* Melbourne: Cambridge University Press, 1994.

Turner, Ann. *Historical Dictionary of Papua New Guinea.* Metuchen, N.J.: Scarecrow Press, 1994.

Viviani, N. M. *Nauru: Phosphate and Political Progress.* Canberra: Australian National University Press, 1970.

28. ECONOMIC HISTORY: GENERAL

Alford, K. *Production or Reproduction? An Economic History of Women in Australia, 1788-1850.* Melbourne: Oxford University Press, 1984.

Bell, Stephen. *Australian Manufacturing and the State: The Policy of Industrial Policy in the Post-War Era.* Melbourne: Cambridge University Press, 1993.

————. *Ungoverning the Economy: The Political Economy of Australian Economic Policy.* Melbourne: Oxford University Press, 1997.

Blainey, Geoffrey N. *A Land Half Won.* Melbourne: Sun Books, 1983. First published in 1980.

Boehm, E. A. *Twentieth Century Economic Development in Australia.* 3rd ed. Melbourne: Longman Cheshire, 1993.

Butlin, Noel G. *Forming a Colonial Economy: Australia, 1810-1850.* Melbourne: Cambridge University Press, 1994.

Butlin, Noel G., Alan Barnard, and J. J. Pincus. *Government and Capitalism: Public and Private Choice in Twentieth Century Australia.* Sydney: Allen and Unwin, 1982.

Butlin, S. J., and C. B. Schedvin. *War Economy, 1942-1945.* Canberra: Australian War Memorial, 1977.

Capling, Ann, and Brian Galligan. *Beyond the Protective State: The Political Economy of Australia's Manufacturing Industry Policy.* Cambridge: Cambridge University Press, 1992.

Coghlan, Timothy A. *Labour and Industry in Australia from the First Settlement in 1788 to the Establishment of the Commonwealth in 1901.* 4 vols. Oxford: Oxford University Press, 1918. Reissued by Macmillan, Melbourne, in 1969. This is still the classic work on the last half of the nineteenth century.

Day, David. *The Customs History of Australia.* 2 vols. Canberra: Australian Government Publishing Service, 1992.

Duncan, Tim, and John Fogarty. *Australia and Argentina: On Parallel Paths.* Melbourne: Melbourne University Press, 1984.

Dyster, Barrie, and David Meredith. *Australia in the International Economy in the Twentieth Century.* Cambridge: Cambridge University Press, 1989.

Fagan, Robert, and Michael Webber. *Global Restructuring: The Australian Experience.* Sydney: Oxford University Press, 1994.

Findlay, C., and R. Garnaut (eds.). *The Political Economy of Manufacturing Protection: Experiences of ASEAN and Australia.* Sydney: Allen and Unwin, 1986.

Gregory, R. G. and N. G. Butlin (eds.). *Recovery from the Depression: Australia and the World Economy in the 1930s.* Melbourne: Cambridge University Press, 1988.

Groenewegen, Peter and Bruce McFarlane. *A History of Australian Economic Thought.* London: Routledge, 1990.

Jackson, R. V. *Australian Economic Development in the Nineteenth Century.* Canberra: Australian National University Press, 1977. A useful introduction to the approach of N. G. Butlin.

Lloyd, Peter J., and Lynne S. Williams. *International Trade and Migration in the APEC Region.* Melbourne: Oxford University Press, 1996.

Maddock, R., and I. McLean (eds.). *The Australian Economy in the Long Run.* Cambridge: Cambridge University Press, 1987.

Pinkstone, Brian, and David Meredith. *Global Connections: A History of Exports and the Australian Economy.* Canberra: Australian Government Publishing Service, 1992.

Raby, Geoff. *Making Rural Australia: An Economic History of Technical and Institutional Creativity, 1788-1860.* Melbourne: Oxford University Press, 1996.

Rattigan, Alfred. *Industry Assistance: The Inside Story.* Melbourne: Melbourne University Press, 1986. An important contribution to the making of Australian government economic policy making.

Schedvin, C. B. *Australia and the Great Depression: A Study of Economic Development and Policy in the 1920s and 1930s.* Sydney: Sydney University Press, 1970.

Snooks, Graeme. *Portrait of the Family within the Total Economy: A Study in Longrun Dynamics: Australia 1788-1990.* Melbourne: Cambridge University Press, 1994. A pioneering contribution to economic history which presents social accounts for Australia from 1788 to 1990 and traces the contribution of households to the total economy over that period.

Tweedie, Sandra. *Trading Partners: Australia and Asia, 1790-1993.* Sydney: University of New South Wales Press, 1994.

Wells, Andrew. *Constructing Capitalism: An Economic History of Eastern Australia, 1788-1901.* Sydney: Allen and Unwin, 1989.

Wilson, R. K. *Australia's Resources and Their Development.* Sydney: Southward Press, 1980.

29. INDUSTRY AND BUSINESS HISTORIES

Bach, John P. S. *A Maritime History of Australia.* Melbourne: Nelson, 1976.

Beeston, John, and Guy Mirabella. *A Concise History of Australian Wine.* 2nd ed. Sydney: Allen and Unwin/Rathdowne, 1995.

Blainey, Geoffrey. *The Golden Mile.* St. Leonards, New South Wales: Allen and Unwin/Rathdowne, 1993. A centenary history of the gold fields of Kalgoorlie, Western Australia.

———. *The Rush That Never Ended: A History of Australian Mining.* 4th ed. Melbourne: Melbourne University Press, 1993. Despite its title, this well-known work does not deal with coal mining.

———. *White Gold: The Story of ALCOA in Australia.* Sydney: Allen and Unwin, 1997. Deals with the aluminum industry.

Bowen, Jill. *Kidman: The Forgotten King.* Melbourne: HarperCollins Publishers/Imprint Lives, 1992.

Broomham, Rosemary. *On the Road: The NRMA's First Seventy-Five Years.* Sydney: Allen and Unwin, 1996. A history of the National Roads and Motorists' Association.

Buckley, Ken, and Kris Klugman. *The Australian Presence in the Pacific: Burns Philip, 1914-1946.* Sydney: Allen and Unwin, 1983.

Bureau of Industry Economics. *Australia Steel and the Steel Industry Plan, 1984-1987.* Canberra: Australian Government Publishing Service, 1988.

Carew, Edna. *Fast Forward: The History of the Sydney Futures Exchange.* Sydney: Allen and Unwin, 1993.

————. *Westpac: The Bank that Broke the Bank.* Sydney: Doubleday Australia, 1997.

Cannon, Michael. *That Disreputable Firm: The Inside Story of Slater and Gordon.* Melbourne: Melbourne University Press, 1998. Deals with notable law firm.

Davidson, B. R. *European Farming in Australia: An Economic History of Australian Farming.* Amsterdam: Elsevier Scientific, 1981.

Falkus, Malcolm. *Called to Account: The History of Cooper and Lybrand in Australia.* Sydney: Allen and Unwin, 1993.

Firkins, Peter (ed.). *A History of Commerce and Industry in Western Australia.* Nedlands, Western Australia: University of Western Australia Press, 1979.

Garden, Don. *Builders to the Nation: The A. V. Jennings Story.* Melbourne: Melbourne University Press, 1992.

Garran, J. C., and L. White. *Merinos, Myths and Macarthurs: Australian Graziers and Their Sheep, 1788-1900.* Canberra: Australian National University Press, 1985.

Gimsey, Oscar. *Built from Nothing: A History of the Building Industry in Australia.* Carlton, Melbourne: Building Careers Resource Centre of Australia, 1992.

Harcourt, Edgar. *Taming the Tyrant: The First 100 Years of Australia's International Telecommunications Services.* Sydney: Allen and Unwin, 1987.

Johnston-Lik, E. M., George Lik, and R. G. Ward. *A Measure of Greatness: The Origins of the Australian Iron and Steel Industry.* Melbourne: Melbourne University Press, 1998.

Jones, Colin. *Watch for Trams.* Sydney: Kangaroo Press, 1993. A history of street cars in Australia from 1861 to 1961.

Kingston, Beverley. *Basket, Bag, and Trolley: A History of Shopping in Australia.* Sydney: Oxford University Press, 1994.

Linge, Godfrey J. R. *Industrial Awakening: A Geography of Australian Manufacturing, 1788-1890.* Canberra: Australian National University Press, 1979. The main work on the subject for the nineteenth century; see also Rich, David in this section.

Mackersey, Ian. *Smithy: The Life of Sir Charles Kingsford Smith.* New York: Little, Brown, 1998.

Morley, I. W. *Black Sands: A History of the Mineral Sand Mining Industry in Eastern Australia.* St. Lucia, Brisbane: Queensland University Press, 1981.

Moyal, Ann M. *Clear Across Australia: A History of Telecommunications since 1788.* Melbourne: Nelson, 1984.

Murray, Robert. *From the Edge of the Timeless Land: A History of the North West Shelf Project.* Sydney: Allen and Unwin, 1991.

Murray, Robert, and Kate White. *A Bank for the People: A History of the State Bank of Australia.* Melbourne: Hargreen Publishing, 1992.

Mylrea, P. J. *In the Service of Agriculture: A Centennial History of the New South Wales Department of Agriculture, 1890-1990.* Sydney: New South Wales Department of Agriculture and Fisheries, 1991.

Rich, David. *The Industrial Geography of Australia.* Sydney: Methuen, 1987. A large scale study which complements the earlier work of Godfrey J. R. Linge listed in this section.

Rolland, Derrick B. *Aerial Agriculture in Australia: A History of the Use of Aircraft in Agriculture and Forestry.* Sydney: McMatton Publishing, 1996.

Salsbury, Susan and Kay Sweeney. *The Bull, the Bear, and the Kangaroo: The History of the Sydney Stock Exchange.* Sydney: Allen and Unwin, 1988.

Schedvin, C. B. *In Reserve: Central Banking in Australia, 1945-1975.* Sydney: Allen and Unwin, 1992.

———. *Shaping Science and Industry: A History of Australia's Council for Scientific and Industrial Research, 1926-49.* Sydney: Allen and Unwin and CSIRO, 1987.

Sykes, Trevor. *Two Centuries of Panic: A History of Corporate Collapses in Australia.* Sydney: Allen and Unwin, 1988.

———. *The Bold Riders: Behind Australia's Corporate Collapses.* Sydney: Allen and Unwin, 1994.

Tranter, Deborah. *Cobb and Co.: Coaching in Queensland.* Toowoomba, Queensland: Queensland Museum, 1991.

Trengove, Alan. *"What's Good For Australia!" The Story of BHP.* Sydney: Cassell Australia, 1975.

Turner, John W. *Coal Mining in Newcastle, 1801-1900.* Newcastle: Council of the City of Newcastle, 1982.

Walsh, Gerald. *Pioneering Days: People and Innovations in Australia's Rural Past.* Sydney: Allen and Unwin, 1993.

Williams, D. B. *Agriculture in the Australian Economy.* 2nd ed. Sydney: Sydney University Press, 1982.

Whitmore, R. L. *Coal in Queensland: From Federation to the Twenties, 1900-1925.* Brisbane: Queensland University Press, 1990.

Whitwell, Greg, and Diane Sydenham. *A Shared Harvest: The Australian Wheat Industry, 1939-1989.* Melbourne: Macmillan, 1992.

Wilkinson, R. *Where God Never Trod: Australia's Oil Explorers Across Two Centuries.* Sydney: David Ell Pty Ltd., 1991.

Wood, Rodney. *The Commercial Bank of Australia Ltd.* Melbourne: Hargreen Publishers, 1990.

30. EMPLOYMENT AND LABOR RELATIONS

Beasley, Margo. *The Missos: A History of the Federated Miscellaneous Workers' Union.* Sydney: Allen and Unwin, 1996.

―――. *Wharfies: A History of the Waterside Workers' Federation of Australia.* Sydney: Halstead Press in association with the Australian National Maritime Museum, 1996.

Bowden, Badley. *Driving Force: The History of the Tansport Workers' Union of Australia, 1883-1992.* Sydney: Allen and Unwin, 1993.

Broomhill, C. R. *Unemployed Workers: A Social History of the Great Depression in Adelaide.* St. Lucia: University of Queensland Press, 1978.

Bunbury, Bill. *Timber for Gold: Life on the Goldfield Woodlines, 1899-1965.* Fremantle: Fremantle Arts Center Press, 1997. A history of the West Australian Goldfields Firewood Supply Company and its employees.

Callus, Ron, and others. *The Australian Workplace Industrial Relations Survey.* Canberra: Australian Government Printing Service, 1991. See also the entry for Morehead in this section.

Curthoys, Anne, and others (eds.). *Women At Work.* Canberra: Australian Society for the Study of Labour History, 1975.

Deery, Stephen J. and David Plowman. *Australian Industrial Relations.* 3rd ed. Sydney: MacGraw-Hill Book Company, 1992.

Ellem, Bradon. *In Women's Hands: A History of Clothing Trades Unionism in Australia.* Sydney: University of New South Wales Press, 1989.

Frances, Raelene. *The Politics of Work: Gender and Labour in Victoria, 1880-1939.* Melbourne: Cambridge University Press, 1993.

Graves, Adrian. *Cane and Labour: The Political Economy of the Queensland Sugar Industry, 1862-1906.* Edinburgh: Edinburgh University Press, 1993.

Hagan, James. *The History of the ACTU.* Melbourne: Longman Cheshire, 1981. A history of Australia's national labor body, the Australian Council of Trade Unions.

Hearn, Mark and Harry Knowles. *One Big Union: A History of the Australian Workers' Union.* Melbourne: Cambridge University Press, 1996. A general account of Australia's largest labor union from the 1900s to 1969.

Hince, K. *Conflict and Coal: A Case Study of Industrial Relations in the Open-Cut Coal Mining Industry of Central Queensland.* St. Lucia: Queensland University Press, 1982.

Hyams, Bernard. *From Compliance to Confrontation: 140 Years of Teachers' Unions in South Australia, 1851-1991.* Blackwood, South Australia: Auslib Press, 1992.

Juddery, Bruce. *White Collar Power: A History of the ACOA.* Sydney: Allen and Unwin, 1980. A history of the main white collar union in the federal bureaucracy, then called the Administrative and Clerical Officers' Association.

Kirby, Diane. *Barmaids: A History of Women's Work in Pubs.* Melbourne: Cambridge University Press, 1997.

Lever-Tracy, C., and Michael Quinlan. *A Divided Working Class: Ethnic Segmentation and Industrial Conflict in Australia.* London: Routledge and Kegan Paul, 1988.

MacIntyre, Stuart, and R. Mitchell (eds.). *Foundations of Arbitration: The Origins and Effects of State Compulsory Arbitration, 1890-1913.* Melbourne: Oxford University Press, 1989.

McMurchy, M., and others. *For Love or Money: A Pictorial History of Women and Work in Australia.* Ringwood: Penguin, 1983.

Morehead, Alison and others. *Changes at Work: The 1995 Australian Workplace Industrial Relations Survey.* Melbourne: Longman, 1997. See also the entry for Callus in this section.

Murray, Robert, and Kate White. *The Ironworkers: A History of the Federated Ironworkers' Association of Australia.* Sydney: Hale and Iremonger, 1982. One of the best histories of an Australian labor union.

Ryan, E. and A. Conlon. *Gentle Invaders: Australian Women At Work, 1788-1974.* Melbourne: Nelson, 1975.

Selby, Hugh. *Long Service Leave.* Sydney: Law Book Company Limited, 1983.

Sheridan, Thomas. *Mindful Militants: The Amalgamated Engineering Union in Australia, 1920-1972.* Cambridge: Cambridge University Press, 1975.

Svensen, Stuart. *The Sinews of War: Hard Cash and the 1890 Maritime Strike.* Sydney: University of New South Wales Press, 1995.

Turner, Ian and Leonie Sandercock. *In Union is Strength: A History of Trade Unions in Australia, 1788-1983.* Melbourne: Nelson, 1983.

United States Department of Labor, Bureau of International Affairs. *Foreign Labor Trends: Australia.* Washington, D.C.: Government Printing Office issued annually from 1986-87 to date.

Wright, Christopher. *The Management of Labour: A History of Australian Employers.* Melbourne: Oxford University Press, 1995.

31. SOCIAL INVESTIGATION AND ANALYSIS

1989 Australian Youth Survey: First Results. Canberra: Australian Government Publishing Service, 1991.

Bryson, Lois, and Faith Thompson. *An Australian Newtown: Life and Leadership in a New Housing Suburb.* Melbourne: Penguin Books, 1972. A pioneering study of a new, outer Melbourne suburb.

Connell, R. W. and T. H. Irving. *Class Structure in Australian History: Poverty and Progress.* 2nd ed. Melbourne: Longman Cheshire, 1992.

———— (eds.). *Class Structure in Australian History: Documents, Narrative and Argument.* Melbourne: Longman Cheshire, 1980.

Cuffley, Peter. *Australian Houses of the Twenties and Thirties.* Melbourne: Five Mile Press, 1993.

Dempsey, Ken. *A Man's Town: Inequality Between Women and Men in Rural Australia.* Melbourne: Oxford University Press, 1992.

Dempsey, Ken. *Smalltown.* Melbourne: Oxford University Press, 1992.

Denholm, David. *The Colonial Australians.* Ringwood: Penguin, 1979.

Fabian, S. and M. Loh. *Children in Australia: An Outline History.* Melbourne: Oxford University Press, 1980.

Fitzpatrick, James. *The Bicycle and the Bush: Man and Machine in Rural Australia.* Melbourne: Oxford University Press, 1980.

MacIntyre, Stuart. *Winners and Losers: The Pursuit of Social Justice in Australian History.* Sydney: Allen and Unwin, 1986.

McCalman, Janet. *Journeyings: The Biography of a Middle-Class Generation.* Melbourne: Melbourne University Press, 1993.

McGregor, Craig. *Class in Australia.* Melbourne: Penguin Books, 1997.

Peel, Mark and Janet McCalman. *Who Went Where in Who's Who 1988: The Schooling of the Australian Elite.* Melbourne: History Department, University of Melbourne, 1992.

Powell, Diane. *Out West: Perceptions of Sydney's Western Suburbs.* Sydney: Allen and Unwin, 1993.

32. SOCIAL WELFARE

Ashton, Paul. *Laying the Foundations: A History of the House With No Steps.* Belrose, Sydney: Paul Ashton, 1991.

Baldcock, C. V., and Bettina Cass. *Women, Social Welfare, and the State in Australia.* Sydney: Allen and Unwin, 1983.

Barbalet, M. *Far From a Low Gutter Girl: The Forgotten World of State Wards, South Australia, 1887-1940.* Oxford University Press, 1983.

Cage, Robert. *Poverty Abounding, Charity Aplenty: The Charity Network in Colonial Victoria.* Sydney: Hale and Iremonger, 1992.

Clark, Joan. *Just Us: A History of the Association of Civilian Widows of Australia.* Sydney: Hale and Iremonger, 1988.

Dickey, Brian. *No Charity There: A Short History of Social Welfare in Australia.* Melbourne: Nelson, 1980.

Hunt, Harold. *The Story of Rotary in Australia, 1921-1971.* Melbourne: The Regional Rotary Institute, 1971.

Mendelsohn, Ronald. *The Condition of the People: Social Welfare in Australia, 1900-1975.* Sydney: Allen and Unwin, 1975.

Menedue, John E. *A Century History of the Australian Natives' Association, 1871-1971.* Melbourne: Horticultural Press, 1971.

Moore, Allan. *Growing up with Bernardo's.* Sydney: Hale and Iremonger, 1990.

Norris, Ada. *Champions of the Impossible: A History of the National Council of Women of Victoria, 1901-1977.* Melbourne: Hawthorn Press, 1978.

Ollif, Lorna. *Archway to Vision: A History of the Royal Blind Society of New South Wales, 1880-1980.* Sydney: Ollif Publishing, 1992.

Organisation for Economic Co-Operation and Development. *The Battle against Exclusion: Social Assistance in Australia, Finland, Sweden, and the United Kingdom.* Paris: Organisation for Economic Co-Operation and Development, 1998.

Ramsland, John. *Children of the Back Lanes: Destitute and Neglected Children in Colonial New South Wales.* Sydney: University of New South Wales Press, 1986.

Rathbone, Ron. *A Very Present Help: The History of the Benevolent Society of New South Wales.* Sydney: State Library of New South Wales, 1994.

Reiger, Kerreen, *The Disenchantment of the Home: Modernising the Australian Family, 1880-1940.* Melbourne: Oxford University Press, 1985.

Stratton, Jon. *The Young Ones: Working-Class Culture, Consumption and the Category of Youth.* Perth: Back Swan Press, Curtin University of Technology, 1992.

Summers, Anne. *Damned Whores and God's Police: The Colonization of Women in Australia.* Ringwood: Penguin, 1975.

Wild, Ronald A. *Bradstow: A Study of Status, Class and Power in a Small Australian Town.* Sydney: Angus and Robertson, 1974. An influential social investigation of Bowral, New South Wales, in the late 1960s.

Wilson, John, and others (eds.). *The Australian Welfare State: Key Documents and Themes.* Melbourne: Macmillan Education, 1996.

33. EDUCATION

Barcan, Alan. *A History of Australian Education.* Oxford University Press, 1980.

Connell, W. F. *Reshaping Australian Education, 1960-1985.* Hawthorn, Victoria: Australian Council for Educational Research, 1993.

Connell, W. F., and others. *Australia's First: A History of the University of Sydney,* Volume 2, *1940-1990.* Sydney: Hale and Iremonger, 1995.

Crickmore, Barbara L. *Education of the Deaf and Hearing Impaired: A Brief History.* Mayfield, New South Wales: Education Management Systems, 1995.

Foster, Stephen G., and Margaret M. Varghese. *The Making of the Australian National University, 1946-1996.* Sydney: Allen and Unwin, 1996.

Harris, David R. (ed.). *The Archaeology of V. Gordon Childe.* Melbourne: Melbourne University Press, 1994.

Kenny, Joan M. *Prologue to the Future: Christ College: The Foundation and Early Development of Australian Catholic University's Christ Campus, 1967-1990.* Melbourne: Lovell (David) Publishing, 1996.

Mansfield, Bruce, and Mark Hutchinson,. *Liberality of Opportunity: A History of Macquarie University, 1964-1989.* Sydney: Macquarie University with Hale and Iremonger, 1992.

Marginson, Simon. *Educating Australia: Government, Economy, and Citizen since 1960.* Melbourne: Cambridge University Press, 1997.

Pybus, Cassandra. *Gross Moral Turpitude: The Orr Case Reconsidered.* Melbourne: William Heinemann, 1992.

Quirke, Noel. *Preparing for the Future: A History of Griffith University, 1971-1996.* Brisbane: Boolarong Press, 1996.

Theobald, Marjorie. *Knowing Women: Origins of Women's Education in Nineteenth Century Australia.* Melbourne: Cambridge University Press, 1996.

Turney, Clifford, and others. *Australia's First: A History of the University of Sydney,* Volume 1, *1850-1939.* Sydney: Hale and Iremonger, 1991.

Turney, Clifford, and Judith Taylor. *To Enlighten Them Our Task: A History of Teacher Education at Balmain and Kuring-Gai Colleges. 1946-1990.* St. Ives, New South Wales: Sydmac Academic Press, 1996.

Whitelock, Derek. *The Great Tradition: A History of Adult Education in Australia.* St. Lucia, Queensland: Queensland University Press, 1974.

34. SPORT AND GAMBLING

Adair, Daryl, and Wray Vamplew. *Sport in Australian History.* Melbourne: Oxford University Press, 1997.

Cashman, Richard, and others (eds.). *Australian Sport through Time: The History of Sport in Australia.* Sydney: Random House, 1997.

———. *The Oxford Companion to Australian Sport.* 2nd ed. Melbourne: Oxford University Press, 1994.

———. *Paradise of Sport: The Rise of Organised Sport in Australia.* Melbourne: Oxford University Press, 1995.

Egan, Jack. *The Story of Cricket in Australia.* 3rd ed. Sydney: ABC Enterprises, 1996.

Galton, B. *Gladiators of the Surf: The Australian Surf Life Saving Championships: A History.* Sydney: Reed, 1984.

Gordon, Harry. *Australia and the Olympics.* St. Lucia, Queensland: Queensland University Press, 1994.

Hickie, Thomas V. *They Ran with the Ball: How Rugby Football began in Australia.* Melbourne: Longman Cheshire, 1993.

Le Quesne, A. L. *The Bodyline Controversy.* London: Secker and Warburg, 1984. Concerns cricket.

Moore, Andrew. *The Mighty Bears! A Social History of North Sydney Rugby League.* Sydney: Pan Macmillan, 1996.

O'Hara, John. *A Mug's Game: A History of Gambling in Australia.* Sydney: University of New South Wales Press, 1988.

Perry, Roland. *The Don: A Biography.* rev. ed. Melbourne: Pan Macmillan/Ironbark, 1998. A life of Australia's legendary cricketer, Donald Bradman.

Phillips, Dennis H. *Australian Women at the Olympic Games, 1912-92.* Sydney: Kangaroo Press, 1996.

Pollard, Jack. *The Complete Illustrated History of Australian Cricket.* Melbourne: Penguin/Pelham, 1992.

————. *The Pictorial History of Australian Horse Racing.* Sydney: Lansdowne, 1981.

Whittington, R. S. *An Illustrated History of Australian Tennis.* Melbourne: Macmillan, 1975.

Wilkinson, Michael. *The Phar Lap Story.* Sydney: Budget Books, 1983.

Wilson, T. *The Luck of the Draw: A Centenary of Tattersall's Sweeps, 1881-1981.* Melbourne: T. Wilson Publishing, 1980.

35. POPULATION AND IMMIGRATION

Bartrop, Paul. *Australia and the Holocaust, 1933-45: Entry Denied.* Kew, Victoria: Australian Scholarly Publishing, 1994.

Bean, Philip, and Joy Melville. *Lost Children of the Empire.* London: Unwin Hyman, 1989.

Bell, Martin. *Internal Migration in Australia, 1981-1986.* Canberra: Australian Government Publishing Service, 1992.

Bogle, Joanna. *Caroline Chisholm: The Emigrant's Friend.* London: Gracewing, 1993.

Borrie, Wilfred D. *The European Peopling of Australia: A Demographic History, 1788-1988.* Canberra: Research School of Social Science, Australian National University, 1994.

Burnett, Linda. *Issues in Immigrant Settlement in Australia.* Sydney: Macquarie University, 1998.

Burnley, Ian H., Peter Murphy and Bob Fagan. *Immigration and Australian Cities.* Sydney: Federation Press, 1997.

Campbell, Malcolm. *Kingdom of the Ryans: The Irish in Southwest New South Wales, 1816-1890.* Sydney: University of New South Wales Press, 1997.

Carmichael, Gordon A. (ed.). *Trans-Tasman Migration: Trends, Causes and Consequences.* Canberra: Bureau of Immigration Research, Australian Government Publishing Service, 1993. A major study carried out with the New Zealand Immigration Service.

Davidson, Alastair. *From Subject to Citizen: Australian Citizenship in the Twentieth Century.* Melbourne: Cambridge Unviersity Press, 1997.

Day, Lincoln, and Donald T. Rowland (eds.). *How Many More Australians? The Resource and Environmental Conflicts.* Melbourne: Longman Cheshire, 1988.

Economic and Social Commission for Asia and the Pacific, *Population of Australia: Country Monograph Series No. 9.* 2 vols. New York: United Nations, 1982.

Erickson, Rica. *The Bride Ships: Experiences of Immigrants Arriving in Western Australia, 1849-1889.* Carlisle, Western Australia: Hesperian Press, 1992.

Ferdinands, Rodney. *Proud & Prejudiced: The Story of the Burghers of Sri Lanka.* Melbourne: R. Ferdinands, 1995. An immigration study concerning the descendants of European traders in Ceylon.

Freeman, Gary P., and James Jupp (eds.). *Nations of Immigrants: Australia, the United States, and International Migration.* Melbourne: Oxford University Press, 1992.

Gittins, J. *The Digger from China: The Story of the Chinese Diggers on the Goldfields.* Melbourne: Quartet Books, 1981.

Haines, Robin F. *Emigration and the Labouring Poor: Australian Recruitment in Britain and Ireland, 1831-60.* Basingstoke, England: Macmillan, 1997.

Hicks, Neville. *"This Sin and Scandal" Australia's Population Debate, 1891-1911.* Canberra: Australian National University Press, 1978.

Hoban, M. *Fifty-One Pieces of Wedding Cake: A Biography of Caroline Chisholm.* Melbourne: Lowden Publishing Co., 1973.

Hogg, Robert, and Neil Thomson. *Fertility and Mortality of Aborigines Living in the Queensland Aboriginal Communities, 1972-1990.* Canberra: Australian Government Publishing Service, 1992.

Hokanson, Stig, and Birgitta Sharpe (eds.). *One Way Passage: Swedish Migrants to Australia in the James Sanderson Archive.* Sydney: Word Wright Texts and Translations, 1996. Documents 3,000 individuals.

Hollinsworth, David. *Race and Racism in Australia.* 2nd ed. Katoomba, New South Wales: Social Science Press, Australia, 1998.

Hugo, Graeme. *The Economic Implications of Emigration from Australia.* Canberra: Australian Government Publishing Service, 1994.

Hyams, Bernard. *The History of the Australian Zionist Movement.* Melbourne: Zionist Federation of Australia, 1998.

Inglis, Christine, and others (eds.). *Asians in Australia: The Dynamics of Migration and Settlement.* Sydney: Allen and Unwin, 1993.

Jordens, Ann-Mari. *Alien to Citizen: Settling Migrants in Australia, 1945-75.* Sydney: Allen and Unwin in association with the Australian Archives, 1997.

Jupp, James. *Immigration.* Sydney: Sydney University Press, 1991.

———— (ed.). *The Australian People: An Encyclopedia of the Nation, Its People and Their Origins.* Sydney: Angus and Robertson, 1988. The major work on the subject.

Kunz, Egon F. *Displaced Persons: Calwell's New Australians.* Canberra: Australian University Press, 1988.

MacDonald, Peter, F. *Marriage in Australia: Age at First Marriage and Proportions Marrying, 1860-1971.* Canberra: Department of Demography, Australian National University, 1974.

MacGregor, Paul (ed.). *Histories of the Chinese in Australasia and the South Pacific.* Melbourne: Museum of Chinese Australian History, 1995.

Markus, Andrew. *Fear and Hatred: Purifying Australia and California, 1850-1901.* Sydney: Hale and Iremonger, 1979.

National Population Inquiry. *Population and Australia: A Demographic Analysis and Projection.* 2 vols. Canberra: Government Printer of Australia, 1975. A landmark study.

O'Farrell, Patrick. *The Irish in Australia.* 2nd ed. Sydney: University of New South Wales Press, 1993.

Palmer, Glen. *Reluctant Refuge: Unaccompanied Refugee and Evacuee Children in Australia, 1933-45.* Sydney: Kangaroo Press, 1997.

Prentis, M. D. *The Scots in Australia: A Study of New South Wales, Victoria and Queensland, 1788-1900.* Sydney: Sydney University Press, 1983.

Price, Charles A. *The Great White Walls Are Built: Restrictive Immigration to North America and Australasia, 1836-1888.* Canberra: Australia National University Press, 1974.

Reitz, Geoffrey G. *Warmth of the Welcome: The Social Causes of Economic Success for Immigrants in Different Nations and Cities.* Boulder, Colorado: Westview Press, 1998. A study of Australia, Canada, and the United States.

Robinson, Portia. *The Hatch and Brood of Time: A Study of the First Generation of Native Born White Australians, 1788-1828.* 2 vols. Sydney: Oxford University Press, 1985.

Roe, Michael. *Australia, Britain and Migration: A Study of Desparate Hopes.* Cambridge: Cambridge University Press, 1995.

Ruzicka, L. T., and J. C. Caldwell. *The End of Demographic Transition in Australia.* Canberra: Department of Demography, Australian National University, 1977.

Ryan, Jan. *Ancestors: The Chinese in Colonial Australia.* Fremantle, Western Australia: Fremantle Arts Centre Press, 1995.

Sheehan, Paul. *Among the Barbarians: The Dividing of Australia.* Sydney: Random House Australia, 1998.

Shukert, Elfrieda B. *The War Brides of World War II.* Novato, Calif.: Presidio Press, 1988. Has some material on Australian war brides in the United States.

Sinclair, Keith (ed.). *Tasman Relations: New Zealand and Australia, 1788-1988.* Auckland: Auckland University Press, 1987.

Tomasi, Lydio, Piero Gastaldo, and Thomas Row (eds.). *The Columbus People: Perspectives in Italian Immigation to the Americas and Australia.* New York: Center for Migration Studies, 1994.

Viviani, Nancy. *The Indochinese in Australia: From Burnt Boats to Barbeques.* Melbourne: Oxford University Press, 1996.

Wang, Sing-wu. *The Organization of Chinese Immigration with Special Reference to Chinese Emigration to Australia.* San Francisco: Chinese Materials Center Inc., 1978.

Watson, Don. *Caledonia Australia: Scottish Highlanders on the Frontier of Australia.* Sydney: Collins, 1984.

Webb, Janeen, and Andrew Enstice. *Aliens and Savages: Fiction, Politics, and Prejudice in Australia.* Sydney: HarperCollins, 1998.

36. RELIGION

Adam, Enid, and Philip J. Hughes. *The Buddhists in Australia.* Canberra: Australian Government Publishing Service, 1996.

Baker, Donald W. A. *Days of Wrath: A Life of John Dunmore Lang.* Melbourne: Melbourne University Press, 1985.

Bentley, Peter, and Philip J. Hughes. *The Uniting Church in Australia.* Canberra: Australian Government Publishing Service, 1996.

Bilimoria, Purushottama. *The Hindus and Sikhs in Australia.* Canberra: Australian Government Publishing Service, 1996.

Blombery, Tricia. *The Anglicans in Australia.* Canberra: Australian Government Publishing Service, 1996.

Bolton, B. *Booth's Drum: The Salvation Army in Australia, 1880-1980.* Sydney: Hodder and Stoughton, 1980.

Breward, Ian. *A History of the Australian Churches.* Sydney: Allen and Unwin, 1993.

Broome, Richard L. *Treasure in Earthen Vessels: Protestant Christianity in New South Wales Society, 1900-1914.* St. Lucia, Queensland: Queensland University Press, 1980.

Burke, David, and Phillip J. Hughes. *The Presbyterians in Australia.* Canberra: Australian Government Publishing Service, 1996.

Bygott, Ursula M. *With Pen and Tongue: The Jesuits in Australia, 1865-1939.* Melbourne: Melbourne University Press, 1980.

Byrne, Neil. J. *Robert Dunn 1830-1917: Archbishop of Brisbane.* Brisbane: Queensland University Press, 1991.

Carey, Hiliary M. *Believing in Australia: A Cultural History of Religions.* Sydney: Allen and Unwin, 1996.

Dixon, Robert E. *The Catholics in Australia.* Canberra: Australian Government Publishing Service, 1996.

Ely, R. *Unto God and Caesar: Religious Issues in the Emerging Commonwealth, 1891-1906.* Melbourne: Melbourne University Press, 1976.

Engel, Frank. *Christians in Australia.* 2 vols. Melbourne: Joint Board of Christian Education, 1984, 1993.

Gardiner, Paul. *An Extraordinary Australian: Mary MacKillop—The Authorised Biography.* Sydney: E. J. Dwyer/David Ell Press, 1993. The official life of Australia's first saint.

Godley, Stephen and Philip J. Hughes. *The Eastern Orthodox in Australia.* Canberra: Australian Government Publishing Service, 1996.

Goosen, Gideon C. *Religion in Australian Culture: An Anthropological View.* Sydney: St. Pauls, 1997.

Hogan, Michael. *The Sectarian Strand: Religion in Australian History.* Ringwood, Victoria: Penguin, 1987.

Hughes, Philip J. *The Baptists in Australia.* Canberra: Australian Government Publishing Service, 1996.

———. *The Pentecostals in Australia.* Canberra: Australian Government Publishing Service, 1996.

Jackson, Hugh R. *Churches and People in Australia and New Zealand, 1860-1930.* Auckland, New Zealand: Allen and Unwin, 1987.

McKernan, Michael. *Australian Churches at War: Attitudes and Activities of the Major Churches, 1914-1918.* Canberra: Australian War Memorial, 1980.

Mol, Hans. *Religion in Australia: A Sociological Investigation.* Melbourne: Nelson, 1971. A report on the first survey of religion undertaken in Australia.

O'Farrell, Patrick. *The Catholic Church and Community: An Australian History.* 2nd ed. Sydney: New South Wales University Press, 1992.

Omar, Wafia, and others. *The Muslims in Australia.* Canberra: Australian Government Publishing Service, 1996.

Rubinstein, W. D. *Judaism in Australia.* Canberra: Australian Government Publishing Service, 1995.

Rutland, Suzanne D. *Edge of the Diaspora: Two Centuries of Jewish Settlement in Australia.* 2nd rev. ed. Sydney: Brand and Schlesinger, 1997.

Santamaria, Bartholemew, A. M. *Mannix: A Biography.* Melbourne: Melbourne University Press, 1984.

Schild Maurice, and Philip J. Hughes. *The Lutherans in Australia.* Canberra: Australian Government Publishing Service, 1996.

Turner, Naomi. *Catholics in Australia: A Social History.* 2 vols. North Blackburn, Victoria: Collins Dove, 1992.

Ward, Rowland, S. *The Bush Still Burns: The Presbyterian and Reformed Faith in Australia, 1788-1988.* Wantirna, Victoria: Rowland Ward, 1989.

Wright, Don, and Eric G. Clancy. *The Methodists: A History of Methodism in New South Wales.* Sydney: Allen and Unwin, 1993.

37. SCIENCE

Bhathal, Ragbir. *Australian Astronomer: John Tebbutt: The Life and World of the Man on the $100 Note.* Sydney: Kangaroo Press, 1993.

Cockburn, Stewart, and David Ellyard. *Oliphant: The Life and Times of Sir Mark Oliphant.* Kent Town, South Australia: Axiom Publishers and Distributors, 1981.

Dougherty, Kerrie, and Matthew L. James. *Space Australia: The Story of Australia's Involvement in Space.* Sydney: Powerhouse Publishing, 1993.

Duyer, Edward, and Per Tingbrand (eds. and trans.). *Daniel Solander: Collected Correspondence, 1733-1782.* Melbourne: Melbourne University Press, 1995.

Finney, Colin. *Paradise Revealed: Natural History in Nineteenth-Century Australia.* Melbourne: Museum of Victoria, 1993.

Kelly, Farley. *On the Edge of Discovery: Australian Women in Science.* Melbourne: Text Publishing, 1993.

MacLeod, Roy (ed.). *The Commonwealth of Science: ANZAAS and the Scientific Enterprise in Australia, 1888-1988.* Melbourne: Oxford University Press, 1988.

Schedvin, C. B. *Shaping Science and Industry: A History of Australia's Council for Scientific and Industrial Research, 1926-49.* Sydney: Allen and Unwin, 1987.

Walker, David, and Jürgen Tampke (eds.). *From Berlin to the Burdekin: The German Contribution to the Development of Australian Science, Exploration, and the Arts.* Sydney: University of New South Wales Press, 1991.

38. HEALTH AND MEDICINE

Bassett, Jan. *Guns and Brooches: Australian Army Nursing from the Boer War to the Gulf War.* Melbourne: Oxford University Press, 1992.

Bessant, Judith, and Bob Bessant. *The Growth of a Profession: Nursing in Victoria, 1930s-1980s.* Melbourne: La Trobe University Press, 1992.

Bickel, L. *Rise Up to Life: A Biography of Howard Walter Florey Who Gave Penicillin to the World.* London: Angus and Robertson, 1972.

Butler, A. G. (ed.). *The Australian Army Medical Services in the War of 1914-1918.* 3 vols. Canberra: Australian War Memorial, 1930, 1940, 1943. The major source on the subject.

Crichton, Anne. *Slowly Taking Control: Australian Governments and Health Care Provision, 1788-1988.* Sydney: Allen and Unwin, 1990.

Cumpston, J. H. L. *Health and Disease in Australia: A History.* Canberra: Australian Government Publishing Service, 1989. Covers the period from 1788 to 1928.

Gillespie, James A. *The Price of Health: Australian Governments and Medical Politics 1910-1960.* Melbourne: Cambridge University Press, 1991.

Glover, John, and Tony Woollacott. *A Social Health Atlas of Australia.* 2 vols. Kent Town, South Australia: Sunrise Press, 1992. Distributed by the Australian Bureau of Statistics (ABS Catalogue No. 4385.0). The first comprehensive work of its kind for Australia.

Howie-Willis, Ian. *A Century for Australia: St. John Ambulance in Australia, 1883-1983.* Canberra: Priory of the Order of St. John in Australia.

Lewis, Milton. *Managing Madness: Psychiatry and Society in Australia, 1788-1980.* Canberra: Australian Government Publishing Service, 1988.

O'Keefe, Brendan, and F. B. Smith. *Medicine at War: Medical Aspects of Australia's Involvement in Southeast Asian Conflicts, 1958-1972.* Sydney: Allen and Unwin in association with the Australian War Memorial, 1994.

O'Neil, William M. *A Century of Psychology in Australia.* Sydney: Sydney University Press, 1987.

Pensabene, T. S. *The Rise of the Medical Practitioner in Victoria.* Canberra: Australian National University, 1980.

Rudolph, Ivan. *John Flynn: Of Flying Doctors and Frontier Faith.* Melbourne: HarperCollins Melbourne/Dove, 1996

Ryan, K., and others. *Australasian Radiology: A History.* Sydney: McGraw-Hill, 1996.

Snow, D. J. R. *The Progress of Public Health in Western Australia, 1829-1977.* Perth: Public Health Department, 1981.

Tipping, John. *Back on Their Feet: A History of the Commonwealth Rehabilitation Service, 1941-1991.* Canberra: Australian Government Publishing Service, 1992.

Walker, A. S. *Australia in the War of 1939-1945.* Series 5 (Medical). 4 vols. Canberra: Australian War Memorial, 1952-61. The official military history.

Walker, Robin B. *Under Fire: A History of Tobacco Smoking in Australia.* Melbourne: Melbourne University Press, 1984.

Webb, Stephen. *Palaeopathology: Health and Disease Across a Hunter-Gatherer Continent.* Melbourne: Cambridge University Press, 1995.

Wilson, George. *The Flying Doctor Story: A Pictorial History of the Royal Flying Doctor Service of Australia.* Melbourne: Magazine Art, 1989.

39. LAW AND CRIME

Bennett, J. M., and Alex C. Castles (eds.). *A Source Book of Australian Legal History: Source Materials from the Eighteenth to the Twentieth Centuries.* Sydney: Law Book Co., 1979.

Bennett, J. M. *Keystone of the Federal Arch: An Historical Account of the High Court of Australia to 1980.* Canberra: Australian Government Publishing Service, 1980.

Bennett, J. M. *A History of the Supreme Court of New South Wales.* Sydney: Law Book Co., 1974.

Castles, Alex C. *An Australian Legal History.* Sydney: Law Book Co., 1982.

Finnane, Mark. *Police and Government: Histories of Policing in Australia.* Sydney: Oxford University Press, 1994.

————. *Punishment in Australia.* Sydney: Oxford University Press, 1997.

Golder, Hilary. *High and Responsible Office: A History of the New South Wales Magistracy.* Sydney: Oxford University Press, 1991.

Haldane, Robert K. *The People's Force: A History of the Victoria Police.* Melbourne: Melbourne University Press, 1986.

Johnston, W. Ross. *The Long Blue Line: A History of the Queensland Police.* Brisbane: Boolarong Publications, 1992.

Kirby, Diane (ed.). *Sex, Power, and Justice: Historical Perspectives on Law in Australia.* Sydney: Oxford University Press, 1995.

McQuilton, John. *The Kelly Outbreak 1878-1880: The Geographical Dimension of Social Banditry.* Melbourne: Melbourne University Press, 1979.

Mukherjee, S. K. *Crime Trends in Twentieth Century Australia.* Sydney: Australian Institute of Criminology with Allen and Unwin, 1981.

Solomon, David. *The Political Impact of the High Court.* Sydney: Allen and Unwin, 1992.

40. WAR AND DEFENSE

Adam-Smith, Patsy. *Prisoners of War: From Gallipoli to Korea.* Melbourne: Penguin/Viking, 1992.

Australia in the War of 1939-1945. 22 vols. Canberra: Australian War Memorial, 1952-77. The official history.

Baker, Clive, and Greg Knight. *Milne Bay, 1942.* Loftus, New South Wales: Baker-Knight Publications, 1992.

Bean, C. E. W. (ed.). *The Official History of Australia in the War of 1914-1918.* 12 vols. Sydney: Angus and Robertson, 1921-42. Many of these volumes have been reprinted by Queensland University Press in the 1980s.

Bevege, Margaret. *Behind Barbed Wire: Internment in Australia during World War II.* St. Lucia, Queensland: Queensland University Press, 1993.

Bowden, Tim. *Changi Photographer: George Aspinall's Record of Captivity.* Sydney: Australian Broadcasting Commission, 1984. Contains unique and remarkable photographs.

Brune, Peter. *The Spell Broken: Exploding the Myth of Japanese Invincibility: Milne Bay to Bun-Sanananda, 1942-43.* Sydney: Allen and Unwin, 1997.

Coulthard-Clark, C. D. *Duntroon: The Royal Military College of Australia, 1911-1986.* Sydney: Allen and Unwin, 1986.

———. *The Third Brother: The Royal Australian Air Force, 1921-39.* Sydney: Allen and Unwin, 1991.

Courtney, G. B. *Silent Feet: The History of Z Special Operations, 1942-1945.* Melbourne: R. J. and S. P. Austin, 1993.

Cowling, Anthony. *My Life with the Samurai.* Sydney: Kangaroo Press, 1996.

Darian-Smith, Kate. *On the Home Front: Melbourne in Wartime, 1939-1945.* Melbourne: Oxford University Press, 1990.

Dean, Penrod. *Singapore Samuri.* Sydney: Kangaroo Press, 1998.

Dennis, Peter and Jeffrey Grey. *Emergency and Confrontation: Australia's Military Operations in Malaya and Borneo, 1950-1966.* Sydney: Allen and Unwin/Australian War Memorial, 1996.

Department of Defence. *Australia's Strategic Policy.* Canberra: Department of Defence, 1997. An official statement of Australia's defense policy and vital interests.

Edbury, Sue. *Weary: The Life of Sir Edward Dunlop.* Melbourne: Penguin Books/Viking, 1994.

Edwards, Peter. *A Nation at War: Australian Politics, Society, and Diplomacy During the Vietnam War, 1965-1975.* Sydney: Allen and Unwin/Australian War Memorial, 1997.

Frost, Frank. *Australia's War in Vietnam.* Sydney: Allen and Unwin, 1987.

Gallaway, Jack. *Last Call of the Bugle: The Long Road to Kapyong.* St. Lucia, Queensland: Queensland University Press, 1994. Deals with the Korean war.

Gammage, Bill. *The Broken Years: Australian Soldiers in the Great War.* Canberra: Australian National University Press, 1974.

Garton, Stephen. *The Cost of War: Australians Return.* Melbourne: Oxford University Press, 1996.

Goot, Murray, and Rodney Tiffen (eds.). *Australia's Gulf War.* Melbourne: Melbourne University Press, 1992.

Grey, Jeffrey. *A Military History of Australia.* Melbourne: Cambridge University Press, 1990.

————. *Up Top: The Royal Australian Navy and South-East Asian Conflicts, 1955-1972.* Sydney: Allen and Unwin/Australian War Memorial, 1998.

Grey, Jeffrey, and Jeff Doyle (ed.). *Vietnam: War, Myth, and Memory: Comparative Perspectives on Australia's War in Vietnam.* Sydney:

Allen and Unwin, 1992. Includes comparisons with the United States and New Zealand.

Hall, Leslie. *The Blue Haze: The POWs on the Burma Railway.* Sydney: Kangaroo Press, 1996.

Hamill, Ian. *The Strategic Illusion: The Singapore Strategy and the Defence of Australia and New Zealand, 1919-1942.* Singapore: Singapore University Press, 1981.

Henning, Peter. *Doomed Battalion: Mateship and Leadership in War and Captivity.* Sydney: Allen and Unwin, 1995.

Hill, Alec J. *Chauvel of the Light Horse.* Melbourne: Melbourne University Press, 1978. A life of Australia's first field marshal.

Horner, David M. *Blamey: The Commander-in-Chief.* Sydney: Allen and Unwin, 1998. A biography of Australia's commander-in-chief during World War II.

———. *High Command: Australian and Allied Strategy 1939-1945.* Sydney: Allen and Unwin, 1982.

Hyslop, Robert. *Aye Aye, Minister: Australian Naval Administration, 1939-59.* Canberra: Australian Government Publishing Service, 1990.

Inglis, Amirah. *Australians in the Spanish Civil War.* Sydney: Allen and Unwin, 1987.

Inglis, K. S. *Sacred Places: War Memorials in the Australian Landscape.* Melbourne: Miegunyar Press/Melbourne University Press, 1998.

Jenkins, David, and Peter Sullivan. *Battle Surface: Japan's Submarine War against Australia, 1942-44.* Sydney: Random House, 1992.

Lake, Marilyn. *The Limits of Hope: Soldier Settlement in Victoria, 1915-1938.* Melbourne: Oxford University Press, 1987.

Lloyd, Clem, and Jacqui Rees. *The Last Shilling: A History of Repatriation in Australia.* Melbourne: Melbourne University Press, 1994.

Long, Gavin M. *The Six Years War: A Concise History of Australia in the 1939-45 War.* Canberra: Australian War Memorial and Australian Government Publishing Service, 1973.

McAulay, Lex. *Blood and Iron: The Battle for Kakoda.* Sydney: Hutchinson Australia, 1991.

———. *To the Bitter End: The Japanese Defeat at Buna and Gona, 1942-43.* Sydney: Random House Australia, 1993.

McCormack, Gavan, and Hank Nelson (eds.). *The Burma-Thailand Railway: Memory and History.* Sydney: Allen and Unwin, 1993. 668 Americans were also among the thousands of Allied prisoners of war and Asian laborers who were forced to build this railway.

McKernan, Michael. *All In! Australia During the Second World War.* Melbourne: Nelson, 1983.

Mordike, John. *An Army for a Nation: A History of Australian Military Developments, 1880-1914.* Sydney: Allen and Unwin with Department of Defence, 1992.

Morton, Peter. *Fire Across the Desert: Woomera and the Anglo-Australian Joint Project, 1946-1980.* Canberra: Australian Government Publishing Service, 1989.

Murphy, John. *Harvest of Fear: A History of Australia's Vietnam War.* Sydney: Allen and Unwin, 1993.

Nelson, Hank. *P.O.W. Prisoners of War: Australians Under Nippon.* Sydney: Australian Broadcasting Commission, 1985.

Oliver, Bobbie. *War and Peace in Western Australia: The Social and Political Impact of the Great War, 1914-26.* Nedlands, Western Australia: University of Western Australia Press, 1995.

O'Neill, Robert J. *Australia in the Korean War 1950-53.* 2 vols. Canberra: Australian War Memorial and Australian Government Publishing Service, 1981 and 1984.

———. *Japan and British Security in the Pacific, 1904-1942.* Oxford: Oxford University Press, 1993.

Park, Tedition *Angels Twenty: A Young American Flyer a Long Way from Home.* St. Lucia, Queensland: Queensland University Press, 1994. Recollections of a United States army pilot during World War II.

Pedersen, P. A. *Monash as Military Commander.* Melbourne: Melbourne University Press, 1985.

Perry, F. W. *The Commonwealth Armies: Manpower and Organization in Two World Wars.* New York: St. Martin's Press, 1988. Contains a chapter on Australia.

Powell, Alan. *War by Stealth: Australia and the Allied Intelligence Bureau, 1942-45.* Melbourne: Melbourne University Press, 1996.

Rasmussen, Carolyn. *The Lesser Evil? Opposition to War and Fascism in Australia, 1920-1941.* Melbourne: History Department, University of Melbourne, 1991.

Robertson, John. *Australia Goes to War, 1939-1945.* Sydney: Doubleday, 1985.

Ross, Andrew T. *Armed and Ready: The Industrial Development and Defence of Australia, 1900-1945.* Wahroonga, New South Wales: Turton and Armstrong, 1995. Argues that Australia was far better prepared for defending itself against Japanese invasion by virtue of its industrial base than has been previously acknowledged.

Royal Australian Air Force Historical Section. *Units of the Royal Australian Air Force.* 10 vols. Canberra: Australian Government Publishing Service, 1995.

Scott, Jean. *Girls with Grit: Memories of the Australian Women's Land Army.* 2nd ed. Sydney: Allen and Unwin, 1995.

Serle, Geoffrey. *John Monash: A Biography.* Melbourne: Melbourne University Press in association with Monash University, 1982.

Silver, Lynette R. *Sandakan: A Conspiracy of Silence.* Burra Creek, New South Wales: Sally Milner Publishing, 1998.

Somerville, Christopher. *Our War: How the British Commonwealth Fought the Second World War.* London: Weidenfeld and Nicholson, 1998.

Stanley, Peter. *Tarakan: An Australian Tragedy.* Sydney: Allen and Unwin, 1997.

Stephens, Alan. *Power Plus Attitude: Ideas, Strategy and Doctrine in the Royal Air Force, 1921-1991.* Canberra: Australian Government Publishing Service, 1992.

Stevens, David (ed.). *The Royal Australian Navy in World War II.* Sydney: Allen and Unwin, 1996.

Thompson, Joyce. *The WAAAF in Wartime Australia.* Melbourne: Melbourne University Press, 1991. A history of the Women's Auxiliary Australian Air Force.

Tyquin, Michael B. *Gallipoli: The Medical War: The Australian Army Medical Services in the Dardallelles Campaign of 1915.* Sydney: University of New South Wales Press, 1993.

Uhr, Janet. *Against the Sun: The AIF in Malaya, 1941-42.* Sydney: Allen and Unwin, 1998.

Walker, A. S. *Australia in the War of 1939-1945.* Series 5 (Medical). 4 vols. Canberra: Australian War Memorial, 1952-61.

Warner, Denis, Peggy Warner, and Sadao Seno. *Disaster in the Pacific: New Light on the Battle of Savo Island.* Sydney: Allen and Unwin, 1992.

White, Michael W. D. *Australian Submarines: A History.* Canberra: Australian Government Publishing Service, 1992.

Wood, James. *The Forgotten Force: The Australian Military Contribution to the Occupation of Japan, 1945-1952.* Sydney: Allen and Unwin, 1998.

41. LANGUAGE AND LITERATURE

Ackland, Michael. *Henry Kendall: The Man and the Myths.* Melbourne: Melbourne University Press/Miegunyah Press, 1995.

Bennett, Bruce and Strauss, Jennifer (eds.). *The Oxford Literary History of Australia.* Melbourne: Oxford University Press, 1998.

Brady, Veronica. *South of My Days: A Biography of Judith Wright.* Melbourne: HarperCollins, 1998.

Brooks, Barbara, and Judith Clark. *Eleanor Dark: A Writer's Life.* Melbourne: Pan Macmillan, 1998.

Clancy, Laurie. *A Reader's Guide to Australian Fiction.* Melbourne: Oxford University Press, 1992.

Clark, Axel. *Christopher Brennan: A Critical Biography.* Melbourne: Melbourne University Press, 1980.

Cochrane, Kathie. *Oodgeroo.* St. Lucia, Queensland: Queensland University Press, 1994. A biography of the Aboriginal poetess formerly known as Kath Walker.

Davis, Joseph. *D. H. Lawrence at Thirroul.* Sydney: Collins Australia, 1989.

De Groen, Frances. *Xavier Herbert.* St. Lucia, Brisbane: University of Queensland Press, 1998.

Dixon, Robert. *Writing the Colonial Adventure: Race, Gender and Nation in Anglo-Australian Popular Fiction, 1875-1914.* Melbourne: Cambridge University Press, 1995.

Docker, John. *Australian Cultural Elites: Intellectual Traditions in Sydney and Melbourne.* Sydney: Angus and Robertson, 1974.

Fitzpatrick, P. *After"The Doll": Australian Drama since 1955.* Melbourne: Edward Arnold (Australia), 1979.

Fotheringham, Richard. *In Search of Steele Rudd: Author of the Classic Dad and Dave Stories.* St. Lucia, Queensland: Queensland University Press, 1995.

Goldberg, S. L., and F. B. Smith (eds.). *Australian Cultural History.* New York and Melbourne: Cambridge University Press, 1989.

Head, Brian, and James Walter (eds.). *Intellectual Movements and Australian Society.* Melbourne: Oxford University Press, 1988.

Healy, J. J. *Literature and the Aborigine in Australia, 1770-1975.* St. Lucia: Queensland University Press, 1978.

Hergenhan, Laurie (ed.). *The Penguin New Literary History of Australia.* Ringwood, Melbourne, Victoria: Penguin, 1988.

Heyward, Michael. *The Ern Malley Affair.* St. Lucia, Brisbane: University of Queensland Press, 1993. Deals with a significant incident in the history of Australian poetry.

Holt, Stephen. *Manning Clark and Australian History.* St. Lucia, Queensland: Queensland University Press, 1982.

Hooton, Joy, and Harry Heseltine. *Annals of Australian Literature.* 2nd ed. Melbourne: Oxford University Press, 1992

Kiernan, Brian. *David Williamston: A Writer's Career.* Melbourne: William Heinemann Australia, 1990.

Kramer, Leonie (ed.). *The Oxford History of Australian Literature.* Melbourne: Oxford University Press, 1981.

Lees, Stella, and Pam Macintrye (eds.). *The Oxford Companion to Australian Children's Literature.* Melbourne: Oxford University Press, 1993.

Lock, F., and A. Lawson. *Australian Literature: A Reference Guide.* 2nd ed. Melbourne: Oxford University Press, 1980.

Lyons, Martyn, and Lucy Taska. *Australian Readers Remember: An Oral History of Reading, 1890-1930.* Melbourne: Oxford University Press, 1992.

MacIntyre, Stuart. *A History for a Nation: Ernest Scott and the Meaning of Australian History.* Melbourne: Melbourne University Press, 1994.

Marr, David. *Patrick White: A Life.* Sydney: Random House Australia, 1991.

———— (ed.). *Patrick White: Letters.* Sydney: Random House, 1995.

Moorehead, Alan. *A Late Education: Episodes in a Life.* Sydney: Text Publishing, 1998. Autobiographical study of an important expatriate author of the 1950s and 1960s.

Mudrooroo. *The Indigenous Literature of Australia: Milli Milli Wangka.* Melbourne: Hyland House, 1997.

Pierce, Peter (ed.). *The Oxford Literary Guide to Australia.* rev. ed. Melbourne: Oxford University Press, 1993.

Ramson, W. S. (ed.). *The Australian National Dictionary: A Dictionary of Australianisms on Historical Principles.* Melbourne: Oxford University Press, 1988.

Rees, L. *A History of Australian Drama.* Sydney: Angus and Robertson, 1978.

Rickard, John. *Australia: A Cultural History.* New York: Longman Inc., 1988. An introductory text.

Roderick, Colin. *Banjo Patterson: Poet by Accident.* Sydney: Allen and Unwin, 1993.

————. *Henry Lawson: A Life.* Sydney: Angus and Robertson, 1991.

Russell, Roslyn. *Literary Links: Celebrating the Literary Relationship between Australia and Britain.* Sydney: Allen and Unwin, 1997.

Wilde, William H., and others (eds.). *The Oxford Companion to Australian Literature.* 2nd ed. Melbourne: Oxford University Press, 1994.

Wilkes, G. A. (ed.). *A Dictionary of Australian Colloquialisms.* 4th ed. Melbourne: Oxford University Press, 1996.

Yarwood, A. T. *From a Chair in the Sun: The Life of Ethel Turner.* Melbourne: Penguin Books/Viking, 1994.

42. POPULAR CULTURE

Cockington, James. *Mondo Weirdo: Australia in the Sixties.* Melbourne: Reed Books Australia/Mardarin, 1992.

Craven, Ian (ed.). *Australian Popular Culture.* Melbourne: Cambridge University Press, 1994.

Joel, Alexandra. *Parade: The Story of Fashion in Australia.* Melbourne: HarperCollins, 1998.

Luck, Peter. *A Time to Remember.* Melbourne: Mandarin Australia 1991. First published in 1988.

Thorpe, Billy. *Most People I Know (Think That I'm Crazy).* Melbourne: Pan Macmillan/Macmillan, 1998. The autobiography of a pop singer of the 1960s and 1970s.

Waterhouse, Richard, and Addison Wesley. *Private Pleasures, Public Leisure: A History of Australian Popular Culture since 1788.* South Melbourne: Longman Australia, 1996.

43. ART, ARCHITECTURE, MUSIC, AND THE PERFORMING ARTS

Adams, Brian. *Portrait of an Artist: A Biography of William Dobell.* Sydney: Random House Australia/ Vintage, 1992. First published in 1983.

Astbury, Leigh. *City Bushmen: The Heidelberg School and Rural Mythology.* Melbourne: Oxford University Press, 1985.

Brisbane, Katherine (ed.). *Entertaining Australia: The Performing Arts as Cultural History.* Sydney: Currency Press, 1993.

Chaloupka, George. *Journey in Time: The World's Longest Continuing Art Tradition.* Sydney: Reed Books, 1994. A history of Aboriginal rock art in Arnhem Land, Northern Territory.

Cochrane, Grace. *The Crafts Movement in Australia: A History.* Sydney: University of New South Wales Press, 1992

Docker, John. *The Nervous Nineties: Australian Cultural Life in the 1890s.* Sydney: Oxford University Press, 1991.

Ellis, Elizabeth, and Helen Bonglorno (eds.). *Conrad Martens: Life and Art.* Sydney: State Library of New South Wales Press, 1994.

Freeland, J. M. *Architecture in Australia: A History.* Ringwood: Penguin, 1972. First published in 1968.

Gyger, Alison. *Opera for the Antipodes: Opera in Australia, 1881-1939.* Sydney: Currency Press, 1990.

Hardy, Jane, and others (eds.). *The Heritage of Namatjira: The Watercolourists of Central Australia.* Port Melbourne: Octopus/William Heinemann, 1992.

Hetherington, John A. *Melba: A Biography.* London: Faber, 1973. First published in 1967.

Hilton, Margot, and Graeme Blundell. *Brett Whiteley: An Unauthorised Life.* Melbourne: Pan Macmillan, 1997.

Hughes, Robert. *The Art of Australia.* rev. ed. Ringwood: Penguin, 1970.

Isaacs, J. *Arts of the Dreaming: Australia's Living Heritage.* Sydney: Lansdowne, 1984.

Irvin, Eric. *Dictionary of Australian Theatre, 1788-1914.* Sydney: Hale and Iremonger, 1985.

Irving, I. *The History and Design of the Australian Home.* Melbourne: Oxford University Press, 1985.

Johnson, D. L. *The Architecture of Walter Burley Griffin.* Melbourne: Macmillan, 1977.

Kerr, Joan. *The Dictionary of Australian Artists: Painters, Sketchers, Photographers and Engravers to 1870.* Sydney: Oxford University Press, 1992.

Love, H. (ed.). *The Australian Stage: A Documentary History.* Sydney: University of New South Wales Press, 1984.

Major, Norma. *Joan Sutherland: The Authorised Biography.* Melbourne: Penguin Books, 1994.

McCulloch, Alan and McCulloch, Susan (eds.). *Encyclopedia of Australian Art.* 3rd ed. Sydney: Allen and Unwin, 1994.

McQueen, H. D. *Tom Roberts.* Melbourne: Pan Macmillan/Macmillan, 1996.

Mellers, Wilfrid. *Percy Grainger.* Melbourne: Oxford University Press, 1992.

Murdoch, J. *A Handbook of Australian Music.* Melbourne: Sun Books, 1983.

Newton, Gael. *Shades of Light: Photography and Australia, 1839-1988.* Canberra: Australian National Gallery, Collins Australia with assistance from Kodak, 1988.

Pask, E. H. *Ballet in Australia: The Second Act, 1940-1980.* Melbourne: Oxford University Press, 1982.

————. *Enter the Colonies, Dancing: A History of Dance in Australia, 1835-1940.* Melbourne: Oxford University Press, 1979.

Prunster, Ursula. *The Legendary Lindsays.* Sydney: Beagle Press and the Art Gallery of New South Wales, 1995.

Salter, Elizabeth. *Helpman: The Authorised Biography of Sir Robert Helpman, CBE.* Brighton, Eng.: Angus and Robertson, 1978.

Serle, Geoffrey. *Robin Boyd: A Life.* Melbourne: Melbourne University Press, 1995. A biography of one of Australia's leading architects.

Smith, Bernard W. *Australian Painting, 1788-1990.* Melbourne: Oxford University Press, 1991.

———. *Documents on Art and Taste in Australia: The Colonial Period, 1770-1914.* Melbourne: Oxford University Press, 1975.

Sturgeon, G. *The Development of Australian Sculpture, 1788-1975.* London: Thames and Hudson, 1978.

Thomson, J. M. *A Distant Music: The Life and Times of Alfred Hill, 1870-1960.* Melbourne: Oxford University Press, 1980.

Topliss, Helen. *The Artists' Camps: "Plein Air" Painting in Australia.* Melbourne: Hedley Australia, 1992.

Walker, Clinton. *Stranded: The Secret History of Australian Independent Music, 1977-79.* Melbourne: Pan Macmillan, 1996. Deals with punk rock.

Walsh, Maureen. *May Gibbs, Mother of the Gumnuts: Her Life and Work.* Sydney: Angus and Robertson, 1985.

Williams, John F. *The Quarantined Culture: Australian Reactions to Modernism, 1913-1939.* Melbourne: Cambridge University Press, 1995.

Williams, M. *Australia on the Popular Stage, 1829-1929: An Historical Entertainment in Six Acts.* Melbourne: Oxford University Press, 1980.

Willis, A. M. *Picturing Australia: A History of Photography.* Sydney: Angus and Robertson, 1988.

Zubans, Ruth. *E. Philips Fox: His Life and Art.* Melbourne: Melbourne University Press/Miegunyay Press, 1995.

44. FILM

Allen, Yolanda, and S. Spencer. *The Broadcasting Chronology, 1809-1980.* Sydney: Australian Film and Television School, 1983.

Bertrand, I. (ed.). *Cinema in Australia: A Documentary History.* Sydney: University of New South Wales Press, 1989.

Edmondson, R., and A. F Pike. *Australia's Lost Films: The Loss and Rescue of Australia's Silent Films.* Canberra: National Library of Australia, 1982.

Hall, Sandra (ed.). *Australian Film Index: A Guide to Australian Films Since 1900.* Melbourne: D. W. Thorpe, 1992.

Lansell, R., and P. Beilby (eds.). *The Documentary Film in Australia.* Melbourne: Cinema Papers in association with Film Victoria, 1982.

McFarlane, Brian, and Geoff Mayer. *New Australian Cinema: Sources and Parallels in American and British Film.* Cambridge: Cambridge University Press, 1992.

Murray, Scott. *Australian Film, 1978-1992.* Melbourne: Oxford University Press, 1993.

Paterson, Barbara. *Renegades: Australia's First Film School: From Swinburne to VCA.* Melbourne: Helicon Press, 1996. A history of the Swinburne Film and Television School from 1966 to its transfer to the Victorian College of the Arts.

Pike, Andrew, and Ross Cooper. *Australian Film, 1900-1997: A Guide to Feature Film Production.* Melbourne Oxford University Press, 1998.

Tulloch, J. *Australian Cinema: Industry, Narrative and Meaning.* Sydney: Allen and Unwin, 1982.

45. THE PRESS AND TELEVISION

Beilby, P. (ed.). *Australian TV: The First 25 Years.* Melbourne: Nelson in association with Cinema Papers, 1981.

Black, Jenny. *The Country's Finest Hour: Fifty Years of Rural Broadcasting in Australia.* Sydney: ABC Enterprises, 1995.

Hodge, Errol. *Radio Works: Truth, Propaganda, and the Struggle for Radio Australia.* Melbourne: Cambridge University Press, 1995.

Inglis, Ken. *This is the ABC: The Australian Broadcasting Commission, 1932-1983.* Melbourne: Melbourne University Press, 1983.

Jones, Colin. *Something in the Air: A History of Radio in Australia.* Sydney: Kangaroo Press, 1995. Includes some hard-to-get statistics.

Munster, G. *Rupert Murdoch: A Paper Prince.* Ringwood: Viking, 1984.

O'Brien, D. *The Weekly: A Lively and Nostalgic Celebration of Australia Through 50 Years of Its Most Popular Magazine.* Ringwood: Penguin, 1982.

Pullan, Robert. *Four Corners: Twenty-Five Years.* Sydney: ABC Enterprises, 1986. An account of Australia's longest-running television investigative program.

Souter, Gavin. *Heralds and Angels: The House of Fairfax, 1841-1990.* Melbourne: Melbourne University Press, 1991.

Walker, R. B. *Yesterday's News: A History of the Newspaper Press in New South Wales from 1920 to 1945.* Sydney: Sydney University Press, 1980.

APPENDIXES

GOVERNORS-GENERAL

Title and name	Period of office
Earl of Hopetoun (John Adrian Louis Hope) (1860-1908)	1901-02
Lord Tennyson (Hallam Tennyson) (1852-1928) [Acted as Governor-General, 1902-03]	1903-04
Lord Northcote (Henry Stafford Northcote) (1846-1911)	1904-08
Earl of Dudley (William Humble Ward) (1867-1932)	1908-11
Lord Denman (Thomas Denman) (1874-1954)	1911-14
Sir Ronald Craufurd Munro-Ferguson (1860-1934)	1914-20
Lord Forster (Henry William Forster) (1866-1936)	1920-25
Lord Stonehaven (Sir John Lawrence Baird) (1874-1941)	1925-31
*Sir Isaac Alfred Isaacs (1855-1948)	1931-36
Lord Gowrie (General Alexander Gore Harkwright Hore-Ruthven) (1872-1955)	1936-45
Prince Henry William Frederick Albert (H.R.H. Duke of Gloucester, Earl of Ulster and Baron Culloden) (1900-1974)	1945-47
*Sir William John McKell (1891-1985)	1947-53
Sir William Joseph Slim (1891-1970)	1953-60
Viscount Dunrossil (William Shepherd Morrison) (1893-1961)	1960-61
Viscount De L'Isle (William Philip Sidney) (1909-1991)	1961-65
*Lord Casey (Richard Gardiner Casey) (1890-1976)	1965-69
*Sir Paul Meernaa Caedwalla Hasluck (1905-1993)	1969-74
*Sir John Robert Kerr (1914-1991)	1974-77
*Sir Zelman Cowen (1919-)	1977-82
*Sir Ninian Martin Stephen (1923-)	1982-89
*Bill (William George) Hayden (1933-)	1989-96
*Sir William Patrick Deane (1931-)	1996-

* Australian-born.

Appendix 2   PRIME MINISTERS

Name	Party of government	Period(s) of office
*Edmond BARTON (1849-1920)	Protectionist	1901-03
*Alfred DEAKIN (1856-1919)	Protectionist	1904-04
		1905-08
John Christian WATSON (1867-1941)	Labor	1904
George Houston REID (1854-1918)	Free Trade-	
	Protectionist	1904-05
Andrew FISHER (1862-1928)	Labor	1908-09
		1910-13
		1914-15
Joseph COOK (1860-1947)	Liberal	1913-14
William Morris HUGHES (1862-1952)	Labor	1915-16
	National Labor	1916-17
	Nationalist	1917-23
*Stanley Melbourne BRUCE (1883-1967)	Nationalist-Country	1923-29
*James Henry SCULLIN (1876-1953)	Labor	1929-32
*Joseph Aloysius LYONS (1879-1939)	United Australia	1932-38
	United Australia-Country	1938-39
*Earle Christmas Grafton PAGE (1886-1961)	Country-United Australia	1939
*Robert Gordon MENZIES (1894-1978)	United Australia	1939-40
	United Australia-Country	1940-41
	Liberal-Country	1949-66
*William Arthur FADDEN (1895-1973)	Country-United Australia	1941
*John Joseph CURTIN (1885-1945)	Labor	1941-45
*Francis Michael FORDE (1890-1983)	Labor	1945
*Joseph Benedict CHIFLEY (1885-1951)	Labor	1945-49
*Harold Edward HOLT (1908-1967)	Liberal-Country	1966-67
*John McEWEN (1900-1980)	Liberal-Country	1967-68
*John Grey GORTON (1911-)	Liberal-Country	1968-71

*William McMAHON (1908-1990)	Liberal-Country	1971-72
*Edward Gough WHITLAM (1916-)	Labor	1972-75
*John Malcolm FRASER (1930-)	Liberal-Country	1975-83
*Robert James Lee HAWKE (1929-)	Labor	1983-91
*Paul John KEATING (1944-)	Labor	1991-96
*John Winston HOWARD (1939-)	Liberal-National	1996-

* Australian-born.

Appendix 3   HISTORICAL STATISTICS

Australian official statistics

Australia has an impressive heritage of high quality official statistics covering long periods of time and its current official statistics are regarded as among the best in the world. Australia's European beginnings as an expensive British jail unwittingly inaugurated a strong official tradition of monitoring and accounting. The upsurge of interest in official statistics in Britain from the 1830s was faithfully followed and continued in its Australian colonies. Australia's isolation also made it relatively easy for governments to monitor accurately the movement of people and goods from overseas. The 1988 edition of the *Year Book Australia* published by the Australian Bureau of Statistics contained a special article (pp. 1-95) on the evolution of Australian official statistics.

The tables are designed to complement and extend the text and to be used in their own right. They bring together much information which is not easily obtainable elsewhere. Some of the information has not been previously published. Table 2, for instance, presents a general view of the number of works published in or about Australia since 1784, a task not apparently attempted before. Another argument for this appendix is that the cost of obtaining official Australian statistics has risen greatly in recent years.

For an excellent general guide to international statistical sources, the reader is referred to Jacqueline W. O'Brien and Steven R. Wasserman (eds.), *Statistical Sources,* 10th ed. 2 vols. (Detroit, Michigan: Gale Research Company, 1986).

Structure of the appendix

The following tables set out some important features of Australian history, but they are only a selection of what is available. Technical notes have been kept to a minimum; specialist readers should consult the sources listed after the tables in the form of endnotes. Estimates, where used, are conservative.

A.   Australia: General

1. Australia: Evolution of States and Territories, 1770-1911
2. Australia: Published Works, 1784-1993
3. Australia: Population Interchange with Selected Countries, 1901-1991
4. Australia: Visitors by Country of Residence, 1925-1997
5. Australians Visiting Other Countries, 1925-1997

B.   Australia and the United States

6. Australia and United States: Area, Population, Foreign-born, Urbanization and Home Ownership, 1920, 1950, 1970, and 1990
7. Australia and United States: Gross Domestic Product per Head, United States Dollars, 1891-1996
8. Australia and United States: Population Interchange, 1860-1996
9. Australia and United States: Trade, 1891-1998
10. Australia and United States: Labor Union Members as a Percentage of Employees, 1891-1997

C.   Population

11. Australia: Population: Sources of Change, 1788-1998
12. Australia: Birthplace of Population, 1828-1996
13. Australian Citizenship, 1949-1998
14. Australia: Population, Ages, 1841-1996
15. Australia: Population Sex Ratios, Fertility, and Mortality, 1840-1997
16. Australia: Population by Colony/State, 1841-1996
17. Australia: Religious Affiliations, 1828-1996

D.   Urbanization and Home Ownership

18. Australia: Urban/Rural Population by Percentage, 1841-1996
19. Australia: Population of Capital Cities (Thousands), 1841-1996
20. Australia: Distribution of Urban Population by Size of Center, (Percentage), 1841-1996
21. Australia: Home Ownership for Selected Places, 1871-1911
22. Australia: Home Ownership, 1911-1996

E.   Economy

23. Australia: Gross Domestic Product by Industry, 1841-1998
24. Australia: Foreign Investment by Country, 1896-1997
25. Australia: Exports by Country of Destination, 1891-1998
26. Australia: Imports by Country of Origin, 1891-1998
27. Australia: Trade Indicators, 1891-1998
28. Australia: Index of Retail Prices, 1851-1998
29. Australia: Exchange Rates with the United Kingdom and the United States, 1851-1998

F.   *Labor*

1. AUSTRALIA: EVOLUTION OF STATES AND TERRITORIES, 1770-1911

State or Territory and date of British annexation	Separate colony or Territory by Britain	Granted self-government	Present area (thousands square kilometres)
New South Wales (1770)	1786	1855	801.6
Victoria (1770)	1851	1855	227.6
Queensland (1770)	1859	1859	1,727.2
South Australia (1770, 1827)	1834	1856	984.0
Western Australia (1829)	1829	1890	2,525.0
Tasmania (1788)	1825	1855	67.8
Northern Territory (1770, 1827)	1863[a]		1,346.2
Australian Capital Territory (1770)		1911[b]	2.4
Total			7,682.3

Notes and sources can be found at the end of the appendix.

2. AUSTRALIA: PUBLISHED WORKS, 1784-1993

Period[a]	Number of works (thousands)	Annual average
1784-1800	0.3	21
1801-50	5.7	115
1851-1900	13.9	279
1901-10	5.2	520
1911-20	8.2	818
1921-30	7.1	706
1930-40	11.4	1,140
1941-50	17.6	1,760
1951-60	24.6 [b]	2,456
1961-70	30.5	3,054
1971-80	68.3	6,828
1981-90	105.7	10,565
1991-93	29.5	9,812

Notes and sources can be found at the end of the appendix.

3. AUSTRALIA: POPULATION INTERCHANGE WITH SELECTED COUNTRIES, 1901-1991

Country	1901	1921	1951	1971	1991
	Australian-born (thousands)				
United Kingdom	24.5	29.1	33.7	57.0	74.3
United States	7.0	10.9	19.9	24.3	52.5
Canada	1.0	2.9	4.2	14.8[b]	14.0
New Zealand	27.0	48.0	35.8	44.1	48.7
South Africa	6.5	7.2	5.3[a]	4.9[c]	4.0[d]
Papua-New Guinea	-	0.7	4.2	28.6	5.2
	Foreign-born in Australia (thousands)				
United Kingdom	685.8	681.7	543.8	1,170.1	1,118.7
United States	7.5	6.6	6.2	34.0	50.5
Canada	3.2	3.7	4.1	12.8	24.1
New Zealand	25.8	38.6	43.6	176.7	276.1
South Africa	1.5	5.4	5.9	28.0	49.4
Papua-New Guinea	-	0.5	1.2	19.5	23.7

Notes and sources can be found at the end of the appendix.

4. AUSTRALIA: VISITORS BY COUNTRY OF RESIDENCE, 1925-1997

Year	Country				
	New Zealand	United Kingdom and Ireland	Asia	United States	Total [a]
	Number (thousands)				
1925	12.5	3.7	-	0.4	23.2
1930	12.2	2.8	-	0.4	22.2
1935	11.0	3.1	-	1.0	22.5
1940	5.3	1.6	-	0.5	18.7
1950	18.6	8.5	6.1	1.9	43.6
1955	19.8	8.6	9.0	4.3	53.6
1960	33.3	10.5	14.6	9.5	84.6
1965	62.9	22.8	19.0	23.8	173.3
1970	96.8	39.8	35.0	64.3	416.1
1975	154.4	72.6	72.3	64.4	516.0
1980	307.1	131.5	122.8	111.4	904.6
1985	245.3	158.9	265.3	196.5	1,142.6
1990	418.5	288.3	820.5	250.7	2,214.9
1996	671.9	388.3	2,091.5	316.9	4,164.8
1997	685.7	435.9	2,127.9	329.6	4,317.9

Notes and sources can be found at the end of the appendix.

5. AUSTRALIANS VISITING OTHER COUNTRIES, 1925-1997

Year	Country				
	New Zealand	United Kingdom and Ireland	Asia	United States	Total[a]
	Number (thousands)				
1925	6.5	7.5	-	0.6	20.7
1930	6.2	6.4	-	0.5	23.4
1935	5.7	5.8	-	1.4	20.3
1940	3.0	0.1	-	0.3	4.7
1950	11.0	9.9	3.2	1.0	31.4
1955	13.3	15.2	8.1	2.1	52.2
1960	17.2	13.4	14.6	7.7	77.8
1965	44.3	17.1	36.1	13.3	161.7
1970	81.0	25.6	83.1	29.8	352.5
1975	217.4	154.9	162.0	66.4	911.8
1980	217.7	188.3	283.8	144.1	1,203.6
1985	279.2	218.5	265.3	134.9	1,512.0
1990	320.2	264.7	713.9	290.5	2,169.9
1996	415.0	307.8	1,022.0	331.1	2,732.0
1997	406.9	343.4	1.121.3	351.9	2,932.8

Notes and sources can be found at the end of the appendix.

6. AUSTRALIA AND UNITED STATES: AREA, POPULATION, FOREIGN-BORN, URBANIZATION, AND HOME OWNERSHIP, 1920, 1950, 1970, AND 1990

Year/Feature	Australia	United States
Area (thousands of square kilometres)	7,682	9,363 (7,884 without Alaska)
Population (millions)		
1920	5.3	105.7
1950	8.2	150.7
1970	12.7	203.2
1990	17.1	248.7
Percentage of population foreign-born		
1920	15.5	13.2
1950	9.8	6.9
1970	20.2	4.7
1990	24.5	7.9
Percentage of population urban dwellers		
1920	55.4	51.2
1950	70.2	64.0
1970	81.4	73.6
1990	81.7	75.2
Percentage of home ownership		
1920	52.4	45.6
1950	52.6	55.0
1970	68.7	62.9
1990	68.8	73.7

Notes and sources can be found at the end of the appendix.

7. AUSTRALIA AND UNITED STATES: GROSS DOMESTIC PRODUCT (GDP) PER HEAD, UNITED STATES DOLLARS, 1891-1996

Year	Australia (Australian dollars)	Australia (U.S. dollars)	United States	Australian GDP per head (U.S. dollars) as a percentage of U.S. GDP per head
1891	115	279	210	133.1
1901	111	268	267	100.2
1911	154	370	382	96.9
1921	254	478	641	74.6
1931	198	372	611	60.9
1939	257	411	691	59.5
1951	816	914	2,129	42.9
1961	1,403	1,641	2,831	58.0
1971	2,666	3,039	5,283	57.5
1981	9,088	10,452	13,177	79.3
1991	21,758	16,754	22,565	74.2
1996	24,188	19,109	28,422	67.2

Notes and sources can be found at the end of the appendix.

8. AUSTRALIA AND UNITED STATES: POPULATION INTERCHANGE, 1860-1996

Date[a]	United States-born in Australia	Australian-born in United States
	Thousands	
1860-1861	4.3	1.4
1870-1871	4.3	3.1
1880-1881	5.9	4.9
1890-1891	8.0	6.0
1900-1901	7.5	7.0
1910-1911	6.7	9.0
1920-1921	6.6	10.9
1930-1933	6.1	12.7
1940	-	11.0
1947-1950	6.2	19.9
1960-1961	10.8	22.2
1970-1971	30.0	24.3
1980-1981	32.6	36.0
1990-1991	43.8	52.5
1996	49.5	-

Notes and sources can be found at the end of the appendix.

9. AUSTRALIA AND UNITED STATES: TRADE, 1891-1998

Year	Imports from United States (percentage of total)	Exports to United States (percentage of total)
1891	6.8	7.6
1901	13.3	3.4
1911	13.8	2.1
1920-21	22.0	5.4
1930-31	18.8	3.2
1940-41	16.0	18.0
1950-51	8.2	14.3
1960-61	20.0	6.7
1970-71	25.1	10.3
1980-81	22.0	9.8
1990-91	23.5	11.0
1995-96	22.6	6.1
1996-97	22.3	7.0
1997-98	21.9	8.8

Notes and sources can be found at the end of the appendix.

10. AUSTRALIA AND UNITED STATES: LABOR UNION
MEMBERS AS A PERCENTAGE OF EMPLOYEES, 1891-
1997

Year	Australia	United States
1891	23	8
1901	9	6
1913	34	9
1920	46	17
1930	51	9
1940	46	16
1950	59	28
1960	58	26
1970	50	27
1980	49	22
1990	41	16
1996	31	15
1997	30	14

Notes and sources can be found at the end of the appendix.

11. AUSTRALIA: POPULATION, SOURCES OF CHANGE, 1788-1998

Period	Population at end of period	Sources of change	
	Thousands	Natural increase (births less deaths)	Migration
		Percentage of total change	
1788-1800	5.2	-14.3	114.3
1801-10	11.6	9.5	90.5
1811-20	33.5	4.5	95.5
1821-30	70.0	7.1	92.9
1831-40	190.4	7.9	92.1
1841-50	405.4	31.4	68.6
1851-60	1,145.6	20.7	79.3
1861-70	1,647.8	66.8	33.2
1871-80	2,231.5	67.2	32.8
1881-90	3,151.4	58.4	41.6
1891-1900	3,765.3	96.1	3.9
1901-10	4,425.1	93.9	6.1
1911-20	5,411.2	78.8	21.2
1921-30	6,500.8	71.4	28.6
1931-40	7,077.6	92.9	7.1
1941-50	8,307.5	70.2	29.8
1951-55	9,311.8	59.7	40.3
1956-60	10,391.9	63.1	36.9
1961-65	10,391.9	61.5	38.5
1966-70	12,663.5	60.6	39.4
1971-80	14,601.8	75.9	24.1
1981-90	17,044.7	52.1	47.9
1991-98	18,709.7	62.3	37.7

Notes and sources can be found at the end of the appendix.

12. AUSTRALIA: BIRTHPLACE OF POPULATION, 1828-1996

Year	Australia	British Isles	Other	Total Population
	Percentage			(million)
1828	23.8	-	-	0.04
1841	23.9	-	-	0.2
1851	37.1	60.0	2.9	0.4
1861	37.2	54.7	8.1	1.2
1871	54.5	40.9	5.6	1.7
1881	63.2	31.0	5.8	2.3
1891	68.2	26.1	5.7	3.2
1901	77.2	18.2	4.6	3.8
1911	82.9	13.5	3.6	4.5
1921	84.5	12.5	3.0	5.4
1933	86.4	10.8	2.8	6.6
1947	90.2	7.2	2.6	7.6
1954	85.7	7.4	6.9	9.0
1961	83.1	7.2	9.7	10.5
1966	81.6	7.8	10.6	11.6
1971	79.8	8.5	11.7	13.1
1976	79.9	7.8	12.3	14.0
1981	79.1	7.9	13.0	14.9
1986	77.6	7.2	15.2	15.6
1991	75.5	6.9	17.6	16.9
1996	75.5	6.3	19.2	17.8

Notes and sources can be found at the end of the appendix.

13. AUSTRALIAN CITIZENSHIP, 1949-1998

Total persons granted citizenship			
Period ending 30 June	**Number (thousands)**	**Period ending 30 June**	**Number (thousands)**
1949-56	49.6	1976-81	333.8
1956-61	283.4	1981-86	473.5
1961-66	161.8	1986-91	519.5
1966-71	207.9	1991-96	582.8
1971-76	359.8	1996-98	220.6
Australian citizenship by birthplace (percentage), 1996			
Greece	97.3	Germany	78.3
Croatia	95.5	Canada	66.2
Vietnam	93.4	Ireland	63.7
Papua New Guinea	91.3	United Kingdom	62.2
Hong Kong	86.8	United States	57.3
South Africa	86.2	New Zealand	35.1
Taiwan	83.5	Japan	25.3
Italy	79.3	All countries	73.2

Notes and sources can be found at the end of the appendix.

14. AUSTRALIA: POPULATION, AGES, 1841-1996

Year	Age groups in years (percentage)				Median age[a]
	0-14	15-44	45-64	65 and over	Years
1841	25	67[b]	7[c]	2[d]	25
1851[e]	36	53[b]	9[c]	2[d]	22
1861	37	53	9	1	23
1871	42	45	11	2	20
1881	39	46	13	2	20
1891	37	48	12	3	22
1901	35	49	12	4	23
1911	32	49	15	4	24
1921	32	47	17	4	26
1933	28	47	19	6	28
1947	25	46	21	8	31
1954	29	43	20	8	30
1961	30	41	20	9	29
1966	29	42	29	9	28
1971	29	43	20	8	28
1976	29	43	29	8	28
1981	27	44	20	9	30
1986	23	47	19	11	31
1991	22	47	19	12	32
1996	22	45	21	12	34

Notes and sources can be found at the end of the appendix.

15. AUSTRALIA: POPULATION SEX RATIOS, FERTILITY, AND MORTALITY, 1840-1997

Average for period	*Males per 100 females*	*Fertility*		*Mortality per thousand population*	
		Births per 1,000 population	Births per 1,000 women aged 15-44	Infant deaths per 1,000 births	Deaths
1840-42	206	30.8	194	-	15.9
1850-52	142	34.8	173	-	14.5
1860-62	138	43.8	209	-	18.6
1870-72	121	41.2	193	111.1	15.2
1880-82	117	35.3	170	120.8	15.2
1890-92	116	34.6	159	109.5	14.1
1900-02	110	27.2	117	103.6	12.2
1910-12	109	27.8	117	71.6	10.9
1920-22	103	25.0	107	62.5	9.2
1932-34	103	16.7	71	41.5	8.9
1946-48	100	23.6	104	28.4	9.7
1953-55	102	22.7	109	22.6	9.1
1960-62	102	22.5	112	20.0	8.5
1965-67	101	19.5	95	17.3	8.8
1970-72	101	20.8	100	13.8	8.7
1980-82	99	15.7	71	10.3	7.3
1985-87	99	15.2	67	9.2	7.3
1990-92	99	15.1	65	7.4	7.0
1995-97	99	13.9	63	5.6	6.9

Notes and sources can be found at the end of the appendix.

16. AUSTRALIA: POPULATION BY COLONY/ STATE, 1841-1996

Year	NSW	Vic	Qld	SA	WA	Tas	NT	ACT
	Thousands							
1841	118.9	11.7	0.2	14.6	3.9	57.4	-	-
1851	178.7	77.3	8.6	63.7	4.6	70.1	-	-
1861	350.9	538.6	30.1	126.8	15.6	90.0	-	-
1871	503.0	730.2	120.1	185.6	24.8	99.3	0.2	-
1881	749.8	861.6	213.5	276.4	29.7	115.7	3.5	-
1891	1,124.0	1,139.8	393.7	315.5	49.8	146.7	4.9	-
1901	1,354.8	1,201.1	498.1	358.3	184.1	172.5	4.8	-
1911	1,646.7	1,315.6	605.8	408.6	282.2	191.2	3.3	1.7
1921	2,100.4	1,531.3	756.0	495.2	332.7	213.8	3.9	2.6
1933	2,600.8	1,820.3	947.5	580.9	438.9	227.6	4.9	8.9
1947	2,984.8	2,054.7	1,106.4	646.1	502.5	257.1	10.9	16.9
1954	3,423.5	2,452.3	1,318.3	797.1	639.8	308.8	16.5	30.3
1961	3,917.0	2,930.1	1,518.8	969.3	736.6	350.3	27.1	58.8
1966	4,233.8	3,219.5	1,663.7	1,091.9	836.7	371.4	37.4	96.0
1971	4,601.2	3,502.4	1,827.1	1,173.7	1,030.5	390.4	86.4	144.1
1976	4,777.1	3,647.0	2,037.2	1,244.8	1,144.9	402.9	97.1	197.6
1981	5,126.2	3,832.4	2,295.1	1,285.0	1,273.6	419.0	123.3	221.6
1986	5,531.5	4,160.9	2,624.6	1,382.6	1,459.0	446.5	154.4	258.9
1991	5,732.0	4,244.2	2,977.8	1,400.6	1,586.8	452.8	175.9	279.3
1996	6,038.7	4,373.5	3,369.0	1,427.9	1,726.1	459.7	195.1	299.2

Notes and sources can be found at the end of the appendix.

17. AUSTRALIA: RELIGIOUS AFFILIATIONS, 1828-1996

Year	Denominations					No religion
	Church of England	Catholic	Methodist	Presby- terian	Judaism	
	Percentage of total population					
1828	69.2	30.8	-	-	-	-
1836	70.7	24.0	1.4	2.4	0.2	-
1841	56.5	21.1	2.8	8.9	0.6	-
1851	52.7	28.2	5.6	10.3	0.5	-
1861	42.8	23.6	7.8	13.4	0.5	-
1871	38.4	24.6	11.8	12.4	0.4	-
1881	38.4	24.2	11.3	11.5	0.4	-
1891	38.9	22.5	12.6	11.1	0.4	2.7
1901	39.7	22.7	13.4	11.9	0.4	1.7
1911	38.4	22.4	12.3	12.5	0.4	3.0
1921	43.7	21.6	11.6	11.7	0.4	2.1
1933	38.7	19.6	10.3	10.8	0.4	13.0
1947	39.0	20.9	11.5	9.8	0.4	11.2
1961	34.9	24.9	10.2	9.3	0.6	10.9
1971	31.0	27.0	8.6	8.1	0.5	12.8
1981	26.1	26.0	3.4	4.4	0.4	21.8
1991	23.9	27.3	8.2	4.4	0.4	23.1
1996	21.8	26.8	7.5	3.8	0.4	25.1

Notes and sources can be found at the end of the appendix.

18. AUSTRALIA: URBAN/RURAL POPULATION BY PERCENTAGE, 1841-1996

Year	Urban	Rural	Total population (thousands)
1841	38.6	61.4	206.7
1851	38.1	61.9	403.0
1861	33.2	66.8	1,151.9
1871	35.7	64.3	1,663.2
1881	40.6	59.4	2,250.2
1891	47.5	52.5	3,174.4
1901	47.7	52.3	3,773.8
1911	50.6	49.4	4,455.0
1921	55.4	44.6	5,435.7
1933	63.5	36.5	6,629.8
1947	70.2	29.8	7,579.4
1954	74.7	25.3	8,986.5
1961	78.3	21.7	10,508.2
1966	80.9	19.1	11,550.5
1971	81.4	18.6	13,067.3
1976	80.1	19.9	14,033.1
1981	80.7	19.3	14,923.3
1986	80.0	20.0	16,018.4
1991	81.7	18.3	16,852.3
1996	82.3	17.7	17,892.4

Notes and sources can be found at the end of the appendix.

19. AUSTRALIA: POPULATION OF CAPITAL CITIES, (THOUSANDS), 1841-1996

Year	Sydney	Melbourne	Brisbane	Adelaide	Perth	Hobart	Canberra
1841	35.5	4.5	0.2	11.6	-	14.6	-
1851	54.0	29.0	3.0	18.0	1.0	23.1	-
1861	96.0	125.0	6.0	35.0	5.0	25.0	-
1871	138.0	191.0	15.0	51.0	5.0	26.0	-
1881	225.0	268.0	31.0	92.0	9.0	27.0	-
1891	400.0	473.0	87.0	117.0	16.0	33.0	-
1901	496.0	478.0	92.0	141.0	61.0	35.0	-
1911	648.0	586.0	117.0	169.0	107.0	40.0	-
1921	899.1	766.5	210.0	255.4	154.9	52.4	2.5
1933	1,235.3	991.9	299.7	312.6	207.4	60.4	7.3
1947	1,484.0	1,226.4	402.0	382.5	272.5	76.5	15.2
1954	1,863.2	1,524.1	502.3	483.5	348.6	95.2	28.3
1961	2,183.7	1,914.0	621.8	588.1	420.3	115.9	56.4
1966	2,446.3	2,110.2	718.8	727.9	500.0	119.5	92.3
1971	2,935.9	2,503.0	869.6	842.7	703.2	153.2	142.9
1976	3,022.0	2,604.0	957.7	900.4	805.7	162.1	196.5
1981	2,379.5	2,806.3	1,096.2	954.3	922.0	171.1	226.5
1986	3,472.7	2,913.9	1,196.0	1,003.8	1,050.4	179.0	257.7
1991	3,538.7	3,022.4	1,322.2	1,023.6	1,143.2	185.6	278.9
1996	3,741.3	3,138.1	1,488.9	1,045.9	1,244.3	189.9	298.8

Notes and sources can be found at the end of the appendix.

20. AUSTRALIA: DISTRIBUTION OF URBAN POPULATION BY SIZE OF CENTER (PERCENTAGE), 1841-1996

Year	Size of center						
	Under 10,000	10,000-24,999	25,000-49,999	50,000-99,999	100,000-499,999	500,000-999,999	1 million or more
1841	22.7	32.8	44.5	-	-	-	-
1851	12.1	33.9	18.9	35.2	-	-	-
1861	12.9	13.5	15.7	25.1	32.7	-	-
1871	13.2	11.5	11.2	8.6	55.5	-	-
1881	16.5	3.0	16.5	10.1	54.0	-	-
1891	11.7	7.0	10.0	13.5	57.8	-	-
1901	12.2	6.0	11.3	8.5	62.0	-	-
1911	14.1	5.3	6.0	2.4	17.4	54.7	-
1921	11.6	5.1	2.9	4.5	20.6	55.3	-
1933	13.1	4.6	5.9	1.4	22.0	23.6	29.4
1947	11.8	6.7	5.7	2.6	22.3	0.0	51.0
1954	11.0	6.8	5.3	3.9	15.0	7.5	50.5
1961	10.9	7.3	4.5	3.1	10.7	13.7	49.8
1966	9.7	7.6	2.5	4.0	12.0	15.5	48.7
1971	9.0	6.7	3.8	3.0	7.9	18.4	51.1
1976	8.2	6.5	3.8	3.8	9.1	22.1	46.7
1981	8.6	7.0	3.3	4.7	9.3	21.9	45.3
1986	8.0	8.2	2.5	4.6	10.4	14.2	52.1
1991	8.2	8.4	3.3	3.7	11.4	6.9	58.0
1996	8.0	7.4	4.7	4.2	11.6	6.6	57.5

Notes and sources can be found at the end of the appendix.

21. AUSTRALIA: HOME OWNERSHIP FOR SELECTED PLACES, 1871-1911

Location	1871	1881	1891	1901	1911
Capital city					
Melbourne					
Owned (%) [a]	-	-	59	65	63
Number (thousands)	-	-	88.1	91.1	119.6
Sydney					
Owned (%) [a]	-	-	28[b]	-	31
Number (thousands)	-	-	79.5	-	118.4
Municipalities outside capital cities in New South Wales					
Hamilton					
Owned (%) [a]	31[c]	32	47	50	49
Number (thousands)	0.1	0.4	0.9	1.2	1.7
Newcastle City					
Owned (%) [a]	27	15	33	22	21
Number (thousands)	1.3	1.6	2.2	2.2	2.3
Tamworth					
Owned (%) [a]	-	79	47	49	45
Number (thousands)	-	0.5	0.7	0.9	1.2
Northern Illawarra					
Owned (%) [a]	35	27	35	53	44
Number (thousands)	0.1	0.1	0.5	0.6	1.0

Notes and sources can be found at the end of the appendix.

22. AUSTRALIA: HOME OWNERSHIP, 1911-1996

Year	Owned	Being bought	Total	Rented [a]	Total
	Percentage of occupied private dwellings				Thousands
1911	45.0	4.4	49.2	45.2	894.2
1921	39.9	12.5	52.4	40.6	1,107.0
1933	40.0	12.6	52.6	41.0	1,509.7
1947	44.7	7.9	52.6	43.4	1,873.6
1954	47.9	15.1	63.0	34.1	2,343.4
1961	47.5	22.4	69.9	27.4	2,781.9
1966	n. a.	n. a.	70.6	26.4	3,151.9
1971	n. a.	n. a.	68.7	26.4	3,533.3
1996	40.9	25.9	66.4	27.3	6,496.1
	Percentage of households				
1976	31.5	34.7	66.6	25.2	4,140.5
1981	33.2	33.0	68.1	24.9	4,668.9
1991	41.1	27.7	68.8	26.8	5,586.7

Notes and sources can be found at the end of the appendix.

23. AUSTRALIA: GROSS DOMESTIC PRODUCT BY
INDUSTRY, 1841-1998

Year	Sector				Total
	Rural	Mining	Manufacturing	Services	$ million
	Percentage of total				
1841	51.2	0	9.8	39.0	6
1851	40.5	6.2	13.0	40.3	24
1861	23.3	17.8	2.5	56.4	113
1871	29.8	10.1	9.0	51.1	145
1881	27.8	12.1	5.6	54.4	249
1891	27.2	6.2	11.7	55.0	365
1901	21.6	11.5	13.5	53.5	419
1911	28.4	6.1	14.2	51.3	684
1921	30.0	2.6	13.2	54.1	1,382
1931	25.7	2.3	17.3	54.7	1,287
1939	21.4	3.6	20.3	54.6	1,819
1950-51	29.8	2.2	24.4	43.6	6,776
1960-61	13.8	1.8	29.9	54.5	14,576
1970-71	7.2	3.7	27.4	61.7	33,758
1980-81	5.9	6.6	20.7	66.8	132,705
1990-91	4.4	8.4	18.3	69.0	370,859
1995-96	3.7	4.4	14.0	77.9	436,917
1997-98	3.7	4.3	13.2	78.8	468,934

Notes and sources can be found at the end of the appendix.

24. AUSTRALIA: FOREIGN INVESTMENT BY COUNTRY, 1896-1997

Year	United Kingdom	United States	Japan	Other	Total
	Percentage				$ million
1896-97	99.9	0.1	-	-	3,774
1914	93.5	0.9	-	5.5	4,446
1938	70.7	5.3	-	24.0	7,308
1950-59	60.2	29.1	-	29.1	1,743
1960-69	42.7	40.9	-	40.9	5,837
1970-75	27.4	34.1	3.3	35.2	5,977
1975-76	33.8	33.2	4.4	28.6	10,692
1980-81	30.8	27.6	8.7	32.9	47,343
1985-86	24.4	26.0	17.4	32.2	122,805
1990-91	18.7	19.0	17.6	44.7	290,499
1995-96	19.6	23.1	13.1	44.1	438,090
1996-97	23.2	25.0	11.8	40.0	481,957

Notes and sources can be found at the end of the appendix.

25. AUSTRALIA: EXPORTS BY COUNTRY OF DESTINATION, 1891-1998

Year	Country of destination				
	United Kingdom	Other Europe	Japan	United States	Total $million
	Percentage				
1891	70.8	12.0	-	7.6	72
1901	53.5	18.7	0.3	3.4	71
1911	49.5	32.6	11.9	2.1	135
1920-1	53.2	14.6	2.3	5.4	254
1930-1	44.0	22.5	10.6	3.2	180
1940-1	42.7	0.0	3.9	18.0	270
1950-1	30.7	21.7	5.9	14.3	2,087
1960-1	21.4	14.3	14.9	6.7	2,166
1970-1	9.8	7.9	23.7	10.3	5,032
1980-1	3.2	7.5	23.8	9.8	22,003
1990-1	3.4	9.2	27.4	11.0	52,399
1995-6	3.7	7.4	21.6	6.1	76,005
1997-8	3.5	8.2	20.0	8.8	87,734

Notes and sources can be found at the end of the appendix.

26. AUSTRALIA: IMPORTS BY COUNTRY OF ORIGIN, 1891-1998

Year	Country of origin				
	United Kingdom	Other Europe	Japan	United States	Total $ million
Percentage					
1891	70.1	4.7	-	6.8	75
1901	57.5	10.3	0.8	13.3	80
1911	50.2	21.7	1.3	13.8	119
1920-21	46.9	7.6	3.2	22.0	298
1930-31	38.4	12.4	3.9	18.8	124
1940-41	45.4	1.3	3.3	16.0	248
1950-51	48.1	23.8	2.1	8.2	1,483
1960-61	31.4	28.6	6.0	20.0	2,172
1970-71	21.4	32.8	13.8	25.1	4,146
1980-81	8.4	36.0	19.1	22.0	18,965
1990-91	6.7	19.7	18.1	18.9	48,912
1995-96	6.3	18.6	13.9	22.6	77,792
1997-98	6.2	17.9	14.0	21.9	90,685

Notes and sources can be found at the end of the appendix.

27. AUSTRALIA: TRADE INDICATORS, 1891-1998

Year	Exports (percentage)		Exports/Gross Domestic Product	Imports/Gross Domestic Product
	Wool	Gold		
	Percentage of total exports		Percentage	
1891	56.1	15.8	17.8	18.6
1901	43.1	38.2	24.6	20.3
1911	38.7	6.5	24.4	18.7
1921	26.7	4.2	19.4	25.5
1931	35.6	6.3	15.6	11.7
1941	29.4	16.2	17.6	17.0
1950-51	64.9	0.4	31.2	25.5
1960-61	37.0	0.4	14.9	17.8
1970-71	13.0	0.4	15.4	15.6
1980-81	10.0	0.3	16.8	18.9
1990-91	6.1	7.1	14.0	13.1
1995-96	3.3	7.4	17.6	18.0
1997-98	3.5	7.1	18.7	19.3

Notes and sources can be found at the end of the appendix.

28. AUSTRALIA: INDEX OF RETAIL PRICES, 1851-1998

Year	Index number (1945=100)	Year	Index number (1945=100)
1851	56	1931	78
1861	71	1936	75
1866	60	1941	89
1871	47	1946	102
1876	51	1951	167
1881	46	1956	224
1886	56	1961	252
1891	50	1966	276
1896	42	1971	332
1901	47	1976	579
1906	48	1981	926
1911	53	1986	1,370
1916	71	1991	1,898
1921	103	1996	2,141
1926	90	1998	2,199

Notes and sources can be found at the end of the appendix.

29. AUSTRALIA: EXCHANGE RATES WITH THE UNITED
KINGDOM AND THE UNITED STATES, 1851-1998[a]

Year	United Kingdom (pound)	United States (dollar)
1851	0.495	-
1861	0.498	-
1871	0.496	-
1881	0.499	-
1891	0.497	2.43
1901	0.494	2.41
1911	0.496	2.41
1921	0.498	1.88
1931	0.388	1.75
1941	0.398	1.60
1950-51	0.398	1.12
1960-61	0.398	1.17
1970-71	0.465	1.14
1980-81	0.567	1.15
1990-91	0.471	0.77
1995-96	0.509	0.79
1996-97	0.448	0.75
1997-98	0.368	0.61

Notes and sources can be found at the end of the appendix.

30. AUSTRALIA: EMPLOYMENT BY INDUSTRY, 1841-1998

Year	Sector				Total employed
	Rural	Mining	Manufacturing	Services	
			Percentage		Thousands
1841	37.3	-	—62.7—		110.2
1851	27.5	3.1	5.5	64.4	196.7
1861	27.3	19.4	3.4	49.9	547.8
1871	32.6	11.4	7.7	48.3	674.4
1881	32.1	7.2	11.7	49.1	917.9
1891	25.5	6.0	15.0	53.6	1,220.0
1901	24.2	7.3	11.7	56.8	1,611.0
1911	25.4	5.6	20.6	48.4	1,754.3
1921	24.3	2.7	21.6	51.4	2,007.8
1931	25.7	2.2	18.3	53.8	2,100.0
1941	19.0	2.1	24.9	54.0	2,829.1
1951	14.3	1.7	28.6	55.5	3,503.4
1961	11.3	1.3	28.2	59.2	4,091.9
1971	7.5	1.6	24.7	66.2	5,515.7
1981	6.5	1.6	19.4	72.6	6,379.3
1991	5.3	1.2	14.4	79.0	7,559.2
1996	5.1	1.1	13.5	80.3	8319.7
1997	5.0	1.0	13.8	80.2	8,315.5
1998	5.0	1.0	12.9	81.1	8,535.9

Notes and sources can be found at the end of the appendix.

31. AUSTRALIA: OCCUPATIONAL STATUS OF EMPLOYED
LABOR FORCE, 1891-1998

Year	Employer	Self-employed	Wage and salary earners	Total employed
		Percentage		Thousands
1891[a]	11.3	14.9	68.5	1,085.5
1901[a]	9.9	15.9	67.0	1,345.2
1911	12.1	10.1	73.5	1,837.9
1921	6.9	17.0	74.4	2,042.8
1933	9.3	16.5	72.2	2,245.9
1947	7.2	12.6	79.3	3,112.9
1954	6.9	11.3	81.1	3,647.0
1961	6.6	10.2	82.7	4,052.5
1966	6.5	8.0	84.5	4,778.8
1971	5.3	7.2	86.9	5,240.4
1976	5.1	8.7	84.7	5,788.1
1981	5.4	10.1	84.1	6,393.1
1986	5.0	10.8	83.2	6,918.6
1991	4.5	10.2	84.4	7,669.2
1996	4.1	9.9	85.1	8,319.7
1997	4.3	10.8	84.9	8,315.5
1998	4.1	9.6	85.5	8,535.9

Notes and sources can be found at the end of the appendix.

32. AUSTRALIA: WHITE/BLUE OCCUPATIONS, 1891-1998

Year	White collar	Blue collar
	Percentage of employed labor force	
1891	18.8	81.2
1901	20.7	79.3
1911	22.1	77.9
1921	24.2	75.8
1933	24.7	75.3
1947	32.7	67.3
1954	n.a.	n.a.
1961	36.3	63.7
1966	38.0	62.0
1971	42.0	58.0
1976	45.2	54.8
1981	47.4	52.6
1986	59.9	40.1
1991	61.2	38.8
1996	66.1	33.9
1997	66.4	33.6
1998	67.2	32.8

Notes and sources can be found at the end of the appendix.

33. AUSTRALIA: LABOR UNIONS, 1913-1998

Feature	1913	1920	1950	1970	1998
Number of unions	432	388	360	305	132[a]
Members (thousands)	497.9	684.4	1,605.4	2,314.6	2,037.5
	Percentage				
Female	4.1	11.4	18.9	24.4	41.6
Members/employees	34.2	46.1	59.1	54.3	28.1
State/Territory - New South Wales	46.3	40.5	40.0	39.4	34.9
Victoria	26.1	27.3	25.3	25.6	25.3
Queensland	10.4	15.2	16.4	14.3	18.3
South Australia	8.1	8.2	8.6	8.8	8.2
Western Australia	7.1	6.4	6.5	7.3	7.8
Tasmania	2.0	2.2	2.8	3.2	2.7
Northern Territory	-	0.1	0.1	0.3	0.8
Australian Capital Territory	-	-	0.4	1.2	2.0
Industry - Mining	8.1	6.1	3.0	1.5	1.2
Manufacturing	29.5	32.5	38.3	35.4	17.4
All other industries	62.4	61.4	58.7	63.1	81.4

Notes and sources can be found at the end of the appendix.

34. AUSTRALIA: LABOR DISPUTES, 1913-1997

Period [a]	Disputes in mining	Disputes over wages	Days lost	Days lost
	Percentage of days lost		Thousands	Per 1,000 employees
1913-20	45.1	44.0	2,132.9	1,728
1921-25	56.2	27.1	1,067.6	821
1926-30	61.3	43.7	1,954.8	1,472
1931-35	59.0	50.1	287.2	205
1936-40	73.7	19.8	871.8	526
1941-45	35.6	21.1	1,077.0	538
1946-50	29.1	54.9	1,669.2	712
1951-55	31.5	33.4[b]	1,000.0	373
1956-60	25.1	33.7[b]	656.3	222
1961-65	15.2	50.5[b]	684.9	203
1966-70	9.9	46.9	1,373.7	326
1971-75	8.2	73.2	3,503.2	729
1976-80	15.7	40.6	2,973.9	596
1981-85	21.7	30.2	2,110.1	376
1986-90	27.4	27.7	1,384.6	228
1991-95	17.6	11.8	847.3	130
1996	17.3	26.5	928.5	131
1997	18.3	20.5	528.8	74

NOTES AND SOURCES FOR TABLES

1. AUSTRALIA: EVOLUTION OF STATES AND TERRITORIES, 1770-1911

[a] Previously part of New South Wales; transferred to South Australia and then to the federal government in 1911.

[b] Previously part of New South Wales.

SOURCES: Maps in G. Greenwood (ed.), *Australia: A Social and Political History* (Sydney, 1955), pp. 82-83; Australian Bureau of Statistics, *Year Book, Australia* 1977-78 ed., p. 6; 1988 edition, p. 206.

2. AUSTRALIA: PUBLISHED WORKS, 1784-1993

[a] The data in this table before 1901 are indicative only and underestimate the total number of works published in or about Australia, but they are presented here in the absence of anything better.

[b] The "old" series for 1951-60 shows a total of 6,648 works; based on the "new" series for 1961, this indicates that an upward adjustment of 3.7 times is required for comparability with the previous series.

Note: This table attempts to measure the total output of books published in or about Australia, a task not apparently attempted before. Reliable national figures only date from 1960. The figures show before this date have been estimated from the sources listed below.

SOURCES: John A. Ferguson, *Bibliography of Australia.* 7 vols. Canberra, National Library of Australia, 1975-77; Australian Bureau of Statistics, *Catalogue of Australian Statistical Publications, 1804 to 1901* (Canberra: Australian Bureau of Statistics, Catalogue Number 1115.0); Australian Bureau of Statistics, *Year Book Australia*, No. 58, 1972, p. 681; National Library of Australia, *Australian National Bibliography, 1901-1950.* Canberra: National Library of Australia, 1988; National Library of Australia, *Australian National Bibliography.* Canberra: National Library of Australia, 1961 to 1996. From 1996 this valuable work was no longer to be published and the statistics ceased to be published after 1993.

3. AUSTRALIA: POPULATION INTERCHANGE WITH SELECTED COUNTRIES, 1901-1991

[a] 1946.
[b] 1981.
[c] Estimated from Oceanian-born in 1970.
[d] 1985.

SOURCES: **Foreign data:** *Census of the British Empire*, 1901 (London: HMSO, 1906), pp. 54 ff. Central Statistical Office (UK), *Annual Abstract of Statistics*, No. 85, 1937-47, p. 12; *Census of Population and Housing, 1951* (England and Wales, General Report, p. 104; Census of Scotland, 1951, Vol. III, p. 54; Census of Northern Ireland, 1951, General Report, p. 21); *Statistical Abstract of the United States*; *Census of Canada, 1951*, Vol. I, p. 44-1; *1981 Census of Canada*, Catalogue 92-913, Vol. I, National Series, pp. 18-19; Statistics Canada, *Immigration and Citizenship: 1991 Census of Canada.* Catalogue No. 95-316 (Ottawa: Supply and Services Canada, 1992), p. 32. Gordon A. Carmichael (ed.), *Trans-Tasman Migration: Trends, Causes and Consequences* (Canberra: Australian Government Printing Service, 1993), p. 37; *New Zealand Official Year Book*, 1993 ed., p. 106; *Official Year Book of South Africa*, 1923 ed., p. 157, 1950 ed., p. 1167; United Nations, *Demographic Yearbook*, 1983 ed.,, pp. 811 ff., 1989 ed., pp. 723 ff. Data for Papua-New Guinea for 1921 and 1947 was taken from the *Census of the Commonwealth of Australia* (1933 *Census Bulletin*, No. 2, p. 6; 1947 *Census Bulletin*, No. 6, p. 5) and the 1990 census for Papua New Guinea. **Australian data**: Wray Vamplew (ed.), *Australians: Historical Statistics* (Sydney: Fairfax, Syme and Weldon, 1987), pp. 8-9; Australian Bureau of Statistics, *1991 Census of Population and Housing, Expanded Community File: Australia* (ABS Catalogue No. 2722.0), p. 3.

4. AUSTRALIA: VISITORS BY COUNTRY OF RESIDENCE, 1925-1997

[a] Includes other countries not specified. These data first become available in 1924.

SOURCES: Commonwealth Bureau of Census and Statistics, *Australian Demography*, 1925-79: Australian Bureau of Statistics,

Overseas Arrivals and Departures (Reference Number 4.23; Catalogue Number 3404.0, 3401.0).

5. AUSTRALIANS VISITING OTHER COUNTRIES, 1925-1997

[a] Includes other countries not specified. These data first become available in 1924.

SOURCES: As for Table 4.

6. AUSTRALIA AND UNITED STATES: AREA, POPULATION, FOREIGN-BORN, URBANIZATION AND HOME OWNERSHIP, 1920, 1950, 1970, AND 1990

SOURCES: *Statistical Abstract of the United States*; Australian Bureau of Statistics, *Year Book Australia*.

7. AUSTRALIA AND UNITED STATES: GROSS DOMESTIC PRODUCT PER HEAD, UNITED STATES DOLLARS, 1891-1996

Note: The data are expressed in current prices (that is, at the time) and then adjusted for the exchange rate for the year shown. For many and various reasons—such as international politics, changes in population size, and exchange rates—they provide only a rough measure of the economy, but they are still useful for general comparative purposes.

SOURCES: Wray Vamplew (ed.), *Australians: Historical Statistics* (Sydney: Fairfax, Syme and Weldon Associates, 1987), pp. 133, 244; U.S. Department of Commerce, *Historical Statistics of the United States* (U.S. Government Printing Office: Washington D.C., 2 vols., 1975), Part I, p. 224; International Monetary Fund, *International Financial Statistics Yearbook*, 1997 ed., pp. 199, 857.

8. AUSTRALIA AND UNITED STATES: POPULATION INTERCHANGE, 1860-1996

[a] Years ending in zero refer to the United States; other years refer to Australia.

SOURCES: **Australian data** for 1861-1981 in Wray Vamplew (ed.), *Australians: Historical Statistics* (Sydney: Fairfax, Syme and Weldon Associates, 1987), p. 9, and the Census of Population for 1986, 1991, and 1996; **U.S. data** for 1860-1950 census population data *Statistical Abstract of the United States*; 1950 data were taken from the *U.S. Census of Population 1950: Special Report P-E 3A*, pp. 71-74; 1960 data from U.S. Census 1960, Detailed Characteristics, Vol. 1, p. 366; 1970 data for the U.S. *Census of Population 1970: United States Summary*, p. 1-598; 1980 and 1990 census data: *Statistical Abstract of the United States, 1992*, p. 42.

9. AUSTRALIA AND UNITED STATES: TRADE, 1891-1998

SOURCE: Wray Vamplew (ed.), *Australians: Historical Statistics* (Sydney: Fairfax, Syme and Weldon Associates, 1987), pp. 188-89, 193, 196, 201, 204; Australian Bureau of Statistics, *Australian Economic Indicators* (ABS Catalogue No. 1350.0), 1991 to date.

10. AUSTRALIA AND UNITED STATES: LABOR UNION MEMBERS AS A PERCENTAGE OF EMPLOYEES, 1891-1997

SOURCES: James C. Docherty, *Historical Dictionary of Organized Labor* (Lanham, Md.: Scarecrow Press, 1996), pp. 263-64 (the Australian data for 1901 have been slightly revised); Australian Bureau of Statistics, *Trade Union Members, August 1996* (ABS Catalogue No. 6325.0), p. 9; Australian Bureau of Statistics, *Weekly Earnings of Employees (Distribution) Australia*, August 1997 (ABS Catalogue No. 6310.0), p. 40; U.S. Department of Labor, Bureau of Labor Statistics, *Employment and Earnings*, January 1997, p. 211, January 1998, p. 215.

11. AUSTRALIA: POPULATION, SOURCES OF CHANGE, 1788-1998

SOURCES: Wray Vamplew (ed.), *Australians: Historical Statistics* (Sydney: Fairfax, Syme and Weldon Associates, 1987), pp. 44, 50-51, 56; Australian Bureau of Statistics, *Year Book, Australia* 1983 edition, p. 119; Australian Bureau of Statistics, *Australian Demographic Statistics* (ABS Catalogue No. 3101.0), 1982 to date.

12. AUSTRALIA: BIRTHPLACE OF POPULATION, 1828-1996

SOURCES: Census of Population and Housing; Wray Vamplew (ed.), *Australians: Historical Statistics* (Sydney: Fairfax, Syme and Weldon Associates, 1987), pp. 8-9.

13. AUSTRALIAN CITIZENSHIP, 1949-1998

SOURCES: Commonwealth Department of Immigration, *Statistical Bulletin* (Canberra), 1952-65; Commonwealth Department of Immigration and Multicultural Affairs, *Australian Immigration Consolidated Statistics* and *Annual Reports*; Research and Statistics Unit, Department of Immigration and Multicultural Affairs.

14. AUSTRALIA: POPULATION, AGES, 1841-1996

[a] The median age is the age that divides the population into two equal halves: one half is less than the age shown and one half is older.
[b] 14-44 years.
[c] 45-60 years.
[d] 60 and over years.
[e] Excludes Victoria.

SOURCES: Wray Vamplew (ed.), *Australians: Historical Statistics* (Sydney: Fairfax, Syme and Weldon Associates, 1987), pp. 50-51, 56-57; Australian Bureau of Statistics, *Year Book Australia*, 1988 ed., p. 258; Census of Population and Housing.

15. AUSTRALIA: POPULATION SEX RATIOS, FERTILITY, AND MORTALITY, 1840-1997

SOURCES: Wray Vamplew (ed.), *Australians: Historical Statistics* (Sydney: Fairfax, Syme and Weldon Associates, 1987), pp. 50-51, 56-57; Australian Bureau of Statistics, *Australian Demographic Statistics* (ABS Catalogue No. 3101.0), 1982 to date.

16. AUSTRALIA: POPULATION BY COLONY/STATE, (THOUSANDS), 1841-1996

Note: Before federation in 1901, the Australian states were British colonies. The population totals used here exclude external territories.

SOURCE: Census of Population and Housing.

17. AUSTRALIA: RELIGIOUS AFFILIATIONS, 1828-1996

Note: Although it was not compulsory to answer the census of population and housing question on religious affiliation, this was not explicitly stated in the questionnaire until 1933. The data shown for Methodism for 1981 to 1996 refer to the Uniting Church of Australia which was formed in 1977 by the amalgamation of the Methodist, Congregationalist, and Presbyterian churches. However, a significant part of the Presbyterian church continued to be separate.

SOURCES: Wray Vamplew (ed.), *Australians: Historical Statistics* (Sydney: Fairfax, Syme and Weldon Associates, 1987), pp. 421-27. Convenient summaries of historical census data on religious affiliation can also be found in Hans Mol, *Religion in Australia: A Sociological Investigation* (Melbourne: Nelson, 1971), p. 5; and Australian Bureau of Statistics, *Year Book Australia*, 1996 ed., p. 348; 1996 Census of Population and Housing.

18. AUSTRALIA: URBAN/RURAL POPULATION BY PERCENTAGE, 1841-1996

SOURCE: Author's calculations from the Census of Population and Housing using the U.S. definition of a minimum urban population of 2,500.

19. AUSTRALIA: POPULATION OF CAPITAL CITIES, (THOU-SANDS),1841-1996

SOURCE: Census of Population and Housing. For the pre-1921 figures, the figures used have are those in J. W. McCarty in C. B. Schedvin and J. W. McCarty, *Urbanization in Australia: The Nineteenth Century* (Sydney: Sydney University Press, 1970), pp. 31-39.

20. AUSTRALIA: DISTRIBUTION OF URBAN POPULATION BY SIZE OF CENTER (PERCENTAGE), 1841-1996

SOURCE: Author's calculations based on the Census of Population and Housing and using the U.S. definition of a minimum urban population of 2,500. The data from 1933 included urban centers which were not incorporated as municipalities as well as those which were.

21. AUSTRALIA: HOME OWNERSHIP FOR SELECTED PLACES, 1871-1911

[a] Includes homes being purchased.
[b] Based on a sample of 20 municipalities covering 28,000 houses.
[c] Based on data for 1872.

SOURCES: R. V. Jackson, "Owner-Occupation of Houses in Sydney, 1871 to 1891," *Australian Economic History Review*, 1970, X, No. 2 p. 141; A. E. Dingle and D. T. Merrett, "Home Owners and Tenants in Melbourne, 1891-1911," *Australian Economic History Review*, 1972, XII, I, pp. 28-29; and B. F. Rees, "Home Ownership in Tamworth and Tenterfield," *Armidale and District Historical Society Journal*, No. 21, January 1978, p. 142. For the other places, the data were derived from systematic sampling of municipal rate books by the author.

22. AUSTRALIA: HOME OWNERSHIP, 1911-1996

[a] Excludes not stated and undefined forms of home occupancy.

Note: 1911 was the first year when home ownership was first asked at the census of population. Before 1911, the only source of these data was the rate books of municipal governments and water and sewerage authorities. This becomes available after about 1870. Table 21 presents a selection of these data.

SOURCES: Wray Vamplew (ed.), *Australians: Historical Statistics* (Sydney: Fairfax, Syme and Weldon Associates, 1987), p. 353; summary publications from the population census from 1976 to 1996.

23. AUSTRALIA: GROSS DOMESTIC PRODUCT BY INDUSTRY, 1841-1998

Note: Totals before 1991 are expressed in current prices whereas prices after 1991 are expressed in average prices for 1989-90.

SOURCES: Wray Vamplew (ed.), *Australians: Historical Statistics* (Sydney: Fairfax, Syme and Weldon Associates, 1987), pp. 131, 133. W. E. Norton and P. J. Kennedy, *Australian Economic Statistics, 1949-50 to 1984-85* (Canberra: Reserve Bank of Australia, 1985), p.

116. Australian Bureau of Statistics, *Australian Economic Indicators* (ABS Catalogue No. 1350.0), 1991 to date.

24. AUSTRALIA: FOREIGN INVESTMENT BY COUNTRY, 1896-1997

Note: The level of foreign investment refers to the estimated total value of investments which can be attributed to a particular country. The data for 1976 onward exclude foreign investment by international capital markets, international institutions and unallocated investment. The data before 1950 and after 1975 refer to stock estimates. For 1950 to 1975 they refer to totals of flow data.

SOURCES: William Woodruff, *Impact of Western Man: A Study of Europe's Role in the World Economy, 1750-1960* (New York: St. Martin's Press), 1966, pp. 152, 154, 156, 158 [Woodruff's data were expressed in U.S. dollars which have been converted to Australian dollars according to the exchange rates for that year]; Donald T. Brash, *American Investment in Australian Industry* (Canberra: Australian National University Press, 1966), p. 22; W. E. Norton and P. J. Kennedy, *Australian Economic Statistics, 1949-50 to 1984-85* (Canberra: Reserve Bank of Australia, 1985), pp. 24-5. Australian Bureau of Statistics, *Year Book Australia*, 1992 ed. p. 725; Australian Bureau of Statistics, *Balance of Payments and International Investment Position,* June Quarter 1998, (ABS Catalogue No. 5302.0), p. 23.

25. AUSTRALIA: EXPORTS BY COUNTRY OF DESTINATION, 1891-1998

Note: Total includes other countries not specified.

SOURCES: Wray Vamplew (ed.), *Australians: Historical Statistics* (Sydney: Fairfax, Syme and Weldon Associates, 1987), pp. 188, 193-95, 201; Australian Bureau of Statistics, *Year Book Australia*, 1997 ed., pp. 701-2, 708; 1998 ed., pp. 769-71; *Australian Economic Indicators* (ABS Catalogue No. 1350.0), 1991 to date.

26. AUSTRALIA: IMPORTS BY COUNTRY OF ORIGIN, 1891-1998

Note: Total includes other countries not specified.

SOURCES: Wray Vamplew (ed.), *Australians: Historical Statistics* (Sydney: Fairfax, Syme and Weldon Associates, 1987), pp. 189, 196, 204; Australian Bureau of Statistics, *Year Book Australia* 1994 ed., pp. 768-9; *Australian Economic Indicators* (ABS Catalogue No. 1350.0), 1991 to date.

27. AUSTRALIA: TRADE INDICATORS, 1891-1998

Note: The totals for exports and imports used in this table are significantly higher than those given in Tables 25 and 26 which mainly refer to totals where the destination of country was known.

SOURCES: Wray Vamplew (ed.), *Australians: Historical Statistics* (Sydney: Fairfax, Syme and Weldon Associates, 1987), pp. 133, 139, 188-89; Australian Bureau of Statistics, *Year Book Australia*, 1997 ed., p. 708; 1998 ed., p. 776; Australian Bureau of Statistics, *Australian Economic Indicators* (ABS Catalogue No. 1350.0), 1991 to date; *International Merchandise Trade*, Australia (ABS Catalogue No. 5422.0).

28. AUSTRALIA: INDEX OF RETAIL PRICES, 1851-1998

SOURCES: Australian Bureau of Statistics, *Year Book Australia*, 1998 ed., p. 702; Australian Bureau of Statistics, *Australian Economic Indicators* (ABS Catalogue No. 1350.0), 1991 to date.

29. AUSTRALIA: EXCHANGE RATES WITH THE UNITED KINGDOM AND THE UNITED STATES, 1851-1998

[a] Rates are given in terms of the Australian dollar which was made the basic currency unit in February 1966.

SOURCES: W. Vamplew (ed.), *Australians: Historical Statistics* (Sydney: Fairfax, Syme and Weldon Associates, 1987), pp. 244-45; Australian Bureau of Statistics, *Australian Economic Indicators* (ABS Catalogue No. 1350.0), February 1991 to date.

30. AUSTRALIA: EMPLOYMENT BY INDUSTRY, 1841-1998

SOURCES: Census of Population and Housing, 1841-1891; G. J. R. Linge, *Industrial Awakening* (Canberra, 1973), p. 708; Wray Vamplew (ed.), *Australians: Historical Statistics* (Sydney: Fairfax, Syme and

Weldon Associates, 1987), pp. 72, 147, 288, 290; Michael Keating, *The Australian Workforce, 1910 to 1960-61* (Canberra, 1973), pp. 356-57; Australian Bureau of Statistics, *Labour Force, Australia: Historical Summary, 1966 to 1984* (ABS Catalogue No. 6204.0) and *Labour Force, Australia* (ABS Catalogue No. 6203.0), 1985 to date [August data].

31. AUSTRALIA: OCCUPATIONAL STATUS OF EMPLOYED LABOR FORCE, 1891-1998

[a] The data for 1891 and 1901 have been partly estimated using the totals for those colonies/states where the data are available. The total includes unpaid helpers.

SOURCES: Census of Population and Housing (data for 1891 to 1971); Australian Bureau of Statistics, *Labour Force, Australia* (ABS Catalogue No. 6203.0), 1981 to date [August data].

32. AUSTRALIA: WHITE/BLUE COLLAR OCCUPATIONS, 1891-1998

Note: although data on occupations were collected at the 1954 population census, they were not compiled or published and were merely used as a check on the industry question.

SOURCES: Author's calculations from the Census of Population and Housing, 1891 to 1966; Australia Bureau of Statistics, *Labour Force, Australia* (ABS Catalogue Number 6203.0) 1971 to date [August data].

33. AUSTRALIA: LABOR UNIONS, 1913-1998

[a] Data are for 1996. This is the last year when these data were published.

SOURCES: Commonwealth Bureau of Census and Statistics, *Labour Reports*; Australian Bureau of Statistics, *Trade Union Statistics, Australia* (ABS Catalogue No. 6323.0); Australian Bureau of Statistics, *Employee Earnings, Benefits, and Trade Union Members, Australia* (ABS Catalogue No. 6310.0).

34. AUSTRALIA: LABOR DISPUTES, 1913-1997

[a] Annual averages.

[b] Data include disputes over hours and leave.

SOURCES: Commonwealth Bureau of Statistics/Australian Bureau of Statistics, *Labour Report*, 1913-73; Australian Bureau of Statistics, *Industrial Disputes, Australia* (ABS Catalogue No. 6322.0), 1974 to date.

About the Author

JAMES C. DOCHERTY was born in Gosford, New South Wales, Australia, in 1949. Like many Australians, he is a second-generation Australian. Both of his parents were born in Scotland, his father in St. Andrews and his mother in Milngavie, north of Glasgow. He is a graduate of the University of Newcastle, New South Wales, (B.A.) and the Australian National University (M.A., Ph.D.). Before joining the Australian Bureau of Statistics in 1978, he worked as a research assistant with the Australian Dictionary of Biography at the Australian National University. In 1978 he joined the Australian federal public service and is currently the administrator of the national database for citizenship with the Department of Immigration and Multicultural Affairs. He was an honorary research associate with the National Centre for Australian Studies at Monash University from 1990 to 1996.

His publications include *Selected Social Statistics of New South Wales, 1861-1976* (1982); *Newcastle: The Making of an Australian City* (1983); "English Settlement in Newcastle and the Hunter Valley" in *The Australian People: An Encyclopedia of the Nation, Its People and Their Origins*, edited by James Jupp (1988); and *Historical Dictionary of Australia* (1992). He was an editorial consultant to *Australians: Historical Statistics* (1987), contributing the entries on Australian history, politics, labor relations, and institutions in *The Cambridge Encyclopedia*, edited by David Crystal (1990), and was an editor and contributor to *Workplace Bargaining in the International Context* (1993). He is the author of *Historical Dictionary of Organized Labor* (1996) and *Historical Dictionary of Socialism* (1997).